Critical Tales

Critical Tales

New Studies of the *Heptameron* and Early Modern Culture

Edited by John D. Lyons and Mary B. McKinley

University of Pennsylvania Press

Philadelphia

Jacket illustration: Ink drawing on parchment from a sixteenth-century manuscript edition of *L'Heptaméron* (Pierpont Morgan Library M.242, f. vi verso). Courtesy of the Pierpont Morgan Library, New York.

Library of Congress Cataloging-in-Publication Data
Critical tales: new studies of the Heptameron and early modern culture / edited by
  John D. Lyons and Mary B. McKinley.
     p.   cm.
  Includes bibliographical references and index.
  ISBN 0-8122-3206-2
     1. Marguerite, Queen, consort of Henry II, King of Navarre, 1492–1549.   Heptaméron.
     2. Characters and characteristics in literature.   3. Narration (Rhetoric).   4. Rhetoric—
  1500–1800.   5. Literary form.   I. Lyons, John D., 1946–   .   II. McKinley, Mary B.
  PQ1631.H4C75   1993
  843'.3—dc20   93-26575
                                                                              CIP

Contents

Preface

These new studies of the *Heptameron* are intended to be useful both to scholars and to new readers of Marguerite de Navarre's work. In many cases readers of *Critical Tales* will find it useful to consult an English translation of her work. To facilitate access to the text of the *Heptameron* without burdening our book with a myriad of quotations in both languages, we have chosen to provide the original French text and to indicate the relevant page of the most recent English translation. French quotations and other references to the *Heptameron* are from the edition by Michel François (Paris: Classiques Garnier, 1966). Page references show the page number of the François edition first, followed by a semicolon and the page number of Paul Chilton's English translation, *The Heptameron* (Harmondsworth: Penguin Books, 1984).

Three chapters of this work were originally written in French and translated for publication. Michel Jeanneret's "Modular Narrative and the Crisis of Interpretation" was translated by John Lyons. Philippe de Lajarte's "The Voice of the Narrators in Marguerite de Navarre's Tales" was translated by Mary McKinley and John Lyons. André Tournon's "Rules of the Game" was translated by George Hoffmann.

The publication of *Critical Tales* would not have been possible without the generous support of the Center for Advanced Study of the University of Virginia. We thank the Center and its director, Paul Gross, for this substantial assistance.

Introduction

Appearing in print for the first time in 1558, the book that we now know as the *Heptameron* represents in microcosm the conflicts, tensions, and beliefs of early modern French society as viewed from one part of the court. The "tales of the queen of Navarre," as Brantôme called the work, present a forum where different elements of Renaissance and Reformation culture meet and, at times, collide. Often the encounters are ideological. The stories and discussions of the *Heptameron* depict confrontations based on, among other elements, gender. Contradictory suppositions about women emerge repeatedly from the stories and discussions as the *devisants* or fictional storytellers—five men and five women—delineate attitudes both feminist and misogynist. At the same time, similarly conflicting notions about men emerge to be debated. Whether echoing the late medieval *querelle des femmes*, the contemporary *querelle des amyes*, the evolving currents of Neoplatonism and Petrarchism, or the attitudes toward sexual roles put forth in Reformation polemics, deeply felt beliefs about gender inform and animate the *Heptameron*.

Ideological confrontations in the *Heptameron* often echo evangelical efforts at church reform. Here, conflicts among the storytellers are less oppositional, for even if some seem more fervent in their religious ardor than others and some more concerned with the corporal than with the spiritual, none of them advocates a theological position opposed to that of the evangelical reformers. The stories the *devisants* tell are often cautionary tales conveying their hostility and dismay about the state of the Catholic church: decadent priests and monks, most often lubricious and venal; unfortunate Christians whose belief in the efficacy of good works leads to disaster and death. Both the stories and the discussions often center on differing attitudes toward sin and virtue, alienation and reconciliation, eros and *caritas*, pleasure and honor—alternatives that the storytellers and their characters present as conflictual states and values within which they must negotiate a tenable place in their fictional world. If some have found a haven of tranquillity in the steadfast convictions of their evangelical faith, others are still playing out restless scenarios of unsatisfied desire. The climate of unrest, menace, and hostility that characterizes the prologue also portrays the world of the *Heptameron* in general, the physical world from which the storytellers flee and to which they wait to return, and their overall view of the human condition as well. The conflicts of the Reformation loom over the *Heptameron* as a prominent symptom of larger, related disruptions and new departures that marked mid-sixteenth-century Europe.

This volume proposes that the *Heptameron* both records and contributes to those changes. The queen of Navarre's tales signal new ways of thinking and writing. The words *vérité* and *véritable* recur frequently in these pages, but if the stories are all true, as the prologue decrees they must be and their tellers insist they are, the lessons they ostensibly convey contradict each other so relentlessly that the very notion of truth in human experience is subverted. The differing connotations of such pivotal words as love and honor—and the way the stories and discussions foreground those differences—point to a crisis in language and epistemology. That semantic instability mirrors, in turn, a precarious ontology. If we were to define the human condition on the basis of what the *Heptameron* shows us, we would have to conclude with Montaigne that it is vain, diverse, and undulating. Only the theological belief system set forth in the book offers an anchor, in the promise of Christ the Logos. We are frequently reminded of the other textual activity that structures the storytellers' days, the morning scriptural readings that, while they are ostensibly apart from the *Heptameron*'s text, surface repeatedly in both the stories and the discussions.

Our contributors show how shifts in structures of thinking manifest themselves not just thematically but formally, linguistically, and aesthetically as well. Discontinuity is also a structural principle of the *Heptameron*. Stories alternate with discussions. Poetry interrupts prose. Editors' glosses shape our reading of each new tale. Stylistic tics occur in one story that reappear nowhere else in the book. Within this literary heterogeneity emerge new ways of generating and manipulating narrative. These are, indeed, critical tales.

Like the *Heptameron*, this volume is a forum bringing together different views and approaches. Their very diversity is a measure of the *Heptameron*'s rich complexity. Our contributors use various words to refer to the book's contents. Are these stories, tales, or novellas? Do they alternate with discussions, conversations, dialogues, debates, or commentaries? Such changing terminology reflects the problem of assigning the *Heptameron* to a standard generic category. Just as several literary genres leave their traces on its pages, the question of genre recurs in different forms in the pages of this volume. Likewise, most of our contributors make their own discussions places of convergence, because they raise critical questions of more than one kind: rhetorical, semiotic, feminist, historical, narratological—like so many *devisants*, different voices come together in these pages. Questions of gender join with other critical perspectives in several of the articles. Cathleen Bauschatz examines the gendered figurations of readers and reader response inscribed in the book and argues that the *Heptameron*'s narrative and rhetorical strategies undercut men's authority as teachers and preachers to women. François Cornilliat and Ullrich Langer relate the naked female body to the uncovering that is central to all narrative. Paula Sommers shows how androgynous structures and energies shape and animate the *Heptameron*. Hope Glidden focuses on one dramatic transgression of gender typing, the character of Jambicque, who dares to be a desiring subject. Robert Cottrell, while showing how the drama of Christ's passion is violently replayed on the bodies of the women in the stories, investigates the ways in which Marguerite's evangelical spirituality redefines the notion of Logos.

The presence of Reformation theology and polemic is the major concern of several of the chapters. But their authors show that religious belief functions as much more than a thematic element of the *Heptameron*. Edwin Duval proposes a radically evangelical reading that addresses the structure and coherence of the book, as well as offering a new definition of the genre, *nouvelle*. Mary McKinley argues that the confession stories, while reflecting Reformation disputes about the sacrament of penance, figure the emerging voice of women's narrative. François Rigolot shows the evangelical iconography that underlies one of the most compelling tales, but his discoveries also point to a tension between medieval allegory and humanist philology in the Renaissance.

From their various points of departure, several of the essays explore the new ways of structuring thought that the book implies. Their discoveries, in turn, lead to new insights about the *Heptameron*'s originality as writing. Both Donald Stone and Marcel Tetel examine the juxtaposition of lyric and narrative in Marguerite's work. Daniel Russell shows how changing presuppositions about social relationships lead to new possibilities for fictional characterization. Tom Conley proposes that notions of the text shaped by early print culture create graphic games of inscription that leave their signatures on the work. Michel Jeanneret argues that new "modular" structures of thinking reshape the structures of narrative in the Renaissance, and that the *Heptameron* manifests that radical shift. Both André

Tournon and Philippe de Lajarte focus on the narrative strategies of the book, Tournon exploring the generic innovations implicit in its frame structure and de Lajarte elaborating on its original staging of narrative and authorial voice.

As in the shady meadow of Notre Dame de Sarrance, there are some disagreements among the voices in this volume. However, they have deepened and altered our understanding of the *Heptameron* so much that we have endeavored, in our afterword, to assess their implications for the book's place in the history and theory of narrative. In so doing we do not attempt to foreclose the voices of our contributors but to open a dialogue that we hope readers of this volume will want to continue.

Part I

Generic Transformations and Graphic Transgressions

Robert D. Cottrell

1. Inmost Cravings: The Logic of Desire in the *Heptameron*

"Nous sommes tous encloz en peché."

—Novella 26, *Heptameron*

"Omnes peccaverunt."

—Romans 3.23 (Vulgate)

In the Prologue to the *Heptameron*, the ten stranded travelers—that is to say, the *devisants* in the frame-narrative—ask Oisille, the most venerable of the group, how they might best occupy themselves during the several days they must spend together while waiting for a bridge to be built. Oisille answers that the only remedy she has ever found for boredom and sorrow is "la lecture des sainctes lettres" (7;66) and explains that she spends her days reading Scripture, "contemplant la bonté de Dieu" (7;66), and singing "les beaulx psealmes et canticques que le sainct Esperit a composé au cueur de David et des autres aucteurs" (7;66). The other *devisants* observe that Oisille's remedy is not appropriate for them, for they, being younger and more deeply committed to worldly pursuits, need amusement and diversion. Eventually they decide to assemble for one hour each morning in Oisille's room to listen to her read a biblical "lesson" and then to reassemble in the afternoon in a beautiful meadow where they will tell each other stories, the only stipulation being that all the stories must be true. Oisille's biblical "lessons" are not recorded in the text itself, which, except for brief prologues that introduce each "journée," consists of the stories the *devisants* tell each other and the discussions that follow each novella.

In his important work on the *Heptameron*,[1] Philippe de Lajarte distinguishes two discursive registers that, in his view, mark textual practice in Marguerite de Navarre's text. Calling one register "the sacred" and the other "the profane" ("Le Prologue de *l'Heptaméron*," 410), de Lajarte claims that the prologue to the *Heptameron* stages the disappearance of "the sacred" from the profane world of phenomena. Pointing out that the *devisants* choose not to follow Oisille's example, de Lajarte argues that Marguerite de Navarre's text is a semantic field from which "the sacred" has withdrawn, leaving behind, however, faint traces, which are discernible mainly in Oisille's speech. Because "the sacred" has retreated from the world of the text, the *Heptameron*, according to de Lajarte, circumscribes a space that has been invaded by phenomena, by "the profane." To emphasize his point, de Lajarte contrasts the *Heptameron* sharply with *Les Prisons*, the long poem Marguerite de Navarre wrote while composing the *Heptameron*, and maintains that whereas *Les Prisons* is informed by what he calls the "archaic" ideology of a transcendent Logos, the *Heptameron* unfolds outside the "monologisme logocentrique" ("Le Prologue de *l'Heptaméron*," 419) of sacred speech.

In this chapter, I shall present a different view. I shall suggest that the *Heptameron*, like *Les Prisons* (and, indeed, like every one of Marguerite de Navarre's texts) is powerfully informed by "the sacred," by the Logos, by a Real that is situated eternally beyond the world of phenomena but that is simultaneously always inscribed in it. That Real is, of course, Christ, the Word made flesh, which, from the Christian perspective that shapes Marguerite's views as well as those of all the protagonists in the *Heptameron*, operates in the *hic et nunc* of phenomena, in the fleshy, sinful, suffering world of the desiring body.

Throughout the *Heptameron*, the stress on physicality and on pain conforms to the traditions of a culture whose signifying center is occupied by the figure of the Passion. All other figures derive their meaning from the figure of Christ's body, which is a testimony to God's humanization and which is displayed in spectacular, public suffering. As Caroline Walker Bynum has noted, late medieval and Renaissance piety was deeply experiential.[2] Devotional writers of the fifteenth and sixteenth centuries displayed Christ's suffering body, making of it, and of the human body generally, the privileged place where the Christian can experience Christ.[3] As Paul reminded the Romans (8:17), the only way to share Christ's glory is to share his suffering. Christians, Paul affirmed, must offer their bodies to God as a living sacrifice (Rom. 12:1).

The Logos inscribed in the *Heptameron* is mediated mainly by Paul.[4] In the prologue to the sixth day, we learn that the scriptural text the *devisants* studied and meditated on during the previous five mornings was Paul's Epistle to the Romans. (During the morning of the sixth day, they read 1 John; during the morning of the seventh day, Acts and the beginning of

Luke; during the morning of the eighth day, they prolonged their devotions in order to read the Epistles of John all the way through.) The biblical text most massively present in the *Heptameron* is, then, Romans, which, more than any other book in the New Testament, stresses the sinful fleshiness of man's fallen state, from which faith alone can save him. The exemplum that informs the *Heptameron* from beginning to end is the figure of Christ, who, as Paul explained to the Philippians, humiliated himself and emptied himself of his divinity—or rather of the glory to which his divinity entitled him—and became incarnate in a human body: "He emptied himself, taking the form of a slave, becoming as human beings are; and being in every way like a human being, He was humbler yet, even to accepting death, death on a cross" (Phil. 2:7–8).[5]

In the theologically rich discussion that follows the apparently foolish and trivial novella 34 (finding wisdom in what appears foolish is an important Christian topos to which the *devisants* themselves here allude), Hircan, often thought to be the most cynical and "materialist" of the *devisants*, declares that "la nature des femmes et des hommes est de soy incline à tout vice, si elle n'est préservée de Celluy à qui l'honneur de toute victoire doibt estre rendu" (254;345). Oisille, referring to Paul's observation in Romans 1:24 that "inmost cravings" compel the flesh to do what the spirit abhors (Oisille notes that this was the very text they had read that morning), remarks that the absence of grace and faith is registered on the body as "desordre" (254;344), as unruly graphemes that are visible and legible. And Longarine, the youngest and usually considered to be the most frivolous of the *devisants*, notes that God's grace, operating through a scopic economy, often makes the sin that is hidden in our heart visible across the surface of our body so that we can *see* it, thus allowing us to "experimenter [notre] nature pecheresse, par les effectz du dehors" (254;344).

Human beings, then, are "naturally" sinful. The *Heptameron* is a record of human sinfulness writ large enough for all to see. Pursuing in their individual ways "le chemin où Dieu les conseilloit" (3;62), the *devisants* find themselves assembled "miraculeusement" (6;65, the text says that God bestowed his grace upon them) at Notre Dame de Sarrance, a site that is constituted as a place of momentary exile that the travelers will soon leave as they go forth and continue to look for a road that will take them back home. They thank God for his great mercy and beseech him to assist them on their return journey, adding that if they return home safely it will not be their doing but rather God's.

If the flood from which they were saved evokes the image of the flood from which Noah was saved, it also evokes the waters of baptism.[6] In Romans 6, which Briçonnet interpreted at length in his letter of May 18, 1522, to Marguerite, Paul explains that baptism joins us to Christ's Passion and initiates us into his death.[7] In baptism we are "joined to Him by dying a death like His" (Rom. 6:5). Baptism is a sacrament that, to use a favorite word of the late fourteenth-century English anchoress, Juliana of Norwich, "ones"[8] us with the figure of Christ's suffering and humiliated body, so like ours in every respect. Salvation, which becomes a virtuality at the time of baptism, depends upon our willingness to "one" ourself with his tormented body and to acknowledge the sinfulness of the flesh, which, as long as we are in this world, will bear the marks of Adam's disobedience.

Like the human creature whose body registers visible signs of the Fall, the *Heptameron* is a script across whose surface are inscribed the signs of sin rendered legible. It is a confession of "la fragilité de noz cueurs" (221;306), to cite Longarine, who here echoes the words Hircan had just spoken: "En bien nous mirant, n'aurons besoing de couvrir nostre nudité de feulles, mais plustost confesser nostre fragilité" (221;305). In its own materiality, in its splits, divisions, gaps, ruptures, and contradictions, the text is a body that re-presents the human body, which, burdened with fleshiness, with its cravings for pleasure and for pain, is the site God chose for his incarnation, the place where, according to God's plan, the Christian encounters Christ. For, as Monseigneur d'Avannes, restating the Augustinian topos that God makes use of the visible and the fleshy to lead us to the invisible and the divine, explains in novella 26: "Dieu, incongneu de l'homme, sinon par la foy, a daigné prendre la chair semblable à celle de peché, afin qu'en attirant nostre chair à l'amour de son humanité, tirast aussi notre esprit à l'amour de sa divinité; et s'est voulu servyr des moyens visibles, pour nous faire aymer par foy les choses invisibles" (214;298).

The Politics of Gender

Although the *devisants* in the *Heptameron* all belong to the same aristocratic circle, antagonisms emerge, the most important of which is what may seem at first to be an ontological split between men and women. The tension between men and women in the *Heptameron* reflects no doubt the mores of a sixteenth-century aristocratic society shaped by the masculine ethos of conquest, honor, and military glory, an ethos that the increasingly powerful bourgeoisie appropriated for its own purposes and translated into the language of economic and, according to Michel Foucault, sexual power.[9] Indeed, throughout the *Heptameron* women are figured as possessors of a precious commodity (chastity) that men seek to despoil. Addressing with astonishing frankness the five aristocratic women present among the *devisants*, Geburon claims to speak for men when he says that "nostre gloire, nostre felicité et nostre contentement, c'est de vous veoir prises et de vous oster ce qui vous est plus cher que la vie" (133;208). Female honor, on the other hand, is shaped by a different dynamic, for, as the text points out several times, a woman's honor depends on denying men access to the priceless commodity she possesses, metaphorized variously as a treasure (37;100) and, in a tradition that was codified in *Le Roman de la rose*, a flower (182;261).

Although there is no doubt that the relationship between men and women in the *Heptameron* reflects to some degree the social environment in which the text was produced, that relationship is reduced so obsessively, so repetitively, so *phantasmatically*, to what Scripture calls "lust of the flesh" (1 John 2:16, King James version) that surely it is—to use the psychoanalytic term—overdetermined. Surely the "meaning" of the relationship between men and women in the *Heptameron* exceeds any meaning that can be secured in sixteenth-century social conventions or in the contemporary praxis of secular power.

Such overdetermined "meaning" can, I believe, be secured only in the discourse of divine power. This is simply another way of saying what the text itself says over and over—namely, that the visible and material things of this world are informed with the invisible presence of the Logos, which, operating through the mechanics of desire and of sin, humiliates and annihilates the flesh and thereby draws the beloved creature closer to Christ.

In a scriptural passage that resonates with particular force in devotional literature throughout the late Middle Ages and Renaissance, John declares in his First Epistle (2:16) that the world of matter is marked by "concupiscentia carnis," "concupiscentia oculorum," and "superbia vite," words that Briçonnet, who comments on this passage twice in his letters to Marguerite, renders with only partial accuracy as "luxure, avarice et orgueil" (2.270), and which the New Jerusalem Bible translates as "disordered bodily desires, disordered desires of the eyes, pride in possession." Although this passage is by John, the dynamics of concupiscence preoccupied

Paul far more than it did John, who focused primarily on the efficacy of love. Indeed, Paul's Epistle to the Romans is an especially powerful statement of the way flesh and sin function in the economy of salvation.

Paul uses the term "flesh" to designate the matter of which the body is composed. Occasionally he uses other terms, such as "human nature," "natural inclinations," "physical descent," to designate the body or various of its attributes, but they are all subsumed in the word "flesh."[10] "Flesh," therefore, is constituted primarily as the arena in which the passions and sin operate. Augustine, elaborating on Paul, saw in sexual desire the passion that overrides all others. In the tradition derived from Augustine, sexual desire, therefore, epitomizes sin in general.[11] Often rendered as "pleasure," it is the primary stigma of the Fall.

Marguerite, working within the theological tradition that goes back through Briçonnet to Augustine and Paul, uses the term "plaisir" in the *Heptameron* to designate, mainly, sex outside of marriage. But if extramarital sexual activity is a sign of our fallen state, so is sexual activity in marriage, which both Paul and Augustine tolerate only with reluctance. Indeed, love for the creature is, as Scripture teaches, incompatible with love for the Creator (1 John 2:16), and in the *Heptameron* neither marriage nor love of another creature is a source of "joy," this term being reserved almost exclusively for union with Christ. Briçonnet, in a passage that stresses the necessity of submitting the flesh to mortification, had explained to Marguerite that God, wanting men and women to see their insufficiency, to recognize their lack, had mingled salt and bitterness in marriage so that they would not become prisoners of passion and of pleasure. Briçonnet explains that, in accordance with God's design, the bitterness inscribed in marriage will cause the creature ultimately to reject human love and turn to Christ, the fountain of divine love:

> Et pour ce que l'unyon du mary et de la femme n'est que l'ombre du mariage spirituel, qui est umbre du divin avec nature humaine . . . , ne voulant la bonté divine nature humaine se acoquiner et tant effriander à l'umbre, qu'elle laissast et oubliast la verité, à laquelle est appellée, et pour icelle crée, *a meslé en la première umbre* (*qui est la mariage charnel*) *de l'amertume*, pour suspirer et desirer l'unyon du spirituel, qui est sans *amertume*, umbre toutesfois de l'infinye, inexpressible doulceur, verité des deux. . . . Et, combien que *la tristesse et douleur viegne a cause du peché* . . . , toutesfois doulceur sans amertume n'eust esté si bon resveille matin pour congnoistre sa nature pellerine et desirer autre pays et region, où est nature humaine apellée. Et sainct Paul estime *le mariage charnel* (*combien que embridé de tristesse*) estre empechement du spirituel et, par ce, conseille se rettirer de l'umbre, pour plus commodement vaquer en orai-

son. Quel eust il esté sans avoir *du sel au pot, qui est la tristesse*, et le souvienne vous de moy, estant lors nature immortelle, eust par infidellité voulu demourer en l'ombre, sans desirer la lumiere et verité. Ce sçachant, la bonté divine, jalouze de nature humaine (de laquelle desiroit la totalle et parfaicte unyon), par *la mixtion de tristesse avec plaisir*, luy a donné lumiere de congnoissance qu'il y autre plaisir, pur et sans enuy, en abisme et source de toute joye et consollation. (2.251–52, emphasis added)

Marguerite's depiction of human love in the *Heptameron* and, indeed, elsewhere throughout her work is informed with Briçonnet's revelation that bitterness marks the relationship between men and women. Parlamente remarks that there is "pour le moins autant de peyne que de plaisir [dans le mariage]" (277;371), and Madame de Loué, the protagonist of novella 37, speaking in even broader terms, observes "qu'il n'est plus grand desespoir que l'amour" (267;359). Similarly, Dagoucin says that marriage is often "un fauxbourg d'enfer" (280;374). For Marguerite, human love does not in any consistent way lead to or shade into love for Christ, which is what generally happens in works marked strongly by Neoplatonism.

There is of course an occasional Neoplatonic cast to Marguerite's thought.[12] But as Christine Martineau points out, it is important to distinguish between two fundamentally different currents of Neoplatonism in the sixteenth century.[13] One is a religious current that runs back through Briçonnet, Lefèvre d'Etaples, a host of late medieval mystics, Cusa, Pseudo-Dionysius, and the patristic fathers. In this current, "Platonism" had been so deeply absorbed into Christianity that it was seldom thought of as being a form of "Neoplatonism." It was simply "Christian." The other current is what Martineau calls "un néo-platonisme amoureux," which was mainly a literary, especially poetic, phenomenon that was a powerful force in Italian literature at the end of the fifteenth century (the key figure here is Ficino) and that marked French literature of the sixteenth century. "Néo-platonisme amoureux" became increasingly important in French literature from around 1540, the date at which Marguerite seems to have become interested in it. Throughout the 1540s, scholars in her entourage wrote texts in which Neoplatonic elements figured more or less prominently (Héroët's *La Parfaicte amye* and Pontus de Tyard's *Solitaire premier*, for example). The Neoplatonism of these texts derives almost exclusively from the Ficinian model (Martineau's "néo-platonisme amoureux"), according to which human love serves as a stepping stone to divine love.

Marguerite herself, however, never embraced the fundamental tenets of "le néo-platonisme amoureux." In her work during the 1540s, she occasionally mentions Plato (for example, novellas 18 and 34), always unfavorably however, with the exception of two laudatory passages in the last book of *Les Prisons*. In any case, Marguerite never suggests, as does Ficino, that human love can mutate into love for Christ. On the contrary, throughout her work she stresses that human love, which in the *Heptameron* is articulated most often in the syntax of sexual desire, is an obstacle that must be annihilated before the Christian can arrive at Christ. Even Dagoucin, the most Platonizing of the *devisants*, points out that one has every reason to fear "ce petit dieu [Cupidon], qui prent son plaisir à tormenter autant les princes que les pauvres, et les fortz que les foibles, et qui les aveuglit jusque là d'oblier Dieu et leur conscience, et à la fin leur propre vie" (94;163). And Madame du Vergier in novella 70, realizing that her love for a certain "gentil homme" had turned her away from Christ, apostrophizes her soul before dying of grief: "Helas! ma pauvre ame, qui, par trop avoir adoré la creature, avez oblié le Createur, il fault retourner entre les mains de Celluy duquel l'amour vaine vous avoit ravie" (414;528). Insofar as we equate "Neoplatonism" with the Ficinian model (which is what twentieth-century readers nearly always do, collapsing the religious current of Neoplatonism into Augustinianism or more generally into Christianity), we must say that Marguerite is not in the least "Neoplatonic." Her positioning of human love within the arena of sinful flesh is a mark of her profound rejection of Ficinian "Neoplatonism."

"Woman as Symbol of Humanity"[14]

Nearly all the men in the *Heptameron* are driven by "la fureur de la concupiscence" (189;269), by a peculiarly masculine "malice"[15] that compels them to satisfy their desire in a paroxysm of what the text calls "jouissance" (140;217) on the conquered and humiliated, often raped and wounded, female body. The occasional woman in the *Heptameron* who is driven by sexual desire (for example, Jambicque in novella 43) ends up not by conquering the body of the Other as men do, but by being herself subjected to humiliation, the marks of which are inscribed on her body. (To discover the identity of his mysterious masked mistress, Jambicque's lover makes a chalk mark on the back of her shoulder as they embrace so that he can later identify her at court.)

Throughout the *Heptameron*, the humiliated body is far more often female than male, although there are examples of humiliated male bodies, too. The violence done to the female body in the *Heptameron* is not only, perhaps not even mainly, the violence of sexual politics grounded in a patriarchal order that, equating woman with matter and man with spirit, exercized repressive control over woman's body. It is also the sacramental violence that Christ demands of all humans, men and women, who seek to join him in "joy." Paul had declared that "in Christ . . . there can be neither male nor female" (Gal. 3:28). Male and female share in Christ an identity where opposites meet and are negated. To relate the treatment of the female body in the *Heptameron* only to the sexual politics of the Valois court is to restrict meaning to mimesis. In the devotional and representational practices of the fifteenth and sixteenth centuries, the female body was not legible first of all as mimesis but as *sign*. To read images of the "mortified" female body mimetically only, that is, to see in them nothing more than reflections of reified female bodies exploited by males in a patriarchal society, is to bracket out the function of desire, physicality, and *mortificatio* in the economy of salvation.

Recent studies of late medieval piety demonstrate that women theologians and mystics (and an increasing number of male mystics) saw woman as the symbol of all humanity, where humanity was understood as physicality.[16] Mary, redeeming and recuperating Eve, was the human source of salvation. Through her, the Word was made flesh. Ambrose had explained that although Christ "did not take His origin from the Virgin," he did take his body from her; Christ may be "white . . . for He is the brightness of the Father," but he is also "ruddy, for He was born of a Virgin."[17] All medieval theologians agreed that Christ, who did not have a human father, took his flesh from Mary. Hildegard of Bingen even argued that since Christ's body was formed from Mary's flesh it is identical with female flesh.[18] In Hildegard's view, female flesh, therefore, restores the world. Briçonnet repeatedly identified woman with the earth, with flesh, with *humanity*: "Terre, chair et femme (qui est ung)" (2.259); "le Verbe superceleste [chemine] en terre (en nature humaine)" (2.239). Elsewhere he observed that God used a woman to save the world, "car de la femme (qui est la sacrée Vierge) est le doux Jhesus vraye semence de vie, venu pour nous retirer de Sodome et Gomorre, mer et abisme de peché" (2.249).

Given that the dynamics of salvation required a "taking on" of Christ's pain (*mortificatio*), women often sought to join with Christ by emphasizing their own physicality and weakness. In the spirituality of the fifteenth and sixteenth centuries, the *imitatio Christi*, tracing an arc that moves from the pain of *mortificatio* to the jubilation of *illuminatio*, was staged more often than not across flesh that was theorized as female. Registering the mystical imperative to annihilate the body in order to accede to union with Christ, woman's body represented the flesh of *all* humans. As such, it was the supreme carnal site for securing Christian experience.

In both her poetry and prose, Marguerite de Navarre conforms to a tradition (going back through Augustine to the Bible) in which spiritual processes are articulated in the syntax of bodily functions. Here Briçonnet, once again, was Marguerite's mentor, for in his letters to her he presented the functions of the body as paradigms of spiritual operations. Eating was one of the most important of those functions and one of the richest in spiritual implications. Images of eating and drinking abound in Briçonnet's letters to Marguerite, who repeats them and elaborates on them in her letters back to him. In part, Briçonnet is making artful use of a biblical tradition, for images of food as metaphors for spiritual nourishment appear throughout the Bible. In part, he is following a tradition codified by Augustine, who, as Kenneth Burke points out, repeats almost to the point of obsession images of God as food, as, for example, in the invocation of Book Four of the *Confessions*, where he speaks of himself as sucking God's milk.[19]

Throughout the late Middle Ages, writers of mystical persuasion dwelled on the mystery of the Eucharist, which entailed, of course, eating Christ's body and drinking his blood. Recent scholarship has shown that blood, in particular, became an increasingly powerful symbol in late medieval and Renaissance devotional works.[20] Caroline Walker Bynum has argued that "all human exuding—menstruation, sweatings, lactation, emission of semen, etc.—were seen as bleedings."[21] Furthermore, all bleedings were viewed as food and nourishment. Artists and devotional writers often represented the wound in Christ's side as a breast spurting nourishing blood into a chalice held by Mary. Catherine of Siena spoke of drinking blood from the breast of mother Jesus.[22] For male writers, too, Christ's body was metaphorized as food. The preacher Jean Geiler, for example, devoting a series of sermons to the Passion, allegorized Christ's crucified body as rabbit stew that God prepared for the faithful.[23]

Read in the context of that tradition, which, moreover, Marguerite exploited in *Le Miroir de Jhesus Christ crucifié*, contemporaneous with the *Heptameron*, the alimentary and gustatory metaphors in the *Heptameron* acquire a rich resonance.[24] Over and over the text metaphorizes woman's body as a "viande," a "bonne chere," a "friandise" that arouses and satisfies desire. Moreover, woman's body is linked metonymically to other objects that are also figured as "viande," the most important of which is the Bible, identified as a "viande" (328;428) that sustains us, a "norriture" (393;503) that God gave humanity. Scripture is the Word made flesh, where flesh (inseparable from the female body) is understood as nourishment.

In the spirituality of the late Middle Ages and the Renaissance, "le corps alimentaire"[25] was indistinguishable from the eroticized body. Bernard (1091–1153) had linked the eating of Christ's body and the drinking of his blood to erotic experience. Around 1200, women mystics began to articulate with increasing frequency their experience of Christ in the register of erotic desire and sexual fulfillment. They stressed their joy at feeling their body pressed against Christ's body, their ecstasy at pressing their lips against his wound, often figured as a mouth that uttered ineffably beautiful sounds. From around 1400 on, male mystics began to express their experience of Christ in similar terms. Given the "female" nature of Christ's body, it is not surprising that late medieval artists, isolating Christ's wound for specific, almost fetishistic depiction, represented it in some instances very like a vulva.[26] At the heart of "le sacré médiéval" there is, as Jean Wirth has noted, "une série d'équivalences symboliques entre la nourriture, le sexe et la parole. L'acte sacré par excellence est l'union fécondante due à la manducation du Verbe."[27]

If in the *Heptameron* the word "plaisir" designates primarily sexual gratification and is sharply distinguished from "amour," it also designates the gratification that is derived from speech. "Le plaisir de parler" is often linked with "le plaisir de faire bonne chere," one of the text's euphemisms for sexual activity. In the *Heptameron*, speaking, like eating, is eroticized. Several times Longarine, whose name suggests skillful speaking (*langue orine*: "golden tongue"), declares that, for men at least, sexual gratification is incomplete until it is articulated in the register of discourse. "Il n'y a veneur qui ne prenne plaisir à corner sa prise" (322;422), she says, referring to the practice of sounding a horn when the animal pursued in a hunt is caught. In novella 18, speech is a substitute for sex. The lady in the novella demands that her suitor spend the night with her in bed, without, however, seeking to obtain any sexual favors other than kisses and speech. Although he was tempted to seize the "bonne chere qu'elle luy feist" (138;215), he kept his promise to restrain his passion and spent the night talking to her.

In the prologue, the *devisants* discussed how they might spend the ten days waiting for the bridge to be built. (Catherine of Siena spoke of Christ's body as a bridge the Christian must cross.)[28] Politely rejecting Oisille's suggestion that they spend their time in meditation and devotion, Hircan proposed that they engage in "les passetemps ou deux seullement peuvent avoir part" (9;68). Parlamente, in turn, rejected this proposal as inappropriate and suggested that they tell each other stories. Accepting Parlamente's suggestion, the *devisants* relate stories that turn out, however, to be substitutes for the very activities they had rejected. Their stories and the discussions that follow are informed by the imperatives of both spiritual and erotic desire, displaced now from devotion (Oisille's solution to the temporality of existence) and from sex (Hircan's solution to the same problem) into speech and textual production.

The *Heptameron* can be viewed, then, as a phantasy generated in part by erotic desire that is openly avowed in the prologue and then repressed. In the economy of the text, the "repressed" returns in a discourse where speech itself becomes an erotic act. But if erotic desire is displaced onto the text, so too is what one might call "devotional" desire. The *Heptameron* can be read as a commentary on—a staging, embodiment, or "enfleshment" of—the scriptural passages (Romans, mainly) that the *devisants* reflect upon every morning. Though not overtly manifest in the text except in an occasional citation, Scripture circulates through the interstices of human speech, filling discourse with the invisible presence of the Word.

The devotional nature of the *Heptameron* becomes even more apparent if we read the text in light of devotional practices in the late Middle Ages and Renaissance. In an article entitled "The Humanity and the Passion of Christ," Ewert Cousins points out that "the roots of meditation on the life of Christ can be traced to the monastic *lectio divina*,"[29] a slow and meditative reading of Scripture that, throughout the late Middle Ages, focused more and more on Christ as the man of sorrows. Stress on Christ's body, on his suffering flesh, resulted in devotional practices in which visual images played an increasingly important role. In line with the tendency toward greater affectivity in devotion, the notion of *pietas* became inseparable from the sense of compassion and pity: the pity of Christians before the image of the crucified Christ and the pity of Christ and his saints before the image of human misery and suffering.[30] Devotion merged into what Alois Maria Hass calls "an urgent 'passion-mysticism.'"[31]

With increasing frequency, wealthier Christians sought to provoke Christ's pity and to express their own compassion by commissioning paintings in which they were represented as penitents. Given to churches, these paintings were not only expressions of devotional impulses but also emblems of social status, wealth, and power. Put on display, they served as the focus of public, sometimes spectacular, devotional practices that became increasingly theatrical in nature. Wirth has pointed out the extent to which devotion became "performative": "Visant à un gain spirituel, la dévotion peut être assimilée symboliquement au travail ou au jeu, mais c'est l'assimilation au jeu qui l'emporte, vu la disproportion du gain et l'engagement affectif. Les écrits dévots opposent Marthe et Marie, le travail et la dévotion oisive; ils utilisent le symbolisme du jeu érotique en développant les metaphores du *Cantique des cantiques*. La parenté entre la dévotion et le jeu est non moins évidente dans l'utilisation du terme *devozione*, en Italie, pour désigner le théâtre religieux."[32]

Of Marguerite de Navarre's poems, *Le Miroir de Jhesus Christ crucifié* is a particularly forceful demonstration of the mechanics of devotion expressed in the register of the private and the individual.[33] Articulated in the language of tears, it illustrates how pity flows back and forth between Christ and the Christian, between the image that is the object of devotion and the spectator who, at the termination of the devotional exercise, is the recipient of Christ's pity. Insofar as the *Heptameron* is informed by a devotional urge, the text is legible as a representation of devotion cast now in the register of the *public* and the *social*. Read through the grid of devotional practices, the novellas function as images that do indeed often draw tears from those present. The elegance of the assembled *devisants*, the elaborate orchestration of each afternoon's performance (the order of the speakers, the alternation of male and female voices, and so on), and the beauty of the site where each performance takes place all point to a sumptuousness and a *spectacularity* that, because of sumptuary laws and prohibitions against games, had been confined to devotion, which in Wirth's words, "apparaît ainsi comme la seule pratique somptuaire et ludique qui soit légitime et honorable."[34]

Theatricality is heightened by the fact that the *devisants* carefully rehearse their parts before each performance. Furthermore, they perform before an audience, for with the permission of the *devisants*, monks from the monastery lie in a ditch behind a row of bushes that separates them from the aristocratic storytellers and listen, spellbound, to everything that is said. Here the theatrical shades off into the confessional. The claim that all the stories are true is consistent with the confessional format within which the performances take place. "Confession," as Foucault has pointed out, "is one of the main rituals we rely on for the production of truth."[35] Moreover, the stress on *concupiscentia carnis* is also consistent with the confessional format, for (quoting Foucault again) from the Middle Ages on "sex [has been] a privileged theme of confession."[36]

The *Heptameron*, then, is deeply informed with the problematic of penance, which, as Paul suggests in his letter to the Romans, is inseparable from the phantasmatic of "fleshy" desire. As creatures of "flesh and blood," we are "slaves to sin" (Rom. 7:14). But if Paul stresses the weakness of flesh, inevitably driven to sin, he also stresses salvation through faith. Eschatology is central to the Pauline tradition. It is also central to all of Marguerite de Navarre's work. The *Heptameron* generates its most powerful meanings when the relationship the text maps out between man and woman is seen in light of Pauline eschatology, when, that is to say, it is situated in the economy of salvation.

In Romans 5 (the biblical chapter Briçonnet and Marguerite mention most often in their correspondence), Paul says that because of Adam's disobedience, sin and death "spread through the whole human race" (5:12) only to be overcome in turn by the obedience and sacrifice of another man, Jesus, who, performing his father's will, delivered from death those who have faith in him. "Christ," Paul says, "died for the godless" (5:6); "we have been justified by His death" (5:9). Throughout her poetry, Marguerite maps the journey from sin to salvation (a road each Christian, guided by faith, seeks to follow) as a progression away from the old Adam, figure of the reign of sin and the harsh retribution of the Law, to the new Adam, to Christ, to the "new man," figure of a salvation that is effected through suffering and *mortificatio*, divestiture and loss.[37]

The same journey, I believe, is mapped out in the *Heptameron*. The increased devotional fervor of the *devisants* (manifested, for example, by the enthusiasm with which they extend their morning devotions on the eighth day) and the shift away from Romans after the fifth day toward the letters of John, redolent with the spirit of love and grace, point powerfully to progress along the *via Christi*.[38] Compelled by the storm to remain for ten days at Notre Dame de Sarrance, the *devisants* undertake a spiritual journey that, like all spiritual journeys, depends on the arrest of time. Or rather, on the perception that time, like flesh, is a medium designed to be "used" (*uti*), as Augustine says, "used up" or "annihilated" (*anichilé*), as Briçonnet puts it.

The Poetics of Chastity

Augustine stressed that the road the Christian travels is not "a road from place to place but a road of the affections."[39] What propels the Christian forward is desire. Analyzing the nature of desire, Augustine distinguished between "things that are to be enjoyed" and "things that are to be used" (*DDC* 1.4.9). The only "things" that are to be enjoyed are "the Father, the Son, and the Holy Spirit" (*DDC* 1.5.10). All other "things" are to be "used." Now desire, which is harbored in the flesh, constantly exerts a pull toward "fleshy" things that ought be "used" but that, because of their "perverse sweetness" (*DDC* 1.4.10), lure the Christian toward improper "enjoyment," that is to say, toward sin. In the *Heptameron*, the drive that propels the human creature toward the improper "enjoyment" of "fleshy" things is figured mainly, but by no means exclusively, in males. Moving in the immediacy of appetitive time, males represent, in one sense at least, the old Adam. On the other hand, the drive that propels the human creature toward the only "things" that can properly be "enjoyed" is figured primarily in those females whose overwhelming desire is for chastity.

Chastity, of course, signals purity. "What," Ambrose asked, "is virginal chastity but purity free from stain?"[40] In the *Heptameron*, however, chastity denotes also (and more crucially) an enjoyment that is *potential* and therefore not yet realized. Chastity is the supreme emblem of Christian "enjoyment," an "enjoyment" that is deferred and that will be experienced in a future that lies outside of time itself, beyond flesh and beyond discourse. The unfinished state of the *Heptameron*, whatever the reasons, translates with uncanny accuracy the perception that "enjoyment," in the Augustinian sense, can occur only beyond the "fleshy" words on the page.

Of course, not all women in the *Heptameron* strive to resemble Christ; and, naturally, a number of men do. Still, throughout the text, "woman" far more often than "man" is figured as that part of the human creature that strives to resemble the new Adam, or Christ, whose humanity, as we have seen, late medieval spirituality gendered as female. It is surely not by accident that the spiritual journey undertaken by the *devisants* during their several days together occurs at Notre Dame de Sarrance, a site to which they were miraculously led by God. In the economy of the text, the trajectory from Romans to John is identical with the movement from the old Adam to the new Adam, to Christ, figured as (female) flesh that suffers.

Although Marguerite distinguishes between chastity and virginity, early church fathers tended to use the terms interchangeably. In patristic texts, virginity always contains a reference to the blissful state of Adam and Eve before the Fall. The "paradise of virgins" to which Jerome refers is, in theological terminology, the "angelic," or asexual, state.[41] As Peter Brown points out, angels and virgins (because of the "abnormal" state of the virgin body) were viewed as "mediator[s] between the human and the divine."[42]

In the "angelic" state, the human creature is not yet—or no longer—a sexual being. Virginity, moreover, was linked to Mary, who, by bringing Life into the world, redeemed Eve. Jerome explains that it is because of Mary that "the gift of virginity has been bestowed most richly upon women, seeing that it has its beginning from a woman."[43] And Ambrose, in a passage that links Christ's humanity with female flesh, identifies Christ as "the Virgin Who bare us, Who fed us with her own milk." "From Christ," he observes, "the teats fail not."[44]

The desire for virginity is the desire to transcend the corporeal, a wish that amounts to a yearning to return to an original state. Though it is not inaccurate to claim, as R. Howard Bloch does, that "in this desire for totality lies the unmistakable symptom of a death wish,"[45] it is misleading, for the register in which the desire for virginity, for chastity, for totality, must be situated is not Freudian but Christian. Central to the Christian tradition is the concept of reversal. What Bloch identifies as the symptom of a death wish is an overwhelming desire for life in Christ.[46] In his letter of August 31, 1524, to Marguerite, Briçonnet, explaining that life is death and death is life, shows how the properties of each of the terms of what one would have thought to be a binary opposition cross over and come together in such a way that their opposition is inscribed into a system of exchange that is structured like a trope, chiasmus, the figure that, more than any other, deeply informs Christianity.

Peter Brown has pointed out that "the debate about virginity [in the early church] was in large part a debate about the nature of human solidarity. It was a debate about what the individual did and did not need to share with fellow creatures."[47] From the pagan point of view, sexuality was (in theory, at least) a desire that led to a *social* act. Marriage was an investment in the future of the social order. By refusing marriage, and more drastically, sexuality, Christians claimed for themselves a "freedom" that loosened the bonds of community. The body that was maintained in a virgin state was kept out of circulation and could not be recruited by society for its own benefit. It resisted the demands that society made on it and thus represented a threat to the sexual social contract that held society together. As the pagan elite recognized, the Christian advocacy of virginity implied a new social order that was radically different from the old.

In a key passage, Ambrose explains that "virginity is not praiseworthy because it is found in martyrs, but because *itself makes martyrs*" (emphasis added).[48] The supreme virtue of virginity is that it effects the annihilation and mortification of the body that allows accession to Christ. That is precisely the function of chastity in the *Heptameron*: it makes martyrs and thereby accomplishes the operation of grace. The woman in novella 2 is an exemplar of the many chaste women in the *Heptameron*. A mule-driver's wife, she resisted the advances of her husband's servant. Enraged by her resistance and inflamed by an "amour bestialle" (19;79), the servant stabbed the woman several times. Bleeding profusely, she grew weaker and prayed to Christ, asking him to accept her soul, secure in her faith that her sins had been effaced by the blood of his sacrifice. The servant then raped her, and she, "une martire de chasteté" (21;81), died "avecq un visaige joyeulx" (20;81), a joyful death being an infallible sign of salvation in Marguerite's works.[49]

Something of the debate about what one owes society and what one can (or even must) withhold from society lingers on in Marguerite's advocacy of chastity. Distinguishing chastity from virginity, Marguerite seldom, if ever, praises virginity per se. Nor does she ascribe positive value to chastity in the sense of sexual abstinence. Throughout the *Heptameron*, chastity means *fidelity* (*fides*, the first of the ecclesiastical virtues). It denotes a fidelity so absolute that it "makes martyrs." Often marriage is the scene within which fidelity—or its lack—is demonstrated. But not always. In novella 70 (a retelling of the thirteenth-century poem *La Chastelaine de Vergi*), the young and beautiful widow Madame du Vergier is secretly the mistress of a young and handsome "gentil homme." Their love, which is "chaste, honneste et vertueuse" (413;527) and which "[n'est] tachée de nul vice" (414;528), depends on being kept secret. The young man's fidelity is manifested by his refusal to speak about his love, by his willingness to withdraw from the public arena in order to experience passion in a wholly private and inward space, figured in the text as a room in a tower of the chastelaine's castle, which is located at some distance from the court. To approach the tower, the lover must pass through a small garden door, which he locks after him. When his master, the duke, driven on by his wife's jealousy, compels the young man to reveal his love, the chastelaine dies of grief. The lover, apostrophizing his tongue as the instrument of his infidelity, kills himself for having spoken. The duke, realizing that it was his wife's speech that had made him force a confession from the young man, turns on his wife and stabs her to death. In novella 70, as elsewhere in the *Heptameron*, silence and chastity are inseparable, one serving as a metaphor for the other and both functioning as metaphors for the inwardness of a faith so strong that, as Paul explained to the Romans, it alone separates the saved from the damned.[50]

Indeed, two races inhabit the world of the *Heptameron*: the damned and the elect. The damned, like the Serpent, live out their lives in dust and filth, driven forward through time by the discourses of concupiscence and garrulity. Like "la mauvaise femme" in novella 1, they die "miserablement" (17;77). The elect, too, are driven by a desire they cannot control. They do not choose their election; rather, they are *marked* for election.[51] They are driven toward Christ by the fire of a faith that traverses them and consumes them, that in fact destroys their humble dreams of happiness (in marriage, family, friends, social respectability) and leaves them with no desire save the wish to be annihilated in him. God, as Briçonnet repeated over and over to Marguerite, is a consuming fire. Christ is "la fournaize virginalle" (2.231) in which the elect are burned until, reduced to "pouldre," they are "semblables au doux Jhesus" (2.249). They are projected upward, away from the axis of metonymic succession, by the desire Paul articulated when he said, "Cupio dissolvi et esse cum Christo" (Phil. 1:23). Plotting the Christian trajectory from sin to salvation across the human body, Marguerite sees in the cry of desire (*cupio*) the means whereby grace, operating mysteriously and miraculously, rotates the elect away from "la terre" and propels them toward Christ.

The intense desire to escape from desire is itself the source of the desire that projects the elect toward Christ. Though the desire for chastity, for totality, for deferred enjoyment, may hold the phantasy of an escape from desire, it is itself inscribed in the logic, in the *theatrics*, of desire. And it is through this logic, which brings together in chiastic concatenation the violence of desire and the desire for violence, that God operates his will and draws those he has chosen to him.

Notes

1. Philippe de Lajarte, "L'*Heptaméron* et la naissance du récit moderne: Essai de lecture épistémologique d'un discours narratif," *Littérature* 17 (1975): 31–42; "Le Prologue de l'*Heptaméron* et le processus de production de l'oeuvre," in *La Nouvelle française à la Renaissance*, ed. Lionello Sozzi (Geneva: Slatkine, 1981), 397–423 (henceforth "Le Prologue de l'Heptaméron"); "Modes du discours et formes d'altérité dans les 'Nouvelles' de Marguerite de Navarre," *Littérature* 55 (1984): 64–73.

2. Caroline Walker Bynum, "The Body of Christ in the Later Middle Ages: A Reply to Leo Steinberg," *Renaissance Quarterly* 39 (1986): 399–439, esp. 413. See also Bynum, *Holy Feast and Holy Fast* (Berkeley: University of California Press, 1986).

3. Speaking about the evangelical attitude toward death and suffering,

Claude Blum, *La Représentation de la mort dans la littérature française de la Renaissance* (Paris: Champion, 1989), vol. 1, 259, notes: "Dans cet immense jeu de significations, le corps humain tient un rôle central: il est 'modèle,' lieu originel de toutes les figures de Péché et de la Mort. Il devient, pour les Evangéliques, un élément privilégié d'insertion du récit de la Chute et de la Rédemption dans l'espace et le temps du monde."

4. On the biblical intertext in the *Heptameron*, see Nicole Cazauran, Les Citations bibliques dans l'*Heptaméron*," in *Prose et prosateurs de la Renaissance: Mélanges offerts à Robert Aulotte* (Paris: SEDES, 1988), 153–61. Also Mary B. McKinley, "Scriptural Speculum: The Biblical Sub-texts in Marguerite de Navarre's *Heptaméron*," unpublished paper read at the annual meeting of the Renaissance Society of America, Boston, 1989.

5. Unless indicated differently, all English translations of the Bible are from *The New Jerusalem Bible* (Garden City, N.Y.: Doubleday & Company, Inc., 1985). The theological term for Christ's "humiliation" is kenosis. On the prominence accorded the concept of kenosis in evangelical texts, see Robert D. Cottrell, "The Poetics of Transparency in Evangelical Discourse: Marot, Briçonnet, Marguerite de Navarre, Héroët," in *Lapidary Inscriptions: Renaissance Essays for Donald Stone, Jr.*, ed. Barbara C. Bowen and Jerry C. Nash (Lexington, Ky.: French Forum, 1991), 40–41.

6. On the thematics of water in the *Heptameron*, see Claude-Gilbert Dubois, "Fonds mythique et jeu des sens dans le 'prologue' de l'*Heptaméron*," in *Etudes seiziémistes offertes à M. le professeur V.-L. Saulnier par plusieurs de ses anciens doctorants*, Travaux d'Humanisme et Renaissance 177 (Geneva: Droz, 1980), 151–68.

7. Guillaume Briçonnet and Marguerite d'Angoulême, *Correspondance (1521–1524)*, ed. Christine Martineau, Michel Veissière, and Henry Heller. 2 vols. Travaux d'Humanisme et Renaissance 141 (Geneva: Droz). 1 (1975), 2 (1979). 1:195–214. Subsequent references to the *Correspondance* will be identified in the text by volume and page number.

8. Juliana of Norwich, *Revelations of Divine Love* (London: Kegan Paul, Trench, Trübner and Co., 1902), 143.

9. Michel Foucault, *The History of Sexuality, Volume I: An Introduction*, trans. Robert Hurley (New York: Vintage, 1980).

10. For a discussion of Paul's term "flesh," see *The New Jerusalem Bible*, p. 1877.

11. Elaine Pagels, *Adam, Eve, and the Serpent* (New York: Random House, 1989), 109–11.

12. Blum, *La Représentation de la mort*, vol. 1, 279: "Le platonisme fournit aux Evangéliques des images, des formules, non une spiritualité."

13. Christine Martineau, "Le Platonisme de Marguerite de Navarre?" *Réforme, Humanisme, Renaissance* 2, no. 4 (1976): 13–14.

14. The phrase is by Bynum, *Holy Feast and Holy Fast*, 261.

15. The words "la malice des hommes" appear at least twice in the text, 75;143 and 295;390.

16. The literature is extensive. See in particular Caroline Walker Bynum, *Jesus as Mother: Studies in the Spirituality of the High Middle Ages* (Berkeley: University of California Press, 1982); Bynum, *Holy Feast and Holy Fast*; Bynum, "'. . . And Woman

His Humanity': Female Imagery in the Religious Writing of the Later Middle Ages," in *Gender and Religion: On the Complexity of Symbols*, ed. Caroline Walker Bynum, Steven Harrell, Paula Richman (Boston: Beacon Press, 1986), 257–88. Also Richard Kieckhefer, *Unquiet Souls: Fourteenth-Century Saints and Their Religious Milieu* (Chicago: University of Chicago Press, 1985), and Eleanor McLaughlin, "'Christ My Mother': Feminine Naming and Metaphor in Medieval Spirituality," *Nashota Review* 5 (1975): 229–48.

17. Ambrose, "Concerning Virgins," in *A Select Library of Nicene and Post-Nicene Fathers of the Christian Church*, 2d series, ed. Philip Schaff and Henry Wace, vol. 10 (New York: The Christian Literature, 1896), 366.

18. See Elisabeth Gössmann, "Das Menschenbild der Hildegard von Bingen und Elisabeth von Schönau vor dem Hintergrund der frühscholastischen Anthropologie," in *Frauenmystik im Mittelalter*, ed. Peter Dinzelbacher and Dieter R. Bauer, Wissenschaftliche Studientagung der Akademie der Diözese Rottenburg-Stuttgart, February 22–25, 1984, in Weingarten (Osfildern bei Stuttgart: Schwabenverlag, 1985), pp. 24–47, and Bynum, *Holy Feast and Holy Fast*, 264–65.

19. Kenneth Burke, *The Rhetoric of Religion* (Boston: Beacon Press, 1961), 66, 119.

20. See James H. Marrow, *Passion Iconography in Northern European Art of the Late Middle and Early Renaissance: A Study of the Transformation of Sacred Metaphor into Descriptive Narrative* (Kortrijk, Belg.: Van Ghemmert, 1979); Lionel Rothkrug, "Popular Religion and Holy Shrines: Their Influence on the Origins of the German Reformation and Their Role in German Cultural Development," in *Religion and People, 800–1700*, ed. James Obelkevich (Chapel Hill: University of North Carolina Press, 1979); Bynum, "The Body of Christ in the Later Middle Ages"; Bynum, *Holy Feast and Holy Fast*.

21. Bynum, "The Body of Christ in the Later Middle Ages," 436.

22. See Bynum, *Holy Feast and Holy Fast*, 271.

23. See Jean Wirth, *L'Image médiévale: Naissance et développements (VIe–XVe siècles)* (Paris: Méridiens Klincksieck, 1989), 326.

24. Marcel Tetel, *Marguerite de Navarre's Heptaméron: Themes, Language and Structure* (Durham, N.C.: Duke University Press, 1973), 43–54, discusses food metaphors in the *Heptameron*. See also Colette H. Winn, "Gastronomy and Sexuality: 'Table Language' in the *Heptaméron*," *Journal of the Rocky Mountain Medieval and Renaissance Association* 7 (1986): 17–25. On food metaphors in the Briçonnet-Marguerite *Correspondance*, see Robert D. Cottrell, *The Grammar of Silence: A Reading of Marguerite de Navarre's Poetry* (Washington, D.C.: The Catholic University of America Press, 1986), 19–21.

25. The phrase is by Wirth, *L'Image médiévale*, 325.

26. See the illustrations in Wirth, *L'Image médiévale*, 329–31.

27. Wirth, *L'Image médiévale*, 340.

28. Catherine of Siena, *Il Dialogo della Divina Provvidenza ovvero Libro della Divino Dottrina*, ed. Guiliana Cavallini (Rome: Edizioni Cateriniane, 1968), 179.

29. Ewert Cousins, "The Humanity and the Passion of Christ," in *Christian Spirituality: High Middle Ages and Reformation*, ed. Jill Raitt (New York: Crossroad, 1987), 377.

30. See Hans Belting, *Das Bild und sein Publikum im Mittelalter* (Berlin: Gebr. Mann Verlag, 1981), 14–23. Also F. O. Büttner, *Imitatio Pietatis* (Berlin: Gebr. Mann Verlag, 1983).

31. Alois Maria Hass, "Schools of Late Medieval Mysticism," in *Christian Spirituality: High Middle Ages and Reformation*, ed. Jill Raitt (New York: Crossroad, 1987), 155.

32. Wirth, *L'Image médiévale*, 279–80.

33. See Robert D. Cottrell, "The Gaze as the Agency of Presence in Marguerite de Navarre's *Miroir de Jhesus Christ crucifié*," *French Forum* 13, no. 2 (1988): 133–41.

34. Wirth, *L'Image médiévale*, 280. On sumptuary laws in Renaissance France, see Louise Godard de Donville, *Signification de la mode sous Louis XIII* (Aix-en-Provence: Edisud, 1976), esp. "Annexe I: les édits somptuaires," 205–13.

35. Foucault, *The History of Sexuality, Volume I: An Introduction*, 58.

36. Ibid., 61.

37. On the old Adam/new Adam opposition and on the *mortificatio* in Marguerite's poetry, see Robert D. Cottrell, *The Grammar of Silence*, esp. 51, 107, 117, 174–75. On the journey metaphor and on the importance of time in the *Heptameron*, see Glyn P. Norton, "Narrative Function in the 'Heptaméron' Frame-Story," in *La Nouvelle française à la Renaissance*, ed. Lionello Sozzi (Geneva: Slatkine, 1981), 435–47.

38. Paula Sommers, "Marguerite de Navarre's *Heptaméron*: The Case for the Cornice," *The French Review* 57, no. 6 (1984): 786–93, argues that the increased spiritual fervor in the prologues is systematically deconstructed in the epilogues.

39. Augustine, *De doctrina christiana*, trans. D. W. Robertson, Jr. (Indianapolis: The Bobbs-Merrill Co., Library of the Liberal Arts, 1958), Bk. I, Chap. 17, p. 6. Henceforth identified in the text as *DDC*, the numbers referring to book, chapter, and page.

40. Ambrose, "Concerning Virgins," 366.

41. Jerome, "Letter 22," in *A Select Library of the Nicene and Post-Nicene Fathers of the Christian Church*, 2d ser., ed. Philip Schaff and Henry Wace, vol. 6 (Grand Rapids, Mich.: Eerdmans, 1961), 29.

42. Peter Brown, "The Notion of Virginity in the Early Church," in *Christian Spirituality: Origins to the Twelfth Century*, ed. Bernard McGinn and John Meyendorff (New York: Crossroad, 1985), 433. See also Peter Brown, *The Body and Society: Men, Women, and Sexual Renunciation in Early Christianity* (New York: Columbia University Press, 1988), and Jane Tibbets Schulenburg, "The Heroics of Virginity: Brides of Christ and Sacrificial Mutilation," in *Women in the Middle Ages and the Renaissance*, ed. Mary Beth Rose (Syracuse: Syracuse University Press, 1986), 29–72. Because angels were "superior" to humans, virginity, which made humans angel-like, could be a source of power. On this, see Philippa Berry, *Of Chastity and Power: Elizabethan Literature and the Unmarried Queen* (London: Routledge, 1989).

43. Jerome, "Letter 22," 30.

44. Ambrose, "Concerning Virgins," 366–67.

45. R. Howard Bloch, "Chaucer's Maiden's Head: 'The Physician's Tale' and the Poetics of Virginity," *Representations* 28 (1989): 120.

46. Bloch is aware of this and footnotes the sentence quoted above with the words: "I am not unaware of the fact that according to a certain Christological logic, virginity can also be said to triumph over death."

47. Brown, "The Notion of Virginity in the Early Church," 436.

48. Ambrose, "Concerning Virgins," 365.

49. Citing verses from Marguerite de Navarre's poetry, Blum, *La Représentation de la mort*, vol. 1, 280, observes, "L'heure de la mort retrouve alors une signification: elle est l'heure sans mensonges, l'instant où l'on peut distinguer les fidèles de ceux qui ne le sont pas."

50. Virginity and silence were linked from the time of the church fathers on. Thus Georges d'Esclavonie, "chanoine et penencier de l'eglise de Tours," in a work entitled *Le Chasteau de la virginité* (Paris: 1505) writes to a young girl who has just entered a convent: "Tu garderas la virginité de la langue." Relying heavily on Jerome and especially Ambrose, d'Esclavonie notes that "la virginité a fait les anges & celuy qui la garde est devenu ange." Observing that angels do not speak in human tongues, d'Esclavonie tells the girl that if she wishes to be like an angel she must refrain from speaking.

51. Blum, *La Représentation de la mort*, 213, insists on the difference between the evangelical notion of predestination and that of Calvin. He points out, however, that certain verses in Marguerite de Navarre's late poetry suggest the influence of Calvin. Calvin's influence is even stronger, I believe, in the *Heptameron*, a text Blum never mentions.

2. Gender, Essence, and the Feminine (*Heptameron* 43)

> On dict que place qui parlamente est demy-gaingnée.
> —Novella 18, *Heptameron*

Pierre Jourda noted long ago that Marguerite de Navarre's *Heptameron* marks a clear regression away from the brutality of medieval tournaments and toward the culture of wit and intellectual dueling.[1] The *Heptameron* self-consciously marks its investment in speech as characterization, with Parlamente, its most complex voice, punningly inscribed in the siege language which opens this essay: "on dict que place qui parlamente est demy-gaingnée" (142;219). As speech projects itself into exteriority, thus unmaking the purity of silence, it gives of itself at its risk and peril, just as the commander who would negotiate with the enemy may be taken in through dissembling and betrayal. In the sexual terms of medieval siege allegory, a recurrent topos in the *Heptameron*, chastity is half-lost when speech begins, Marguerite's recognition of the yoking of discourse and desire.

Femininity as bastion is variously assailed, provoked, and celebrated in this most dialogic of collections, the issue of feminine identity being at once self-evident and contested in the stories and their frame discussions. What I explore in this chapter is gender as a classificatory system in Marguerite's text, in particular, the aggressive female character who disrupts neat boundaries between what the culture designates as models of femininity and masculinity. It is perhaps too frequently overlooked that our critical vocabulary for discussing the *Heptameron* is heavily shaped by the language of its first editors. When Adrien de Thou affixed summaries to the beginning of each tale, he offered a gloss of its contents, much in the way that medieval scribes rubricated their manuscripts, often moralizing them.[2] Marguerite wrote in a time of class realignments, gender redefinition, and confusion as to sexual protocols, one root of which was the decline of courtly love as a social institution. De Thou's headings project an illusion of stability based on the recurrence of such words as honor, hypocrisy, nature, and *dissimulation*, the meanings of which seem agreed upon but far from absolute in the discussions following the tales. Initially, then, we must recognize a potential bias, even closural effect, generated by the prefatory material which works to exclude in a subtle way other strategies of reading.

To illustrate this point, I want to turn to the story of Jambicque, a lady of the court whose sexual desire is the subject matter of novella 43. De Thou's summary, the text of which follows, sets the terms in which later critics conceive the heroine and her plight: "Jambicque, preferant la gloire du monde à sa conscience, se voulut faire devant les hommes autre qu'elle n'estoit; mais son amy et serviteur, descouvrant son hypocrisye par le moyen d'un petit trait de craye, revela à un chascun la malice qu'elle mectoit si grand peine de cacher." Following de Thou, recent critics of the *Heptameron* have emphasized Jambicque's hypocrisy, pride, and degeneracy, viewing her as a woman rivaled only by the foreign countess of novella 49 in her duplicity. Nicole Cazauron, for one, echoes De Thou when she attributes Jambicque's fate and that of the countess to their foolish desire to please men instead of pleasing God: "La condamnation de Jambicque . . . tire ainsi tout son sens de cet abaissement qui les remet à leur *vraie place*, celle qui est la leur au regard de Dieu, après qu'elles ont été montrées dans tout l'éclat de leur 'gloire' ou de leur crédit parmi les hommes" (emphasis added).[3] Cazauron locates Jambicque's sin in her not knowing her place, a failing which stems from her assumption that God is not present in earthly affairs. But there is another sense in which Jambicque does not know her place, and that is with regard to protocols of feminine and masculine desire. Jambicque shocks the world by taking the place of a man in her pursuit of pleasure, and it is this changing of place in the sexual paradigm that creates the scandal in the story. Indeed, when another critic, writing about Jambicque's desire, describes her as a "nymphomaniac," a norm is posited beyond which the concept of the feminine cannot go without veering into pathology.[4]

Indeed, novella 43 tests the idea of gender as a classificatory practice, asking implicitly how accommodating the categories of the feminine and the masculine can be and still offer themselves as determinative of difference. I propose that Jambicque be read in this light, as Marguerite's exercise in the "outing" of feminine desire in the unlikely force field of an aristocratic culture. Desire—feminine desire—labors under taboos which disallow the expression of that desire within a matrix conceived along masculine, courtly lines. This drama is played out on several fronts in the

Heptameron: in avowal as a privileged act, in speech and silence as tropes of disclosure, and elsewhere, in desire spoken only at the arrival of death, thus signaling its disappearance at the very moment of its articulation. To these may be added the split between public and private selves—a further sign that desire is shameful when exhibited within a configuration of masculine power relations. The Jambicque story puts the female body at the center of desire, thematizing it as disembodied but paradoxically empowering it by means of masking, a variation on the trope of woman as effaced in courtly love. Jambicque's performance of femininity will be taken up in the final section of this chapter. First, however, let us turn to the story and its framing of gender questions in terms of the plot and the discussion which it generates.[5]

Geburon, the story's narrator, includes much that defines Jambicque as a slave of her passions. She is "fort audatieuse," and is feared at court as an enemy of love. She frowns on "folle amour," reports on those who give in to love, and generally ingratiates herself with her mistress as a woman who stands above passion. Indeed, she appears to be something of a Hippolytus in her arrogant rejection of sex, thus setting herself up for the charge of hypocrisy when she later makes an overture to a gentleman at court. Jambicque thus practices a double standard, but it is her impiety which sets her apart. For Jambicque it is better to have honor before men than before God. She contrives to present a virtuous face to her public, but dismisses God's judgment because he is far away. In the evangelical world of Marguerite's *devisants*, the sin of pride sets Jambicque apart from other desiring women because she not only gives in to desire; she plans and executes her tryst with conscious intent to deceive others. What Jambicque does not admit, however, is that God is all-knowing and that he sees all.

Jambicque is all too familiar in the fabliau tradition as the wanton female. Geburon portrays her as dissatisfied with the pleasures habitually accorded to women, that is, loving chastely through "le regard et la parolle" (297;392). Instead, she seeks both to have sex and to keep her good reputation, a goal she achieves for a long time by insisting that the tryst be conducted in the dark. The crisis in the story comes when the *gentilhomme*, impatient to know who she is, marks her shoulder with chalk during an embrace, so that she may be readily identifiable as his lover when she next appears in court. The lover is astonished to see that his sexual partner is in fact Jambicque, and when he confronts her, he is denounced as a liar and ultimately banished from the court.

The *Heptameron*, as K. Kasprzyk reminds us, does not adopt a facile schematization of male and female natures in regard to love. There are men who love "parfaictement," just as there are women like Jambicque who are lustful and unscrupulous, experience showing that virtue is not the exclusive property of one sex or the other.[6] Nevertheless, Marguerite's *devisants* often apply fixed notions of femininity and masculinity to the stories they hear, thus running what Diana Fuss calls "the risk of essence," that is, a conception of man and woman "which stands outside the sphere of cultural influence and historical change."[7] According to the women, honor defines women as superior to men, whereas men declare themselves in harmony with nature because they love openly, without hypocrisy.[8] The Jambicque story presents just such a challenge to the prevailing courtly construct of women as chaste. Within the courtly code by which Jambicque lives, there can be no question of the open display of affection, let alone sexual desire. What she demands of her lover is that he enjoy her without asking who she is and that, correlatively, he not speak of their love to anyone. In other words, she demands silence: "si vous me voulez promectre de m'aymer et de jamais n'en parler à personne, ne vous vouloir enquerir de moy qui je suys, je vous asseureray bien que je vous seray loyalle et bonne amye, et que jamais je n'aymeray autre que vous" (297;393).

In a second phase of the story, after their sexual union has been consummated, the lover again raises the issue of his lady's identity. He wonders out loud how he can "pourchasser," or be a good servant to her, when he does not even know who she is. Jambicque again reminds him of his promise: "Et, sur tout, je vous prye ne serchez jamais de me congnoistre" (298;394). Reiterated at this second stage of phrasing, Jambicque's command takes on another significance, and that is as a sign of woman's resistance to the male desire to know, and thus master, the woman who eludes him. Jambicque's story then becomes not an emblem of deceit or shame but a self-conscious challenge to gender-typing associated with courtliness.

As a theoretical framework for this reading, let us recall what Roland Barthes calls the "maleness of all narrative movement," that is, the plotting of stories as sequences wherein the protagonist's goal, explicitly acted upon, is to discover the answer to a secret. In Barthes's telling, the paradigmatic example is Sophocles' Oedipus who arrives at the knowledge of his own identity by solving the riddle of the Sphinx, but the same impulse to know propels all narrative, a movement whose culmination is seen in the hero's unveiling of a truth which has remained hidden from him.[9] The appropriateness of Barthes's observation to the *Heptameron* is evidenced in the numerous stories in which a male protagonist eavesdrops, spies, or physically intrudes into the space which his lady occupies. The extreme case of this is *viol*, rape, in which transgression occurs literally on the site of the female body. But elsewhere, Marguerite shows a pattern of forced entry which is serious by virtue of its near invisibility; each time a confession is overheard, or a secret wrested from its hiding place, the subject finds herself mastered, which is to say exposed, in such a way as to threaten her autonomy as a subject.

Now eavesdropping/spying may present itself as nongendered and nonviolent, as when a *damoiselle* in novella 70 listens to a lady's lament "à travers le rideau," and subsequently reports what she has heard.[10] In such cases a relay among speakers and listeners is set up, and the network that results may very well mirror in scriptural terms the passing of stories by word of mouth in the oral tradition. But a far more representative case occurs in the same story when the duke, "le plus curieux homme du monde," spies from behind a tree while his young courtier woos a lady.[11] Here, as repeatedly elsewhere, the desire to know appears to be motivated by curiosity alone, quite apart from the specific insight which may be obtained. The duke as spectator shares the storyteller's pleasure in gazing, a pleasure which is intensified by mastering the subject through visual objectivation. This "capturing of the female body," as Mary Ann Doane calls it,[12] only anticipates the power of the gaze later theorized by Foucault as a constituent force in the discourse of institutionalized power; on the other hand, it gestures beyond itself to writing as a compensatory form of power, as a strategy to take back the power that is lost when women will not let themselves be seen/known. In Jambicque's story, male power asserts itself through the well-worked trope of inscription. During an embrace, the lover marks Jambicque with chalk so that he may identify her when he sees her next at court. Jambicque is the passive feminine "blank page" who, far from being a user of language, becomes instead the surface on which the lover marks. If women are denied their status as subjects when they become the objects of spectral pleasure, they may found a feminine subjectivity on the body's claim to visibility.[13] Only a radical retroping of the metaphor of the gaze could mark this shift, and it is precisely this shift which Marguerite attempts in her story of Jambicque.

Barthes's remark on narrative is pertinent to our analysis because it refocuses the reader's attention on the male protagonist, with his desire to know, rather than on Jambicque and her hypocrisy. Indeed, there has been undue attention paid to whether women in the stories live up to the virtuous ideal of femininity prescribed for them by the courtly code, and rather little on the male role as aggressor. That disbalance may be attributed in part, as noted above, to the moralizing rubrics of the tales. But it may also stem from another source: our willingness as readers to assent to the belief that, as one pious character puts it elsewhere, "l'honneur des hommes et des femmes n'est pas semblable" (218;302). Now it is not just the men who proclaim the difference between the sexes to be based on sexual appetite; to the contrary, they make the universalist claim that women too are desiring subjects and would act upon their desires like the men if they could do so without hurting their reputations. It is rather the women in the *Heptameron* who insist on their uniqueness and derive their sense of identity from a self-conscious reflection on the honor that defines them as a sex. It is for this reason—their investment in honor—that counterexamples such as Jambicque and the lady of Pampluna are so troubling. The pious lady of Pampluna, it may be recalled, was caught when her devotion to a priest shifted abruptly into lust. Jambicque, on the other hand, exhibits lust as part of her "nature," and thereby challenges the notion that women place honor above all.

Indeed, it is so unthinkable for a woman to display desire that when she does, she is redescribed as a male. The appeal to fixed categories occurs often enough in the *Heptameron* to suggest that male and female are grounded in essentialist notions that cannot be rethought without putting into question the entire economy of sexual difference. As one example, consider the tempestuous duchess of Burgundy, again in novella 70, whose passion provokes a "sex change" of sorts, as the text's only way of accommodating her desire within a system that apportions sexuality and chastity according to canons of gender definition: "oubliant qu'elle estoit femme qui debvoit estre priée et refuser, princesse qui debvoit estre adorée, desdaignant telz serviteurs, print le cueur d'un homme transporté pour descharger le feu qui estoit importable" (401;513). Given this striking example, we may agree with Paul Smith who writes elsewhere that "patriarchy has defined and placed women as the other with the result that, if women begin to speak and act from the same ground of cerned objectivity and identity as men have traditionally enjoyed, a resistance is automatically effected."[14] For Smith, women have not been accorded status as properly "full" subjects, their role as other serving rather as the means through which male self-definition is negotiated. The lover fantasizes about whom his partner might be, believing that all women want to be seen, but his conflation of *voir/savoir* is none other than the self-serving exercise of his own narcissistic need to be affirmed in his identity as a courtly lover. Both parties participate in each other's self-representations, but the lover is at a risk of emasculation in the profound sense of not being allowed to play the cultural role to which he has been assigned, that is, as the one who gazes.

Now within the courtly paradigm, there is a practical reason why the lover must know whom it is he loves, and that is the obligation to actively pursue the good that the beloved by convention withholds from him. Allusion is made to this courtly code by the lover when he asks Jambicque how he can "pourchasser" under such constraints of anonymity. But on an entirely different plane altogether is the problem of Jambicque's "otherness," that strange quality which remains forever unassimilable, but which the lover feels compelled to discover by making her reveal herself. There is a way, moreover, in which the "enigma" of Jambicque anticipates Freud's view of woman as the "dark continent," with the lover being no more able to know his lady than Freud was able to penetrate the secrets of female sexuality. In his lecture "Femininity," Freud characterized woman as passive but also posited the notion of bisexuality to account for the exceptionally intelligent, active woman. According to his essay, the intelligent woman could be seen as an exception to the rule of woman as passive, she being more masculine than feminine in makeup. The strategic effect of Freud's move was the contaminant of feminine complexity, insofar as the idea of woman was not expanded to include a full range of desire, power, and other male-identified characteristics. Whereas Marguerite's *devisants* think of Jambicque as a man, Freud, too, could not regard the active woman as belonging to the category of the feminine.[15]

Freud's solution to the case of the intelligent woman, viewing her as an anomaly, demonstrates just how absolute the categories of masculine/feminine could be, so as to force the creation of a new category, bisexuality, to account for exceptions. Jambicque's resistance to her lover's gaze is related to this complex issue, insofar as she "saves face," but also loses face, by being redefined as a body having no identity apart from her sexual organs. On the other hand, Jambicque retains her enigmatic character, her "darkness" (in Freud's terms). But it is also true that Jambicque remains invisible as a condition of her erotic self-expression, and will even be read out of the category of woman all together in the ensuing discussion—and by Parlamente, no less. If women served men as mirrors for men's self-definition, as has recently been observed, why is it that men did not do the same for women, making the body a part of their sense of self?[16]

*   *   *

A return to the character of Jambicque defined not as a hypocrite, but as a resistant subject, permits other elements of the story to surface, and in particular, Jambicque's determination to escape the stigma of sexuality defined as dishonorable in a courtly setting, that is, to keep her secret. Here, the feminine resistance to male knowing reasserts itself, as noted above. Jambicque's strategy is couched in terms of the gaze, meaning that she will literally not allow her lover to see her face when they are making love. What Jambicque asks of her lover, then, is to treat her with anonymity, and most important, to forgo any attempt to discover who she is: "si vous me voulez promectre de m'aymer et de jamais n'en parler à personne, ne vous vouloir enquerir de moy qui je suys, je vous asseureray bien que je vous seray loyalle et bonne amye. . . . Mais, j'aymerois mieulx morir, que vous sceussiez qui je suys" (297;393). The urgency of Jambicque's command, repeated more than once, recalls the lady's power to set the terms of an adulterous union, her prerogative according to courtly convention. But there is more to Jambicque's command than the exercise of privilege accorded to ladies, and that is a certain archaism underscored by the text's repetition of the demand on several occasions that her lover not seek to know her. What Jambicque does, in effect, is to institute a taboo, the transgression of which will cause her lover to lose her favors forever. As she says, "Et, sur tout, je vous prye ne serchez jamais de me congnoistre, si vous ne voulez la separation de nostre amityé" (298;394).

The taboo enjoining the male lover not to look at his lady is a recurrent theme in folklore, and would have been known to Marguerite's contemporaries both in high cultural and popular sources. Ovid's story of Orpheus recounted the latter's loss of his beloved when he turned back to look at her, in violation of his promise not to do so. In the popular legend of the serpent-fairy Mélusine, Mélusine flies away forever after her husband spies on her in her bath, again in defiance of a taboo. The Mélusine legend is of particular interest to our story. Mélusine was the supernatural ancestor of the Lusignan family of Poitou and a builder of castles and churches. More importantly, Mélusine was also known as a monster who could only be saved if she married a mortal man and led a normal, human life. This she did when she married Raimondin, but not before he had promised to adhere solemnly to a singular command: that he not look at her on Saturdays, her day.

In the late medieval novel of Jean d'Arras, still popular in Marguerite's time, it is recorded that Raimondin did not obey his wife's command but spied upon her naked body, thus discovering her ugly serpent's tail. Moreover, the scene of Raimondin's spying underscores the sexual nature of his discovery, in that what Mélusine is made to show are her private parts which were at other times hidden from him. The text thus presents us with an anomalous creature who looks like a woman but is in fact double, being both feminine and masculine in her anatomy. Indeed, folklore sources accord an explicit phallic signification to Mélusine's tail, so that, by means of her feminine/masculine attributes, she may be said to escape classification, belonging to both sexes at the same time. It was to this tradition that Rabelais appealed when he described Niphleseth, the queen of the Andouilles, as an androgynous Mélusine figure, and called her by the Hebrew word for phallus.[17] The nature of Mélusine thus harks back to a primordial myth of androgyny.[18] Endowed with a composite nature, Mélusine escapes the dualist logic of sexual differentiation, to those, that is, who know how to see through the figure of femininity to the darker, masculine nature within.

The Jambicque who commands her lover not to know her belongs to this folktale type. When he later disobeys her wish he, like other curious males, including Orpheus, sustains the loss he knew only too well would occur if he did not heed the warning: "qu'il la perdroit, de l'heure qu'il la chercheroit" (300;396). The myth focuses the idea of loss, but it does more: it demystifies the image of woman as pure, exposing as well her hidden sexuality. Jambicque's mixed nature is announced indirectly early in the story when she plays the role of voyeur typically accorded to males. Geburon points out that gazing is at the source of her desire: "ung jour qu'elle estoit en la chambre de sa maistresse regardant sur une terrace, veit pourmener celluy qu'elle aymoit tant; et, après l'avoir regardé si longuement que le jour qui se couchoit en emportoit avec luy la veue, elle appella ung petit paige . . ." (297;392). By sighting her lover in a transfixing gaze, Jambicque assumes the libidinous male role in defiance of the presumed chastity of her sex.

Looked at from an anthropological perspective, Jambicque's double nature positions her between worlds of courtliness and nature. To this is added the in-between of boundaries between male/female and honor/lust.

Hayden White has noted that wildness is characterized in the Western tradition as "species pollution," that operation by which things that God ordained to remain apart are mixed together.[19] Chief among the separation of kinds in creation is the division of the human race into two sexes, a division which is observed as biologically operative in nature but complicated in mythology by the strange couplings of gods with mortals, men with beasts, and others whose monstrosities confirm the fallenness of human nature.[20] As noted above, the Mélusine myth states forcefully the mixed nature of woman, and it could be argued that myths function culturally in just this way, to show that sexual categories are not so rigid as patriarchal structures of language have made them appear. It is understandable, then, that the Jambicque case prompts the *devisants* to revisit the operating principle that surfaces at important junctures in the book, and that is the typology of male/female natures as mutually exclusive: Jambicque should be called a man, because she desires. There is no questioning of the supposition that woman as defined is too restrictive and in need of a more complex definition, one that includes desire. Parlamente reiterates the reigning paradigm of sexual difference that remains fixedly in place: "celles qui sont vaincues en plaisir ne se doibvent plus nommer femmes, mais hommes, desquelz la fureur et la concupiscence augmente leur honneur. . . . Mais l'honneur des femmes a autre fondement: c'est doulceur, patience et chasteté" (301;396).

$$* \quad * \quad *$$

Thus far, the *Heptameron*'s steadfast observance of gender boundaries has been stressed, in particular, the boundary separating femininity and masculinity as natural, or essential, categories. Is sexual desire expressible for a woman, then, only when she is rendered nameless and faceless, the implication being that female sexuality is shameful? This would seem borne out by Jambicque's self-erasure, the eclipse of her identity through masking her face. But it is by no means certain that masking is a sign of shame, and we would do well to investigate further how the mask functions in its complex relation to femininity, hypocrisy, and *dissimulation*, all topics bound up with gender definition in the book.

To do this, let us recall again that Jambicque is not just a courtly lady, but literally a *masked* lady whose status as a sexual object is inseparable from the "touret de nez" she wears when she meets her lover. Significantly, the mask is presented as a redundancy within the story. It functions overtly to hide its wearer's face so that she will not be recognizable. But, the mask is in fact a mask upon the darkness which already obscures Jambicque's face, it being that hour in the winter when the sun has already set.[21] In other words, the mask is a supplement which has no functional role in the plot, but points beyond itself toward role playing, performance, and the carnivalesque. A sizable literature on festivals in early modern Europe confirms the subversive role played by masking, cross-dressing, and other seasonal rituals. We are by now familiar with the overturning of hierarchies that such festivity presupposes, as well as with the limited efficacy of carnival in terms of social transformation, given its status as ritualized play in the liturgical calendar.[22] However, as Stallybrass and White have established for the nineteenth century, carnivalesque props, such as masks, could be freed up and reabsorbed into new sites, such as the court, thus making available a ready source of subversive energy where there had not been one before.[23] Jambicque's mask is just such a token which is incorporated and reworked to new effect in the story. Jambicque wears a mask to hide her identity, but the mask also frees the subject to become a locus of sexual desire. To desire is to turn herself into an active agent in defiance of all courtly ritual, but this is possible only through the ruse of masking which both affirms her femininity and parodies it at the same time, by effacing her.

The mask as ambivalent has its modern roots in the discourse of psychoanalysis. In a classic essay dating from 1929, Joan Riviere described women who wish for masculinity as "put[ting] on a mask of womanliness to avert anxiety and the retribution feared from men."[24] This double movement, so much in keeping with the inner/outer topos of humanist writing, may be seen psychoanalytically as ambivalence deriving from Jambicque's unique situation as a desiring woman in a culture praising female chastity. Jacques Lacan refers to Riviere's important essay when he argues that women seek to enter into the symbolic order of language by means of masquerade, in his terms, the signifier of the desire of the "Other": "masquerade has another meaning in the human domain, and it is precisely to play not at the imaginary, but at the symbolic, level."[25] Both Riviere and Lacan build upon the Freudian characterization of woman as passive, Riviere stressing in particular the intellectual woman's need both "to hide possession of masculinity and to avert the reprisals expected if she was found to possess it."[26] A psychoanalytic approach to Jambicque does not deny the sociocultural significance of the mask as wearing apparel or its strategic use as a defense against the male gaze. But what the mask also signifies is the ambiguous status of *dissimulation* as both woman's "nature" and, conjointly, a strategy to hide the appropriation of masculine forms of power. The mask is thus double-edged: it endorses the cultural construction of woman as deceitful; but it also uses that trope to subvert patriarchy in its claims to know the feminine in the *Heptameron*.[27]

An analogous example of masking will help shed further light on the Jambicque story. In novella 20, a gentleman courts a proper widow, but the courtship ends abruptly when he finds that she has betrayed him by lying with a stable boy. The lover's discovery takes the familiar form of trespassing into his lady's private space, her pavilion, a vantage point from which he gazes on the couple. To cover her shame, the lady then makes a symbolic mask with her hand, interpreted by Saffredent the storyteller, as follows: "puisqu'elle ne povoit couvrir sa honte, couvrit-elle ses oeilz, pour ne veoir celluy qui la voyoit trop clairement, nonobstant sa dissimullation" (154; 232). Once again, masking is affirmative of feminine desire but is interpreted otherwise as a sign of shame—the patriarchal culture's way of foreclosing the idea of women's pleasure. To be fair, it may be recalled that the women in the *Heptameron* hold the view of womankind as morally superior, but that in itself derives from a cultural imperative, some canonical texts being defenses of women which idealized them as chaste.[28]

Thus far, masking has been associated with "bad" people in the *Heptameron*, specifically, ladies who act upon their desire. But the virtuous Parlamente also wears a "touret de nez" in the discussion following novella 20, and its use is clearly inseparable from the sexual dynamics of the gathering whose complications include courtships, coqueteries, and disappointments at unrequited love. The witty stories and discussions are themselves masks to hid phallic ambitions, particularly those of Saffredent who regards women in the medieval siege terms as bastions to be broken down. Following novella 20 he boasts that he "knows" women and that he has a repertoire of stories gleaned from eyewitness testimony ("du cerf à veue d'oeil"). This inscribes him within the voyeuristic male strategy of seeing and knowing, and it is surely not by chance that Saffredent is first identified in the prologue as an onlooker. Following the bandits' attack on the travelers, he first caught sight of Parlamente, much like the Duke of Nemours will later glimpse the Princess of Clèves, "regardans aux fenestres." His aggressivity is met in the frame-discussion to novella 20 by Parlamente donning a mask. Parlamente uses her mask ironically in anticipation of the way Jambicque will use it later, to assert the female subjectivity which can only be construed as masculine in the prevailing economy of gender roles.

The mask as sign in novella 20 is just one instance of the text working out its own gender confusion, one focus of which is woman as a writing subject.

Jambicque can only banish her lover/writer with a daring lie, or *dissimulation*, that undoes the mark he has written upon her. But, whereas she may erase his script, she does not become a writing subject who breaks out of the social obligation to play the role of honorable lady. Marguerite, however, appropriates the corpus of Boccaccio in a transformative move that establishes her own authority to write. The caution expressed in our epigraph may stand as an allegory of writing the self into visibility as a storyteller. *Imitatio* as a practice demands risk-taking, insofar as the effort to emulate is fraught with the potential loss of self-identity as a writing subject. "On dit que place qui parlemente est demi-gagnée," counsels prudence in treaty-making, acknowledging the inherent loss in speech. As speech projects itself into exteriority, thus unmaking the purity of silence, it gives of itself at its risk and peril, just as the commander who would negotiate may be taken in through dissembling and betrayal. Parlamente takes the risk with Saffredent, among others, just as Marguerite enters into parlay with the corpus of Boccaccio, at once a meeting halfway and a potential threat to women's nature as honorable. Parlamente's name conflates *parler/mentir* in recognition of the proximity of speech and *dissimulation*, otherwise known as the in-between space of negotiation where dangerous parlays may lead to seduction and betrayal. In the psychoanalytic terms employed above, she is the narcissistic double who allows Marguerite to "take the place of the Father in public discourse as a speaker."[29] She is Marguerite's assertion of the privilege to displace the male corpus by inserting her own writing, so that rather than being written upon, as Jambicque was, she produces her own new body of texts. Marguerite is positioned somewhere between flirtation and manliness, both of which are available to women only in the role-playing of masquerade, and which, if "demi-gagnée," in siege terms, is also grounded and preserved in the open-ended *Heptameron*.

This chapter has attempted to show that fiction writing, even in the imitative culture of humanist poetics, is a *dissimulation*—of sources, of *realia*, of the contradictions that move its plots. The female author, as woman, is thus twice a dissimulator, as a woman, and functionally as a male in her appropriation of language. The Jambicque story brings to light the mixed nature of woman and, hence, the idea of writing as androgynous. But it also asserts an unwelcome truth—that honor is, in the 1550s, no longer viable as a mode of female self-definition. To the contrary, "honor" never has been compatible with female agency because it denies, even represses, the male element in the feminine makeup. The Jambicque story may then be seen as a caution that exceptional women—outlandish in their vices, as well as their virtues—may also be strangely close to that other anomaly: the feminine writer who reaches inside to find sources of desire from which to write.

Notes

1. "... les hommes ne sont plus exclusivement préoccupés des tournois et des chasses. La littérature conquiert les soldats mêmes. Les guerres d'Italie y sont pour beaucoup." See Pierre Jourda, *Marguerite d'Angoulême: Etude biographique et littéraire* (Paris: Honoré Champion, 1930), 2: 982.

2. For rubrication as a mode of textual interpretation, see the fine study by Sylvia Huot, *From Song to Book: The Poetics of Writing in Old French Lyric and Lyrical Narrative Poetry* (Ithaca, N.Y.: Cornell University Press, 1987), 27–49.

3. Nicole Cazauron, *L'Heptaméron de Marguerite de Navarre* (Paris: SEDES, 1976), 64.

4. The norm for gendered behavior of either sex presupposes a conception of natural law, as Marcel Tetel assumes when he views Jambicque's passion as "unnatural." See Tetel, *Marguerite de Navarre's Heptaméron: Themes, Language, and Structure* (Durham, N.C.: Duke University Press, 1973), 82.

5. Among recent treatments of the face and effacement in the *Heptameron*, see Carla Freccero, "Rape's Disfiguring Figures: Marguerite de Navarre's *Heptaméron*, Day 1:10," in *Rape and Representation*, ed. Lynn A. Higgins and Brenda R. Silver (New York: Columbia University Press, 1991), 227–247; and Lawrence D. Kritzman, *The Rhetoric of Sexuality and the Literature of the French Renaissance* (Cambridge: Cambridge University Press, 1991), 45–56.

6. "La probité et la perspicacité de Marguerite l'empêchent de se ranger, dans ce 'conflit des sexes,' entièrement du côté des femmes. Les arguments et les griefs masculins ont eux aussi un fondement psychologique et réel," in K. Kasprzyk, "L'Amour dans *l'Heptaméron*: De l'idéal à la réalité" (*Mélanges d'histoire littéraire (XVIe–XVIIe) offertes à Raymond Lebègue* [Paris: Nizet, 1969]), 54.

7. Diana Fuss, *Essentially Speaking: Feminism, Nature and Difference* (New York and London: Routledge, 1989), 3.

8. Philippe de Lajarte locates the conflict between the two thought systems—essentialist and dialogic—in "le pratique idéologique de l'écriture." See "*L'Heptaméron* et le ficinisme: Rapports d'un texte et d'une idéologie," in *Revue des Sciences Humaines* 147 (July–September 1972): 342.

9. On the Oedipal structuration of narrative, see Roland Barthes, *Le Plaisir du texte* (Paris: Seuil, 1973), 75–76.

10. This is the Chastelaine de Vergi story (413;527).

11. ". . . tant pour satisfaire à son soupson que pour entendre une si estrange histoire, [le duc] le pria de le vouloir mener avecq luy" (409;523).

12. Mary Ann Doane, "Woman's Stake: Filming the Female Body," *October* 17 (Summer, 1981): 23–36.

13. Teresa De Lauretis, *Alice Doesn't: Feminism, Semiotics, Cinema* (Bloomington: Indiana University Press, 1984), 26–27.

14. Paul Smith, *Discerning the Subject*, foreward by John Mowitt (Minneapolis: University of Minnesota Press [Theory and History of Literature, vol. 55], 1988), 137.

15. See "Femininity," in *The Standard Edition of the Complete Psychological Works of Sigmund Freud*, ed. James Strachey, 24 vols. (London: The Hogarth Press, 1953–74), 22:116–17.

16. See Ann Rosalind Jones, *The Currency of Eros* (Bloomington: University of Indiana Press, 1990), 11.

17. "Là trouvverez tesmoings vieulx de renom et de la bonne forge, lesquelz vous jureront sus le braz sainct Rigomé que Mellusine, leur premiere fondatrice, avoit corps foeminin jusques aux boursavitz, et que le reste en bas estoit andouille serpentine ou bien serpent andouillicque," François Rabelais, *Oeuvres complètes*, ed. Guy Demerson (Paris: Seuil [l'Intégrale], 1973), 687–88.

18. See Jean Markale, *Mélusine ou l'androgyne* (Paris: Editions Retz, 1983), 131–72.

19. Hayden White, "The Forms of Wildness: Archaeology of an Idea," in *The Wild Man Within: An Image in Western Thought from the Renaissance to Romanticism*, ed. Edward Dudley and Maximillian E. Novak (Pittsburgh: University of Pittsburgh Press, 1972), 24–25.

20. Ibid.

21. The lover cannot see his partner in the dark: "L'heure estoit de cinq et six en yver, qui entierement lui ostoit la veue d'elle" (298;393).

22. See Mikhail Bakhtin, *L'Oeuvre de François Rabelais et la culture populaire au moyen âge et sous la Renaissance*, trans. Andrée Roblel (Paris: Gallimard, 1970); Peter Burke, *Popular Culture in Early Modern Europe* (New York: New York University Press, 1978); and Peter Stallybrass and Allon White, *The Politics and Poetics of Trangression* (Ithaca, N.Y.: Cornell University Press, 1986).

23. Stallybrass and White, *The Politics and Poetics of Transgression*, 180.

24. Joan Riviere, "Womanliness as a Masquerade," in *Formations of Fantasy*, ed., Victor Burgin, James Donald, Cora Kaplan (London: Methuen, 1986), 35. The original article appeared in *The International Journal of Psychoanalysis* 10 (1929). Citations in the text refer to the reprinted article as it appeared in *Formations of Fantasy*.

25. Jacques Lacan, "From Love to the Libido," in *The Four Concepts of Psycho-Analysis*, ed. Jacques-Alain Miller, trans. Alan Sheridan (New York: Norton, 1981), 193.

26. Riviere, "Womanliness as a Masquerade," 38.

27. The lover scolds Jambicque as follows: "Madame, vous ne m'estes pas tousjours si rigoreuse que maintenant. De quoy vous sert de user envers moy de telle dissimulation?" (299–300;395).

28. See Constance Jordan, *Renaissance Feminism: Literary Texts and Political Models* (Ithaca, N.Y.: Cornell University Press, 1990).

29. Judith Butler, *Gender Trouble: Feminism and the Subversion of Identity* (New York and London: Routledge, 1990), 51. Butler's discussion of Lacan, Riviere, and masquerade is offered in support of her theory of gender as "performative," by which she means improvised without reference to a necessarily heterosexual matrix of desire.

3. The Rhetoric of Lyricism in the *Heptameron*

Marguerite de Navarre's texts clearly fall into two categories of written media: prose and poetry. Until recently, her prose (primarily the *Heptameron*) received substantial attention, but critics often did not know what to make of her poetry.[1] Yet four novellas of the *Heptameron* (13, 19, 24, 64) stand out, for in each one of them is inscribed a lengthy poem in the guise of a letter. Immediately, two questions arise: Why does Marguerite de Navarre deliberately choose to insert a poem when many long prose soliloquies pepper the novellas and seem to serve the same purpose, namely a declaration of love to a scornful or dejected lover?[2] And why in the first three instances is it a man who addresses a woman—regardless of the storyteller's gender—but in the last a woman addresses a man?

This last question is intriguing because of the change in gender of the epistolary writer. Marguerite de Navarre follows the literary tradition of the love letter dating back to Ovid's *Heroids*, wherein the lovers are represented in epistolary exchanges purveying various sentiments.[3] Yet in this epistolary setting she assumes the more traditional role of the male in the poetic love discourse. And in contrast to the later epistolary novel, Balzac's letters, or the Ovidian tradition, Marguerite does not allow the female recipients of the epistolary poems to return answers in kind; the male recipient, however, does answer. All the same, these poems have reached a certain *terminus ad quem*. Yet they are also, in Lacanian terms, *lettres en souffrance* that go astray and are thus available to any recipient; in the *Heptameron*, the recipients will be the discussants/storytellers who are going to read these versed epistles in different ways. In a very literal sense, the poems are also *lettres de souffrance*, because they express the lover's sufferings.

Ultimately, despite their textual presence in the novellas, and despite the fact that they eventually reach their intended addressees, these poems become "purloined letters" because they acquire a further, "prolonged" life in the hands of the storytellers and, in one case (novella 13), in the hands of a subsequent recipient.[4] These poems call attention to themselves by their very extended presence, their centrality, within the prose text. This focal situation makes them assume the appearance of a "tableau élaboré de toute sa suffisance" surrounded by "crotesques," as Montaigne would say in "De l'amitié" (1.28).[5] From them are then generated multiple interpretations of semantic frames, as the protagonists react to the messages or as the storytellers interpret them. These centers, then, are soon decentered; these purveyors of a truth are at some point subverted. Their verse form conveys a strong lyricism, a pathos, a "drame réel" that in turn produces "des effets de cadre" and undoubtedly triggers in these novellas, especially in the short term, drastic results, which dismantle the epistle's message—whose effects are examined later by the addressee or the discussants.[6]

By their very prolixity these poems raise the question of the arbitrariness of the referent or the unsatisfactory semantic fluidity of the logos, and thus each epistle articulates a decided repetitiveness that may be seen as an additional means of subverting a persuasive, rhetorical purpose. On the other hand, this wordiness can also manifest an intense lyricism intended to achieve the epistolary poem writers' catharsis. In the first such poem, which occurs in a novella narrated by Parlamente, the logos/Logos dichotomy is clearly posited, albeit in a significant allegorical setting. Here, indeed, as elsewhere in the *Heptameron*, the vagaries of the human word are opposed to the unicity of the divine Word.

This hermeneutical difference appears in novella 13 in the guise of a projected pilgrimage to Jerusalem. A childless and devout couple (an aged husband and a young wife) falls under the spell of a soldier of fortune, a "capitaine" who proposes to be their guide but who in fact uses this undertaking to advance other designs toward the lady: "avoit le cueur si serré entre crainte de parler et desir, que souvent il perdoit la parolle. Mais, à fin qu'elle ne s'en aperceust, se mectoit à parler des sainctz lieux de Jerusalem où estoient les signes de la grande amour que Jesus-Christ nous a portée. Et, en parlant de ceste amour couvroit la sienne" (99;168–69). If the captain is deceptive here, Parlamente/Marguerite interposes herself with the gloss on Jerusalem ("où estoient les signes de la grande amour que Jesus-Christ nous a portée"). This may be the captain's indirect discourse, but it is also an explicit interruption of the authorial voice. Moreover, it introduces the fundamental sign/word dichotomy. On that topic it should be noted that, until the verbal explosion of the epistolary poem (165 lines), the only time the captain speaks directly and deceptively is when he promises the eager couple that he will never abandon them in their realization of the pilgrimage, when in fact he will leave soon thereafter. Thus the captain's mutism in the presence of the couple, representing here his deceptive purpose and forcedly repressed desire, is apposed to the outburst of the letter after his departure, during which the "speaking" takes place more for the benefit of the reader than of the lady.

The epistolary poem is directed to a double addressee: the lady (the reader of letter) and the reader of the novella, the text itself, and in both instances it focuses on their insufficiency and shortcomings, which come to include the sender (*je*) as well. This fluidity of referents is crystallized around the repetition within the poem of "parler" that also refers to the captain's/lover's lyrical declaration, and to the lady's conversations with the captain: "Ce parler-là . . . son parler . . . Ce sot parler . . . O Parler trop hardy . . . Parler foible et plein de langueur . . . O mon Parler! tu n'as pas la practicque / De luy compter . . ." (100–102;170–72). Before the letter begins there is a reference to "ces longs parlemens," an expression that evokes the conversations between the couple and the captain, as well as the narrator of this tale, Parlamente, who tends to recount some of the longest novellas (see novellas 10 and 70). The length of the letter is made analogous to the captain's lengthy "servitude" to the lady (103;173) just as the letter itself is represented as the "serviteur" (103;174) of the lady. Thus the epistolary poem, in addition, is represented not only as the intercessor before the lady but as the textual mediation to efface her since she will never respond to him. Ultimately the addressee is not merely the reader within the novella itself but the reader of the printed text with whom Marguerite is engaged in a metatextual dialogue.

Or perhaps this poem is one of several exercises in the writing of love letters, a popular Renaissance genre that may even be pastiched here, to some degree. Indeed, the poem, already hyperbolically inflated, ends by purveying a sign, a quintessential reduction of the text itself—its synecdoche—but it does so by rhetorical means, by a verbal pun that is a worn-out topos of the period, hence a somewhat questionable vehicle: "O diamond, dy: 'Amant si m'envoye,'" (104;174).[7] It is now the diamond ring accompanying the letter, "pierre de fermeté," the sign of "Ma loyauté, ma ferme seureté," that addresses and beseeches the lady. However, since the captain will be killed in a battle against the Turks, the truth about his "loyauté" will never be tested or known.

Henceforth the ring, the synecdoche of the letter and its uncertainty, will become the manipulated sign open to interpretation by the protagonists of the story, by the storytellers, and by the reader. Upon receiving the poem and the ring, the lady forwards the latter, along with a note, to the captain's wife, informing her deceptively that he wished it so because of "le regret de ne vous avoir tant aymée comme il debvoit" (104;175). The synecdochic ring then continues its communicative (albeit strictly fabricated) purpose after the captain's death, seeming to consecrate the bond of marriage. Later, when the lady meets the deceived wife, she had "tant d'envye de rire veu que de sa tromperie estoit sailly ung tel bien . . . et se retira en une chapelle, où elle passa l'envye qu'elle avoit de rire" (107–8;178). As the tale itself ends here, the lady is represented in a diabolic role, for she has manipulated the image of the other; she has played the role of an ambiguous *fortuna*; she has abused the traditional meaning of a sign—even if perhaps this was not her original intent. This transgression, oscillating between a seemingly well-meaning intention and a seemingly fortuitous sense of cruel superiority, invites an analogy between ring/lady and text/reader. The ring/sign/text assumes a life of its own; it is interpreted differently as it moves from one receiver to another.

On what kind of finger can the ring fit? As usual, no agreement emerges. Parlamente's interpretation of the story she has just told is somewhat surprising because she indulges in self-deception by attributing only good intentions to the lady and promotes her exemplarity for other women: "car elles trouveroient que les bienfaictz sont les joyes des bien faisans. Et ne fault poinct accuser ceste dame de tromperie mais estimer de son bon sens, qui convertit en bien ce qui de soy ne valloit riens" (108;178–79). Even the lady's need to laugh can be construed by the listeners as a manifestation of joy. No wonder then that Parlamente is taken to task by her listeners, especially Hircan. Was the captain a true 'serviteur"? Did the lady love him? Was she well-intentioned toward his wife? Is Marguerite trying to rewrite some autobiographical event or history around her? At any rate, Oisille puts the questions to rest by proposing the fundamentalist Pauline precept that pervades the *Heptameron*, namely that God manifests himself in ways that are not always comprehensible to humans who can—or should—limit themselves to judge only actions and not motivations: "Vous en direz ce qu'il vous plaira . . . Dieu peult juger le cueur de ceste dame; mais quant à moy je treuve le faict très honneste et vertueux" (109;180). In a way, Oisille negates any possibility of interpretations of the text, whereas other storytellers are to varying degrees more hermeneutically inclined as they focus on the multiple metaphoricial meanings of the ring—and, hence, on the poem.

The centrality and the verbal abundance of the epistolary poem provide the axis of the novella's *facteur de la vérité*,[8] for here are revealed, rhetorically at least, the captain's "true" and heretofore hidden feelings by means of the *conduplicatio* (the repetition of a word throughout a text) of "parler" whose value is going to be questioned. Similarly, in the narrative itself, the desired pilgrimage to Jerusalem, expressed through the repetitive punctuation of "voyage," never materializes except, in a perverted way, for the captain who meets betrayal and death while fighting the Turks. Therefore, literally and allegorically the return to the Promised Land or to the "native country" fails. Does this mean, allegorically, that here *logos* is not a mediating step toward *Logos* as it usually is in Marguerite's poetry?[9] Or, is the promise of the "voyage" a mere rhetorical use of others' religious faith in order to achieve one's own physical desire? Or does Marguerite, as the authorial voice, ironize at the expense of Saffredent at the end of the commentaries, when she has him assert that: "Par ma foy . . . je ne veiz oncques mefaict pugny, sinon la sottise . . . souvent la malice est si grande . . . qu'elle les aveugle; de sorte qu'ilz deviennent sotz et comme j'ay dict. Seulement les sots sont punis, et non les vicieux" (108–9;179–80)? Who is prone to *sottise* and *malice*? The captain or the lady? Or both? The Logos is still within reach for the *sots* but certainly not for the *vicieux*. And thereby Marguerite could speak the truth through the usually sexist Saffredent.

As for the poem in novella 19, it is very much a letter of seduction, a seduction by a man already in a monastery who attempts to convince a woman to leave the earthly, conventional, and constrained life and join him in his spiritual realm. This "seduction" will succeed because society's socio-economic hierarchical norms, if not exigencies, had already forbidden the couple's marital union. The poem itself functions both as a synecdoche, even a *mise en abyme* of a reconciliation of the earthly and spiritual realms, and as a message/letter since ultimately it is addressed to and reaches the lady, Poline. As a poem, it is a "chanson spirituelle," closely associated with Marguerite's poetic production since it mimics the ascending ladder from the earthly to the spiritual[10] and is punctuated by an identical refrain at the beginning of the poem and at the end of each stanza: "Que dira-elle, / Que fera-elle, / Quand me verra de ses oeilz / Religieux?" (146 et seq.;223). The lyrical pace of the text is quickened by alternating four- and seven-syllable verses. The reference in the stanzas shifts from *elle*, to *eux/ils*, *eux/nous*, to *tu* and finally to the "parfaicte amityé" (148;225), thus reproducing the trajectory from conflict to spiritual concord or *contentements*—the key emblematic word(s) of the novella.

Yet the balance does not tilt totally toward "parfaicte amityé."[11] In the epistolary poem itself, the refrain repeats the concern of the lover within the walls for the world outside the walls; in fact, it continues to provide the terrestrial echoes that the new monk hears. And before Poline formally joins him, "se donnerent par vraye charité le sainct baiser de dilection. Et, en ce contentement, se partit Poline et entra en la religion" (150;227). Of course, the comments of the storytellers dramatize the dichotomies of the logos/Logos, the earthly/divine, the fallen human being/exemplary human being who has faith. Parlamente asserts that man/woman must experience earthly desires in order to realize faith and spiritual love (151–52;229). And Dagoucin maintains, as Parlamente had already (151;229), that on earth man and woman lovers must never forsake "honneur et conscience" (152;230).[12] Notwithstanding these dichotomies, should the reader then dismiss Hircan's counterpointing with the "melencolie et desespoir" (151;228) resulting from the lover's unrequited love which leads him to take the monastic path? If Poline and the Mantuan nobleman had been able to marry, the spiritual union would have become a moot point, although "honneur et conscience" would remain constant.

In this novella the epistolary poem is neither an idealized nor an essentially problematized text but rather an ideal text; it is not prolix, but self-contained and self-enclosed; it is simultaneously limited in scope and reductively representative of the whole span of the novella. While enacting the gradual emancipation of desires from earthly contingencies, the poem still counterbalances this ascension with the earthly experiences, reminiscences, and uncertainties that reverberate throughout the novella and on which some of the storytellers will focus. Here the exemplarity of the epistolary poem (its condensed and intense lyricism, its persuasive power, and its *concordia oppositorum*) is called into question, but not allowed to succumb to the forceful deconstructive enterprise exercised by some of the storytellers in their discussions following each story, or to social and hierarchical structures underlying the bias of this novella. However, many of the novellas that follow continue to focus on the human inability to climb the spiritual ladder.

If the epistolary poem reveals a truth and thereby replaces silence, it can, in another instance (novella 24) manifest self-knowledge. However, even as it calls attention to itself and focuses on a precise message, the poem's initial and apparent semantic clarity plays with words through rhetorical devices. Its causes, meaning, and effects will always shift according to the addressee or interpreter—particularly according to the storyteller discussing the novella. Thus after waiting seven years, the "serviteur" in novella 24 decides to reveal his love for the queen of Castille by having her look in a mirror he has fashioned, but she does not "recognize" herself; for the moment, attempted specularity does not achieve its purpose. When Elisor, her lover, finds himself compelled to verbalize his sentiments, she informs him that now that she is aware of his love, she will need her own seven years to reciprocate. The two then share one of her rings, each taking a half for safekeeping. When these seven years have elapsed, she receives an epistolary poem that ends with a curt: "Adieu, madame" (200;282). Elisor has decided to leave the earthly temporality for the serenity of the monastery.

Just as in novella 13, *conduplicatio* and *antistasis* punctuate the epistle in novella 24; here it is *temps* that is repeated, at least fifteen times, and disseminated in convergent and antithetical meanings in a text of less than seventy verses. One function of these rhetorical devices is to show Elisor compensating for the abuses and manipulations that the queen imposed on him and that he endured until he opted for an earthly atemporality:

> Le temps m'a faict veoir l'amour veritable,
> Que j'ai congneu en ce lieu solitaire,
> Où par sept ans m'a fallu plaindre et taire,
> J'ay, par le temps, congneu l'amour d'en hault
> Lequel estant congneu, l'autre deffault.
> Par le temps suis du tout à luy rendu,
> Et par le temps de l'autre deffendu.
>
> (199;281)

If the burden and materiality of earthly time (old time) is opposed to the ethereal nature of spiritual time (new time), it also serves as the medium, the necessary experience for arriving at spiritual enlightenment. The queen will not achieve this understanding of divine atemporality.

In the course of their discussions after the story is told, the storytellers' narrative function, by way of their interpretations, is to bring the story back to its earthly realm by focusing on the queen's behavior and motivations. Most significant is the comment by Oisille, the voice closely associated with the authority of the Scriptures: "Je croy qu'elle ne vouloit aymer ny estre aymée" (201;283), an opinion diametrically opposed to Parlamente's: "il me semble qu'elle ne luy faisoit poinct de tort de vouloir esprouver sept ans s'il aymoit autant qu'il luy disoit" (201;282), given man's inherent deception.

Otherwise, the queen is condemned by all the other storytellers, both men and women. Yet what the tale itself demonstrates is the queen's redemptive—albeit excessive—performance, and it is thus in complete accord with Oisille's general perspective in the *Heptameron* as well as with that of the tale's narrator, Dagoucin. Indeed, the queen's testing results in Elisor's union with the divine, atemporal sphere. This *non-dit*, a quintessential narrative interstice, of course, finds its contrapuntal *dit*, specificity, in the epistolary poem.

The important point is that the epistolary poem generates a narrative strategy that challenges both the modern and the Renaissance reader. Structured around the antithetical axis of temporality and atemporality, the old and the new, the earthly and the spiritual, the epistle ultimately privileges the ascending spiritual destination, and is immediately and surprisingly eschewed by the narrator Dagoucin's admonition: "Par ceste exemple, ne doibt le serviteur confesser ce qui luy peult nuyre et en rien ayder. Et encore moins, mes dames, par incredulité, debvez-vous demander preuves si difficiles que, en ayant la preuve, vous perdiez le serviteur" (200;282). Neither the male lover nor the queen is praised, and, as noted, the latter will become the target of a universal attack that disregards the existential merits of the poem and proceeds to subvert it—although the epistolary poem reaches a contrite first reader, the queen of Castille. The reader, however, is faced with a *concordia oppositorum*, the letter and its deconstruction, with the juxtaposition of a crucial semantic locus expressed via the poem on the one hand and, on the other hand, a dispersing counterpart. Here the epistle dramatizes only one side of the equation by bringing it into a relatively condensed and intense lyrical focus. But it would be perhaps too facile to opt for one side of the *concordia* when this Renaissance topos, applied in this context, aims to represent the simultaneity of the humanity and the divinity of man.

It may be significant that Parlamente tells the first (13) and the last (64) of the tales that contain epistolary poems because, among other reasons, this trajectory also points to a shift in tone in the *Heptameron*; from a grayness to a darkness of the human condition, from a possible hopefulness in the 1520s, when the first tales were written, to a pessimism in the queen of Navarre's last years (the 1540s). Of course, of further note is that this time a woman writes the letter to a man who, having been overly tested for his loving intentions by this lady, has finally decided to seek solace in a monastery. Despite his perfect conduct, the lady had refused to marry him because "ou cuydant trouver mieulx, ou voulans dissimuler l'amour qu'elle luy avoit portée, trouve quelque difficulté" (383;492). This time, assuming the role usually assigned to the male figure, she implores forgiveness and, repentant, agrees to be his in rhetorical terms that are reminiscent of the Grands Rhétoriqueurs, and which are not unusual in Marguerite de Navarre's poetry:

> C'est requerir celluy dont fuz requise,
> Et d'acquerir celluy dont fuz acquise.
> Or doncques, amy, la vie de ma vie,
> Lequel perdant, n'ay plus de vivre envye. . . .
>
> (384;493)

Thus it is now her turn to seek reciprocity, although to no avail:

> Or ay-je faict de toy l'experience:
> Ta fermeté, ta foy, ta patience
> Et ton amour, sont cogneuz clairement,
> Qui m'ont acquise à toy entierement.
> Viens doncques, amy, prendre ce qui est tien:
> Je suis à toy, sois doncques du tout mien.
>
> (385;494)

Indeed it is quite possible to read this epistolary poem, if not the novella itself, in allegorical terms that reflect the themes of much of Marguerite de Navarre's poetry: namely, as the story of the pitiful and weak earthly being seeking to be reunited with the One Husband in another world. Or the lady can be seen as the sister seeking reconciliation or reunion with her brother, King François I, either before or after his death.

Of course, the unusual nature of this missive, translated from Catalan, is that it elicits from the addressee, a man of God, a terse answer in the original language: "Volvete don venesti, anima mia, /Que en las tristas vidas es la mia" (387;496). Again, on an allegorical level, the wordiness and suggested vacuity of daily language is opposed to a quintessential, meaningful other language. Furthermore, on the same level, the meaning that these two Catalan verses convey reiterates a leitmotiv of Marguerite de Navarre's poetry: the longing for an ethereal spiritual life, on earth or after death, in order to flee a turgid earthly life.

Then, as often occurs, the discussants' comments bring the tale back to an empirical sphere that manipulates the meaning(s) of the tale. Thus the discussion reverts to the vagaries of marriage and conjugal life, faintly suggested at the very beginning of the tale, and features above all the sardonic observations by Hircan, the husband of Parlamente, who is the tale's narrator: "Il me semble . . . qu'elle faisoit tort à ung homme si foible, de la tanter de mariage; car c'est trop pour le plus fort homme du monde. Mais si elle luy eust tenu propos d'amityé, sans l'obligation que de volunté, il n'y a corde qui n'eust esté desnouée. Et, veu que pour l'oster de purgatoire, elle luy offroit ung enfer je dis qu'il eut grande raison de la refuser et luy faire sentir l'ennuy qu'il avoit porté de son refuz" (387;496). Although the wife provides her husband the opportunity to judge their marriage in no uncertain mischievous terms, the wife has on numerous occasions also bemoaned the difficult state of marriage that is subject to husbands' infidelities even as she identifies the necessity for and unique benefits of this institution. Yet at this late point in the *Heptameron* it is evident that these comments on marriage, and those previously made on *contemptus mundi* by a "fictitious" couple, carry a markedly autobiographical, authorial stamp.

*   *   *

The epistolary poems create a notion of perspective, a textual third dimension. They divide the novella and they train a special focus on the discussants' comments. The poems function on a dichotomous plane. In novella 13, the epistle is balanced on *parler*, which it puts into question to produce the opposition of logos/Logos. And only Parlamente could be its narrator because she is the persona that reflects Marguerite the writer giving in to the temptations of *plaire*, while not overlooking *instruire*. The lyrical text in novella 19 both foreshadows and reenacts a couple's "success" in freeing themselves from the materiality and pettiness of society in order to find spiritual solace in a monastery. Since, in the course of this ascending journey, the protagonists continue to cast their eyes and minds on earthly concerns, it is no wonder that during the discussion Ennasuite still wonders who can live so perfectly. Thus this epistolary poem may have achieved its persuasive purpose by uniting the couple, and yet strangely enough the narrator of this tale questions what she has told—or what Marguerite had her narrate.

Temps provides the fulcrum of the poem in novella 24. Here time, weighted down by desire, by excesses of "parfaite amitié," and by societal norms, is opposed to an ethereal atemporality. The last epistolary poem, in novella 64, reverses the gender of the addressee and literally transmits the fervent wish for an earthly union within the institution of marriage, and yet it articulates the female sender's desire (also that of the queen of Navarre, on an allegorical level) to be reunited with God in an afterlife. It reveals thereby the queen's dominant disillusion, in her last years, with the course of her own life and with the generally desolate state of earthly life. Thus each poem manifesting an intense lyrical outburst of both emotion and liberation is cast against normative flaws, be they human, societal, or communicative, in the prose narrative; these four novellas become chantefables.

The poems, therefore, figure a series of vertical emotive movements, a succession of lyrical ladders that are representative of Marguerite's poetry as a whole. Meanwhile the narrative prose, mitigating the ascension and representing the terrestrial, builds a bridge to attempt to reconcile the two, the spirit and the flesh. The narrative prose is in fact the bridge under construction that is missing from the prologue to the *Heptameron*, and which may have allowed the "mallades" (1;60) to return to terra firma.

Notes

1. The most notable recent exceptions are Robert D. Cottrell's *The Grammar of Silence: A Reading of Marguerite de Navarre's Poetry* (Washington, D.C.: Catholic University of America Press, 1986); Paula Sommers's *Celestial Ladders: Readings in Marguerite de Navarre's Poetry of Spiritual Ascent* (Geneva: Droz, 1989); and Gary Ferguson's *Mirroring Belief: Marguerite de Navarre's Devotional Poetry* (Edinburgh: Edinburgh University Press for the University of Durham, 1992).

2. In dealing with these four novellas, André Tournon notes, on the surface, a "platonisme amoureux," whereas underneath, and more significantly, he detects "l'insistance d'Eros, tache aveugle où travaillent secrètement le péché et la grâce" ("'Amor de lonh': Thème et variations dans un groupe de quatre nouvelles de l'*Heptaméron*," *Réforme, Humanisme, Renaissance* 5 (May 1977), 3, 4).

3. See Bernard Alain Bray, *L'Art de la lettre amoureuse* (Paris-The Hague: Mouton, 1967), p. 14.

4. Jacques Lacan, "Le Séminaire sur 'La lettre volée,'" *Ecrits I* (Paris: Seuil, 1966), 40.

5. Montaigne, *Essais*, ed. Pierre Villey and V.-L. Saulnier (Paris: Presses Universitaires de France, 1978), 183.

6. Jacques Derrida, *La Carte postale de Socrate à Freud et au-delà* (Paris: Flammarion, 1980), 469–71.

7. Cf. Marcel Tetel, *Rabelais et l'Italie* (Florence: Olschki, 1969), 94, esp. n.2.

8. This expression, with its semantic reverberations, is taken of course from Derrida's *La Carte postale*, p. 439 et seq.

9. In this context, see Robert Cottrell's thorough analysis of *Les Prisons* in his *Grammar of Silence*, 247–310; as well as Gary Ferguson's *Mirroring Beliefs*, 216–220.

10. This "désir de la mort corporelle" for Marguerite de Navarre, in the mystical and evangelical traditions, has been well refined by Claude Blum, *La Représentation de la mort dans la littérature française de la Renaissance* (Paris: Champion, 1989), 238–91.

11. The distinction that Paula Sommers makes that Marguerite de Navarre in her poetry emphasizes an inner transformation would also suggest that it may not be quite so in the *Heptameron* (*Celestial Ladders*, 109).

12. Cf. Daniela Rossi, "*Honneur* e *conscience* nella lingua e nella cultura di Margherita di Navarra," *Journal of Medieval and Renaissance Studies* 5 (1975): 63–87.

Donald Stone

4. "La Malice des hommes": "L'Histoire des satyres" and the *Heptameron*

If we are to believe Nicole Cazauran, the time has passed when any respectable scholar would argue for a significant discontinuity between the *Heptameron* and the plays or poems of Marguerite de Navarre.[1] Moreover, to illustrate the validity of modern-day thinking on this point, Cazauran shows how Marguerite's criticism of human pretension crisscrosses the *Heptameron* no less than it does her religious writings.

The demonstration is vigorous and convincing, but for that very reason questions remain, notably concerning the details of this rapprochement of verse and prose. Will an important leitmotiv such as Marguerite's attack on human pretension tend to inspire the same structures for its presentation, regardless of the medium used? Does the motif remain constant in its meaning for the queen as we move from one part of her *oeuvre* to another? If we obtain affirmative answers to these questions, can we feel secure in closing the book on the issue that Cazauran raises? Realizing that such problems are too broad to be resolved satisfactorily within the limits of a short chapter, I have elected to focus my attention on a single example of the pretension Marguerite discusses, that is, "la malice des hommes," a subject which has the added advantage of bringing into play an aspect of the *Heptameron* that for so long appeared to set it apart from the rest of Marguerite's writings.

Whereas her verse returns again and again to the central focus of Marguerite's religious convictions, in the *Heptameron* the storytellers do not speak with one voice. They often posit contradictory yet seemingly valid perspectives on the human condition, such as those we encounter in the quarrel concerning human love that arises between Hircan and Saffredent on the one hand and Parlamente and Oisille on the other. Their disagreement surfaces with particular directness in the discussion following the tenth *nouvelle*.[2] Parlamente underscores Floride's virtuous resistance to the blandishments and physical advances of Amadour; Hircan muses aloud that had Amadour pressed Floride in a place where her cries could not have been heard, "je ne sçay qu'elle eust faict." The story notwithstanding, he is far from shaken in his conviction "que oncques homme qui aymast parfaictement, ou qui fust aymé d'une dame, ne failloit d'en avoir bonne yssue." He even praises Amadour for having performed at least "a part of his duty," an observation which prompts this sarcastic rejoinder from Oisille: "Appellez-vous faire son debvoir à ung serviteur qui veult avoir par force sa maitresse, à laquelle il doibt toute reverence et obeissance?" Here Saffredent enters the fray, distinguishing between the public ritual where the man must play the role of humble servant and the private realm ("Mais, quant nous sommes à part") where love becomes the only judge of one's behavior. There, as the proverb says, "Serving makes the servant master."

This confrontation closely parallels remarks on the preceding tale[3] although there we hear Saffredent, not Hircan, insisting that when a woman loves a man who courts her properly, he will be rewarded: "il n'y a homme, s'il est aymé d'une dame, (mais qu'il le saiche poursuivre saigement et affectionnement), que à la fin n'en ayt du tout ce qu'il demande en partye."[4] Saffredent's argument even includes an equivalent of the proverb to be cited at the close of the tenth tale, that is, two verses from the *Roman de la Rose* spoken by the "vieille" to the effect that we have been created "Toutes pour tous, et tous pour toutes." Despite the prominence of Saffredent here, throughout he is again following the lead of Hircan who scoffs at the fate of the perfect lover in tale 9. Hircan sees no need for men to be reticent about seeking from women what, according to him, God commands them to give.

Saffredent's use of a proverb and verses from the *Roman de la Rose* to make his point need not surprise us (despite the reference by Hircan to God and to God's intentions). These men would ground the discussion in the most pragmatic facts of life. The courtly ritual is just that, a situation in which the sexes assume roles that have no corresponding reality in the world of human emotions. The truth about that world we encounter in the wisdom of accumulated experience (proverbs) or of long-term observers of human behavior, like the old woman of the *Roman*. Even Hircan's reference to God is eventually drawn into this realm of pragmatic observation.

Given that Genesis 2:20–22 relates how God made woman because Adam had no "help meet" ("adiutor" in the Vulgate), Hircan is not wrong to speak of women as "made for man" ("qui ne sont faites que pour nous"). The absence of any form of the word "help" in his description is nevertheless telling. Hircan prefers to speak rather of "ce que Dieu leur commande de nous donner." Like the reference to the "bonne yssue" that always awaits Hircan's perfect lover or to the "ce qu'il demande" that Saffredent's wise and affectionate lover achieves, the phrase implies that God's design in creating woman was to permit the physical union of the sexes. And, despite a certain delicacy in Hircan's language, Parlamente has no difficulty reading a worldly, self-directed bias into his words, as we learn later in the *Heptameron* when Parlamente distinguishes between two kinds of love:

> Car l'amour de la femme, bien fondée sur Dieu et sur honneur, est si juste et raisonnable, que celluy qui se depart de telle amityé, doibt estre estimé lasche et meschant envers Dieu et les hommes. Mais l'amour de la plupart des hommes de bien est tant fondée sur le plaisir, que les femmes, ignorant leurs mauvaises voluntez, se y mectent aucunes fois bien avant; et quant Dieu leur faict congnoistre la malice du cueur de celluy qu'elles estimoient bon, s'en peuvent departir avecq leur honneur et bonne reputation. (174–75;253–54)

That Parlamente's words characterize the larger points of the various tales of "parfaite amour" should be obvious. The passage comes after tale 21, the story of Rolandine and her faithfulness to a man who abandons her for a rich German wife. Here the object of male pleasure is venal rather than carnal, but Rolandine's adventure is for that no less illustrative of basic male behavior than was Floride's. Moreover, each tale portrays the male as deceptive and eventually incapable of hiding from the woman a side of his nature that gives the lie to the honorable tenor of his protestations. Since stories 10 and 21 are told by Parlamente, such consistency contains no surprises. But if Marguerite's prose and poetry are closely aligned, we should expect to find the same consistency outside the *Heptameron*, in other portraits of male behavior, where Marguerite speaks directly to her readers. Thanks to the content of a poem that first appeared in the 1547 *Suyte des Marguerites de la Marguerite des Princesses*, it is possible to observe that this consistency is no accident.

"L'Histoire des satyres et nymphes de Dyane" tells anew the story of the male pursuit of pleasure, here directed at the nymphs of the goddess Diana, and as Marguerite summarizes the action in the early lines of the poem, her characterization of the satyrs and the nymphs returns us to the distinction Parlamente sketches at the close of *nouvelle* 21. "L'Histoire" will depict "des hommes la malice."[5] Such vice will be bested by virtue, however, even though "ignorance / Du mal, couuert soubz honneste apparence, / Souuent deçoit celles qui n'ont apris" (p. 4). Once again ignorance of the male's deeper designs initially engages the woman. In the end she becomes disabused and knows fully the evil she faces. But now the voice we hear is no longer that of a fictional persona. The narrator speaks in the first person in a volume whose title page bears Marguerite's name. No less significant is the content in which Marguerite places this paradigm of male/female interaction.

If the introductory verses to "L'Histoire" point out how the evil of the satyrs will be "couuert soubz honneste apparence," a full explanation of their behavior lies outside the specifics of the "story" in question. It belongs rather to the religious truth that Marguerite wishes to convey with her poem. Defining evil as "l'absence de tout bien," she further associates it with "faux cuyder," her phrase for humanity's vain (and unwarranted) belief in its own worth. According to the poem, that belief engenders "vn depraué desir / Dessoubs l'espoir d'vn incongnu plaisir" (p. 3) and incites one to form subtle strategies to obtain the desired end. The satyrs' careful plan to lure the nymphs away from Diana's protection, all the while hiding their true intent, represents "faux cuyder" in action. So great, in fact, is the power of "faux cuyder" that after the satyrs have failed to seduce the nymphs, they still cannot bring themselves to fault their behavior:

> Lors par orgueil dirent, à qui tient il?
> Auons nous en faute de coeur gentil?
> Si nous auons failly quand à les prendre,
> Failly n'auons à force & diligence.
>
> (p. 34)

The nymphs, too, give substance to Parlamente's words. Beset by the satyrs, the women beg Diana to preserve their honor, using a plea that emphasizes just how firmly their concern is, indeed, grounded in devotion to the goddess and honor:

> Làs, ce n'est pas de noz corps secourir
> De l'aspre Mort où les sacrifions:
> Mais c'est que toy, en qui nous nous fions,
> Par ton honneur vueilles sauuer le nostre.
>
> (p. 17)

Diana hears their cries: "Souffrir ne veux pour nulle passion / Ce qui est mien souffrir corruption" (p. 27). The nymphs will become willow trees, well protected from the lecherous satyrs; yet as willows, they will be trees that bear no fruit, "Car vierges sont sans porter fruit d'enfans" (p. 29).

The goddess's decision to save, not punish her errant followers is intended to juxtapose her merciful nature and the gravity of the nymphs' disobedience. When five members of Diana's band first hear the song of the satyrs, they experience a pleasure that allows them to follow the satyrs farther and farther away from the goddess. In their later plea to Diana, the nymphs recognize that by wandering off they have separated themselves from "repos & ioye" (p. 20), whereas in union with Diana they drew worth from her worth:

> . . . ta grand' vertu
> Nous vnissant à toy nous rendoit telles,
> Que nous estions par ta grand' beauté belles;
> Promptes à bien par ta grand' diligence,
> Prudence ayant aussi par ta prudence;
> Fortes en coeur, par le tien inuincible,
> Et tout pouuant par ton puissant Possible.
>
> (p. 20)

The passage is no rhetorical flourish. It serves to underscore the momentous consequences of that separation of humanity from its creator which prideful "cuyder" can effect. In Diana's words: "Par ce Cuyder, par qui se sont senties / Telles que moy, hors de moy sont sorties" (p. 24).

I have spoken in some detail of the behavior of both the satyrs and the nymphs for a particular reason. Just as the broad lines of the narration of "perfect love" return in "L'Histoire des satyres," so certain details from the poem can be found in the *Heptameron* and in passages that are not related by Parlamente. One means employed by "L'Histoire" to illustrate the force of "cuyder" over the satyrs emerges when they refuse to read into their defeat the lessons outlined by Marguerite, insisting instead on their "coeur gentil," "force & diligence." In the *Heptameron* we hear the men defending the same qualities, whatever the moral cast of the male protagonist being discussed. As long as the "perfect lover" of tale 9 remains in good health, respect for his beloved excludes any union other than through marriage. To Oisille the attitude bespeaks "honneste amityé"; to the men it shows a lack of courage. In Hircan's eyes the man was foolish, fearful; Saffredent affirms that "Fortune ayde aux audatieux" (53;119). On the other hand, it will be remembered, Hircan lauds audacious Amadour for having accomplished "une partie de son debvoir" (a reference, perhaps, to the long span of the lover's service and pursuit). Geburon adds that no amount of criticism will allow him to forget the valor of Amadour, the soldier: "Or, quoy que vous ayez tous dict . . . il me semble qu'Amadour estoit ung aussy honneste et vertueulx chevalier qu'il en soit poinct" (84;154).

Marguerite further underscores the unwillingness of the men to see beyond the worldly concerns of valor and assiduity by allowing the women to espouse very different values. Consider this exchange between Saffredent and Longarine following *nouvelle* 10:

> Mais c'est raison aussy que nostre souffrance soit recompensée, quand l'honneur ne peult estre blessé. —Vous ne parlez pas, dit Longarine, du vray honneur qui est le contentement de ce monde; car, quant tout le monde me diroit femme de bien, et je sçaurois seulle le contraire, la louange augmenteroit ma honte et me rendroit en moy-mesme plus confuse. (84;153–54)

Again the male takes a pragmatic stance. The lover should be rewarded for his efforts if the lady's reputation remains unscathed, that is, if her affair remains hidden. Longarine rejects this amoral use of the word "honor." As with the nymphs of Diana, Longarine's "repos & ioye" are defined by a commitment to the absolute, or, to paraphrase Parlamente, to "God and honor."[6] Indeed, in the Pauline spirit that infuses so much of Marguerite's poetry, Longarine insists on emphasizing that the world's judgment ("quant tout le monde me diroit femme de bien") can be wrong, the contrary of the only truth that matters.

By now the evidence for the principle of a continuum between poetry and prose in Marguerite would seem irrefutable. At least, regarding the specific motif of "faux cuyder," its meaning appears unchanged in the examples that we have examined from both her poems and her prose. Parlamente's words echo Marguerite's own by condemning human self-satisfaction and illustrating that sin through the male's pursuit of pleasure and woman's vulnerability, which, however, a love of God and honor allow her to combat.[7] In addition, both Parlamente and Marguerite are prepared to extol the fullest expression of this love, much in the spirit of the goddess Diana, who effects the metamorphosis of her nymphs into willow trees in order to protect her followers against defilement and to preserve their status as virgins: "De porter fruit, à iamais leur defens, / A celle fin que leur virginité / Soit en memoire" (p. 29).

In two of the stories of "parfaite amour" a woman's unswerving commitment to God brings her to marry the one true spouse. Both Floride and Poline, the heroine of story 19, take the veil. From Marguerite's poetry it is clear that such a mystical union had great appeal for the queen. In one of her spiritual songs, for example, she pens a farewell to this world:

A Dieu pour tout iamais, A Dieu;
A Dieu, ie ne veux plus de vous,
N'autre plaisir ne veux auoir,
Que l'vnion de mon Espoux;
Car mon honneur et mon auoir,
C'est par Foy mon Tout receuoir,
Que ne dois laisser pour le peu.[8]

Note that just as Parlamente's characterization of male and female love opposes pleasure and honor, self and God, so here Marguerite rejects any "other pleasure" than union with Christ. Moreover, she refuses to abandon her "All" for "little," a contrast that should make us think of "L'Histoire" and the enormous loss the nymphs experience as a result of abandoning their goddess. The voice speaking in the song understands, with Floride and Poline or the nymphs, that there is no pleasure to rival life with God. Yet not all the women who exhibit "perfect love" take the veil. Rolandine will marry, as did Marguerite, who gives Parlamente a husband. Should we see in this willingness to take an earthly spouse a betrayal of Parlamente's definition of a love "fondée sur Dieu"? According to what the queen's mentor in religious matters, Guillaume Briçonnet, wrote her on the subject of marriage, the answer is "no."

In a letter dated July 6, 1524, the bishop of Meaux offers Marguerite his explication of certain biblical texts concerning the sacrament of matrimony. The carnal reality of marriage, its function as a means to continue the species are recognized, but Briçonnet emphasizes again and again that carnal union is but "l'ombre de l'ombre du grand mariage."[9] The union of two partners represents that union of every faithful soul with Jesus which is itself a representation of the union of the Church with Christ. Since that love for (and of) Christ is spiritual, not carnal, Briçonnet warns that dangers lurk in not seeing beyond the carnal reality of marriage (2:208); he mentions that Saint Paul sees carnal union as impeding spiritual union (1 Cor. 7:32–35), yet insists that an ascension from one to the other is possible: "O que plaisant est aussi le mariage charnel, . . . le mary congnoissant ne pouvoir satisfaire par adhesion d'amour à sa compagne prinse du vray espoux, et elle reverentement se humiliant et ne se reputant digne de telle amour, . . . tous deux reciproquement refferans leurs actions à Dieu . . ." (2.210).[10]

Thus, even the introduction of marriage into the context of "parfaite amour" or the life of Parlamente does not undo the continuum we have been discussing. Crucial is not the fact of carnal union, but the attitude of the couple. As with the essential distinction contained in Parlamente's remarks after story 21, either the couple falls prey to physical pleasure or it recognizes the infinite superiority of the spiritual. And yet, at this very juncture, where author and Parlamente appear so inextricably linked, Marguerite confounds our analysis.

In a most unexpected passage from "L'Histoire," Diana, goddess of chastity, contrasts the satyrs' behavior under the influence of "cuyder" with the proper way to court a woman: "Cerchez l'amour vertueux et honneste, / Et vous ferez honorable conqueste" (pp. 32–33). Deceived by "cuyder," the satyrs have not understood that in order to win a woman's body, one must win her heart:

> Làs apprenez, que si leur coeur n'est pris,
> Et par amour mis en vn les espritz,
> Il perd le temps qui le corps pense auoir.
>
> (p. 32)

Indeed, when a pure heart and body find themselves pursued in the manner employed by the satyrs, the woman "Par chasteté s'endurcist comme vn mur" (p. 32). If, however, the man seeks to create an "amour vertueux et honneste," Diana suggests that his hope for a physical union will be realized. So read, Diana's advice closely resembles remarks by Hircan and Saffredent that were quoted above but not studied in detail: "oncques homme qui aymast parfaictement, ou qui fust aymé d'une dame, ne failloit d'en avoir bonne yssue" (Hircan); "il n'y a homme, s'il est aymé d'une dame, (mais qu'il le saiche poursuivre saigement et affectionnement), que à la fin n'en ayt du tout ce qu'il demande en partye" (Saffredent).

All three passages share a number of surprising features. They signal important role changes: The goddess of chastity points out the path to physical union; two men relate successful courtship to the presence of mutual sentiments. Diana uses the noun "conqueste," a word that would seem to belong more naturally to the male, especially when, as here, no negative judgment is conveyed. Hircan and Saffredent, on the other hand, speak of loving "parfaictement," of courting "saigement et affectionne-ment," words we do not expect to hear pronounced by a man. But then our expectations have been heavily colored by Parlamente's characterization of the sexes. Indeed, to both men Parlamente has only one answer: "je m'esbahys de vous deux comme vous osez tenir telz propos! Celles que vous avez aymées ne vous sont gueres tenues, ou vostre addresse a esté en si meschant lieu que vous estimez les femmes toutes pareilles" (54;119–20).[11] Parlamente's second sentence is not the easiest passage in the *Heptameron* to decipher. By its first clause she may mean: "Those you loved slept with you, but not because they are beholden to you as attentive suiters" or "Those you loved will never sleep with you since they are not obligated to you." In either case, she denies the link the men would make between ardent courtship and eventual success, adding, as an alternate explanation for their outrageous remarks, that having frequented lewd members of her gender, the men mistakenly calculate that all women will behave accordingly. Parlamente's desire to refute the men's claim could not be clearer, but does she speak for Marguerite as well?

To the degree that the words of Diana and the two men have triggered that question, we already have the outline of an answer. Through them Marguerite appears to hold out the possibility of a range of human actions that is greater than the one traced by Parlamente at the close of tale 21. However we understand the problematic clause in her response, it and the phrase "meschant lieu" betray Parlamente's conviction that (decent) women resist the temptations of courtship. With the three passages spoken by Diana, Hircan, and Saffredent, Marguerite suggests that honest courtship by the man can inspire an honest love, one felt and returned by the woman, and she expresses the idea in ways that carefully avoid feeding Parlamente's prejudices. Had Marguerite chosen Venus to speak of an "honorable conqueste" or allowed the men to affirm that women are just as given to seeking pleasure as are men, such passages could only have upheld the distinction articulated at the end of the twenty-first story. But Marguerite does no such thing. Through the reversal of roles and words we have already discussed above, she relates the notion of an "honorable conqueste" to a female (!) prototype of the godhead and to males (!) who echo Diana's belief in the efficacy of worthy conduct.

These passages are not the only ones in which Marguerite distances herself from Parlamente.[12] Despite Amadour's duplicitous behavior, the text attributes to him more than once the very terms of valor and courage for which the male discussants persist in admiring him. His "vertuz" are cited well before he meets Floride: ". . . la France et l'Ytallie estimerent grandement ses vertuz, pource que, à toutes les guerres qui avoient esté, il ne se estoit poinct espargné; et, quand son païs estoit en repos, il allait chercher la guerre aux lieux estranges, où il estoit aymé et estimé d'amys et d'ennemys" (56;123). In addition, long before any hint appears of a strategy to obtain the woman he desires, the narrator explains the presence of valor in Amadour by means quite exterior to the character: "Si est-ce que Amour et Fortune, le voyans delaissé de ses parens, deliberent de y faire leur chef d'euvre, et luy donnerent, par le moyen de la vertu, ce que les loys du païs luy refusoient" (56–57;124). Well within the development of the story, after Amadour's strategies have been clearly drawn, Marguerite attributes to the man feelings and qualities that do not mesh with Parlamente's portrait of him or of men in general. To cite but one example: "Je n'entreprendz poinct vous dire la douleur que sentoit Amadour escoutant ces parolles; car elle n'est seullement impossible à escripre, mais à penser, sinon à ceulx qui ont experimenté la pareille" (75;143). In Parlamente's schema, defeat of the male should engender not pain, but pique, annoyance, frustration over failure of the strategy. Marguerite's depiction of the satyrs assures us that she, too, felt no compassion when the male had given himself to "faux cuyder." But this recognition of Amadour's "douleur," like certain traits of the narration and of the ensuing discussion, suggests that Amadour is both the victim of "faux cuyder" and a man who inspires respect. Men, it seems, can be pragmatic and wrong; they can be vain and wrong. But in some the amalgam of pragmatism, valor, and honesty may be no less true than the capacity to err.

I am not alone in observing this complexity in Marguerite. Lucien Febvre spoke of it when postulating the existence in the sixteenth century of a psychological vacillation between the sacred and the profane. Jean Frappier dismissed Febvre's claim and replaced it with the idea that Marguerite was simply reflecting the contradictions present in the human heart (and, perhaps, the dangers to women lurking in *fine amor*).[13] If Febvre overstates his claim, surely Frappier underestimates the evidence in the *Heptameron* for Marguerite's awareness that her faith is contending with more than just human frailty. Instructive, for example, is Marguerite's very particular presentation of her "perfect lovers."

As I have pointed out elsewhere, the perfect lovers are often individuals whose inferior birth, rank, or fortune disadvantage them and render them at best marginal players in the game of life, as if Marguerite conceived of them from the outset as intrinsically separate from the rest of society.[14] In any case, with this portrait, Marguerite excludes the possibility for her characters to make a free choice between earthly success and heavenly rewards and creates instead the impression that the lovers retreat into religion to find solace for the pleasures they have otherwise been denied.

Whatever Marguerite actually intended by this distance between the perfect lovers and their society, we are very far here from the world of her plays and poems where abstract, symbolic beings and inner voices reenact (as in "L'Histoire des satyres") a drama that ends in the happy triumph of faith over the flesh. This is not to say that the *Heptameron* offers no such moments of moral victory, but quiet signs are also present to suggest that between the pragmatic, worldly concerns of the men and the religious absolutes of the women lies an area where elements of both may come together in an "honorable conqueste." There the men will seek their God-given "help meet" with honest affection; the women will recognize the acceptability of a carnal union born of mutual caring. Parlamente rejects utterly the validity of such behavior, doubting not only man's capacity for such honesty but also the compatibility of any such relationship with the dictates of true belief. But then the progressive withdrawal of certain "perfect lovers" from the worldly sphere in order to fulfill those dictates could be said to show how much Parlamente's rejection risks denying the reality of this life and its challenges. If only for having traced the outlines of such complexities, the *Heptameron* occupies a special place in Marguerite's literary universe, despite its links to her other works, despite the indisputable importance of those links.

Notes

1. "Personne ne voit aujourd'hui de rupture entre l'oeuvre poétique et théâtrale de Marguerite de Navarre et les contes de l'*Heptaméron*" (Nicole Cazauran, *L'Heptaméron de Marguerite de Navarre* [Paris: SEDES, 1976], 259).

2. In the François edition, that discussion takes place in pages 83–85; Chilton 152–54.

3. François, 53–54; Chilton, 118–21.

4. The text of the edition by Yves Le Hir (Marguerite de Navarre, *Nouvelles* [Paris: Presses Universitaires de France, 1967], 54) is far clearer here: "il n'y a homme, s'il est aymé d'une Dame, més qu'il sçache poursuyure sagement et affectionnément, qu'à la fin n'en ait du tout ou en partie ce qu'il demande."

5. I quote from the text of the original edition (Lyons: Jean de Tournes, 1547) reproduced in 1970 through photo-offset by Ruth Thomas in the series French Renaissance Classics, p. 4. Subsequent references will be identified in text by page number.

6. It is not without interest that the text of the Le Hir edition gives "Car l'amour de la femme[,] bien fondée sur Dieu et son honneur" (*Nouvelles*, 153). Moreover, this exchange between Longarine and Saffredent mirrors a particular moment in Parlamente's story of Amadour and Floride. When the man encounters Floride's resistance, he exclaims: "Ung si long service merite-il recompense de telle cruaulté?" to which Floride replies, "Et où est l'honneur" (p. 73).

7. The vulnerability of the nymphs reappears very clearly in the pages of the *Heptameron* when, in tale 10, Parlamente relates how Floride's growing feelings for Amadour inspire jealousy (p. 63), brings her to write continuously to the absent beloved, begging for his return (p. 64), and even engenders dissimulation, the prime feature of "cuyder" (p. 66).

8. *Marguerites de la Marguerite des Princesses*, Lyon, 1547; rpt. (New York: Johnson Reprint Corp., 1970), p. 518.

9. Guillaume Briçonnet and Marguerite d'Angoulême, *Correspondance (1521–1524)*, ed. Christine Martineau and Michel Veissière (Geneva: Droz, 1979), 2 vols. 2:207. It is important to note that Briçonnet was by no means alone in stressing such ideas in the early decades of the sixteenth century. See, for example, *John Colet's Commentary on First Corinthians*, ed. and trans. Bernard O'Kelly and Catherine A. L. Jarrott (Binghamton, N.Y.: Medieval and Renaissance Texts and Studies, 1985), 191, 195, 197.

10. Briçonnet's influence in this matter seems even clearer if we consider Poline's final words to her beloved. She announces her resolve to take the veil and then adds, "vous priant que vous et moy oblyons le corps qui perit et tient du viel Adan, pour recepvoir et revestir celluy de nostre espoux Jesus-Christ" (150;227). Saint Paul returns more than once to this notion of relinquishing the old Adam for the new life in Christ but the apostle's words do not link that transformation to a discussion of marriage. Such a link we do find, however, in Briçonnet's correspondence with Marguerite: "Les pere et mere ne sont laisséz quand pour les biens, honneur, noblesse, beaulté, se faict adhesion du mariage charnel. Car le vieil Adam regne et en est l'object qu'il fault estre mort auparavant que le mariage charnel puisse estre l'ombre et la figure de la verité" (*Correspondance* 2:207).

11. The François edition ends this sentence with a question mark; the Le Hir edition, with a period. Like Chilton, I see no interrogative value to Parlamente's phrasing. On the other hand, Chilton translates "ne vous sont gueres tenues" as "can scarcely have been faithful to you." Not only does the translation change the tense of the French verb, but Chilton also transforms "tenu" ("débiteur, obligé, redevable, reconnaissant," according to Huguet) into "faithful." In light of the belief held by women in the *Heptameron* that their sex is not beholden to men for the "service" of courtship, I prefer the meanings of "tenu" cited by Huguet.

12. I discussed this phenomenon many years ago in an article on "Narrative Technique in 'L'Heptaméron'" (*Studi Francesi* 33 [1967]: 473–76). Although at that time my analysis did not insist, as it should have, on the signs in the tenth tale of Amadour's deliberate strategies to seduce Floride and on the relationship between that strategy and the notion of "faux cuyder," I remain convinced that the *Heptameron* cannot be reduced to a single perspective such as the one Parlamente expresses at the close of the twenty-first tale.

13. Jean Frappier, "Sur Lucien Febvre et son interprétation psychologique du XVIe siècle," in *Mélanges d'histoire littéraire . . . offerts à Raymond Lebègue* (Paris: Nizet, 1969), 19–31. Febvre's remarks are contained in his study *Amour sacré, amour profane: Autour de l'Heptaméron* (Paris: Gallimard, 1944).

14. See the article cited in note 12.

Tom Conley

5. The Graphics of Dissimulation: Between *Heptameron* 10 and *l'histoire tragique*

In a recent and terse analysis of tale 33 of the *Heptameron*, Ullrich Langer shows how a count uncovers a couple's deception. He sets himself apart from a eucharistic ritual exploited to disguise a wrongdoer's identity and save the criminal from conviction. Langer proposes that the count resembles a literary critic. Not duped by the leveling effects of ritual in which collective identity is gained, the hero reads the imbroglio as a "free subject," detached from the narrative and performative agencies of the stratagem. Like a student of Benveniste, he sorts out the deictic activity that makes the dissimulation possible. Langer suggests that the count saw how the deceit was staged, but also how he was able to interpret it because the characters' voices were *detached* from their origins or referents. They were being performed apart from the aura of presence, if a cinematic term can be used, that "lip synchrony" would have conferred upon them.

The count listened to the deictic agents, the "shifters" or pronouns in the woman's speech, and detected how they did not adhere to their referents. "The count treats the woman's oath as a possibly literary text, as a hypothetical statement, whereas his men are part of the text of the Eucharistic scene."[1] Through a canny reading of performative gestures, the hero (a *conte*) also discovers a dissimulation that appears to be inherent in the context of received belief. In doing so, he emerges from the tale as an interpretive subject with nascent libertine views. The count's position in the text is at least double insofar as his mobile role mimes that of the reader driven to ponder the subjects and objects of enunciation and to sort through dangling constructions. It could be said that the count is also a scriptwriter. He sees how words have simultaneously visual and aural traits; and how, in turn, their play of voice and figure indicates how visibility—insofar as it is a part of narrative—is a mode of deception.

In *Heptameron* 33, the authority of the *conte*, noted as the father of the implied author's brother, King François I, devolves upon his identity as a *conte*, both as an active narrative force or *actant*, and also a mirror of the sum of the tale being told. Both subject and object, the count's title shifts and flickers as an effect glimpsed inside and outside of it at once. He bears a title whose authority comes with the inscription of his name. The ambivalence of its graphic form (*conte* as sign of nobility and as sign of a narrative) gives readers cause to ask if the character is in the story or a summation of it. Thus, because we are not among the community either of *devisants* or the congregation in novella 33, we are, like the *conte*, better able to see the verbal dissimulation on the typographical surface. As readers we cannot be inveigled into believing in the virtues of any communion of narrative. The count's name and function figure in the overall scheme of deceit of the tale, in both secular and theological realms. If we liken ourselves to the hero, we find that attention to surface-effects or graphic traits serves to undo what, in the narrative, the characters' ruses are dissimulating.

Langer suggests, then, that Marguerite's work is self-critical in its logical and diegetic or narrative construction. Its attention to itself can be grasped wherever the reader locates how narrative effects emerge as a pattern of a general camouflage. In this sense he also hints at why Jacques Lacan's attraction for the *Heptameron* is not so fortuitous as the identity that the famous analyst proposes when he puns on the Christian names of Marguerite de Navarre and Marguerite Duras to initiate a study of gender, love, and social position.[2] For Lacan the *Heptameron* is rife with expression of dissimulation. It betrays the structure of communication in general, that is less a passage of messages between senders and receivers than oblique and distorted expressions of desire in dialogue within and across figures who dissimulate their presence before one another. Marguerite's tale displays a compelling narrative of Lacan's dynamics of the protean rhetoric of the self and other. The tale of Floride and Amadour has to do with exclusion that produces desire. The young knight's exploits are sustained by the absence and non-gaze of the woman he chooses to love, or of an occulted vision of her presence he obtains only when his desires to possess his object are frustrated.[3] The drama of amorous mediation also locates where evangelical and rhetorical issues seem to converge.

In both psychoanalytical and historical registers an ocular dimension of the narrative appears to play a role crucial to the patterns of dissimulation. If Ullrich Langer's study of *Heptameron* 33 is compared to Lacan's homage, we discover how a critical privilege seems to be accorded to sight, but how, at the same time, the authority of visibility is rent by the broken articulations of Marguerite's discourse. For historians of literature, as a consequence, we should be able to discern why the *Heptameron* moves away from the *histoire tragique* with which it is associated (that is, by way of Pierre Boaistuau's edited version of the collection under the title of *Histoires des amans fortunez*) and why, too, its graphic condition works in the service of a carefully designed grammatical chiaroscuro. By reading *Heptameron* 10 in view of the ocular traits of the diction, we should be better able to see exactly how the narrative is meshed in multiple inversions of oral and visible orders, and for what ostensive purposes, and with what outcome in respect to the *histoire tragique*.

The tale is long and, as the narrator Parlamente admits, could thus "estre à aucuns fascheuse" (83;152). Its duration appears to sustain its incapacity to come to completion except through the protagonists' suicide or withdrawal from their world. Claude Gruget notes its "maintes ruses et dissimulations" (cited in the François edition, 457), perhaps hinting that the study is not about two characters in love, but of language that captures its subjects—characters and readers, *devisants* and narrators alike—in its webbings. In this light the story gives the lie of its own deception. It must be seen, as the *conte* of tale 33, who saw ruses of enunciation located in the shifters floating between various surfaces of meaning. No other tale appears to use so much equivocation of names to yield effects of shimmering appearance. As in other tales, at first sight it is difficult to determine who speaks, or how the narrator is associated with his or her story. The diction is so dense and mannered that it has led biographers and critics to disparage the "style" of the *Heptameron* when they praise its great psychological complexity as a study of love. Yet the manner of the text is in fact its complexity. Its play of form begins with the dissolution of the characters into the physical form of the discourse telling of their adventures.

The characters' names figure in a style in continuous transformation and movement. They flow into the traits that convey their words at the same time their proper names appear to have a motivated relation with the tenor of their speech. A particular style emerges, one that might be called *anagraphy*, or a rhetoric of graphic traits that bind the physical character of the printed letters to the psychological conditions of the narratives; these qualities are seen "en écharpe," through or about the mimetic field. In this sense the notion of "character" in the *Heptameron* tends to oscillate between an ensemble of actions represented in the narrator's discourse (Amadour being bold, handsome, courtly, admirable, adventurous, as his actions indicate; while Floride is the severely attractive antithesis of all that is "florid" or mere decoration) and the virtuality of associations that the proper name evokes in the printed substance of its letters (onomastically disengaged by its resemblance to other words or verbal patterns in the syntax, in the representation of events, or even in its own anagrammatical range). Seen thus, the names establish sites of tension in the paragrammar and offer glimpses of what a neo-Freudian reader would assign to the story's "unconscious" by way of an atomistic play of letters and spaces. Their inscription in the printed matter both controls the imagistic traits of the writing all the while chance and accident bind the names to figures that move across the grammatical order. These same sites of movement constantly betray the story with fidelity. They reproduce the very order of the deferred, delayed, miscast signs exchanged between Amadour and Floride.

The text begs the reader to discover patterns of events through camouflaged signifiers that flicker between syntax and diegesis. The order is marked in the prologue, in which a poetics of reading is elaborated at the same time the narrative frame is being drawn about the ensemble. Threatened by brigands, the two ladies of the group are saved by two gentlemen. "Comme *deux ours enraigés descendans des montaignes*, frapperent sur ces bandouilliers tant furieusement qu'il y en eut si grand nombre de mortz que le demourant ne voulut plus actendre leurs coups . . ." (3;62, emphasis added).[4] They are soon marked as Dagoucin and Saffredent, but then it happens that two other women (later identified as Nomerfide and Ennasuite) "avoient eu affaire contre bestes non hommes": "à demye lieue deça Peyrehitte, avoient trouvé *ung ours descendant la montaigne, devant lequel avoient prins la course* à si grande haste que leurs chevaux, à l'entrée du logis tomberent morts soubz elles" (4;63). These events not only bring the group together. They mark a signifying process in which verbal matter begs the viewing reader to detect homologies and differences in the shape of print that blends with the material being reported. The two men resemble enraged bears rumbling down a mountainside; their figure becomes literalized in the next episode when a bear pursues two women in the same fashion. That their names are identified only after the event shows how the language intends to be seen as a broad signifying process before it is attached or fixed to a reflector with a given social identity.[5] *Ours* anticipates the *course* they take, while the same path resembles the flow of the Gave that has isolated the group at Cauterets. The text is indicating that the chance bringing the *devisants* together is also determining the signifying matter in the patterns established in the printed letters. It asks the reader thus to decipher speech on two levels and, concurrently, to compare them across the difference of their aural and graphic traits as marked in both word and image. The pertinent differences become the field in which interpretation takes place, but always in a manner such that the ocularity of the discourse is put forward as an element constitutive of the narrative.

The operation might be summed up in Parlamente's last words in the prologue. She chooses the site of the narrative in the shade of trees by a field along the banks of the Gave. There "les arbres sont si *foeillez* que le soleil ne sçauroit percer l'ombre ny eschauffer la frescheur; là, assiz à noz aises, dira chascun quelque histoire qu'il aura *veue* ou bien oy dire à quelque homme digne de foy. Au bout de dix jours aurons perachevé la centaine; et, si Dieu faict que notre labeur soit trouvé digne des *oeilz* des seigneurs et dames dessus nommez, nous leur en ferons present au retour de ce voiage *en lieu d'ymaiges* ou de patenostres . . ." (10;69). The ideal site for the narration is imbued with lenticular properties. The leaves of the trees contain eyes in the peculiar orthography of *foeillez* that rhymes visually with the *oeilz* of the tellers. The trees that the sun dapples bear literal witness to the veracity of the tales that are both seen and heard in memory. The ultimate worth of the passed events will be held up to the participants' view. Further, the tales will take the place of images, such that the plastic qualities of the fiction will become those of an image or, the text implies, the large beads of a rosary. Parlamente's words map out the foundation of the volume at the same time they script a poetics that draws the graphic aspects of the writing into the world of narrative truth and analogy.

In tale 10, Parlamente's centerpiece of the ensemble, the same poetics are held in view. Our search for the two protagonists' "subject positions" in dialogue becomes part of what Langer calls the activity of criticism in the *Heptameron*. Following the anagraphic qualities of Parlamente's words in the prologue, it appeals to the viewer's sight for its measure and substance. In working through the discourse, we recognize over and again—often at the expense of following the narrative continuously—how the verbal matter produces both "noise" and order, or forms simultaneously visible and concealed. These elements are conveyed often by a standard figure of a body and its effects. They remain most intensely ambiguous when a proper name, what is said to stand clear of the grammar by defining a lexical place in the structure of the sentence, is scattered graphically in and about surrounding words. A central field of force is discerned, but then forgotten when the narrative is resumed; but it comes back, returning as if from some repressed areas on the surface of the text, in variation that is further hidden and revealed among other signifiers.

The first moment when Floride and Amadour talk together comes when speech and visibility are seen as components of each other's difference of character, quality, and gender. Amadour, "parlant de Floride, appuyé sur une fenestre" (62;129), seeking to control her in his field of view and of speech, uses rhetoric to impose upon her an ineluctable choice between speech and death. "'M'amye, je vous supplie me conseiller lequel vault mieulx parler ou mourir.' Floride luy respondit promptement: 'Je conseilleray tousjours à mes amys de parler, et non de morir; car il y a peu de parolles qui ne se puissent amender, mais la vie perdue ne se peult recouvrer'" (62;129–30). Language can be modified, but death, an ultimate point or mark, cannot. The remark operates in the narrative as an interpellation masked as dialogue; it also asks the reader to *see* verbal forms flickering on the surface of the paginal world before our eyes.

The lexical properties of *amendement* are focalized in the implicit signature of the narrator. To respect the field of verisimilitude in the tale, the narrator can only make marginal mention of her presence within it. But the structure dictates that she be identified with it, or that both the dilemmas it proposes and its manner somehow be hers. She has to be within and of the story, virtually embodied by it but also, for reason of the perspective she has assigned since the prologue, remain excluded. In order to be suffused by the narration, to be one with the tale, and to transgress the line that separates her from the fiction (that is, to commit a sin of narrative incest), she breaks the laws that we know of representation by *being* the very substance of her words. By the mediation of print she can be what she tells, and be both present and absent in the field of the fiction. Parlamente thus marks a bodily presence through the signature she scripts into the visible or paragrammatical field. Her name is in a subliminal area of the text, like a watermark faintly visible between the blank area of a page and its printed characters.[6] Parlamente appears and vanishes in the syntax by means of the spatial disposition of letters of words floating within the tabular frame. As we have seen, the ocularity of the narration is frequently emphasized wherever figures of visibility mark the narrative. Doors, bedsteads, windows, or thresholds define framing elements in the fiction homologous to the rectangular disposition or, better, the "aspect ratio" of the page. The order of a random play of characters is at odds with any character's fixed position in the syntax. In the same episode just mentioned, Parlamente emerges through the writing as a figure of speech (literally taken to be that which utters, or has spoken, *parl . . . e* or *parla*) and an adverbial mark that can be attached as a suffix to any appropriate stem (*-ement*):

> Floride . . . s'adressoit souvent devant Poline si priveement . . . un jour, parlant à Floride, appuyé sur une fenestre . . . : "M'amye, je vous supplie me conseiller lequel vault mieulx parler ou mourir?" Floride luy respondit promptement: "Je conseilleray toujours à mes amys de parler, et non de morir; car il y a peu de parolles qui ne se puissent amender. . . ." (62;129)

The window cited in the text opens onto the analogical play of figures on the page. Parlamente becomes a perspectival object or transitional form, seen but unspoken in the ultimatum of the choice that Amadour tenders between speech and death.[7]

In the courtly world, to be of Amadour's tenor, the male has to keep before his eyes a mute image of the beloved figure. Like an image in a photo, the figure has to be deprived of speech and stand as an object receiving the lover's gaze. Amadour, however, is displaced from his privileged position gained through the interpellation by the disruption of Parlamente's shadow moving between his and Floride's words. Parlamente is present as the concealed intermediary of the dialogue, a third term who views the couple from *within*, and whom we view through the optic of printed speech. In less anagraphic writing (or in whatever comes with purer modes of representation that tend to make the vehicle of narration invisible or secondary to its tenor or content) print would be "scumble" or an interference that establishes a distance between the reading voyeur and the object of his gaze. Here Parlamente's name becomes the very disorder or phantasm of chaos that elicits both desire and mediation.

For the same reason Floride's matte response to Amadour's first entreaty begging her to abide by his love prompts the reader to consider the silence of the speech that comes with the printed traits of his words. The logic of the scene demands it. If the nature of Amadour's love is as platonic as he says it is, to be sustained it would simply *have to go without saying*. As the tale has to put into view the ineffable nature of the love, it must appeal to stratagems of visibility that are glimpsed obliquely, through the atomized presence of Parlamente's name. The spell of the love is broken by speech, yet the printed characters of the protagonist's words indicate how, if it is to be real, its best mode of expression is mediated between the report of voice and the printed word that silences it. As Floride utters to Amadour about his love, "Car, si vous avec ce que vous demandez, qui vous con-

trainct d'en parler si affectionne<u>ment</u>" (64;132). The statement inscribes a
mannequin of what is mirrored in his reply: "Ma dame, vous parlez très
prud<u>emment</u> . . ." (64;132). Several sentences later, we discover that a go-
between, "Poline" (equivocating perhaps on *Pauline* writing and Scripture), extends the same quadrangular configuration marked between the
two interlocutors, their message, and the presence of the other in the
graphics of the representation. Amadour: "Et quand vous venez parler à
moy devant elle [Poline] si priv<u>emment</u>, j'ai si grand paour de faire quelque
signe où elle fonde jug<u>ement</u>" (64;132). In each of these exchanges, the love
has to remain unnamed where it is named. In the wedge of the paradox is
written Parlamente's name. She literally signs each reply of the dialogue
about which the entire tale is turning. If terms of point of view are used to
explain the scene, it could be argued that the narrative displays a couple in
the intimate space of a whisper; to be sustained, its illusion depends on the
presence of an the additional figure who peers onto the scene in the role of
both spectator and creator. Typography avers to be the mediating agent
that allows Parlamente to be a hidden figure in, as it were, the textual carpet
of the tale.

Amadour dissimulates an ethos of conquest in the name of love.
Because it displaces what would be intact in the ineffable relation, his
motives are projected through the graphic presence of the teller otherwise
excluded from the writing. As we have seen, the lovers' meeting that began
with his disguised interpellation of "speech or death" calls forth the figure
of Parlamente. She does not recur in the same fashion until the very end of
the tale, as a perspectival signature that comes into view, once again, as a
spectator hidden in the writing. When Floride leaves the story, she literally
recedes from a pictorial field. She enters into a monastery in which she
spends the rest of her life. At that very moment the narrator comes forward
as a shape of writing that underscores the optical nature of Floride's
vanishment. "Et, après qu'elle [Floride] eut faict ses obseques honorable-
ment, sans en parler à mere ne à belle-mere, s'en alla randre religieuse au
monastere de Jesus, prenant pour mary et amy Celui qui l'avoit delivrée
d'une amour si veh<u>emente</u> que celle d'Amadour, et d'un ennuy si grand que
de la compagnye d'un tel mary" (83;152, emphasis added). The filigrane
webbing that had been established at the rhetorical center of the text in
which Amadour declared his love (64;132) now recurs at the margin, where
vehemence and speech are *moderated* by the distance we gain from the
sentence in which we see, again, the components of a frame in the first and
last syllables of Parlamente's name. The gap opened in the syntax of the

verbal mannequin becomes the measure of a metaphysical space traversed in the last words of the story.[8] In the celebrated conclusion, Floride "ainsy tourna toutes ses affections à aymer Dieu si parfaictement, que après avoir vescu longuement religieuse, luy rendit son ame en telle joye, que l'espouse a d'aller veoir son espoux" (83;152). The marriage of subject and God comes through the passage in a monastic space. Parlamente reiterates the Cistercian architectural plan of a sacred "marriage" that a believer obtains with God in the vision of depth of light passing through darkness, that Bernard of Clairvaux had formulated to give an aura of erotic austerity to the deep nave of the abbey at Fontenay.[9] We sense the same depth of field in Floride's movement toward the ideal spouse, but it is conveyed by the systematic division and extension of the narrator's proper name dissimulated in the typographical screen.

On the one hand, Parlamente endows writing with perspective while, on the other, she is displayed as the veritable author signing the tale in its last words. She is marked as the speaker of the writing (marking a presence camouflaged in the printed texture) without heralding any obvious signs of omniscient authority over the creation. More in line with a duplicity that moves between naming and its obverse, or of individuality and anonymity (both terms being necessary for the establishment of each other), as a visual cipher, *Parlamente* becomes the critical "operator" of the field of illusion from within and without the text.

We must now ask if and how other proper names are dissimulated in the tale. Do Amadour and Floride command the same virtue of graphic dissemination? If not, what terms, or what verbal fragments might acquire similar roles? Amadour does not appear to scatter in the text. A self-contained name, one with obvious connotations (*amadouer*, a verb of sweet mendacity; *mor*, synonym of *mort*; *ame*, *aimer*, with standard meanings in the courtly tradition), Amadour disperses into the verbal matter only once in the narrative, at the very moment when his impatience precipitates his demise. After making physical advances to Floride ["à chercher ce que l'honneur des dames deffend" (72;140)], he becomes a synonym of the force of love, or of force personified: "*Amadour*, qui avoit perdu toute raison par la force d'amour, luy [to Floride] dict: 'Ung si long service merite-il recompense de telle cruauté?'" (73;141). *La force d'amour* becomes his graphic essence, even the motto or trademark by which, in the diegesis, he has been authenticating his actions. In the self-given name of the "force of love" he can arrogate Floride in body and soul: "Car, par *la force d'amour*, je vous ay si bien gaignée que celluy premier a eu vostre cueur a si mal poursuivy le corps, qu'il a merité de perdre le tout ensemble(. . .) . Ne doubtez poinct que, quant *l'amour force* le corps et le cueur, le peché soyt jamais imputé" (73;142). The narrative proceeds to focalize the name. In Floride's speech it is reduced to the violence of *amour* that, in her experience, resembles what we perceive to be something of a Freudian death-drive.

If it is, Floride's identification of love-as-death in the name of Amadour, the text implies that the difference between a "good" and "bad" love is entwined in the tension of the proper names in play. Floride names Amadour more and more by his proper name as she progressively detaches from him ("Je ne puis croire, Amadour, que . . . ," 74;142ff), thus objectifying him in a deictic act that shows how verbal indication at once focalizes both what it marks *and* the traits of its own expression.[10] In the *Heptameron*, the latter is made manifest as the matter of dissimulation, that is, the written text as seen by us, mediators, in an infinite process of deferment. The same ocular principle is also summoned by the imaginary interference of Floride's name with and against that of Amadour. Her name begins to fragment *into* the text when, in both her eyes and ours, Amadour's emerges *from* it. A turning point occurs when, defending herself during Amadour's penultimate entreaty, she utters to him, "Avez-vous oblyé les bons exemples que vous m'avez donnez des vertueuses dames qui ont resisté à la *folle amour*, et le despris que vous avez faict des *folles*?" (74;142). For the first time the context makes Floride's name available to be turned into *Fol-dire*, or a speech of untruth—dissimulation and, soon, vengeance—that will be undertaken in the narrative of her own death-drive. At that moment "elle se sentoit assez forte pour le [Amadour] pugnir de sa follye" (76;145), that is, in the calculated ambivalence of *sa* (like the *vous* that Langer studies in story 33) referring both to his action and to her name. A common folly is once more mediated by the equivocation of the printed letter, that we can also understand to be the Freudian *ça* that Floride is calling *follye*.

The allegorical dimension of Floride's name thus becomes clear in its affinity with madness that comes as a result of dissimulation. Following Floride's decision to break off from *Amadour* and *amour*, the narrator recasts her name in what seems to be an unproblematic, decorative "effect" of alliteration. Desperate, Amadour clasps Floride's hand not long after she has lapidated her face in an act announcing her decision to vanish from the visible world. "Et en ceste fureur, d'une de ses fortes et puissantes mains, print les deux delicates et foibles de Floride" (78;147). Many hands are in play. Visually, in a literal mannerism recalling the sign of the Fontainebleau school of artists and designers, the description puts one large, male hand over Floride's two delicate hands. The image is remarkably violent in the mimetic register. But it is also ciphered in the graphic movement of the common and proper names.[11] All of a sudden, the image leads the reader's eyes to note how foi is invested into Floride, and how self-mutilation is glimpsed in the effect that faith exercises wrenching force over the body (*foibles* equaling *foi blesse*). In the durational register of the narration, Amadour's and Floride's bodies age over the passage of years. By this point, reaching middle age, she is evinced in the wrinkle, of *ride*, that is left over from the inscription of *foibles* in *Floride*. That her name is Scripture becomes apparent to the degree we are reading and seeing her name in all of its manifold virtue in the mannered twist of the anagram (*Lire*: Floride), subjecting it to the same ocular treatment that she assigns to Amadour in the distance she gains from him.

In an uncanny way our perceptions of the traits of the two characters' names run parallel with the narrative at the same time the treatment of violence is modulated by anthonomasia, the trope that willfully confuses common and proper names. Perhaps the relation of "Floride," "Amadour," and "Parlamente" to the narrative also embodies a virtual cinematic representation of "aftereffects" of a verbal lap-dissolve on the graphic surface of the narrative. In film, a medium that splices sight and narrative, any notion of sequence is problematic. Shots refer to each other both forward and backward, independently of any narrative logic. They show us that the production of sequential order is to a given degree a product of our imagination. The same holds in the relation that graphic dissimulation displays in the patent structure of Floride and Amadour's love story. The names have already spelled out the situation in the tenor of Parlamente's first words sowed in the text ["laquelle fille *se nommoit* Floride . . . et, entre les autres, y en avoit ung *nommé* Amadour" (55;122)]. Their deixis "fixes" the protagonists in a tension of characters the tale takes pain to reiterate at greater length.

If we can claim that the story is thus a *nouvelle qui n'en est pas une*, that mediates itself by calculated concealment of names, we should be better able to see how the tale is located between fiction and history, or how it begins to resemble the ambiguous status of the *histoire tragique*. The *histoire tragique* inevitably makes much of its veracity, as does the prologue of the *Heptameron*.[12] The genre asserts that its material is historical in origin but exemplary in composition. In the same way it cuts between two conditions of proper names that are frequently used to gauge differences of fact and fiction. In the writing of history, it is generally said that the proper name is "full" before being shuffled, emptied, and then reformed according to the results of archival investigation. In contrast, in literature a proper name is "empty" at the outset and is "filled" in the course of narration.[13] Thus Edward II of England (in the first tale of Boaistuau's *Histoires tragiques*) could be known by an informed reader of portraits, annals, or cosmographies, whereas "Romeo and Juliette," the two protagonists of his third tale, would acquire pertinent traits only in the course of the telling. "Amadour" and "Floride" would be somewhere between one pole and the other insofar as the analogical force of Marguerite's evangelical onomastics would confer various and contradictory qualities upon the names born of both fact and fiction. At the same time the markers would have to be dissimulated if Parlamente sticks to her claims about the veracity of the stories. As her name indicates, she has to utter lies in order to be veracious. Her characters have few historical traits fixed in their names at the same time they are replete with them. It is thus up to Parlamente to speak through the characters, their dialogue, and their tales in writing.

On this score two observations can be made. First, few stories of the *Heptameron* stress so redundantly the failure of narrative to resolve itself. A Lacanian story where forms are mirrored into infinity without resolution, *Heptameron* 10 can be seen telling only of its delays in reaching an outcome. Whenever she intercedes to tell us where we are as listeners, or what is conspiring among the characters ("Je n'entreprendz poinct vous dire la douleur que sentoit Amadour escoutant ces parolles," 75;143, for example), Parlamente represents herself as a mediator. A self-conscious narrator, she becomes a figure that suffuses the fiction from within but who also generates it from without.[14] The paradox of a character at once in and out of the work stresses the relation of tale-telling to the production of desire as mediation.

In this light Parlamente's relation to her topic has uncanny parallel with Amadour's position in respect to Floride. The story begins by noting Amadour's paucity of means to gain proximity to his desired object. Having no "moyen poury attaindre" (56;123), or a "moyen de parler à elle" (57;124), he conceives a stratagem to see her "par le moyen de la contesse d'Arande" (57;124). Without a "moyen par lequel il peust retourner en lieu où il peust veoir Floride" (59;126), he seeks in marriage "heureuse couverture et moyen" (60;127) to inhabit Floride's heart. He always looks for a *moyen de parvenir* (the formula varying at least six more times, 62–83;128–152). His *moy*, his self, is determined by the *moyen* or distance afforded between his eyes and the objects in their purview. Through the word the model of courtly love dissolves into a scenario of capital speculation. Amadour's entrepreneurial character is seen in view of the narrator who performs likewise, but in a mode of concealment that works between discourse spoken and written. The print of the tale is thus *not* a relay assuring indirect presence of Parlamente's voice, but a coextensive camouflage of writing that tends to affirm an absence of speech. The printed text "represents" neither the narrator's voice nor the commentary of the *devisants*. It figures, rather, in a general order of dissimulation mirroring those of which the tales are speaking. Ambivalence that the graphic matter generates exceeds control that point of view, voice, or commentary might exert on the narration. If Ullrich Langer's remarks are recalled again, we can say that criticism begins wherever the medium of print contradicts the motives of the characters and reroutes their intentions in directions other than what their desire maps out for them.

Second, two strands of what seem to be the "graphic unconscious" of the text exhibit the ways its surfaces mediate one another. On one meeting with Floride, Amadour tries to reach his goal by wearing a saintly look. "Il luy [to Floride] dist avecq le plus *fainct visage* qu'il peut prendre, 'Ma dame, j'ay toute ma vie desiré d'aymer une femme de bien'" (75;143, emphasis added). Since, in the 1559 and 1560 editions the medial *s* resembles an *f*, and the quasi-identity was already exploited among other writers, the *saintly* face can also be a *faintly* or *feigned* face, a *fainct vifage*.[15] Its air of sanctity happens to be marked by a coextensive *inscription of dissimulation* that the graphics reveal—and mask—by their own means. Since the cause of the narrative is intensified and confirmed by typographical ambiguity, the result is that deception emerges everywhere the text underscores its traits of visibility. Ocularity seems to betray the play of shimmering appearance. When the two protagonists meet, they speak by windows that open onto a void beyond or provide imaginary vectors of vanishment for their desires. "Un jour, parlant à Floride, appuyé sur une fenestre" (62;129), Amadour broaches the topic of speech and death. Inversely, when Floride decides to objectify her relation with Amadour, "se tint à une fenestre, pour le veoir venir de loing" (70;138). Windows provide a frame for confined opening, a momentarily closed perspective, an area in which the other appears as an absence.[16] Like the "sainct" or "fainct visage" that Amadour wore before Floride, the *fenestre* is also an inscription of appearance invested into the scenography and the verbal matter.[17] The staging draws attention to the art of concealment. The power of sight is impugned in its own expression.

Without engaging in extensive analysis of the structure of visibility in the *histoire tragique*, with which Marguerite de Navarre shares affinities, we can now ask how her work figures against the genre, born in 1559, that would dominate for much of the rest of the sixteenth century. When he published the first edition of his translation of Bandello, Pierre Boaistuau inaugurated a serial form. The *histoire* is a matrix or paradigm-tale that stages a condition of imbalance or hubris that the narrative proceeds to correct. The tale displays with panache the righteousness of the established Catholic order to be heeded as an inviolable measure of human conduct. The stories impose a difference—of age between spouses, of social class—coded as a transgression corrected by a spectacle of torture serving as an example for viewers to behold.

The *histoire tragique* is generally constructed in an ocular configuration that intends to "mirror" the world before the reader. Its narratives impose laws of conduct that whenever transgressed bring about severe retribution. In Boaistuau's model, six tales vary on the pattern. The paradigmatic stories (2, 3, 4, 5) lead to a murderous denouement in which scenarios of revenge grant the privilege of torture, dismemberment, or strangulation. The narrator invariably signals the forthcoming conclusion, as a *piteux spectacle* or a *chef d'oeuvre*, whose description draws the reader's eye to the platform of a theater of cruelty. The same formulas recur predictably in the tales and appear to make all narrative lines converge upon a spectacle of torture, focalizing the action according to standard formulas.[18] Ritualized murder crystallizes the narrative as an ocular genre that sets the reader in an assigned place in the social order.

Marguerite de Navarre's tales share many of these traits, but the focalizing elements of the visual or schematic rhetoric of the *histoire tragique* are not mobilized. Both the typographical equivocation within the stories and the prismatic discussions on margins appear intended to call into question the centering devices of the new genre. The design of a fragmentary, mosaic form contrasts with that of Boaistuau. As we have seen in the relation of the proper names to the syntax, typography mediates narrative effects by putting them into a webbing of signifiers that move all over and about the tale rather than toward a *piteux spectacle* of murder.

Literary historians have studied the role Boaistuau played in his aborted rewriting of the *Heptameron* under the name of the *Histoires des amans fortunez*. In 1558 he changed the text, suppressed given passages, rectified infelicities of style, and imposed a new order upon the sequence of stories.[19] Boaistuau, a master of exhortative prose, no doubt endowed the manuscript with a rhetorical purpose of the sort that acquired greater definition when he designed the *Histoires tragiques* of 1559. A style of oratory and of eloquence corrects what Boaistuau called the *sentences tant maigres* of Bandello, the Italian's *phrases rudes* replaced with bravura and pompous brio.

The new elegance of Boaistuau's "French" Bandello, and of the *histoire tragique* in general, it can be added, also depends on the ocularity of its centralizing features. The rhetoric is conditioned by a verbal perspective focusing on the *piteux spectacle* or *chef d'oeuvre* of the work's own printed performance. It may be that Marguerite's analogical style of chiaroscuro did not please the rhetor who tried to mold the manuscript to a style of the signature he was fashioning. If so, the many dangling constructions and equivocations had to be adapted to an oratorical diction. Ambiguities had to be minimized. The author's keen sense of camouflage, learned since her affiliation with the Réforme de Meaux,[20] were subjected to editorial revision in the early days of Boaistuau's budding career. If so, the ambivalence of Marguerite de Navarre's style had to be changed—consciously or unconsciously—for different reasons that further link ocularity with power.

The rhetoric of the *histoire tragique* depends on converging lines of perspective, on the producton of a verbal spectacle, and on the construction of a verbal "world-theater" that loosely follows Boaistuau's own invention of the *Théatre du monde* (1558). The many shapes of mediation that move between narrative and print in the *Heptameron* resist adaptation to centering schemes. Mediation enacts a play of appearance and dissimulation all over the surface of writing and, in doing so, calls for a reader, a "critic" engaged in deciphering motives within and beyond the characters' words, who is impelled to consider the ocular drive in writing itself. Through the *Heptameron* the reader discerns the articulation of power that comes with sight unmediated by speech. The *histoire tragique* begins to format a classical model of authority and confinement, whereas, before the fact, the *Heptameron* analyzes the effects of power and sight in its relations to the imprint of its own verbal form.

Notes

1. Ullrich Langer, "Interpretation and the False Virgin: A Reading of *Heptaméron* 33," in *Women in French Literature*, ed. Michel Guggenheim, Stanford French and Italian Studies 58 (Saratoga, Calif.: Anma Libri, 1989), 64.

2. In Jacque Lacan, "Hommage fait à Marguerite Duras du ravissement de Lol V. Stein," in *Marguerite Duras* (Paris: Albatros, 1980).

3. Sanford S. Ames studies *Heptameron* 10 among Lucien Febvre, Duras, and Lacan in "A Severe and Militant Charity," *L'Esprit créateur* 28, no. 2 (1988): 89–95. He shows that in *Le Ravissement de Lol V. Stein* Jacques Hold and Tatiana Karl make love by virtue of their exclusion of Lol, the third term. Amadour's exclusion of Floride, he argues, is congruent with the Durassian scenario. An "undecidability of visible language" of printed writing puts the object of love at a difficult distance from the viewer (90–91). I should like to add a fourth term to the structure, that of the signature of Parlamente that both marks and authenticates the scenario.

4. Unless indicated otherwise, emphasis is added here and throughout all citations of the French.

5. It can be added that the voluminous debate over the *devisants'* historical identity is symptomatic of the play of differential naming that makes characters' names float as enigmas or vanishing points that never resolve tension between their characters (in an onomastic sense) and their actions or speech. They are fictive and historical at once.

6. It would not be wrong to stress how Parlamente's signature forms part of a "mystical fable" in which she is glimpsed in passage through the writing. Her subliminal movement about and in the characters of writing tells us that she is there, *in them*, in the duration of our retinal suspension of the letters we are scanning. In this way Parlamente indeed shares much with the figure of Duras's heroines who spin off the primal scene of *Le Ravissement de Lol V. Stein*. Michel de Certeau takes up the same relation of mysticism, print, and voice in *La Fable mystique* (Paris: Gallimard, 1982), 48–50.

7. Here Guy Rosolato's concept, elaborated in *Eléments de l'interprétation* (Paris: Gallimard, 1985), is stressed.

8. The concept of *mannequin* follows Jean Starobinski's study of Saussure's notes on the anagram, in *Les Mots sous les mots* (Paris: Gallimard, 1974).

9. See Raymond Oursel, "Erotique de Fontenay," *Corps écrit* 2: Le sacré (Paris: Presses Universitaires de France, 1982), 103–12, in which the longitudinal expanse of space articulates the path followed in the Nuptials of the subject with God.

10. Wlad Godzich and Jeffrey Kittay note that "deixis shows the very instance of discourse; it shows that discourse is taking place. It is a way that discourse can make reference to its own eventfulness," in *The Emergence of Prose* (Minneapolis: University of Minnesota Press, 1987), 20. We can add that in the tenth tale deixis indicates a view of masculine interpellation, but also of the ocularity that goes hand in hand with it. The "eventfulness" of which Godzich and Kittay write appears to be, for Marguerite, that of the production of a secular and typographical Scripture.

11. In *Le Maniérisme*, Claude-Gilbert Dubois speaks of Marguerite's verbal constructions that go "by derivation." In the opening sentence of the first tale, "il n'y a pas de centre, il y a plutôt une tête, à laquelle s'attache un corps constitué de subordonnées rattachés entre elles comme des anneaux et dessinant des replis tortueux par prolifération des expansions: en somme une ligne serpentine" (Paris: Presses Universitaires de France, 1979), 146–50. The line is sinuous, and the transversal elements—letters—move across the sentence in order to map its confusion and clarity. Names work in the service of this "mannered" vision.

12. See Michel Simonin, "Faits divers tragiques," *Studi de letteratura francese* 18 (1990): 142, 149–50. The *histoire tragique*, he notes, is motived in part by contemporaneous pictures that both "represent" and "illustrate" scenes of everyday life. The genre exemplifies model behavior by a dialectical relation between its rhetorical composition and its source in local time and space.

13. In *L'Écriture de l'histoire*, Michel de Certeau shows how the historian will take the name of "Robespierre" as a point of departure in what will attempt to complicate our associations with it, and how Stendhal will inscribe "Julien Sorel" at the beginning of *Le Rouge et le noir* in order then to fill it with a history (Paris: Gallimard, 1982 ed.), 112.

14. Parlamente might acquire daimonic mobility that her model of real life does not possess, at least if Carla Freccero's words on the life story of Marguerite as woman are followed, in "1527," in Denis Hollier, ed., *A New History of French Literature* (Cambridge, Mass.: Harvard University Press, 1989), 145–48.

15. See Samuel Kinser, *Rabelais's Carnival* (Berkeley: University of California Press, 1990), on the equivocation of *s'ensuit/s'enfuyt*, what he calls a writing "en tapinois," chaps. 1 and 3.

16. See Marie-Madeleine La Fontaine, "L'Espace fictif dans *L'Heptaméron*," in *Centre d'art, d'esthétique et littérature de L'Université de Rouen* (Rouen: Presses Universitaires de Rouen, 1974), 233–48, in which the critic studies how discourse is spatialized (or framed) by dint of the emblematic presence of doors and windows.

17. Catherine Randall Coats shows how "foeneste" in d'Aubigné's *Les Aventures du baron Foeneste* indicates both deceptive appearances that bear comparison with the figure of the window, in *Subverting the System: D'Aubigné and Calvinism*, Sixteenth Century Essays and Studies, vol. 14 (Kirksville, Mo.: Sixteenth Century Journal Publishers, Inc., 1990), 141ff.

18. The patterns are studied in greater detail in my "Pierre Boaistuau: *histoire tragique* et point de fuite," forthcoming in *Le Roman de la Renaissance*, ed. Michel Simonin (Actes du xxiiie colloque du Centre d'Etudes Supérieures de la Renaissance, Tours, Summer 1990).

19. See Richard A. Carr's informative introduction to his critical edition of the *Histoires tragiques* (Paris: Champion, 1977), xxxv–xl, that includes a rich bibliographical background (n. 30, xxxvi).

20. Studied at length in Henry Heller, "Marguerite de Navarre and the Reformers of Meaux," *Bibliothèque d'Humanisme et Renaissance* 33 (1971): 271–301, and Robert D. Cottrell, *A Grammar of Silence: A Reading of Marguerite de Navarre's Poetry* (Washington, D.C.: The Catholic University of America Press, 1987), chaps. 1–2.

Part II

Narrative Systems
and Structures

Michel Jeanneret

6. Modular Narrative and the Crisis of Interpretation

As a starting point, here are four elementary observations: (1) the *Heptameron* is in the form of short novellas rather than a long narrative; (2) the book gives many of these novellas and takes the form of a collection; (3) each story is followed by a commentary; (4) the storytellers' interpretations do not agree. While these observations apply specifically to the *Heptameron*, they are also valid and pertinent for a large part of French narrative literature in the sixteenth century. Hence, we can illuminate the *Heptameron* by other narratives and vice versa. I will study the narrative structure of the *Heptameron* as an example of major trends. A better understanding of these large-scale phenomena will allow us to return to the *Heptameron* with a better appreciation of the importance of the four characteristics I have mentioned.

Long Romances and Short Stories

The sixteenth century produced remarkably few long romances while collections of novellas proliferated. Translated, adapted, or newly invented, from previously written sources or from the oral tradition—often it is hard to make such distinctions—short narrative forms were fashionable. This phenomenon, as far as I know, has never been explained. It reveals, nonetheless, a meaningful choice, and deserves to be analyzed—first, through a general survey, then some hypotheses—especially because the *Heptameron* is directly concerned.

The absence of large narrative works is all the more curious in that it appears as an accident, an exception. In the fourteenth and fifteenth centuries, and even into the first decades of the sixteenth, the epic and romance cycles of the Middle Ages inspired many romances in prose—an immense corpus of adventures that combined and grew in endless sequences. Late in the sixteenth century the abundance of long and complex romances returned with renewed vigor, and, as is well known, the first half of the seventeenth century reached unheard-of levels in terms of the number of new titles and the length of narratives.[1] It is still more remarkable that long narratives declined in France during the Renaissance in view of what was happening elsewhere at the same time. While France devoted itself almost exclusively to the short narrative, Italy continued to elaborate, in various forms, large heroic and courtly works—for example, the works of Ariosto and Tasso.

This is the general tendency, to which there are some counterexamples, though nothing more than the exception to confirm the rule. Hélisenne de Crenne's romance *Les Angoyses douloureuses* (1538) and Barthelemy Aneau's *Alector* (1560) were not unimportant, but they were isolated cases. I recognize, of course, that the prose versions of epic material and adaptations of medieval romances were among the first texts to benefit from the discovery of the printing press. They perpetuated in the Renaissance the themes and systems of medieval narrative fiction.[2] Yet creative activity in this domain slowed about 1530, and the rewriting of medieval romances appeared thereafter as an obsolete survival, even though several texts of this type continued to be reprinted.

Rabelais's great romance series was inspired by the same principle of the sequel. From father to son, from quests to discoveries, it seems to present all the features of large and continuous narration. On closer inspection, it appears, though, that the journey from *Gargantua* to the *Quart Livre* (or to the *Cinquième*, if one prefers), is more complicated. It is clear that Rabelais begins by inscribing his project in the tradition of medieval cycles. He refers to the *Grandes et inestimable chronicques du grand et énorme géant Gargantua*, and thus creates a link both with the subject matter of chivalric literature and with its method of grafting onto existing work. In addition to this external support, he articulates the parts of *Pantagruel* as sequels designed to form a solid narrative syntax. Finally, his adoption of the biographical structure, in the first two narratives, underscores his will to provide continuity. But this ambitious plan for a novelistic masterwork soon falls apart. Gaps in the plot's logic appear right from the beginning. The *Tiers* and *Quart Livres* adopt a cumulative mode of composition having little to do with the chronological unfolding of the romance. Equivalent episodes—Panurge's consultations, the stages in the sea voyage—pile up without linkage or progression; the narrative breaks into more or less independent units, in apparently random number and order. It seems as if Rabelais, at first faithful to the medieval tradition of sequence, surrendered, from the *Tiers Livre* on, to the new aesthetic. He broke the narrative succession, published romances which look like collections of short stories, and thus arrived, in his last works, at an arrangement very close to the modular structure of the *Heptameron*.

Another exception should be discussed: the romance cycle of *Amadis de Gaula* had a huge success and persisted through the whole of the sixteenth century, growing, diversifying, and spreading out through its family roots. Though chivalric romances were less fashionable, the *Amadis* series picked up where they left off and, in a new timbre, kept alive in the Renaissance reader's imagination the "matière de Bretagne" and the heroic traditions of feudal epics. Gentlemen, ladies, and the whole cultivated elite found in *Amadis* the representation of an ideal that still held their interest. Yes, the *Amadis* books were a social phenomenon, a commercial event and, if there ever was one, a long romance.[3] But one work, even a best-seller, is not enough to belie a trend. However, popular with the French, the *Amadis* books were, after all, a foreign product, since Nicolas Herberay des Essarts and his continuers translated, or adapted, Spanish and other sources. The French were the consumers, rather than the producers, of this long romance. And anyway, were the *Amadis* books any more than a relic, a survival from another age? Their recent editor has used the terms "archaic narrative form" and a "fossil romance."[4]

A general view must also include one last exception. In the great corpus of novellas which proliferated throughout the century, the predilection for the *histoire tragique*, imitated from Bandello, became pronounced from 1565 on. The plots, at first short, began at this point to become more complicated: the stories became longer, and we can see the beginning of the narrative scheme which heralded the rebirth of the romance during the seventeenth century. It seems as if the *histoire tragique* was getting ready to fill the gap created by the dearth of new long fiction between 1530 and 1590.

The scarcity of romances was not only contemporaneous with but probably related to another surprising deficiency, that of the heroic poem, another ghost haunting the sixteenth century, another proof—by absence—of the crisis which struck at that time the long narrative forms. For Sébillet, the situation was clear: "Of the kind of Poems which can be called the Great Work, as is, of Homer, the *Iliad*, of Vergil, the *Aeneid*, of Ovid, the *Metamorphoses*, you will find few or none attempted or completed by the Poets of our time."[5] Such a lacuna is all the more striking in that the epic model enjoyed an exceptional prestige. The *Arts poétiques* proclaimed its superiority and, to bring about the coming of the great work, handed out encouragements and advice. Peletier du Mans clearly established the relationship between the subject matter of medieval romances and that of the heroic poem: "I find our romances very creative. And I will say here in passing that in certain chosen cases, the heroic poet would be able to make use of them: as of the adventures of Knights, their loves, their travels, their enchantments, their combats, and such things, which Ariosto borrowed from us to transpose in his book."[6] Du Bellay also referred to the example of Ariosto, who had succeeded in constructing a vast romance edifice; in his turn the French poet should choose "one of those beautiful old French romances, like *Lancelot*, like *Tristan* or others: and from them revive for the world a marvelous *Iliad* and a well-wrought *Aeneid*."[7] This exalted challenge appealed to Ronsard. The *Franciade* corresponds, in verse, to the lure of the romance: "this book is a Romance like the *Iliad* or the *Aeneid*," wrote Ronsard.[8]

This great heroic and romantic project would not be completed. Such a failure is all the more significant in that it reveals the literary bankruptcy of poets unable to commit themselves to a monumental creation:

> This deficiency of great and Heroic works is from want of subjects: or from the tendency of each of the Poets reputed for knowledge to prefer following the trail approved by so many ages and by so many sages by translating rather than to undertake a work of his own invention, thus opening a pathway for robbers to steal the honor due to any virtuous toil.[9]

It seems as if the period did not fit the ideological conditions for setting out, and carrying through, great projects, and as if the political instability, the crisis of beliefs, and the explosion of traditional culture deprived writers of the equilibrium necessary for a long-term endeavor. Perhaps it is revealing that in poetry, religious authors like d'Aubigné and Du Bartas were the only ones capable of building large and coherent systems. Was this because they had a global vision, a sustaining ideal, which gave their ventures that conviction, that goal which secular poets seemed to lack?

Yet a phenomenon of this type cannot be explained by a single factor. There are many causes, each of which would require a more detailed inquiry than I have laid out. I would like to develop in what follows two other hypotheses, which, I believe, concern important issues in the history of forms and the history of ideas in the sixteenth century. These considerations will bring us back to the *Heptameron*.

Modules and Collections

The success of short stories and the concomitant eclipse of the romance may have to do, first of all, with the Renaissance taste for short forms and with the widespread tendency to segment discourse, whether narrative or expository, into discrete and mobile units—what I will call modules. The sixteenth-century book rarely took the form of an organic unity, a homogeneous construction whose every part had a necessary place in the whole. It seems often a collection of sundry pieces, more or less independent, without a clear principle of selection and classification. Such a book was not conceived as a closed and definitive structure, but as the assembly, temporary and contingent, of movable pieces available for other uses.

Volumes of unmatched stories, anthologies, and collections were not a sixteenth-century invention. Various types of compilations were made in antiquity and throughout the Middle Ages. This phenomenon, however, became unusually important in the Renaissance, in books for exchange of knowledge as well as in books for recreation.

The distribution of narrative material in compact modules and the arrangement of such modules in more or less mixed volumes, like the *Heptameron*, had a crucial impact on the way fiction was distributed in the second half of the sixteenth century. Despite variations in the narrative structure and in the arrangement of the stories, the anthology principle was constant. Novella collections appeared by the dozen, and most merely retold, with small changes, stories already circulating.

In managing knowledge the Renaissance also took up the modular structure. The humanists published innumerable compilations; they loved lists and anthologies, and they heaped up knowledge in vast encyclopedias. Budé's work and Erasmus's immense collection of *Adages* and his *Colloquies* give an idea of many others. The last decades of the century teemed with compendiums, memorandums, and handbooks. I could mention, more or less at random, the works of Etienne Pasquier, Pierre Messie, La Primaudaye, Boaistuau, Béroalde de Verville, Vigenère—outsized reservoirs of erudite fragments, spare parts of knowledge, available for any possible use.

At the crossroads of narrative collections and scholarly miscellanies were all kinds of "recueils bigarrés" which, in different proportions, mixed short stories and documentary materials, didactic excerpts and a variety of jokes.[10] This protean genre, represented by the work of Du Fail, Bouchet, Cholières and many others, was, in the years from 1560 to 1610, an intellectual phenomenon of still unmeasured importance. In these texts the cumulative modular principle reached an extreme. These books were stockpiles of anecdotes and scholarly notes, news items and moral examples, short stories and puns, doctrinal citations, and pieces of popular culture. They were storerooms of memorable facts and sayings, repertories of cultural goods which belonged to everyone and to no one, volumes of anonymous archives where consumers could pick up, as they wished, a unit of knowledge, a maxim, a narrative kernel. We know that Montaigne explored the resources and the aporias of this use of the book as a collection of examples and as the memory of other books.

Cutting knowledge and fiction into modules provided a mobility that the *Heptameron*'s readers utilized immediately. This is proven by the first edition, by Boaistuau (1558), as well as certain manuscripts, which give the tales in a different order. Some versions not only redistribute the material but truncate it.[11] Here as elsewhere, then, the book was used as a repository for movable units. We can see how risky it would be, in these circumstances, to look for definitive cohesion in the order of the stories.

The advent of printing may be related to the trend toward modular structure. This correlation of printing and modular organization lets us better understand the *Heptameron*'s place in the shift, which was decisive for the humanist movement, from the epoch of the oral tradition to a culture transformed by the new possibilities of written records.

Oral communication is linear and moves within the temporal dimension. A story read out loud links successive moments in a flow from the beginning to the end, in an order that does not deviate. As a consequence the normal reception of a work, in a period of aural and oral transmission, is likely to fall along the syntagmatic axis. Each element has a fixed position within a logic based on continuity.

It is often said that written texts are also dominated by a linear flow, but this is false, or at least simplistic. We can read a book from cover to cover, but we can also use it as a space within which all parts are available simultaneously. The book offers itself as a synoptic system through which the reader moves freely forward and backward, in long sequences or in rapid snatches. The reader may open the book where he wishes, read at random, select a certain passage, go back, select and organize according to his desires this material transmitted without regard for time.

Printing, quite logically, in making books available to more people, utilized this resource: the spatial quality of this object which not only lifts a text out of the flow of time but also serves as a reserve of detachable pieces. The proliferation of anthologies and compilations, far from being an accident, was the best possible use of the book's characteristics. Thanks to the development of printing, each literate person now had at hand a treasure of knowledge, a virtually infinite mass of documents. The principle of the dictionary—perhaps prefigured in Rabelais's famous lists—permeated cultural life. Narrative tradition would also benefit from this mode of storage.

This particular use of the book reveals the close bond between printing and the rise of humanism.[12] From the moment when human memory could rely on the immense stock of information available on the shelves of a library, knowledge and thought advanced swiftly. However, rational use of such extensive, and often poorly organized, material required procedures for each retrieval: titles, tables of contents, indexes, summaries, internal cross-referencing—all marking the available units within collections. Humanist books were provisional gatherings of information, files which lent themselves to various uses, which distributed themselves in new contexts, and in many ways quickened the pace of intellectual life. The modular issue and circulation of information probably explains several aspects of Renaissance ideas and culture.

Scholars, however, were not the only ones to profit from this mode of distribution. As a reserve of documentation, books aided a new public, which aimed at attaining culture without belonging to the specialist milieu: nobles and bourgeois for whom culture was a means of social advancement. Published collections abounded as manuals of popularized knowledge which opened the gates of traditional knowledge to nonprofessionals, the new category of the *honnête homme*, which was to change the face of the social world. Packed with information and useful tips, books were treated as a commodity—or an investment—which the user could make productive. The book was a data bank which, when properly sorted out in functional units, would enhance the mind and beautify speech. Printers and booksellers did not fail to cash in on this market. Among producers of collections as among their clients, the printed book allowed people to stock up on culture and make it profitable. The stress on quantity and mobility reflects the mind-set of property owners.

All of this must seem fairly far from the *Heptameron*. After all, Marguerite de Navarre did not publish her collection herself, and the model she followed, the *Decameron*, did not need the printing press to reach a wide public. Nevertheless the principle of the detachable and profitable unit may apply directly to novella collections. One of the priorities of polite society in the sixteenth century was to improve, vary, and refine conversation. In his *Courtier*, Castiglione defined the type of jokes and amusing talk that fit an enjoyable discussion. He recommends "cheerful narratives" and even specifies, "it seems as if one were telling a novella."[13] In the general context described above, it would not be surprising if the *Heptameron* stories, told separately, had served to ornament a conversation, since the habit of picking up and recycling items from books was widespread at the time.

The printed transmission of cultural goods also encouraged individual consumption and, by fragmenting reception, increased chances that interpretive consensus might be lost. A reader who had direct and solitary access to information was no longer tied to an ideological community. Such a reader had a private relationship to his or her books and assumed personal responsibility for each reading. We are familiar with the decisive importance of the direct contact of the faithful with the Bible in the Reformed church. The *Heptameron* storytellers are not, of course, alone. Nonetheless, their reactions to the stories are personal, as if the idea of a common patrimony leading to a natural collective interpretation was beginning to be lost. Here we touch on the question of the commentaries, which call forth other considerations.

Liberating Interpretation

The romance's disappearance in favor of narrative modules can be explained in light of another change, one that concerned ways of reading and corresponds to an important evolution in the interpretation of texts. The hermeneutic principles inherited from the Middle Ages were called into question, replaced by other expectations reshaping the perception of fiction. The short narrative has the advantage of allowing alternation with commentaries which dramatize the story's reception and problematize it. Of course, continuous narrative form in the romance may also double back and include its own interpretation; but such interpretation, more or less implicit, is woven into the narrative fabric. The short narrative, on the other hand, provokes immediate and open reflection on significance, and functions as a laboratory where different reading styles can be tried out. The structure of a narrative on two levels, a device very much appreciated in the sixteenth century, allows such experimentation. After the story, preferably short, comes a metastory, which raises questions of method, or proposes hypotheses on the meaning of the events told. Dialogue invades the field of the story and gives reading a reflexive dimension. This structure, used in the *Heptameron*, may very well have accelerated the shift in the way fiction was treated. If we now consider the significance of this change, in the general context of humanist thought, we will also see better the historical importance of the *Heptameron*'s narrative structure.

Textual interpretation in the Middle Ages was a prominent activity, but it had to work within narrow limits. There is, after all, a single Truth—Revelation—which all human discourse, if inspired by the Spirit, must ultimately confirm. The vision of a unified and structured world, controlled by faith, gave an *a priori* definition of the work's aim and saturated its meaning. Such a meaning might extend over several levels, according to the hierarchy taught by the church: first, knowledge of the world and its history, then a moral lesson, and finally a message about eschatology. This is the fourfold system of interpretation, a fixed grid with some variations subordinated to a strict program.

This method served both to reveal the hidden doctrines of the Bible and to provide a Christian interpretation of secular texts. Read as fables, the latter were subject to the totalizing process of allegory, which vouched for fiction's adherence to church teaching—for example, the well-known series of *Ovide moralisé*. These were the confines within which the interpreter worked; his problem was not to find a new meaning but to demonstrate how each of the work's details fitted into the familiar features of knowledge and faith. In such a restrictive hermeneutic system, the exegete vanished before a higher authority. The interpreter used his ingenuity to find ways to make it all fit; the finalities did not depend on him but derived from a Truth of which he was the mere spokesperson. Reading in the Middle Ages did not produce something new, did not seek something different, but recognized, in what was unknown, the already known.

Narrative literature, up to the beginning of the sixteenth century, conformed to this program. Legends, tales, novellas—the very material that Marguerite was to take up—were not always assigned a spiritual significance but were routinely given a moral meaning. However frivolous a story might seem, it illustrated a proverb or an edifying precept, it presented itself as an example, and it openly conformed to a didactic program. Antoine Vérard, who published in 1485 Laurent de Premierfait's translation of the *Decameron*, added moralizing commentaries. Poggio's *Facéties* and Gringoire's *Fantaisies* underwent the same treatment, and there are many other cases of such additions.[14]

The humanists were to destroy this system and, consequently, cause a deep-seated change in reading habits. They were uneasy with the rigidity of allegory and rejected the notion that fiction should serve as mere example.

Opposed to the routine application of a teleological method, they tried to restore the individuality of each text. They gradually stopped Christianizing and moralizing ancient works, and it was no longer necessary to justify entertaining works by claiming instructional value. Moreover, in reading the Bible the humanists sought first of all to understand the literal meaning and the historical dimension. Philology would vouch for that first reading, which was supposed to be independent of dogmas. A significant change took place during the sixteenth century in the practice of commentaries: in place of the gloss, which laid out allegorical values, erudite annotations favored a more technical understanding and provided documentary materials without prejudging the deeper meaning of a book. No longer was a moral or instructive outlook to be imposed on readers; readers were instead to be given the means to undertake an interpretation for themselves. Historical and critical analysis replaced ideology; assimilation was followed by respect for difference.[15]

This did not mean that reading fiction was from now on simply a matter of determining the literal sense. The dismantling of the allegorical system did not lead the reader to give up the search for latent significance and hidden meanings. The crisis of the ancient exegetical methods and the evolution of philology led instead to a very acute awareness of the complexities and resources of interpretation. What was new was that people no longer believed that it was possible to systematize and to pin down, once and for all, the productiveness of a text. While humanists argued for a rigorous attention to the letter of a text, they remained ready to discover other readings, without, however, seeking to give them formal status.

Once the restrictions and the security offered by allegorical decoding had been given up, the initiative and the responsibility of the reader of fiction increased. To actualize the potential of a text, one had to trust one's intelligence and knowledge. The text called for the active and unprogrammable participation of a reader, who, freed from theological habits, would accept the challenge and the risks of interpretation. The authority which once belonged to the author alone was now shared with the reader, who was responsible for figuring out the meaning of a text. But this transfer changed the very nature of such authority; it had once been founded on a metaphysical guarantee, on the postulate—even through numerous relays—of a prestigious transcendental origin. Henceforth this authority could only claim the weight of human intuition and experience.[16]

The acting out of textual reception in numerous narratives like the *Heptameron* and the sixteenth century's frequent thematization of the figure of the reader and the reader's activity testify to this shift. The use of short narrative modules with intervening interpretive dialogues is an illustration of this new balance. More generally, prose narratives and poetry frequently constructed representations of reading, as if fiction with its symbolic scenarios was the proper instrument for exploring such a problematic activity, resistant to rules and theories. When Erasmus, Rabelais, or Marguerite in their stories juxtapose a tale and its fictive reception, when they create characters who are also readers, they are building theoretical fictions, or imaginary hermeneutic models, which permit them to test other ways of reading. Like love, death, and religion, reading is perceived as an opaque signified, which can only be approached through figural mediation. Interpretation does not claim to control fiction, but realizes that it participates in fiction's ambiguity. Discourse fuses with narrative: metadiegesis circles back onto diegesis.

What is shown in scenes of reading is more an action than a result, a work in progress, the dynamic interaction of a text which resists and of an individual or a group which wrestles with it. Rather than emphasizing the result of reading, reading itself is presented as a conquest. It supposes reading subjects who engage themselves, who challenge an active work, and who allow themselves to be challenged by it. Such reading is a confrontation, an ambiguous manifestation of subordination and rebellion: it contrasts an ancient authority—a pattern of thought already organized—and a receiver who is seeking himself and becoming conscious of himself through assent, controversy, or objection. This is the context in which the metaphor of imitation as digestion appears, the transformation and appropriation of the earlier work. We recall how the construction of the self, in Montaigne's work, is based on the critical reading of authors, how competition stimulates the mind, moves the pen, and helps form judgment. Here too a major shift has occurred: the moral profit of reading no longer corresponds to the acquired "material"—the static product of a finished process, a definitive meaning which would put an end to inquiry. The benefit of reading is to be found in the activity of questioning, in the exemplary performance of an individual who seeks truth. If there is an ethic to reading, this ethic is found less in the contents of the message than in the act of decoding. The ethic is not in thrall to the ideas but fulfills itself in a *praxis*.

These very general propositions call for much nuance and qualification. Biblical exegesis—the methods of which are much discussed—raises, of course, different problems from the interpretation of secular texts. Even when the Scriptures were freed from the fourfold interpretation, readers still sought a final Truth, the irrefutable evidence of Revelation. Humanist theologians might invoke the mystery of the Word and the freedom of the Spirit, but in their commentaries they submitted to a very strict discipline and attempted above all to consolidate faith and doctrine. All that was said above applies to the genres which escaped from the direct control of the church—the field of history, for example, and of fiction—which could avail themselves of greater room to maneuver in refining new hermeneutic strategies. Just as sacred subjects postulated the oneness of the Word, so mankind's immanent creations and discourse on human affairs left room for conjecture.

Among these, works written for entertainment and comic texts, because of their marginality, offered room for experiment which could be a research laboratory for new reading methods and aims. Such texts used their freedom to foil overly restrictive hermeneutic systems and, in guise of a game, to set forth in a hyperbolic way the difficulties of interpretation.[17] We know how Rabelais both inscribes and demolishes the allegorical model, how he throws readers off track by inviting them to seek a hidden meaning while he blocks any possibility of semantic saturation. Bonaventure Des Périers, in the *Cymbalum mundi*, places himself at the ambiguous boundary between enigma and hoax, while he leaves his *Nouvelles recreations* to the reader's acumen, without a commentary. Jocosity or *substantifique moëlle*? Innocent pastimes or stories full of a higher meaning? The narratives of Erasmus, Rabelais, and many of their contemporaries, including Marguerite, raise this question while suggesting, at the same time, that it is badly framed. Their trick is to show that the opposition serious/nonserious does not work, that play and instruction, the pleasure of the apparent story and the promise of latent values are not mutually exclusive. At the intersection of this false duality, they locate the laughter of the wise, the pleasure of intelligence in its quest for meaning; they sketch out in this way an ethic, give an outline of wisdom, but one that is irreducible to theory. From farce to serious things, from the letter to the spirit, they trace an unbroken line, and without determining the method or the result, turn the initiative over to the reader.

The *Heptameron* and the Problematization of Reading

Anyone who knows recent critical studies of the *Heptameron*—particularly the work of Philippe de Lajarte—will recognize, I hope, the relevance of the general framework that I have laid out.[18] To make the connection clear we need only point out a few significant aspects of Marguerite's book.

When Marguerite was composing her collection, the formula of alternating stories and dialogues was far from established. In France the tendency was rather the opposite: the *Cent nouvelles nouvelles* of Philippe de Vigneulles (between 1505 and 1515), the *Parangon de nouvelles honnestes et delectables* (1531), the *Grand parangon des nouvelles nouvelles* of Nicolas de Troyes (1536), along with the *Nouvelles recreations* of Des Périers (1558) juxtapose novellas without commentary. The choice of Boccaccio's model in the *Heptameron* is thus in keeping with a specific project. Yet the differences between the *Heptameron* and this model are just as significant. The storytellers' discussions expand, to such a point sometimes that they are longer than the stories. And not only does the debate take more space, but it also fits itself closely to the story which precedes or follows. Two genres are placed side by side, interacting and forming an organic unity. Such basic observations are proof enough that Marguerite, far from having wanted only to store up a collection of stories, intended to raise the problem of interpretation itself, by exploiting the flexibility of the modules and the room available for the storytellers' exchanges.

The link between narrative and discussion follows a fairly constant pattern. Before beginning the story, a narrator announces a project: to illustrate some typical form of conduct, to establish some truth about love. The narrator's aim is demonstrative: "L'histoire que j'ay deliberé de vous racompter, c'est pour vous faire veoir comme amour . . ." (88;157). These typical preliminary statements program the way the tale should be received; they have the same function as a preface that aims to control the reading of the text which follows. After telling the story, the narrator intervenes again and, in accordance with the initial project, draws the moral: "Voylà, mes dames, une histoire que voluntiers je vous monstre icy pour exemple, à fin que . . ." (27;88). The narrator speaks to the assembled group, or directly to an individual, to get the greatest number to agree, and to try to guide the debate.

This technique is as simple as it is common: a supposedly true story is segmented in such a way as to serve as an example: an anecdote, treated as an allegory, serves as the basis of a didactic and edifying enterprise. An implicit postulate is at work here: the singular illustrates the general. Beyond the diversity of actions and characters, it is possible to detect laws valid for the whole of mankind. A typical story demonstrates a psychological or ethical truth which is so obvious and universal as to be irresistible to its hearers: "Je vous preuve, par cette histoire, que la finesse des hommes . . ." (42;106). New knowledge and moral improvement go hand in hand, since the event retold contains a lesson that applies to all: "Si à quelqu'une de vous advenoit pareil cas, le remede y est ja donné" (34;96). The verb *devoir* is part of the formulaic structure of exemplary discourse. With its two meanings, it recurs many times in the storytellers' commentary. The expression of verisimilitude and the expression of obligation merge: because such a fact is probable, in conformity with the received ideology and thus worthy of imitation, it has the weight of a rule.

The exemplary model, however, does not work.[19] The whole interest of the exchanges between storytellers is in the way the system fails, in the gap between the theoretical project, which supposes the possibility of a universal discourse on mankind and, on the other hand, empirical reality, which demonstrates fundamental differences between individuals. Should one storyteller count on the obvious demonstrative value of his or her tale to marshal general agreement, right away objections fly—"Ceste histoire fut bien escoutée de toute la compaignye, mais elle luy engendra diverses oppinions" (95;163). *Opinion*: this is the keyword, the one which recurs constantly and betrays the failure of allegorical intentions. In this following brief phrase, with an antithesis that seems perfectly innocent, the conflict of the two epistemologies is crystallized: "Et, pour cest *exemple* icy, je ne me departiray de la forte *opinion* que j'ay" (83;153, emphasis added). As soon as one grants to individual difference enough authority to contest the value of the example, the floodgates of universal disagreement are opened. Personal variations destroy the idea of universal knowledge and of a common ethic. Psychology topples doctrine.

As in the *Decameron*,[20] but in a more radical way, autonomous subjects, capable of judgment, take center stage, and, in the polyphony of their discordant voices, destroy the principle of authority. The discord is not limited to trivial nuances in the evaluation of stories but is deeply connected to the vigorously drawn personality of each speaker. They are differentiated by their gender, their temperament, their experiences—literary critics have made full portraits of them as if they were characters in a novel! On top of their differences in personality are the storytellers' different states of mind, the complexity of their power relationships, and the variety of their strategies for dealing with the group. Numerous individual details and incidental events destroy the collective ideological cohesion and contribute to subvert the very possibility of a totalizing system.

The storytellers are different from one another, they express different opinions, but they belong to the same social milieu, and this similarity only serves to reinforce their disagreement, since no one of them has, *a priori*, the right to decide for the others. Each one has an equal right to speak, no voice imposes itself to dominate or organize the polyphony. Regardless of the possible privileged status of Parlamente in relation to Marguerite, and despite the alleged moral superiority of Oisille, neither of them has any preponderance in the discussions. The rules of the game implicitly call for the players to ignore hierarchies and face opponents on an equal basis.

As a result no belief gets the better of the others, no synthesis settles the dispute. Working from the author's biography or from her poems, critics have often tried to reduce the *Heptameron*'s comments about love to a Neoplatonic or Christian-platonic theory; ultimately this systematic interpretation proved untenable. Courtly love and ribald love, the law of honor or the law of pleasure, the mind's nobility in quest of sublimation and the body's vigor in search for satisfaction . . . all these conflicting theses—and many others—are set forth, and their disharmony remains unresolved. The friendly storytellers carefully distinguished the morning Bible-readings from the afternoon pastimes. Devotion, it may be supposed, unites them in a common act of faith; but the uncertain and contradictory human matters cannot be so easily settled.

Undecidability is not solely a result of the differences among the storytellers but is also inherent in the multiplicity of facts, the immense variety of phenomena. If one story doesn't convince the listeners, another one is told and then another, and each one illustrates a different truth; so that in place of complementing one another, the novellas diverge and contradict one another. The storytellers raise endless questions about love, they circle around the same issue in order to construct a global view, but no coherent picture emerges. There are no constants on which to base laws. The individual event which should have found a place in the pattern turns out to be unclassifiable, neither typical nor imitable; it falls outside the categories of knowledge and morality: it is extraordinary.

The storytellers agreed to tell "nulle nouvelle qui ne soit veritable histoire" (9;68). They have habits from the traditional historiography. For them, data from experience, properly selected, have a typical value and contribute to building or to illustrating an ideology—*Historia magistra vitae*. Factuality and exemplarity should go hand in hand. This fit between reality and morality is exactly what the *Heptameron* works to deconstruct. Not only do the stories, for their hearers, prove nothing beyond themselves, but they can be multiplied to infinity—there are as many stories as there are individuals and events recorded in human memory. As a result, the system into which these stories should be inscribed finds itself submerged in the plurality and the heterogeneity of the known phenomena.

History and experience overwhelm the theories, upset the frameworks. The storytellers discover, without realizing it, a principle of skeptical thought that Montaigne makes explicit: no intellectual construction can, without mutilating it, account for the diversity of the real. The necessarily infinite number of situations or possible actions cannot be reduced to the necessarily finite number of moral laws. The programs of abiding by the "vérité de l'histoire" (9;69) and of constructing a philosophy of love appear incompatible.

An Aesthetic of Variety

The deconstruction of the inscribed model of exemplarity links the *Heptameron* to the current of skepticism and antischolasticism that runs through the sixteenth century. Mankind may accumulate individual truths but not reach Truth. Such a practice of doubt does not contradict Marguerite's faith, because Mankind at the Fall in confessing its confusion and recognizing the disorder of human things only recognizes its weakness and the urgent need of Grace. A skeptical anthropology can be the basis for an even more radical belief.

Moreover, Renaissance skepticism, as expressed here, was not necessarily pessimistic. Out of distrust of the great systematic works of the Middle Ages, Renaissance skepticism renounced systems and demystified dogmatisms but did not give up an interest in the world. The suspension of doctrinal thought even favored the freedom of the human gaze. Even if it was vain to want to put everything in order and understand it, one could still admire the abundance of things, the ingenuity of mankind. It is more appropriate to speak of eclecticism than of skepticism. Faced with the astounding diversity of phenomena, the humanists tended to observe, to gather information and opinions without filtering them or striving for a synthesis. Whether moralists or naturalists, they let themselves be guided by a ceaseless curiosity. The storytellers, in the *Heptameron*, never stop tracing out the endless variations of love. They seem to compensate the failure of doctrine with the quantity and the peculiarity of documentation. If intelligence must recognize that it is incapable of absolute certainty, it can at least enjoy the stimulating spectacle of human inventiveness. The *Heptameron* is not so far away from the euphoric skepticism of the *Apology for Raymond Sebond*.

Hence the style of composition of many books of the period. They are long and profuse because they attempt to include—even to imitate—the proliferation of things. They proceed by accumulation and often remain unfinished, or open, because they do not aim at standardizing or summing up the multiplicity of their components. They are montages that stick together more or less well, pretty much heterogeneous compilations, which derive from a poetics of *varietas* and mixture. The disparity of materials on both levels of the *Heptameron* text—multiplicity of opinions among the storytellers and variety of amorous behaviors in the novellas—comes from the same eclecticism.

So here we are back at the point of departure. The custom of collecting and building with modules not only permitted the enactment of the difficulties of interpretation but provided the proper form for expressing a composite and segmented view of the world. As soon as we take into account the breakdown of totalizing systems and the adoption of a philosophy of variety, the division of narrative material into discrete units appears as a considered choice. The fragment is the preferred format of skeptical or eclectic philosophy—essays, adages, or miscellanea. These are tentative probes into a limited terrain, pinpointing for further consideration elements of empirical data. Lined up, these pieces assemble a series of limited truths, without pretending to lead to more than partial knowledge, in snatches and flashes. This epistemology is organized around the paradigmatic axis and declines to engage in syntagmatic construction.

This is how the *Heptameron* is: The storytellers can reason and moralize about love, about psychology, about the genders, and outline numerous appropriate and useful thoughts. But the picture is never finished. One never stops finding variations, exceptions, and the need for revised conclusions. The modular collection never uses up all the material and never settles the questions. It gathers up knowledge, stories, and ideas to turn over to the discernment of the readers. It is up to them, the readers, to make choices and, if they can, to construct some coherence. Books like the *Heptameron* are books in search of an author, do-it-yourself books.

Notes

This essay, written at Irvine, benefited from the advice of Richard Regosin, to whom I express my heartfelt thanks.

1. "According to the inventory established some time ago by Gustave Reynier, there are only two or three original works worthy of the appellation *roman* during the wars of religion" (Maurice Lever, *Le Roman français au XVIIe siècle*

[Paris: Presses Universitaires de France, 1981], 1). The production started up again quickly and progressed constantly: 32 *romans* from 1589 to 1599 (Reynier); 118 from 1600 to 1610 (Lever); and the number "does not stop increasing in the following years" (Lever, p. 11).

2. The articles "Romans et fabliaux" in the analytical indexes of the *Bibliothèques Françoises* of La Croix du Maine and Du Verdier clearly show the preponderance of medieval romances among the works of fiction distributed in the sixteenth century.

3. See Michel Simonin, "La Disgrâce d'*Amadis*," in *Studi Francesi* 82 (1984), 1–35.

4. Yves Giraud, introduction to *Le Premier Livre d'Amadis de Gaule* (Paris: Nizet, 1986), 9.

5. Sebillet, *Art poétique françoys*, 1555 edition (Geneva: Slatkine Reprints, 1972), chap. 2: 14, "De la version" f. 72r.

6. *Art poétique*, ed. A. Boulanger (Paris: Belles-Lettres, 1930), chap. 2: 8, "De l'oeuvre héroïque," p. 201.

7. *Deffense et illustration de la langue françoyse*, ed. H. Chamard (Paris: Didier, 1948), chap. 2: 5, "Du long poeme françoys," pp. 128–29.

8. "Au Lecteur," in *Les Quatre Premiers Livres de la Franciade*, in *Oeuvres complètes*, ed. G. Cohen (Paris: Gallimard, "Pléiade," 1950), vol. 2, p. 1010.

9. Sebillet, *Art poétique françoys*, chap. 2: 14, f. 72r–v.

10. This is Gabriel-A. Pérouse's expression in "De Montaigne à Boccace et de Boccace à Montaigne: Contributions à l'étude de la naissance de l'essai," in *La Nouvelle française à la Renaissance*, ed. L. Sozzi (Geneva: Slatkine, 1981), 13–40.

11. See the introduction by Michel François in his edition of the *Heptameron* (Paris: Classiques Garner, 1967), pp. xxi–xxv.

12. On this question, but in a different perspective from mine, see Marshall McLuhan, *The Gutenberg Galaxy* (Toronto: University of Toronto Press, 1962), and Walter J. Ong, *Ramus, Method and the Decay of Dialogue* (Cambridge, Mass.: Harvard University Press, 1958).

13. Castiglione, *The Book of the Courtier*, trans. G. Chappuys, 1580, pp. 261–62, quoted by Henri Coulet, *Le Roman jusqu'à la Révolution* (Paris: Colin, 1967), 129.

14. See Yves Giraud and Marc-René Jung, *Littérature française: La Renaissance I (1480–1548)*, ed. Jean Lafond and André Stegmann (Paris: Arthaud, 1972), 162.

15. See Jean Céard, "La Transformation du genre du commentaire," in *L'Automne de la Renaissance* (Paris: Vrin, 1988), 101–15.

16. See Terence Cave, "The Mimesis of Reading in the Renaissance," in *Mimesis: From Mirror to Method, Augustine to Descartes*, ed. John D. Lyons and Stephen G. Nichols (Hanover and London: University Press of New England, 1982), 149–65.

17. See my article, "La Lecture en question: Sur quelques prologues comiques du seizième siècle," in *French Forum* 14, no. 3 (September 1989): 279–89.

18. See especially Philippe de Lajarte's "*L'Heptaméron* et le ficinisme: Rapports d'un texte et d'une idéologie," in the *Revue des Sciences humaines* 37, no. 142 (July–September, 1972), 339–371; "*L'Heptaméron* et la naissance du récit moderne: Essai de lecture épistémologique d'un discours narratif," in *Littérature* 17 (1975): 31–

42; and "Modes du discours et formes d'altérité dans les 'Nouvelles' de Marguerite de Navarre," in *Littérature* 55 (1984): 64–73.

19. On the use of the example in the classical tradition and in the *Heptameron*, see John D. Lyons, *Exemplum: The Rhetoric of Example in Early Modern France and Italy* (Princeton, N.J.: Princeton University Press, 1989).

20. See Karlheinz Stierle, "L'Histoire comme exemple, l'exemple comme histoire," in *Poétique* 10 (1972): 176–98.

Cathleen M. Bauschatz

7. "Voylà, mes dames . . .": Inscribed Women Listeners and Readers in the *Heptameron*

Many critics of the *Heptameron* have appeared frustrated or baffled in their attempts to find a coherent and unified message in the book. Rather than reaching any sort of closure, the stories succeed each other in a narrative process, often seeming to cancel out each other's meaning. Thus the message, if any, to be derived from the book appears ambiguous at best.[1] One way out of this impasse may be to look at stylistic patterns which repeat throughout the collection. These patterns reveal underlying structures not apparent in simply trying to derive the philosophical meaning of each story or of the collection as a whole, separately from the words and phrases which make it up. One such stylistic pattern is the ostensible address of almost every story in the collection to women, contained in phrases like "Voylà, mes dames."[2] What does this address show about what Marguerite thinks of women, readers/listeners, storytelling, and the relationship of these elements to her project in the *Heptameron*?

Marguerite's prologue may give us some information about her "implied audience."[3] Gérard Genette, applying the techniques of narratology to the study of a book's reception, has described the "paratexte," including prologues, as "ce par quoi un texte se fait livre et se propose comme tel à ses lecteurs, et plus généralement au public."[4] He sees the existence of the preface genre itself as linked to the advent of print in the sixteenth century: "une pratique liée à l'existence du livre, c'est-à-dire du texte imprimé" (Genette, 152). Among the tasks accomplished in any preface is the "choix d'un public," learned or unlearned, male or female: "Cette visée-là, qui est à bien des égards aussi ancienne que le roman (*aux hommes l'épique, aux femmes le romanesque*),[5] nous l'avons déjà vue exprimée par Boccace s'adressant à ses 'aimables lectrices,' et l'on peut en lire comme une parodie dans l'adresse du prologue de *Gargantua* aux buveurs et vérolés, emblème et portion non négligeable de l'autre sèxe" (Genette, 197).

A second task accomplished by the Renaissance prologue, again in Genette's eyes starting with Rabelais's *Gargantua*, is the declaration of intention by the author, governing the interpretation of the book to follow, by the reader. Thus, since Rabelais, "la pratique auctoriale . . . consiste bien à *imposer au lecteur* une théorie indigène définie par *l'intention de l'auteur*, présentée comme *la plus sûre clé interprétative*, et à cet égard la préface constitue bien l'un des instruments de la *maîtrise auctoriale*" (Genette, 206). Presumably, then, if the *Heptameron* follows this model, we need only look to Marguerite's prologue in order to find out who her intended audience is, and what her purpose with them will be.

Surprisingly, however, we do *not* find that Marguerite gives many instructions to her reader, or that she singles out women readers specifically, in the prologue. "Maîtrise auctoriale" is *not* what this prologue seems to demonstrate. The few addresses of the reader are with a generalized "vous," but this reader is not really given instructions—if anything, the tone is apologetic.[6] For example, on the first page, sensing that the prologue has been too carried away with a description of the circumstances of the book, the narrator (never explicitly identified as Marguerite) tells the reader: "*Ma fin* n'est de *vous declarer* la scituation ne la vertu desdits baings, mais seullement de racompter ce qui sert à la matiere que *je veulx escripre*" (1;60). This anonymous reader ("vous"), however, like the narrator Marguerite herself ("je"), makes only a very brief appearance, before being replaced by the *devisants* who alternately sit in for both.[7] That is, the *devisants* serve as narrators during the tales, and as listeners/participants during the discussions. They are able to switch roles easily, from authoritative speaker to receptive listener, making the distinction between the two roles much less clear than in most narrative literature. Male and female *devisants* participate equally and democratically in both storytelling and listening/discussion.[8]

Within the stories themselves, however, as well as during the discussions before and after, the repeated phrase, "Voylà, mes dames," implies that *women* are the primary audience intended by the storytellers. Despite the democratic structure whereby male and female speakers alternate, their targeted listeners are not so democratically chosen. An interpretation of this address of women could be that Marguerite has her tellers maintain a convention borrowed from Boccaccio (as we saw suggested above in Genette's attribution), and through him from the medieval courtly tradition of addressing romances and love poetry to women (while, as Genette implies, the epic was theoretically addressed to men). The *Heptameron* was composed during the 1540s, approximately two hundred years after Boccaccio's *Decameron*, which had recently been translated into French by Antoine Le Maçon. In the prologue, Marguerite's Parlamente explicitly suggests that the group write something similar to the *Decameron*, while casting the historical "Madame Marguerite" in a role as reader of Boccaccio.[9] Even though the narrator does not explicitly address her book to women, in invoking Boccaccio she may imply that her storytellers will do this for her.[10]

Boccaccio had stated in *his* preface that his stories were specifically addressed to women: "And who will deny that it is far more fitting to give this [his support and comfort] to beautiful women than to men?[11] Boccaccio also predicted that the ladies would derive both the Horatian pleasure and profit from his tales: "The ladies who read them may find delight in the pleasant things herein displayed," but in addition, "They may also obtain useful advice, since they may learn what things to avoid and what to seek" (Boccaccio, 27). These topoi are maintained in the *Heptameron*, but they are found in the stories themselves or in the discussions afterward, *not* in the prologue, which does not mention listener or reader response, beyond the desire to bring the tales back to court, as a sort of souvenir of the trip. Marguerite thus departs from the narrative conventions established by Boccaccio and followed in most sixteenth-century prologues, from Rabelais to Bonaventure Des Périers to Montaigne.[12] As Marguerite is the first woman writer of the *novella*,[13] she may hesitate to take responsibility for narrative or authorial voice and message, as her male predecessors emphatically did.[14] Rather, she allows the *devisants* to define the intended effects of the stories for her.

The address to women of the stories in the *Heptameron* will be connected with the frequent claim by the tellers that the tales are didactic: "Voylà, mes dames" usually is followed by a moralistic or prescriptive injunction, as we shall see in our analyses.[15] This suggestion of didacticism for women was only partially true for Boccaccio, who stated in his conclusion that if women found some of the stories to be immoral, they could simply read those they liked, and leave the others (for male readers, seemed to be the implication).[16] But despite this bow to the convention that literature written for women should be didactic in nature, pleasure appeared to far outweigh profit in most of the comments about listener or reader reception by women scattered through the *Decameron*.

The prologue to Boccaccio's first day stressed the sense that pleasure and amusement were the author's major objectives, as he tried to distract the ladies from the pain of love. The character Dioneo repeated this understanding, before the fourth tale: "If I have understood your intention rightly, amorous ladies, *we are here to amuse ourselves by telling stories*. So long as we achieve that, I think each of us should be allowed to tell the story he thinks most likely to be *amusing*; and just now the queen said that we could do this" (Boccaccio, 61).

Although the tale itself embarrassed some women, they also found it entertaining: "The tale told by Dioneo at first pricked the hearts of the listening ladies with a little *modest shame*, which appeared by their *chaste blushes*. But, as they glanced at each other, *they could scarcely keep from laughing*. However, *they smiled to themselves as they listened*" (Boccaccio, 64). Boccaccio portrayed his lady listeners as young and receptive—easily entertained—not as women looking for instruction.

Marguerite de Navarre will keep the convention of explicitly addressing the stories to ladies, even though her storytellers and listeners (as in the *Decameron*) are a mixed group of males and females. More importantly, Marguerite will add a discussion after each story, showing male and female reaction to and analysis of them, rather than only limiting herself to Boccaccio's "blushes and laughter." From the start, she will be more aware than Boccaccio of the variety in listener response, especially between males and females. Although Marguerite may inherit from Boccaccio the tradition of addressing her stories to women, she will go much further than he to develop—and test—the implications of this convention. She will go beyond the address of women listener/readers, found in the phrase "Voylà, mes dames," to analyze the response of these same women.

In the *Heptameron*, inscribed women listeners are taken much more seriously than they were in the *Decameron*, and the reactions of the *devisantes*, in their role as interpreters, are described in detail. The authoritative interpretative stance generally assumed by writers of Marguerite's time (like Rabelais or Bonaventure Des Périers) is abandoned in favor of presenting a variety of interpretative stances, on the part of the *devisants*."[17] But the author may keep some of her narrative authority by highlighting the reactions of the *devisantes*, when they respond to the address contained in the expression "Voylà, mes dames."

*   *   *

Marguerite establishes a pattern of female address and response in the first half of her book, and does not depart significantly from this pattern in what she completed of the second half.[18] An important question to consider in analyzing the address of and response by women listeners in the first five days is that of what topics, themes, and characters are thought to interest, and in fact elicit the most reaction from, the *devisantes*. Generally these stories treat the difficult virtue of chastity, or the contrary vice of promiscuity, in a woman character. Are these the only topics interesting to women readers? If so, is there a relationship between sexuality and the *nouvelle*, for women, which may differ from the nature of that relationship for men? An analysis of several tales will help to answer these questions.

The first tale, like the prologue one of the most disjointed elements in the collection, is a clear example of a male teller (Simontaut), who wishes to show as bad a woman as possible.[19] He is open about his desire to seek revenge on women for the suffering they have caused him.[20] Therefore, when he tells us the moral of his story with the loaded pejorative terms "mal," "meschante," "maulx," and "peché," we are automatically skeptical about it: "*Je vous suplie, mes dames*, regardez quel *mal* il vient d'une *meschante* femme et combien de *maulx* se feirent pour le *peché* de ceste cy" (18;78).

His story, and the message he attributes to it, are so outrageous that the women don't even bother to respond.[21] This first story prepares us to be suspicious about the message addressed to women with courteous phrases like "Voylà, mes dames," by the male *devisants*, throughout the book. It establishes the affiliation of the *Heptameron* with the literature of the *querelle des femmes*.[22] Most often, the *devisantes* will respond at length to attacks like this. But in this case, the whole second tale provides a response to the first.

The second tale, told by Oisille, is that of the mule driver's wife ("la muletiere"), who died rather than be unfaithful to her husband. Oisille has already admitted before telling the tale that she has searched her memory for the most virtuous woman imaginable, in order to respond to Simontaut's negative example.[23] In other words, we will now see a positive example, which women should *try* to follow. After the tale, Oisille presents the moral with strongly prescriptive language, as well as the book's typical address of women listeners (21;81): "*Voylà, mes dames*, une histoire veritable qui doibt bien augmenter le cueur à garder *ceste belle vertue de chasteté*."

Unlike the first story, which presented a negative example, this one shows a positive model of chastity (which refers here, as in most cases, to marital fidelity—not virginity), the primary female virtue illustrated in the book. After this explanation of the "moral" of the story by its author, Oisille, we learn the reactions to it by, not surprisingly, the *women* in the group: "Il n'ye eut *dame* en la compaignye, qui n'eut la larme à l'oeil, pour la compassion de la piteuse et glorieuse mort de cette mulletiere. *Chascune* pensa en *elle-mesme* que, si la fortune leur advenoit pareille, mectroient peyne de l'ensuivre en son martire" (21;82).[24] This is far indeed from the simple "blushes and laughter" of Boccaccio's lady listeners. Rather than only reacting affectively to the stories ("la larme à l'oeil"), Marguerite's listeners move on to a cognitive reaction ("chacune pensa"), and try to apply the truths illustrated to their own lives ("si la fortune leur advenoit pareille . . ."). Instead of simply showing a good or bad model of behavior, as in an exemplum, Marguerite demonstrates the additional step of reflection which is needed in order to digest or internalize the model provided.

The reaction of the *devisantes* to Oisille's tale is generally positive. It shows the women listeners making a sincere attempt to apply the example to their own lives (although one may privately doubt whether they could *actually* go this far to protect their chastity). This parallelism between message and reaction will not be true of most of the cases we will examine, when male speakers address women listeners with the phrase "Voylà, mes dames."

The next two stories play with the question of exemplarity for women, although there is very little discussion of the examples.[25] After story 5, that of the ferrywoman ("la bateliere"), told by a male *devisant* (Geburon), he prescribes to the ladies how they are to interpret and, more importantly, to act on his story. The tale is presented with morally loaded vocabulary, particularly words like "bonté" and "vertu":

> *Je vous prie, mes dames*, pensez, si ceste pauvre bastelliere a eu l'esperit de tromper l'esperit de deux si *malitieux* hommes, que doyvent faire celles qui ont tant leu et veu de *beaulx exemples*, quant il n'y auroit que *la bonté* des *vertueuses* dames qui ont passé devant leurs oeilz, en la sorte que *la vertu* des femmes bien nourryes seroit autant appelée coustume que *vertu*? (37;100)

Obviously educated women should be even more virtuous, when they learn the story of a chaste uneducated woman (but in fact they often are not). Interestingly, the *devisantes* then make fun of Geburon's somewhat pompous prescriptions. They point out that it does not really take much virtue to resist a Cordelier—since these friars offer very little temptation.

Nomerfide has the last word, making a final comment on the puzzle of the exemplarity of the story (38;101): ". . . tout ainsy que *la vertu* de la batteliere ne honnore poinct les aultres femmes si elles ne l'ensuyvent, aussi *le vice* d'une aultre ne les peut deshonorer." An example only has meaning if people follow it; otherwise it is just an isolated case of human behavior with no particular implications for others. The implications for others are what turn a story into an exemplum. This story, like the second tale, makes a case for reader reception being demonstrated through actions, rather than simply by laughter, tears; passive approval or disapproval. Presenting a model, as Geburon has done, is not enough. The listener or reader must also analyze, interpret, and apply. Boccaccio never considered these next steps in the *Decameron*, because the mechanism of didacticism did not really interest him there.[26] We begin to sense that, similarly, even if the stories told by male *devisants* present positive models of female behavior, they will not go far enough to indicate how and whether these models may be applied. Despite their use of the phrase "Voylà, mes dames," they do not really take into account women's perspectives as receivers of the stories.

The seventh story, in which a girl and her merchant lover outwit the girl's old mother, is told by Hircan. He intends it to prove the quick-

wittedness of *men*: "Par cecy, voyez-vous, *mes dames*, que la finesse *d'un homme* a trompé une vieille et sauvé l'honneur d'une jeune" (42;106). Hircan is spelling out the moral, for the sake of the ladies, and naturally to the advantage of men. He sees the central character in this story as *male*, and the women characters as *subordinate*. But Longarine reacts to the story as women must actually often have done to similar stories in the *Decameron*, again stressing the dilemma of exemplarity:

> Longarine luy dist: "Vrayement, Hircan, je confesse que le compte est trop plaisant et la finesse grande; mais si *n'est-ce pas une exemple que les filles doyvent ensuivre*. Je croy bien qu'il y en a à qui vous vouldriez le faire trouver bon; mais si n'estes vous pas si sot de vouloir que vostre femme, ne celle dont vous aymez mieulx l'honneur que le plaisir, voulussent jouer à tel jeu. (42;106)[27]

Unlike Hircan, Longarine sees the central character in the story as female—the young girl. And she sees the central action of the story as the moral choice made by the young girl—not as the quick-wittedness and deception brought about by the male character. Frequently the first step for women listeners in reinterpreting a story told by one of the male *devisants* is to reinterpret who the central character is, and what the central action involves. This is a much more active form of reception than simply to agree or disagree with the teller's interpretation of his story.[28]

Longarine has here also astutely analyzed the "double standard" which exists in the novella genre, between "ideal" and "real" women readers, from the viewpoint of a male writer or reader: to say that the stories are for (imaginary) women readers, but then to show the women characters doing things that he does not want his (actual) wife or daughter to do. This double standard was present in the *Decameron*, but was never questioned or analyzed by the listeners, as it is here. The potential bad effect of reading, as well as its positive, inspirational side, both are demonstrated in the *Heptameron*. A model or exemplum may work either positively or negatively, and it is up to the listener to decide of which sort an example is, whether it should be acted upon, and how. This decision is partly the task of the *devisantes* in the *Heptameron*: to sort positive from negative examples, which are all presented with the apparently value-free, nonjudgmental address, "Voylà, mes dames." It is usually assumed by the speaker that the example itself shows what he or she has in mind, but the discussions generally show that the movement from example to lesson is not so simple as that.[29]

In the first day, we have seen women listeners react in a variety of ways to the address contained in the phrase "Voylà, mes dames," when it is used by male *devisants*. Some of these reactions have been: to tell a story which proves the opposite; to question whether the story can or should be applied to their own lives; and to reinterpret what and who the story is actually about. This first day, as one would expect from its explicit treatment of the war between the sexes ("un recueil des mauvais tours que les femmes ont faicts aux hommes et les hommes aux femmes" [83;47]), has established the definition of the power to interpret as another facet of this war. This struggle will be continued throughout the book, as the *devisantes* react to the prescriptions prefaced by "Voylà, mes dames" and similar phrases.

The tales of the second day, like those of the first, involve discussion of women.[30] But in these discussions the women are quick to correct male perceptions of their morality, presented with the phrase "Voylà, mes dames."[31]

The third day, "Des dames qui en leur amytié n'ont cerché nulle fin que l'honnesteté, et de l'hypocrisye et meschanceté des religieux" (156;50), contains many stories about the Cordeliers. Because the listeners generally agree about the hypocrisy and wickedness of these monks, the discussions are often less heated than in the first two days, and provide fewer examples of clear-cut, differing positions by males and females. The third day continues to show, however, that women's psychology is more complex than men would have it,[32] and that women are better in control of their impulses than men are.[33] As Emile Telle describes the conclusion to the third day, "C'est une grande victoire du féminisme de Parlamente" (Telle, 120–21). One might add that this conclusion also provides a victory for her anticlericalism, and that we begin to see a connection between those two themes, during the discussions. The conclusion to the third day finds the monks hidden behind a hedge, listening to salacious stories about the sexual behavior of members of the religious orders. This theme will be expanded during the fourth and fifth days, and will help to shed light on the developing irony in phrases like "Voylà, mes dames."

The fourth day treats the "vertueuse patience et longue attente des dames pour gainger leurs marys" (236;52), as well as the reverse behavior of husbands toward their wives. One example is story 35, told by Hircan, that of the "Dame de Pampelune," who is cured of her love for a Cordelier by a beating from her husband. The story treats the situation of men who preach to women, only to seduce them. But Hircan, the teller, is actually like the Cordelier in the story, as he frequently combines preaching with seduction.[34] The theme of men appearing to correct women, but actually leading them astray, is a central topic of the fourth day.[35] This *topos* has important ramifications for the interpretation of the phrase "Voylà, mes dames" as well as the reception by women of it. It suggests that women should not heed all the prescriptions they receive from men, whoever they may be.[36]

The fifth day pursues the subject of the relationship between honor and pleasure, among women and girls ("de la vertu des *filles* et *femmes* qui ont eu leur honneur en plus grande recommandation que leur plaisir, de *celles* aussi qui ont fait le contraire . . .") (282;54). Thus the subject of this day, unlike most of the others, is specifically *women*, rather than both men *and* women. The subject of the relationship between honor and pleasure for women is central to the interpretation of the way in which women may read or listen to the stories themselves, whether for profit or pleasure. The fifth day concludes with a sort of temporary closure, as Oisille expresses the fear that the group may run out of ideas for stories.[37] Although the *devisants*, of course, do not run out of ideas, still this textual indication appears sufficient to permit tentatively interpreting the fifth day as a conclusion to what was intended to be the first half of the *Heptameron*.

Several discussions in the fifth day reinforce the idea (already noted in the seventh tale) that there is a double standard for men and women, crucial to the moral evaluation of male and female characters in the tales.[38] Parlamente responds to the sermonly forty-third tale, told by Geburon, with a definition of the difference between male and female virtue:

> Si nous n'avions d'autres advocatz, dist Parlamente, que eulx [le plaisir et la folie] avecq vous, nostre cause seroit mal soutenue; mais celles qui sont vaincues en plaisir ne se doibvent plus nommer femmes, mais hommes, desquelz la fureur et la concupiscence augmente leur honneur. . . . Mais l'honneur des femmes a autre fondement: *c'est doulceur, patience et chasteté.* (301;396–97)

Because men's and women's virtues differ, it is difficult for men, including lawyers and preachers, to correct women. Men's honor is closely related to the quest for pleasure, whereas women's involves the rejection of pleasure—chastity.[39] This differing moral code will obviously influence the way in which men and women interpret the actions of others, including those in the stories they hear in the *Heptameron.*

Oisille later tells a tale about the Cordeliers, this time about a monk who rapes the young girl he is sent to discipline (story 46).[40] Her conclusion moves beyond the general attack on the Cordeliers to consider again the issue of men who preach to women:

> Vous voiez, mes dames, quelle seureté il y a à bailler telles charges à ceulx qui ne sont pour en bien user. *La correction des hommes appartient aux hommes et des femmes aux femmes*; car les femmes à corriger les hommes seroient aussi piteuses que *les hommes à corriger les femmes seroient cruelz.* (310;408)

In this speech by Oisille, the attacks on monks and on men in general are related, from the point of view of women who must beware of both. Although Oisille is the most extreme and most conservative proponent of women, in the *querelle des femmes* which runs through the book, still this statement contains much truth about the relationship between men and women, speakers and listeners, in the *Heptameron.*

There is a developing sense, toward the end of the fifth day, that not only the Cordeliers but all men are really incapable of preaching to women, since men's and women's conceptions of virtue differ so much, and because men stand to gain from the folly of women. The frequent negative reaction of women listeners to phrases like "Voylà, mes dames," when uttered by male *devisants*, is not just a coincidental stylistic device. Rather, it reveals an underlying system within the *Heptameron* based on the difference between male and female versions of morality and even perceptions of reality. Given this dual reality with which they must live, women listeners, and by extension readers, are advised to resist almost anything they hear which comes from a male speaker or writer. The message of the phrase "Voylà, mes dames" is actually the *opposite* of what it initially appears to be: while it seems to offer women listeners a secure guide to behavior, the reactions of the women *to* the phrase show that these precepts are suspect, and must often be rejected. This double message is present in *much* literature directed to women in the Middle Ages and Renaissance, but only women writers like Marguerite de Navarre appear to be sensitive to its implications.[41]

*   *   *

In the *Heptameron*, the phrase "Voylà, mes dames" introduces, *for* women, judgments frequently *of* women, who behave in a variety of ways—good, bad, and indifferent. "Voylà, mes dames," throughout the book, is generally used in a prescriptive manner, to spell out the overt message of a story, from the point of view of its teller. All the *devisants*—male and female—take their turn at using this phrase, when they are cast in the authoritative role of storyteller. But the reactions of the *dames* to the phrase vary, depending on who is using it, and how. Generally women listeners react positively to a message delivered by a *devisante*, but negatively to that of a male speaker. The examples studied above demonstrate the existence of this phenomenon in the *Heptameron*, which is closely related to its affiliation with the literature of the *querelle des femmes*.

For what is striking about Marguerite's use of this phrase is not so much the phrase itself as the response to it, by the very women being addressed. In most cases they do not react passively as the speaker intended (and as the exemplum tradition would indicate), but rather reinterpret and reevaluate very actively the picture of human behavior being presented them. The most striking examples of active response by women readers to the phrase "Voylà, mes dames" are after stories told by male *devisants*, who generally fill the authoritative (and somewhat pompous) role outlined by the phrase better than the women speakers do. In addition, their negative reactions to these pompous and frequently chauvinistic pronouncements force the women listeners to define their own positions, more clearly than when they simply agree with their fellow *devisantes*. The critical difference here is a productive one.[42]

The phrase "Voylà, mes dames" itself appears to emanate from an authoritative *male* speaker (despite the fact that women also use the phrase).[43] For the address of women assumes both a sexual and textual difference between speaker and listener: in defining "mes dames" as listeners, it casts the male "other" in a role as speaker or source for the stories. Marguerite the *writer* in fact does not take on a narrative *persona* herself, as we saw in our discussion of the hesitant use of the narrative "je" in the prologue. In the stories and discussions of the *Heptameron*, a writerly "je" is, similarly, almost never found, except in side references to translations which the narrator has made from Spanish or Italian, and very occasionally to the act of transcribing stories taken from elsewhere.[44] This narrative "je" is a very neutral one.

But the phrase "Voylà, mes dames," when uttered by the storytellers, assumes a much stronger relationship of power between male speaker and female listener, not unlike the relationship of male strength to female weakness contained in the many examples of rape and other forms of male violence to women, in the stories themselves. Storytelling, in the *Heptameron*, as in the *Decameron*, is often a substitute or metaphor for the activities described *in* the stories, which are primarily sexual in nature.[45] But while Boccaccio clearly outlined a relationship of flirtation and compliance between male speaker/writer and female listener/reader,[46] Marguerite shows us a darker version of this interaction, which parallels the relationship between men and women in the tales themselves.

Women characters distinguish themselves, in the stories, by resisting male sexual violence. The suggestion is thus made that women listeners or readers should likewise resist the sexually suggestive models found in male literature, whether these models are found in Boccaccio, in the sermons told by the Cordeliers, the stories recounted by the *devisants*, or in medieval French romances.[47] This resistance raises some interesting questions about the representation of listening and reading by women in the *Heptameron*, and in particular about the ostensible exemplarity of the stories, implied by the performative catch-phrase "Voylà, mes dames." Although this phrase seems to suggest that women need only imitate the models contained in the tales in order to derive the Horatian "profit" which they contain, the women characters we are shown, both inside and outside the stories, seem as frequently to react with something akin to another well-known performative phrase, "Just say no."[48]

In illustrating the combination of profit and pleasure which can be derived from the stories in the *Heptameron*, Marguerite seems to distinguish sharply between the reactions of male and female reader/listeners. Pleasure appears to be the reader reaction associated with the body and is generally attributed to male *devisants*. But profit, as a reader reaction, must be associated with the mind or spirit, and thus requires rejecting the more pleasurable, carnal (and obvious) readings, in favor of a fairly austere and difficult interpretation, based on suffering and self-sacrifice.[49] This austere reading is generally provided by the *devisantes*, when the discussions move to reception by women listener/readers, rather than simple address of these same listeners.

Looking at speakers and listeners in the *Heptameron* helps us to sort out some issues of male dominance and female submission in the book on a metatextual as well as textual level. While the phrase "Voylà, mes dames" appears to outline a passive, compliant woman listener, the reactions to it by the inscribed women listeners show a very different sort of woman "reader" who is able to insert her own version of reality into the text. To hope for a unified vision of the meaning of the *Heptameron* is to efface the resistance of the woman reader/listener to the very message she is being so courteously shown with the phrase "Voylà, mes dames." This resistance ultimately is the subject of the *Heptameron*.

Despite the fact that Marguerite de Navarre writes early in the French Renaissance, before the liberating effect of print on the reader described by Marshall McLuhan, Walter Ong, and others,[50] she is far ahead of her contemporaries, notably Rabelais, in the major role she accords to listeners, and by extension, to readers. While Rabelais addresses his listener/readers in an authoritative and even threatening manner, reminiscent of the polemics of oral debate, Marguerite not only shows her listeners to be addressed in a courteous way, but more importantly, demonstrates their ability to answer back, and to challenge the message being presented them. Rabelais never permits his "beuveurs illustres" to go so far, and even threatens the "lecteur calomniateur" with dire consequences. His narrative stance perfectly illustrates Genette's conception of "maîtrise auctoriale," described at the beginning of this chapter.

The way in which the *Heptameron*'s women listeners challenge its male speakers is a model to all readers of the book, male and female. It shows Marguerite as an author to have the ability to relinquish verbal authority not found in Rabelais, and a respect for the intelligence of the reader rarely achieved before Montaigne. This empowerment of the reader is connected in large part with her empowerment of women, the traditional addressees of courtly literature as well as sermons. But its implications go far beyond the confines of the *querelle des femmes* about women's nature, to consider larger issues of power in spoken and written language.[51]

The lack of closure frequently noted in the *Heptameron* (in comparison with the *Decameron*, for example) thus emerges not as a weakness but as a strength. In refusing to adopt the earlier authoritative male conception of narrative closure—or power over the text—Marguerite empowers the reader in a strikingly modern way. This empowerment could be viewed as feminist, but it is not necessarily limited to the feminine.

Notes

This chapter was completed with the help of a grant from the Folger Shakespeare Library, funded by the National Endowment for the Humanities, during academic year 1989–90.

1. Two of the many critics to comment on the lack of closure in the *Heptameron* are Arthur Kinney, "The Poetics of Metaphysics and the Fiction of L'Inquié-

tisme," in *Continental Humanist Poetics: Studies in Erasmus, Castiglione, Marguerite de Navarre, Rabelais, and Cervantes* (Amherst, Mass.: University of Massachusetts Press, 1989); and John D. Bernard, "Realism and Closure in the *Heptaméron*: Marguerite de Navarre and Boccaccio," in *The Modern Language Review*, vol. 84, no. 2 (April 1989): 305–18.

2. There is only one exception, story 9, addressed by Dagoucin to the gentlemen: "Que vous semble-t-il, Messieurs . . ." (53;118). All the other stories are addressed to the ladies, with some version of "Voylà, mes dames."

3. For an explanation of this and other terms of reader-oriented criticism, see *The Reader in the Text*, ed. S. Suleiman and I. Crosman (Princeton, N.J.: Princeton University Press, 1980), especially the introduction by Susan R. Suleiman.

4. Gérard Genette, *Seuils* (Paris: Seuil, 1987), 7.

5. Emphasis added, as will be the case throughout this chapter, unless otherwise indicated.

6. Philippe de Lajarte has carried out a complex analysis of the use of pronouns, particularly "je" and "vous," in Marguerite's prologue, in his "Le Prologue de l'*Heptaméron* et le processus de production de l'oeuvre," pp. 397–423 in *La Nouvelle française à la Renaissance*, ed. Lionello Sozzi (Geneva: Slatkine, 1981).

7. Michel Jeanneret, in a recent article on comic prologues in the French sixteenth century, has commented on the disappearance of the narrator after Marguerite's prologue: "La narratrice de l'*Heptaméron*, quant à elle, se manifeste fugitivement puis, très vite, s'efface devant les devisants, qui exprimeront, sur les contes, des opinions diverses et déjoueront, par la même, le principe d'une autorité qui contrôlerait la réception." (Michel Jeanneret, "La Lecture en question: Sur quelques prologues comiques du seizième siècle," *French Forum* 14, no. 3 [September 1989]: 279–289; esp. 283.)

8. It is striking to note that in the prologue, Hircan admits: "au *jeu* nous sommes tous égaux" (10;70, emphasis added).

9. "Entre autres, *je croy* qu'il n'y a nulle de *vous* qui n'ait leu les cent Nouvelles de Bocace, nouvellement traduictes d'ytalien en françois, que le roy François, premier de son nom, monseigneur le Daulphin, madame la Daulphine, madame Marguerite, font tant de cas, que si Bocace, du lieu où il estoit, les eut peu oyr, il debvoit resusciter à la louange de telles personnes." (Prologue, 9;68). Surprisingly, despite the oral/aural mode of the stories themselves, the prologue speaks specifically about *writing*: "n'escripre nulle nouvelle," and furthermore, "nous leur en ferons present au retour de ce voiage" (10;69). There is a strong suggestion that there will be a *written* product at the end of the ten days, similar to the book by Boccaccio which has provided inspiration.

10. Lionello Sozzi points out that this convention is a typical feature of novella collections at the time, which he attributes to their association with feminism: "Par contre, chose remarquable, onze recueils, de celui de Bocace au *Moyen de Parvenir* de Béroalde de Verville, s'adressent aux femmes, leur sont dédiés, sont offerts comme respectueux hommages aux dames, leur lancent au fond un message de solidarité, un message complice" ("L'Intention du Conteur: Des textes introductifs aux recueils de nouvelles," 71–83, in *L'Ecrivain face à son public en France et en Italie à la Renaissance*, ed. Fiorato & Margolin [Paris: Vrin, 1989], 76).

11. Giovanni Boccaccio, *The Decameron*, trans. Richard Aldington (New York: Dell Publishing Co., 1972), 26.

12. Des Périers, for example, a contemporary of Marguerite, raises in his prologue (actually the first story, subtitled "en forme de preambule") the question already posed by Boccaccio, of whether the effect of his book may be positive or negative for women: "Lisez hardiment, *dames et demoyselles*, il n'y ha rien qui ne soit honneste; mais si d'adventure il y en ha quelques unes d'entre vous qui soyent trop tendrettes et qui ayent peur de tomber en quelques passages trop gaillars, je leur conseille qu'elles se les facent eschansonner *par leurs freres ou par leurs cousins*, affin qu'elles mangent peu de ce qui est trop appetissant" (Bonaventure Des Périers, *Les Nouvelles récréations et joyeux devis* [Paris; Librairie des Bibliophiles, 1874], ii, emphasis added).

13. Except for "Jeanne Flore," whose gender and identity are not certain.

14. See Elizabeth C. Wright, "Marguerite Reads Giovanni: Gender and Narration in the *Heptaméron* and the *Decameron*," *Renaissance and Reformation* 15, no. 1 (Winter, 1991): 21–36. Wright addresses the shift from a male narrator in the *Decameron* to a female narrator in the *Heptameron*, but shows how carefully Marguerite avoids revealing herself as female.

15. The phrase frequently alludes to or shows the *exemplary* nature of the stories, for women. John Lyons has analyzed the use of example in the *Heptameron* in detail, in his "The *Heptaméron* and Unlearning from Example," chap. 2 of *Exemplum: The Rhetoric of Example in Early Modern France and Italy* (Princeton, N.J.: Princeton University Press, 1989).

16. "Some of you [ladies] may say that in writing these tales I have taken too much license, by making ladies sometimes say and often listen to matters which are not proper to be said or heard by virtuous ladies. . . . However, those who read these tales can leave those they dislike and read those they like." (Boccaccio, *The Decameron*, Conclusion, 637–39). This strategy for reading is repeated by Des Périers and other male authors of the sixteenth century (as we saw above).

17. Michel Jeanneret suggests something similar when he says: "Une certaine pratique de la lecture est ainsi illustrée: non celle qui surmonte less difficultés, conduit à des certitudes et des synthèses, mais celle qui reconnaît la pluralité des interprétations possibles et, par là, stimule la recherche du lecteur empirique." ("La Lecture en question," 285)

18. I am indebted to Marcel Tetel for the insight that the first half of what was intended to be Marguerite's version of the *Decameron* forms an identifiable unit. For example: "The circle opened in the prologue is closed at the end of the [fifth] day" (Marcel Tetel, *Marguerite de Navarre's Heptaméron: Themes, Language and Structure* [Durham, N.C.: Duke University Press, 1973], Chap. 5, p. 171).

19. See John Lyons's statement that this story is "an image of women, for women, but made by a male character-narrator" (*Exemplum*, 90).

20. This open admission of hostility by Simontaut provides an interesting departure from Boccaccio's stated desire to offer women *comfort*, since he has also experienced the pain of love himself.

21. Only Parlamente responds, and we are told that this is only because

Simontaut has hidden a message for her there: "Parlamente, faingnant de n'entendre poinct que ce fut pour elle qu'il tenoit tel propos . . ." (18;78).

22. See Emile Telle's treatment of this topic in *L'Oeuvre de Marguerite d'Angoulême, reine de Navarre, et la querelle des femmes* (Geneva: Slatkine Reprints, 1969). See particularly, chap. 4, "La Pensée de la reine de Navarre dans *l'Heptaméron*"; and chap. 10, "Le 'Féminisme' de la reine de Navarre."

23. "Il me semble, mes dames, que celluy qui m'a donné sa voix, a tant dict de mal des femmes par une histoire veritable d'une malheureuse, que je doibtz rememorer tous mes vielz ans pour en trouver une dont la vertu puisse desmentir sa mauvaise opinion; et, pour ce qu'il m'en est venu une au devant digne de n'estre mise en obly, je la vous vois compter" (18;78).

24. This judgment parallels the reaction of the women *in* the story (21;81): ". . . toutes les femmes de bien de la ville ne faillirent à faire leur debvoir de l'honorer autant qu'il estoit possible, se tenans bien heureuses d'estre de la ville où une femme si vertueuse avoit esté trouvée. Les folles et legieres, voyans l'honneur que l'on faisoit à ce corps, se delibererent de changer leur vye en mieulx." I am indebted to Mary McKinley for pointing this passage out (in a talk presented at the Renaissance Society of America, Spring 1989), and for showing that it was the "folles et legieres" who actually thought that they could imitate this "martire de chasteté," *not* the "femmes de bien."

25. Saffredent, after the third tale, shows the ladies how they could get back at their unfaithful husbands in kind, and Ennasuite, after the fourth, presents a straightforward positive example of virtue, which "doibt bien augmenter le cueur aux dames" (34;96).

26. Pierre Jourda comments, in contrasting the two authors, "Il n'y a, dans le *Décameron*—on l'a bien vu, aucune préoccupation religieuse, ou simplement morale" (Pierre Jourda, *Marguerite d'Angoulême, Duchesse d'Alençon, Reine de Navarre* [Paris: Honoré Champion, 1930], 2: 995).

27. John Lyons sees that "Longarine implies that the purpose of the narrative is to provide a pattern of conduct and to make that pattern attractive" (*Exemplum*, 75). I would add that she *resists* that attractiveness, however.

28. This sort of reinterpretation works both ways, and is often the mechanism which drives the discussions after the stories. In day one alone, we find several examples of this phenomenon, in which Hircan and Parlamente dominate. After story 4, told by Ennasuite as an example of "la vertu de ceste jeune princesse," Hircan reinterprets it as actually about the cowardice of the *male*, who was "si despourveu de cueur" (34;96). Story 9, told by Dagoucin, is one of the few addressed to the *men* in the group ("Que vous semble-t-il, *Messieurs* . . . ," 53;118). His story shows how love, when it is concealed, can lead to death by the unsatisfied *male*. Hircan then shows the male to have simply lacked initiative. But Parlamente turns the discussion to the *women*'s role in all this, asking Hircan whether "vous estimez les femmes toutes pareilles?" (54;120). Similarly, story 10, about Amadour and Floride, is told by Parlamente as an example of the virtue of Floride. But Hircan sees that it is *actually* about the cowardice of Amadour (83;153). The struggle to interpret right and wrong in these stories is *also* the struggle to interpret which character, male or female, has the *power* to influence their outcome.

29. This uncertainty about the lesson of an example is part of what John Lyons refers to as the "crisis" of the exemplum in the early modern period: "This common rhetorical practice in the face of contradictory visions of reality leads to lively and often paradoxical texts, revealing the push and pull of various currents of thought" (*Exemplum*, Preface, x). I would add that feminism is one of the currents of thought leading to the crisis of the exemplum in the *Heptameron*.

30. See Telle, *L'Oeuvre de Marguerite d'Angoulême*, 113: "Je remarque que cest vingt premières nouvelles (excepté 11 et 17) sont contées en fonction des femmes: les faits et gestes des hommes n'intéressent la compagnie qu'incidemment."

31. See for example tale 12, in which the "Duc de Florence" is killed in his bed at the very moment when he hoped to enjoy the favors of his best friend's sister. The discussions after this story and the following one examine whether or not women's beauty can *really* kill suffering lovers.

32. See for example tale 26, where Saffredent divides women into "folles" and "saiges," while Longarine points out that feminine psychology is more complex, especially when we consider issues of desire and self-control (221;306).

33. See Telle, *L'Oeuvre de Marguerite d'Angoulême*, 120: "Dans cette journée tout particulièrement, elle s'est élevée contre la conception grossière que se font les hommes de l'amour et de l'honneur. Aux femmes de les civiliser, et d'en faire de bons chrétiens en les guidant sur la voie de l'amour fondé sur la vertu, c'est-à-dire la chasteté. . . ."

34. "Je suys bien ayse, dist Parlamente, de quoy vous estes devenu *prescheur des dames*; et le serois encores plus si vous vouliez continuer *ces beaulx sermons* à toutes celles à qui vous parlez" (260;351). On several other occasions the listeners comment explicitly on the preacherly tone of the male *devisants* who address the women listeners. Earlier, at the end of the sixteenth tale, Geburon warned women to stay away from men: "Et pour ce, mes dames, si vous estes saiges, vous garderez de nous, comme le cerf, s'il avoit entendement, feroit de son chasseur" (133;208). Hircan responded with amusement: "Comment, Geburon? . . . depuis quel temps estes-vous devenu prescheur?"

35. See Telle's comment that the conclusion to be drawn from the fourth day is that "les hommes ne visent qu'à déshonorer les femmes." (*L'Oeuvre de Marguerite d'Angoulême*, 126)

36. Is it possible that Marguerite has written an indirect response to Boccaccio's fourth day, here? The *Decameron* begins that day by admitting that "some who have read these tales, discreet ladies, have said that you are too pleasing to me and that it was not modest that I should take delight in pleasing and comforting you and—others have said worse than this—in commending you, as I do" (Boccaccio, *The Decameron*, 246).

37. ". . . que les cinq Journées estoient accomplies de si belles histoires, qu'elle avoit grand paour que la sixiesme ne fut pareille; car il n'estoit possible, encores qu'on les voulut inventer, de dire de meilleurs comptes que veritablement ilz en avoient racomptez en leur compaignye" (326;427). Emile Telle, in fact, believes that the sixth, seventh and eighth days do not really add many new ideas to the arguments for and against women, in the book (*L'Oeuvre de Marguerite d'Angoulême*, 131–39).

38. Patricia F. Cholakian has shown this for tale 42 when she says, "Saffre-dent's tirade demonstrates how the terms *honesty, perfection*, and *honor* are defined differently by men and women in the *Heptaméron*" (*Rape and Writing in the "Heptaméron" of Marguerite de Navarre* [Carbondale: Southern Illinois University Press, 1991], 181).

39. It is striking to note the way in which Marguerite reverses Saint Paul's association of women with flesh, men with spirit. See Constance Jordan's discussion of chastity perceived as a male virtue, in medieval theology stemming from Paul (*Renaissance Feminism: Literary Texts and Political Models* [Ithaca, N.Y.: Cornell University Press, 1990], chap. 1, "The Terms of the Debate," p. 27).

40. The theme of men who preach to women in order to try to seduce them is a central motif in the fifth day, and one which ties together the themes of language and sexuality which are linked throughout the book, but especially in the fifth day. We are reminded of Saint Paul's Epistle to the Romans (Oisille's text for the sermons of the first five days), 2:21–22: "You then who teach others, will you not teach yourself? . . . You who say that one must not commit adultery, do you commit adultery?" (*Revised Standard Version*).

41. For this reason I would disagree with Lionello Sozzi's claim that the address of women in the Renaissance novella written by men shows the genre's affiliation with feminism—quite the opposite is true (Sozzi, "L'Intention du Con-teur").

42. See Barbara Johnson, *The Critical Difference* (Baltimore: Johns Hopkins University Press, 1981). Elizabeth Abel elaborates on Johnson's concept thus: "Sexu-ality and textuality both depend on difference. Deconstructive criticism has made us attend to notions of textual difference, but the complexities of sexual difference, more pervasively engrained in our culture, have largely been confined to the edges of critical debate" (*Writing and Sexual Difference*, ed. Elizabeth Abel [Chicago: University of Chicago Press, 1982], Introduction, p. 1).

43. It is significant to note that in the prologue, the narrator tells us that the *devisants* are requested to tell stories they have heard from "quelque *homme* digne de foy" (10;69). Part of the authority for these (supposedly true) stories resides in their originally *male* authorship.

44. Examples include: story 19 (of Poline; Ennasuite is the teller), ". . . j'en ay voulu traduire les motz en françoys" (146;223); story 24 (of Elisor; Dagoucin speaks), ". . . *je* ne l'eusse jamais osé traduire . . ." (198;280); story 25 (Longarine speaks), ". . . ce qu'elle *m*'a faict mettre icy en escript" (206;289); and story 5, in the "Appendice" of the "Curé Auvergnat," where the teller explains: ". . . pour la fin de ce dixiesme, que j'en voulsisse *escripre* ung qu'il tenoit aussy veritable que l'evan-gile . . ." (p. 445). These instances of a narrative "je" as *writer*, as in the references to writing in the prologue, break down the fiction that the stories are *told* orally, and return us to Marguerite the actual writer of the book. But this narrative "je" is certainly a hesitant and anonymous one, defining itself in a role as transcriber rather than creator.

45. In the prologue to the *Heptameron*, for example, it was made clear that storytelling, at least for Hircan, was only a second choice to lovemaking (9;68).

46. ". . . one of my women neighbors the other day told me I have the best and

sweetest tongue in the world. But, to speak the truth, when that happened there were not many of my tales left to finish." (Boccaccio, *The Decameron*, 640)

47. Marguerite shares the ambivalence of her time for this medieval genre. While authors of instruction books for women forbade these works (see for example Vives's *Institution de la femme chrestienne*), still women did make up the principal audience for them. We see both attitudes in the *Heptameron*, when characters read romances. In the story of Rolandine, for example, the mother of the *bâtard* comments on what a waste of time reading romances is: "La dame, regardant ce gros livre de la Table ronde, dist au varlet de chambre qui en avoit la garde: 'Je m'esbahys comme les jeunes gens perdent le temps à lire tant de follyes!'" (164;242–43). Throughout the *Heptameron*, reading romances appears as a pretext or substitute for *actual* "romance."

48. This phrase sums up the critical stance described by such feminist reader-oriented critics as Judith Fetterley, whose *The Resisting Reader: A Feminist Approach to American Fiction* (Bloomington: Indiana University Press, 1979) describes a set of strategies for subverting the role in which women readers feel trapped by the expectations of male (chauvinist) authors.

49. This sort of reading is more similar to the Bible reading suggested by Oisille than it is to the reading of "fiction," ostensibly criticized on moral grounds as "rhetoricque," in the prologue. Once again Marguerite reverses the Pauline association of male with spirit, female with flesh. It is impossible to overlook the fact that, in this respect at least, Marguerite is a "resisting reader" of the Gospel itself.

50. Marshall McLuhan, *The Gutenberg Galaxy: The Making of Typographical Man* (Toronto: University of Toronto Press, 1962). Walter J. Ong, S.J., *Orality and Literacy* (London: Methuen, 1982); *Interfaces of the Word* (Ithaca: Cornell University Press, 1977), and so forth.

51. See Peter Rabinowitz's discussion of the close connections between feminist and reader-oriented perspectives, in his *Before Reading: Narrative Conventions and the Politics of Interpretation* (Ithaca, N.Y.: Cornell University Press, 1987). The same sorts of arguments have also been made by Jonathan Culler, in *On Deconstruction: Theory and Criticism after Structuralism* (Ithaca, N.Y.: Cornell University Press, 1982).

François Cornilliat and Ullrich Langer

8. Naked Narrator: *Heptameron* 62

The sixty-second novella starts by locating the scene in a gathering of people surrounding a "dame de sang roial," during the reign of François I. It seems likely that this is Marguerite de Navarre herself. Since everyone knows that the queen likes to recount novellas and likes to laugh about those recounted by others, they are pleased to oblige. A young lady then tells a tale which she says is true and should not be repeated by those present. It goes as follows: A young married noblewoman was assiduously pursued by a young gentleman who was her neighbor. She resisted his advances. One day he saw his chance when her husband left the house. He entered her bedchamber without closing the door, and slipped into her bed without even bothering to take off his boots. She was completely surprised, and after he threatened to tell everyone that she had asked him to come, should she reveal that he was there, he raped her. The chambermaids finally entered the room, and as he hurriedly left, his spur caught on the bedcover and revealed her naked body to them. At this moment in the story the narrator cannot help saying "Jamais femme ne fust si estonnée que moy, quant je me trouvay toute nue" (378;486). The princess, who had been listening to the story without laughing, could not keep from laughing at this admission, remarking that "Ad ce que je voy, vous en povez bien racompter l'histoire" (378;486).

The obvious *mise en abyme* of narration alerts the reader to the fact that this brief novella is an invested moment in the *Heptameron*, when social, sexual, and theological problems engage novella poetics. All of these problems have to do with the possibilities and risks of novella recitation, especially when the narrator is a woman. This chapter will deal with three such issues: first, the imperative to entertain at the court; second, the (im)possibility of speaking of rape; third, the theological subtext to involuntary self-revelation.[1]

Courtly Pleasure and "Truth"

The context of the novella is the court following the princess and her visitors. It is also an assembly whose gender is not specified, in counter-distinction to the evenly mixed court of the *devisants*. The greatest impera-tive for courtly narrative is entertainment (*divertissement*), specifically en-tertainment of the princess: this is underlined by the fact that in the novella itself tales are recounted "pour luy faire passer le temps" (377;485). The duchess's *piacemi* in Castiglione's *Book of the Courtier* (1.12) is of course the model for the princess's centrality. It is of utmost importance not to be boring, and this involves a certain appearance of truth, and the appearance of a certain truth.

A major section of Castiglione's *Book of the Courtier* is devoted to *facezie* (French "facéties," English "jokes" or "pleasantries") recounted by the perfect courtier to help pass the time at the court. There are different types of jokes. Three, according to Bernardo Bibbiena: a long and amusing narrative, a single cutting remark, and practical jokes which can include storytelling, short remarks, and a certain amount of action. The first kind consists in a continuous speech similar to the recounting of a novella ("Quelle prime adunque, che consistono nel parlar continuato, son di maniera tale, quasi che l'omo racconti una novella" 2.48).[2] A *facezia* of this kind is of perfect grace and of true strength or quality ("vera virtù") if it demonstrates without boredom or fatigue ("senza fatica") what the narra-tor wishes to express, such that it appears to those who listen that the things being recounted are in fact being done before their very eyes: "Ma la grazia perfetta e vera virtù di questo è il dimostrar tanto bene e senza fatica, così coi gesti come con le parole, quello che l'omo vole esprimere, che a quelli che odono paia vedersi innanzi agli occhi far le cose che si narrano" (*Cor-tegiano*, 2.49). This figure is known as *evidentia* or *enargeia* in classical rhetoric.[3] The narrator presents material as if he himself were a witness, and as if the audience could witness the events described. The original intention behind the use of this figure is undoubtedly the impression of truth that an eyewitness account lends to the represented events. At the court, the truthfulness of an account is secondary to its value in dissipating boredom, as the courtier is encouraged to add a "bugietta" (little lie) to his tale in order to make it more interesting (2.49). The connection between truthful-ness and escape from boredom is, however, implicit in the presentation of the novellas in Marguerite de Navarre's prologue.[4]

Cicero's *De officiis* is of fundamental importance in the articulation of social etiquette at the sixteenth-century court. His discussion of decorum includes a section on the sense of shame (1.126–29).[5] Human beings possess a sense of shame because they imitate nature's art, its hiding of the human private parts ("Hanc naturae tam diligentem fabricam imitata est hominum verecundia," 1.127). So human beings avoid talking about, and perform in secret, actions that involve parts of the body which nature has hidden. This is why actors on stage always wear something to hide their private parts (a *subligaculum*) lest they be uncovered by chance during a performance, and they be looked upon indecorously ("ne, si quo casu evenerit ut corporis partes quaedam aperiantur, aspiciantur non decore," 1.129).

It is important, then, to make sure one's *subligaculum*, the covering of one's private parts, is in place. In narrative this cover is the distinction between the narrator of a tale and the protagonist of the tale itself. This is already a problem in the framing of the embedded tale. A court lady wishing to add a tale to others told to a visiting lady of royal blood, announces that she will "make a beautiful tale" ("faire ung beau compte"), on condition that no one repeat it ("que vous n'en parlerez poinct"). Why does she place this condition, except to alert the audience to the shameful nature of the tale? But the tale is anonymous, and general enough so that identification would be difficult. Is the tale told *because* she does not wish it to be repeated? Or is it precisely because it should not be repeated that it is both not boring and truthful? The *subligaculum* of the narrator-actor seems to be missing at the outset.

The lady goes on to assure the audience that it will be a true tale ("le compte est très veritable"), and that her conscience vouches for its truthfulness. These protestations of truthfulness fulfill the requirements of the *Heptameron* collection, announcing in its prologue in a double way: "n'escripre nulle nouvelle qui ne soit veritable histoire" (9;68), and "dira chascun quelque histoire qu'il aura veue ou bien oy dire à quelque homme digne de foy" (10;69). It is especially the second condition that will be fulfilled: as a tale which is not to be repeated could not have been repeated to the narrator herself, it is she who must have been the eyewitness, that is, the victim of the rape. For the only other eyewitnesses are the "chambrieres." The very fact that she is a lady narrating an unrepeatable true tale is a trap. The alternative is to say that the admonition to the listeners not to repeat her tale is ironic, an inducement to listen, an advertisement for salacious content. If this is the case, then the lady has already lost her (inner) sense of honor, her sense of conscience, before the tale begins, and has thus violated the decorum of courtly exchange in the *Heptameron*. In this sense the final self-revelation is not the only cause of her loss of honor.

The final self-revelation is timed in a specific way, for it seems displaced or deferred.[6] The narrator reveals her identity (the *sujet de l'énonciation* becomes the *sujet de l'énoncé*), collapses the distance between storyteller and tale, at the moment of discovery. The self-revelation might have come earlier, when she awoke to find the gentleman, wearing his boots, beside her in bed ("quant elle s'esveilla, fut autant marrye qu'il estoit possible," 378;485). This is not the case, however, as the narrator keeps her sangfroid toward the material recounted during the "rape." It is only when the man's spur accidentally pulls away the covers, exposing the lady's naked body to her servant girls, that the narrator loses control and reveals herself as the victim of the attack. The displacement of self-revelation from the rape to its discovery is announced by a sentence preceding the encounter: the gentleman did not have enough sense to close the door when he enters her chamber ("sans avoir le sens de fermer la porte," 378;485). This lapse on the part of the gentleman causes in part the discovery which in turn causes the lapse of the narrator. The lady is in effect repeating the forgetful or imprudent gesture of her attacker. His gestures (the door left open, the boots left on) caused the discovery and recounting of the episode by the servant girls, and the narrator, both by repeating the story herself, and by identifying herself as the victim, makes sure that the ladies listening, and the queen of Navarre, will repeat the story again, in gossip and in print. "Vous n'en parlerez poinct" means "Vous en parlerez, comme moi."[7]

The point of the lady's tale is, then, not the rape itself but the curious way in which it is discovered by the chambermaids. This discovery is so surprising that it provokes the self-revelation of the narrator, although the fact that the witnesses are chambermaids seems to lessen its importance. The emotional charge lies in the connection between the original discovery and the scene of narration. This displaced connection, from the physical violation of her person to the metaphorical violation by the eyes of the chambermaids, is a product of the emotional investment of courtly ideology in observation. As the lady is lying naked on the bed, so the narrator is metaphorically naked in front of the princess and the other listeners. It is the act of exposure that generates surprise or release from boredom, not that which has been exposed. This, of course, works on two levels: first, the surprise of the narrator, then the surprise of the court ladies. The primacy of detachment and observation in courtly ideology implies this aesthetics of *surprise*, which, of course, makes this a very successful tale.

This surprise has to do with shame. Recalling the Ciceronian account, we can say that the shameful is so in relation to a natural disposition of the body, in the sense that shamefulness is not produced by an inherent set of moral values, but is so in imitation of the way the human body is constructed. Thus something is shameful if it is normally hidden from view by nature itself. Surprise is generated, then, by the coming to view of what should be hidden. What should be hidden is equivalent to what is not decorous or fitting, *decens*. The gentleman's spur uncovers the female body; it is this that causes surprise. Surprise is to be distinguished from, say, moral revulsion: one is surprised by what is not in line with a "natural" code of behavior, by what seems inconsistent with decorum. Similarly, the narrator's identification with the attacked lady is what causes relief from boredom. Pronouncing the *moy* of identification is to reveal that which is normally hidden and is shameful. When one tells tales one should not be looked at, for one looks at others.

This is where we return to the rhetoric of courtly pastime. The rhetoric of entertainment through evidential truth is made all the riskier because of the social codes of observation and shame. In order to relieve boredom one tells novellas; a novella is similar to a continuous narrative of a joke; this joke is made effective by the figure of *evidentia*. The eyewitness account shows events as if you were there: but you must be there as *witness*, not as the person who is being looked *at*, or whose actions are being witnessed. The narrator is the place of identification of listeners with the eyewitness; if the narrator turns out to be the naked body exposed to others, this identification is shameful. It causes a reversal of roles which violates one of the fundamental practical maxims of courtly behavior: unless you are the prince, it is far safer to look than to be the object of looking.

The unfortunate lady's tale is also a parable of demonstrative rhetoric, in the sense that the naked body is staged as the primary object of evidential truth, as it is at the same time what is so studiously occulted and so meticulously suggested. When the *devisants* demand that novellas be "true," the conditions for this truth turn out in this case to be the evidence of a naked body. It is that which you can see. The listeners could also see the narrator in front of their eyes. Seeing the narrator use "moy" to identify the naked body is the most perfect guarantee of truth, but it is also the most shameful thing to do. A perfectly true tale is one that should not be told.

The point of Marguerite de Navarre's novella is not, however, the chambermaids' surprising discovery of their mistress's naked body, but the revelation that the narrator is the same person as the victim of the "rape." The story is about the shameful conditions of truth, not about that truth itself. In order to reveal that truth, a certain amount of distancing is necessary; one must make sure one's *subligaculum* is in place. The first and obvious distancing concerns the very act of narrating. If you can talk about someone else, you are not being talked about. That was attempted by the first narrator, and the attempt failed, because she became the object of a witticism, and eventually of a novella. Yet the naked narrator has provided others with a new, metastory to be repeated with pleasure. This repetition also means that it is more likely that successive narrators will not be naked: since the point of the story is the identification of the original narrator with the victim of the rape, not the rape itself, the repeating narrator is already twice-removed from the shameful discovery of the naked body. The subsequent collapsing of victim and (original) narrator *is* the point of the story, so the most dangerous thing that could happen to you can be talked *about*; it does not have to be avoided. As the shameful discovery has already occurred once, it cannot occur again if it is being recounted. You hardly risk repeating the lady's error, as the point of the story *is* her error. The pleasure lies in the conjuring of one's worst fears; the worst fear is not nakedness itself, but its discovery at the court. If that discovery is talked about, not just felt and occulted, then you can feel at remove, safe, while enjoying what is least boring in a courtly setting, the shame of disgrace. What one enjoys, then, is the exposing of truth, not ultimately, truth itself.

Enjoyment is indeed selective: laughter is produced not by the chambermaids' discovery, but by the collapsing of victim and narrator. This laughter is the laughter of the queen. The whole story is framed (once again) by the presence of "une dame de sang roial" during the reign of François I, who "sçavoit bien dire ung compte et de bonne grace, et en rire aussy, quant on luy en disoit quelcun" (377;485). This can hardly not be a reference to Marguerite de Navarre herself. At the end of the unfortunate lady's story, the sister of the king designates the point of the story by adding her motto: "Alors, la dame, qui avoit oy le compte sans rire, ne s'en peut tenir à ce dernier mot, en luy disant: 'Ad ce que je voy, vous en povez bien racompter l'histoire" (378;486). The princess's laughter is highly selective, and highly revealing. She (ironically) praises the lady for having told the tale so well, and she herself is described as someone who knows how to tell a story well ("sçavoit bien dire ung compte"). There is, then, the suggestion of another identification, that of the naked narrator and the princess, an identification which has been occulted and revealed by the fact that the princess reacts with courtly wit to a pleasing but dangerous mistake. This scene of dishonor is in fact the basis for a third story, namely the *facezia* constituted by the princess's witty reply.

In the secular, courtly interpretation of the novella it is discovery and exposure that convey the greatest emotional and ideological investment. The most entertaining tale is one in which the listeners can feel the pleasure of dangerous identification avoided. It is not the learning of truth that is entertaining: the value of the tale as an example of virtue or lack of it is secondary to the conditions of its repetition, and to the risky relation between the *énoncé* and the *énonciation* that repetition involves. In some ways, too, the elaborate frame-story of the *Heptameron* is an aristocratic distancing of shameless material that rehearses courtly pastime.

Rape and Tale: The Case of Lucretia

Up to now we have considered the court and its ethics as a whole, leaving aside the problem of the position of the two genders in relation to narrative activity and its favorite subject, sexual activity. If, for reasons which we have just discussed, the company of the "dame" can allow itself to laugh, the same is not true of Longarine, Parlamente, and Ennasuite. All three judge the foolish woman severely, as if the threat against decorum, deflected by the princess's wit, had reconstituted itself at a higher textual level, in a polemical space that could be defined by the opposition between Parlamente and Hircan, the married couple.[8] "Vostre plaisir gist à deshonorer les femmes, et vostre honneur à tuer les hommes," retorts Parlamente to her husband, in the discussion which follows novella 26 (221;305). In contrast to masculine pleasure and honor, which feed on violence and publicity, women's pleasure and honor require *couverture*, dissimulation.[9] This idea of the *couvert* is also situated in a theological framework, which we will define later. Indeed, this framework is that of novella 62, told by Longarine to illustrate the case of women abandoned by God's grace who "en se coupant, s'accusent." But when the same Longarine declares: "C'est beaucoup que les hommes ne nous puissent accuser" (221;306), she adds the social problem of women's protection by secrecy to the religious problem of the relationship between the sinful soul and its creator.

The female storytellers of the *Heptameron* must jam the narrative machinery which, at least since Jean de Meun (mentioned by Longarine herself [p. 203;285]) and the less-than-truthful Boccaccio, has worked in favor of Hircan and his "loy de Nature": women are just as interested as men in carnal pleasure, but unlike men, they are also hypocritical, seeking to pass for virtuous, like Jambicque in novella 43, told by Geburon. The masculine tale, as practiced by Hircan, Simontaut, or Saffredent, attempts above all to pull up women's dresses "si longues et si bien tissues de dissimulation, qu'on ne peult congnoistre ce qui est dessoubz" (220;305), and to remove the veil or "touret de nez" behind which women hide their laughter at dirty jokes.[10] The feminine tale seeks rather to defend what is secret against the accusation of hypocrisy, by demonstrating the social necessity of secrecy (whether virtuous or not, women stand to lose a great deal by publishing their love affairs and sexual adventures, while men may glory in them shamelessly). This defense also involves sketching a metaphysical background for secrecy (see below).

It is evident that the young female narrator can be defended by recalling that she was raped, as do Geburon and Nomerfide (the senior male and the junior female, the most diplomatic of the men and the least diplomatic of the women). But the problem has several facets: by *telling* the story, she made herself the consenting heroine of the anecdotal genre, which usually indulges in laughter at the expense of women. Freud speaks of the joke that undresses, where woman is the undressed object of narrative commerce between men who, without it, would be rivals.[11] The female narrator in novella 62, who ends up naked first in her bed, then in her story, becomes the involuntary accomplice to the process through which women become the laughingstocks of men. However, in the first group of listeners, the person with the most authority is a woman. Perhaps this is the reason the young woman risks telling such a story. But the problem goes beyond the reception by this first group, which explains the fury of Ennasuite who elsewhere opposes Longarine's and Parlamente's rigorism in questions of virtue. Ennasuite does not care about knowing whether the young woman sinned during the rape. Still, for her, the story and the slip of the tongue are more than ridiculous, they are insufferable: "Voylà la plus grande sotte, dont je oy jamais parler, qui faisoit rire les autres à ses despens" (379;486). Parlamente shortly afterward condemns "ceste sotte" for having "voullu faire rire les aultres" with the rape. The accent is different. Parlamente attacks the very desire to cause laughter. Ennasuite limits herself to criticizing the result. In sum, the laughter machine appears difficult to use, because it can turn against the narrator, especially when she is a woman.

At the first reception of the story, the princess bursts out laughing: she "ne s'en peut tenir." But Longarine's listeners do not laugh. Longarine has taken great care to orient her story to a different end by resuming discussion on the problem of *couverture*. Ennasuite and Parlamente support this effort and the men, who might have been expected to roar with laughter, show extraordinary restraint. Apart from Geburon, who defends the victim, and Dagoucin, the next narrator, they remain quiet. The silence of the infernal trio (Hircan, Saffredent, Simontaut) is perhaps a sign that the opportunity was too golden, too dangerous. Somehow the story speaks by itself, serving as *evidentia* for a latent masculine proof. In any case, their silence leaves the field open to the avenging zeal of Ennasuite and Parlamente, who cut their losses and rush in to crucify the foolish woman.

The pragmatic Ennasuite criticizes her most of all for her stupidity in having revealed that which under all circumstances should remain hidden. But Parlamente goes farther. Developing Longarine's line of thought, she believes that the story and its slip of the tongue prove that sin was committed during the rape. Initially for Longarine, the fact that the young lady allowed herself to tell the story is a sign that she sinned, in this case meaning that she did not experience "grand desplaisir à faire ung tel acte," that she enjoyed letting herself be raped. Geburon takes the rape seriously. He believes that the young woman did not sin at all: "Quel peché avoit-elle faict? Elle estoit endormye en son lict; il la menassoit de mort et de honte: Lucresse, qui estoit tant louée, en feit bien aultant. Il est vray, dist Parlamente; je confesse qu'il n'y a si juste à l'euvre, l'on en prent aussi à la memoire, pour laquelle effacer Lucresse se tua; et ceste sotte a voulu faire rire les autres" (379;487). Lucretia's example produces the opposite of the effect that Geburon had intended: Parlamente refuses to trivialize it. We ought not conclude that in Parlamente's opinion suicide is the only outlet for women who have been raped. But her way of thinking about this "euvre" is locked into the alternative sketched by Longarine. Either there was "desplaisir" or there was pleasure, and sin is committed in the second case.

We are now entering a dangerous zone, one of the critical points to which discourse on women and their sexuality incessantly returns. Does a raped woman enjoy it and is her enjoyment a sin? We recall Montaigne's words:[12] "Des violences qui se font à la conscience, la plus à eviter, à mon avis, c'est celle qui se faict à la chasteté des femmes, d'autant qu'il y a quelque plasir corporel naturellement meslé parmy; et, à cette cause, le dissentement n'y peut estre entier, et semble que la force soit meslée à quelque volonté." Montaigne relates the edifying suicides of Saint Pelagia and Saint Sophronia. But he does not approve of them, and praises Henri Estienne who (in his *Apologie pour Hérodote*) advised women to choose a less cruel alternative. Montaigne adds: "Je suis marry qu'il n'a sceu, pour mesler à ses comptes, le mot que j'apprins à Toulouse, d'une femme passée par les mains de quelques soldats: Dieu soit loüé, disoit-elle, qu'au moins une fois dans ma vie je m'en suis soulée sans peché!" Is it an accident that Montaigne here evokes "comptes" and witticisms? Truth is supposed to come from the mouth of the woman of Toulouse, a truth useful for the little stories of the *Apologie*. In contrast with the story's "truth," which de-dramatizes rape and makes it innocent through pleasure, there is only one other model, edifying and tragic. This model encourages women to kill themselves, before being raped (Pelagia) or after (Lucretia). Which model is the more "feminist"? Between witticism (women reach satiety) and tragedy (women kill themselves), the way left open for the female story-tellers of the *Heptameron* seems narrow.

To clarify: the expression "prendre desplaisir à l'euvre" might at the outside mean to feel "desplaisir" at the pleasure of the act. It is essential that the soul not acquiesce to any possible involuntary bodily pleasure. The problem for Montaigne (adieu, Stoicism) is that the soul always acquiesces a little. As soon as there is bodily pleasure, the will is divided. And, considering the case of the woman of Toulouse, if the soul gives in entirely, the distinction is no longer operative. The whole being enjoys the "jouis-sance" of the body, taking pleasure *like* a body in the removal of a prohibi-tion. The "plaisant" story confirms this removal. Hircan and Saffredent expect nothing else from it, since tragedy, at least *a priori*, is of no use to them. It is enough that women give in to them, preferably while being able to laugh at themselves too. Rape then is not rape.

Confronting the risk of this orientation for the story, Parlamente is left with no other choice but to adopt an extremely rigid attitude. Her ap-proach is not, in principle, that of an inquisitor. Her true stake in the game is not to establish the existence of sexual enjoyment but to limit its effects once it has been revealed. And yet the problem of the *reality* of the pleasure obtained through this "euvre" surfaces in spite of everything. Parlamente goes so far as to say: "Je ne trouve poinct estrange . . . de quoy la parolle ensuict le faict, car il est plus aisé à dire que à faire" (379;486). This remark, woefully inadequate in the case of a rape, provokes Geburon's reaction. Thus it seems that the true sin is one of *fait* and not *parole*. In fact, these distinctions no longer function. The "prendre plaisir" (a kind of acquiescing of the soul) cannot be isolated from original sin, which everyone would like to circumscribe in the body. The pulled-away sheet has in fact only exposed the young woman's body. The scandal was slight; nothing happened. This particular nudity was meaningless because something was lacking for its deciphering. However, when the story exposes the first-person pronoun, it is the soul that appears naked, desiring, and wanting to unmask its desire.

Parlamente's and Longarine's position becomes entrenched when it encounters this icon of sexual pleasure, of "folye." The adultery of novella 61 arouses less anger and more charity. Consider also the double incest of novella 30, which draws only the response of active humility. There are more serious sins, sins more obvious and more spectacular. But few demonstrate in such an economical way that the sin of pleasure (or the pleasure of sin) is a unity, a chain impossible to break apart. Pauline dualism, so effective in other circumstances at keeping fleshly errors from taking root, can only condemn as a whole this nude image where everything appears "libidinal" to the same degree, where it is no longer possible to separate *fait* from *parole*, *oeuvre* from *memoire*, action from story, pleasure from pride, the spirit saying "I" from the flesh saying "Yes."

For Parlamente, the stakes are high. They are simultaneously spiritual (*couvrir* the sinner's nakedness before God), social (*couvrir* women's secrets in front of men), and even literary (to tell without *se découvrir* too much). The scatterbrained young woman, raped or not, carries little weight against Parlamente's chosen political stance: women's power, even at the expense of women's pleasure. Parlamente opposes both Nomerfide's open claiming of the right to pleasure and Ennasuite's reserving of the right to enjoy sexual pleasure in secret. It was she who instituted the *passe-temps* of the novellas, a compromise between the one proposed by Oisille (Scripture reading and prayer) and Hircan's obsession (making love with his wife—or with another woman), and she is in effect the guardian of the temporary space where men and women combat with equal weapons. In order to maintain the balance of truths, women must resist the permanent provocation that the storytelling activity itself constitutes, as a machine for exposing feminine desire in order to excuse/deflect men's violence (through laughter).[13] Parlamente answers with her own peculiar sacrificial violence, condemning the sin "pire que la mort" of the adulterous woman (novella 32). Confronted by the character Jambicque (novella 43), a hypocrite who covers her illicit pleasures with a mantle of virtue, Parlamente concludes that this infamous woman is a man: "celles qui sont vaincues en plaisir ne se doibvent plus nommer femmes, mais hommes, desquelz la fureur et la concupiscence augmente leur honneur" (301;396). In itself, the formula "vaincues en plaisir" brings the answer to our question. For Parlamente, between a woman seeking pleasure and a woman raped, the former has given in more completely to masculine law. This is why the rape in novella 62 might seem a metaphor for a deepest defeat.

Parlamente's standard is always the same: honor. It is a political standard. She is not so much interested in "concupiscence" as concupiscence, but rather in its relationship to honor in the societal code. It so happens that concupiscence increases men's honor and diminishes women's. Thus, Parlamente can briefly use to her advantage Lucretia's suicide, an anti-evangelical example.[14] Lucretia, who experienced "grand desplaisir," did not sin. Still, she kills herself. Lucretia and the foolish woman are thus situated at opposite ends of the alternative facing ordinary women, innocent and guilty. The innocent woman kills herself, the guilty one brags. Moral: a woman should certainly not commit suicide (see the suicide *contre nature* and doubly fatal in novella 23) but of course neither should she brag or try to "faire rire les autres" with her sexuality.

The bothersome aspect of this reasoning is the seesaw movement in the locating of guilt between the act and its recounting. Parlamente seems to be saying two different things at the same time: on the one hand, "she is guilty, and what's more, she brags about it," and on the other, "she brags about it, therefore she is guilty." It is just not possible to stabilize the logic of pleasure.

A contrario, Lucretia's suicide could appear as the ultimate ornament of her innocence, its crowning work, or as proof of her innocence, the only one possible (this paradoxical "solution" and its uses in Italian humanism have been explored by Stephanie H. Jed in a recent book).[15] This story revolves around a problem of medium and semiotics. The heroine expresses herself most clearly in the historian Livy's version.[16] Here, she gave in to Tarquin only to avoid an irreparable scandal—she would have been found dead in the arms of a slave. She chooses a real defilement, of which she can cleanse herself, rather than an alleged but indelible one. She, like Oisille (in novella 25), would also say that scandal is worse than sin—except that for Lucretia, there was no sin at all. To her father and her husband who assert that "mentem peccare, non corpus, et unde consilium afuerit, culpam abesse" (the mind sins, not the body, and where purpose is absent, so is guilt), Lucretia replies: "Ego me etsi peccato absolvo, supplicio non libero; nec ulla deinde inpudica Lucretiae exemplo vivet" (Even if I absolve myself of the sin, I am not free of punishment; and no immodest woman will live hereafter by the example of Lucretia).[17] Even the official patriarchal discourse admits that Lucretia did not sin, but if she lives, her exemplum will be used as a covering for the errors of less virtuous women. If she lives, illicit sexual pleasure will be propagated, because it is unverifiable: the *plaisir corporel* might be enjoyed secretly, excused by use of force, and Montaigne's analysis becomes possible. Who could establish whether or not a woman had tried "se souler sans péché," without apparent sin anyway? Lucretia provides a very radical measuring and detecting instrument, as a truly innocent woman who kills herself. Shortly before she had given the implacable three-term formula:

CORPUS VIOLATUM + ANIMUS INSONS
→ MORS TESTIS

(Violated Body + Innocent Soul → Death Is Witness)

Only death can signify the soul's innocence in a raped female body (or in any female body).

Lucretia's exemplarity comes from her awareness of the exemplum to come. She thinks in terms of the long-range effects, but on women only. She leaves to men the task of deciding her rapist's punishment. As we know, Brutus makes a Roman political decision when over the bloody corpse he suddenly stops feigning insanity in order to ensure the austere triumph of the virtuous republic and of that which Jed calls "chaste thinking." But Lucretia's rape is conceived of by Lucretia herself as an example addressed solely to the *peccatum* to come from feminine sexuality, although she herself did not sin. The tale of her shame is intentional; it leads directly to the suicide which completely restores her honor, her *decus*. This economy is corrupted in the version found in Ovid's *Fasti* (2.761–852). The poet shows Lucretia overcome, a de facto sinner who cannot speak. The story is a supplementary dishonor (*dedecus*) for her. To her father and husband she only says that she refuses their pardon (*veniam*), and kills herself with just one last concern, that of falling with decency (*honeste*). Lucretia is even more reified but less exemplary, incapable as she is of producing reparation herself. On the contrary, story and suicide are suspected of adding to the indecency which the heroine is supposed to bring under control. Ovid offers none of the historical tension of Titus Livy, who legitimizes both story and suicide. He no longer believes in "chaste thinking." He is not interested in virtuous example but rather the image of a wounded, sullied, blushing victim, who preserves the pure pomp of the spectacle, a pomp steeped in a kind of licentious pity.

The problem of medium is most extensively treated in Shakespeare's poem *The Rape of Lucrece*[18]—a long reverie on the fragility of the female soul and body ("For men have marble, women waxen, minds," 1.1240), which bear the marks of errors, especially those made by others, by men. The innocent body is given to be read in the light of day as a sinful text. The "corpus violatum" becomes wholly the sign of the error of which it is the victim. Lucretia's problem is thus to stem the flood of stories and examples which will inevitably be born from the spectacle of outrageous indignity. An indelible, written spectacle forces Lucretia to speak ("my impure tale," 1.1078) then to kill herself, "to clear this spot by death" (1.1053). Story and suicide are thus maintained in the restorative function suggested by Titus Livy, but this debt to him appears trifling when compared to the hyper-trophied motif of the stain-writing on the female body, which seems rather to be an amplification of Ovid. Shakespeare develops the tragic potential in the story of Lucretia. Nothing can be done against the defilement—the act itself or the text. Nothing, save the sacrifice of her own life, is able to reorient the tales to come. Where Titus Livy set up a founding story, Shakespeare uses a "meta-narrative" lyricism, in order to deflect oratorical effects which "will couple my reproach to Tarquin's shame," or verses of "feast-finding minstrels, tuning my defame" (816–17); a lyricism which announces death in order to keep the story on track.

Lucretia's story sets up the problem of the *first* story to be told to father and husband. It is scandalous in a double and contradictory way. Either it is the story of a guilt, which exposes Lucretia's shame, or it is the story of an innocence which, although true, will serve as a blanket for future crimes. The only solution is an exemplary death. But then an even more glaring contradiction appears. Lucretia says at first that her death will prove her innocence, then that it will prevent other women from feigning this same innocence. Logically if Lucretia does not die, her own innocence becomes suspect, and thus less capable of masking future guilt. In every case, death serves to banish the pleasure hypothesis. Death is the only proof that only displeasure took place, what Parlamente calls "desplaisir." On a deeper level, the death, the suicide (of the heroine and female narrator) is the only event by which the story may be stabilized, or rather concluded, in order to keep it from testifying to and prolonging sexual pleasure. Thanks to the death, the story becomes an example, a counterexample.

It is interesting to see what becomes of this strategy when it is joined to an authentically feminist problem, one concerned with the defense and advancement of women. The exemplum is transmitted, intact, from Livy's

Urbe to Christine de Pisan's *Cité des dames*.[19] But Christine uses it first to refute those who claim that women take pleasure in being raped. She emphasizes as well that Lucretia's case inspired Rome to enact strong legislation against rape. In short, she attempts to think the other side of the matter. At the same time, she repeats that the heroine tried to prevent women without honor from invoking her example. All in all, Lucretia's death still allows the balancing of two "causes" of different orders: (1) it proves that women do not enjoy being raped, and (2) it discourages women from letting themselves be "violated" by pleasure. We can see that this rape story, taken literally, might well form a part of the foundation for a serious reflection on rape. But this does not stop it from persisting in its main function, that of moralizing: discouraging women not from being raped but from pursuing their pleasure. Finally, this conjugal exemplum can be used by Christine de Pisan or Marguerite de Navarre as an extreme example for a feminist political stance that analyzes the totality of the sexual problem in terms of power relationships. Lucretia's death, the same and yet other, might still dissuade women from offering themselves up to men's *comptes* and *bons mots*.

Note Parlamente's words: "La mémoire, pour laquelle effacer Lucresse se tua" (379;487). "Mémoire" here refers to personal memory, in other words, to the shame that Lucretia feels. If the word referred to collective memory, to reputation, the word "effacer" (to erase) would not be the one to use. Thus, Parlamente's Lucretia seems closer to Ovid's than to Titus Livy's, but for precise reasons: Parlamente is interested in Lucretia's interior reaction, her relationship with herself. And memory is that which wounds the soul even if it is innocent, that which associates the wound with the sullying of the body in spite of itself. Interestingly, Parlamente this time dodges Lucretia's exemplary narrative activity. In fact, Lucretia hardly sought to erase her *mémoire* but rather to broadcast and direct it among men, at the price of her own life. Parlamente, the better to contrast Lucretia to the foolish woman, refuses to remember that the Roman Lucretia proclaimed her shame (and thanks to this "publication," Parlamente speaks of it today). The fact is that she spoke, in the first person, of the defilement inflicted upon her body. A voluntary story prefaces an equally voluntary suicide, committed with the help of a dagger pulled by surprise from under her robe. One might say that this dagger, "quem sub veste abditum habebat" (which she kept hidden under her garment),[20] stands in contrast to the spur which also by surprise uncovers the female narrator of novella 62. The phallic emblem either undresses the female body by accident and as a joke, or kills it, suddenly appearing out of the clothing which concealed it, wielded by the woman herself. The exposed body (bloody, therefore chaste) in this case is no longer the point of the story. Pulling the dagger from its wound, Brutus will use it to found the Roman republic.

Nomerfide tries to widen the scope of the debate. In order to find a way out of the rape problem, she recalls the young woman's long resistance to the rapist's previous advances. But Parlamente (whom Nomerfide, courted by Hircan, tends to exasperate) hardens her tone more and asserts that the ultimate outcome of every refusal must be considered: "L'on ne doibt poinct faire cas d'une femme si elle ne tient ferme jusques au bout" (379;487).[21] In the context, this sentence strikes an odd note. Does this maxim go so far as to apply to *rape*? Perhaps not, yet one cannot help but recall the famous novella 4, told by Ennasuite, the story of the "dame de Flandres" and the admiral of Bonnivet. This story is exemplary in that it shows that one can, in a case of this type, escape being raped. Hircan confirms this, paradoxically, when Nomerfide forces him to admit that, if he really wanted to prevail in the same situation, he ought to begin by killing the lady-in-waiting. Here, masculine logic goes out of bounds and is obliged to express its own excess, the very excess of Tarquin. Rape is not a funny story, it is nothing less than murder. Within this limit, the princess of Flanders can act as a witness against the foolish woman of novella 62, in *fait* and in *parole*. And this is thanks to the edifying intervention of the lady-in-waiting, the "dame d'honneur."

We know that the princess has just one idea in her head, to tell the affair to her brother in order to have the head of the would-be rapist. And the "dame d'*honneur*," aptly named, after hearing the complete story, convinces her not to do it: "vostre honneur . . . sera mis en dispute en tous les lieux là où cette histoire sera racomptée" (32;94). This is the Lucretia complex: from the society's point of view, telling leads to being accused of having given in to the rapist, even of having provoked him—especially if he is put to death upon the orders of one's brother (François I?). Not every day can a state be founded on the punishment of a rapist. There is therefore no possible story except if one chooses, in order to validate it (or expiate it?), Lucretia's radical solution of voluntary death.

But this fatality of silence has an evangelical justification which the Roman heroine obviously did not know. Rather than pride herself on her virtue, the woman must humble herself before God, for it was he who did all. And should the aggressor start talking, which is unlikely: "Faindrez du tout de ne l'entendre, pour eviter deux dangiers, l'un de la vaine gloire de la victoire que vous en avez eue, l'autre de prendre plaisir en ramentevant choses qui sont si plaisantes à la chair que les plus chastes ont bien à faire à se garder d'en sentir quelques estincelles" (33;95). The glory of victory or the pleasure of defeat. From the princess of Flanders to the foolish young woman, it is the same moral, the same anti-narrative message: the story given or received is a trap for women, because of a network of both societal and spiritual reasons.

Inevitably, this raises the problem of the fourth story's transmission. No one is supposed to know about it and the princess certainly did not commit a slip of the tongue like any foolish young lady. Ennasuite says indeed that the story is quite recent and she gives no names. We are therefore very close to that *vérité* which incurs greater risks to women than to men. But we are brought here with a good motive, since the story is of a woman who (1) resisted the attempts of masculine desire, and (2) said nothing about it, except to her lady-in-waiting. A curious *mise en abyme*, which we must wait until novella 62 to decipher completely! The princess resists the same temptation to which the young woman falls prey, on the levels of *fait* and of *parole*, in such a way that the princess's story is told to us across a void, an enigma, an aporia. In one sense, it could not have been transmitted without betraying the very message it is supposed to convey.

But the message prevails against the constraint for at least two reasons. One is very simple: the company of storytellers has chosen to play the game of truth within precise limits, and women's honor is balanced with men's in this game. Is it an accident that Hircan believes that the hero of this story (Bonnivet) is not "digne d'estre ramentu" (34;96)? For Parlamente and Ennasuite, it represents a victory: a story which should not have been possible has even so been launched against the normal course of masculine *gloire*. The second reason is harder to handle if narrative orthodoxy is followed, since orthodoxy allows no confusion between author, narrator, and protagonist. However, this is exactly what we must do in order to perceive the stakes placed on this strategy and its urgency. If the princess of Flanders is (indirectly) none other than Marguerite de Navarre, she causes a story to be told which is *her* story. We possess in the ruse and the precautions a supplementary sign of the *difficulty* of the feminine story (is this not the very trap into which the foolish young woman falls?), and of its *necessity*: the story will get past the trap.[22] Novella 4 is the story of a resistance which simultaneously averts Lucretia's tragedy (story plus suicide) and, assuming a gap in transmission, the comedy of the young woman (story plus slip of the tongue). Feminine resistance to storytelling manages in this way to tell the story of feminine resistance, without spilling the blood or the ink of scandal. It is a tale that can be repeated.

Involuntary Desire and Sin

If the discussion of Lucretia involves the dangerous position of the *female* narrator, the theological commentary, seemingly universal, in fact also entails a reflection on women's status as sinners. After Longarine has finished she immediately advances a theological explanation for the unfortunate lady's self-inflicted loss of honor: "Je vous asseure, mes dames, que, si elle eut grand desplaisir à faire ung tel acte, elle en eust voullu avoir perdu la memoire. Mais, comme je vous ay dict, le peché seroit plus tost descouvert par elle-mesme, qu'il ne pourroit estre sceu, quant il n'est poinct couvert de la couverture que David dict rendre l'homme bien heureux" (378–79;486). The self-revelation of sin is explained by the fact that the creature is not covered by the cover that makes men happy. The reference is indicated by the mention of David; the Adrien de Thou edition of the *Heptameron* even quotes Clément Marot's translation of Ps. 32:1: "O bien heureux celuy dont les commises / Transgressions sont par grace remises; / Duquel aussi les iniques pechez / Devant son Dieu sont couvertz et cachez" (quoted in François ed., p. 492 n. 771).[23] The metaphor of God's cover of grace is a traditional way of describing the state of man before original sin: Adam and Eve were not embarrassed to be naked in Paradise, as they were covered by God's grace. With the Fall the creature lost that cover, and must hide his private parts, for he is ashamed of them, as he is ashamed of his sins. The classic account is found in Augustine, where we find the connection between the involuntary exposure of sin and the feeling of shame:

> Their [Adam's and Eve's] eyes were not closed, but they were not open, that is, attentive so as to recognize what a boon the cloak of grace afforded them [*quid eis indumento gratiae praestaretur*], in that their bodily members did not know how to oppose their will. When this grace was lost and punishment in kind for their disobedience was inflicted, there came to be in the action of the body a certain shameless novelty [*quaedam inpudens novitas*], and thereafter nudity was indecent. It drew their attention and made them embarrassed [*confusos*].[24]

Shame is not simply caused by the fact that the private parts are exposed, but that the private parts can disobey the will; it is for that reason that they are called *pudenda*: "[It is] reasonable too that those members which it

[lust] moves or does not move by its own right, so to speak, and not in full subjection to our will [*non omni modo ad arbitrium nostrum movet aut non movet*], should be called pudenda or shameful parts as they were not before man sinned" (14.17). Shame is thus a sign of original sin, but in a precise, physical way; it is because the private parts sometimes move themselves involuntarily.

This account of shame is of course "phallocentric," in that Augustine was referring to involuntary erection or flaccidity of the male member. In the *City of God* Augustine does not speak about the female equivalent of unruly desire; when he returns to the discussion of unruliness in other texts, he refers to female desire only to say that it is a "hidden" movement (*in [motu] occulto [Contra duas epistulas Pelagianorum*, 1.16.32]), that it is up to women to know what they feel, and that it is not fitting for men to push curiosity that far (*viderint feminae quid in secretis visceribus sentiant; nos non decet inaniter usque ad ista esse curiosos [De nuptiis et concupiscentia*, 2.13.26]).[25] The novella can then be read as doing what would be indecent or unfitting for men to do. It stages female pleasure and its extremely problematic status in a society where rape is a matter of male pride and the victim automatically incurs a loss of honor. Female desire indeed causes shame, but this desire is a "movement" in language, the identification of the female narrator as the protagonist of a story that exposes her entire body. This identification is an involuntary "movement," transposing into language the unruliness of a body part. The movement of lust is transposed into the movement from *recitatio* to *assertio*, from "faire le compte d'une aultre" to "faire le conte de moi-même." The unruliness of female desire is linguistic, and related in some way to the novella enterprise.

The relationship between female desire and novella production and consumption is perhaps already suggested in the Augustine passage quoted earlier. The action of the body after original sin acquired "a certain shameless novelty," *quaedam inpudens novitas*: the etymological connection to *novella*[26] is relevant precisely because novellas tend in fact to be *inpudentes*, recounting surprising and shameless material. We have suggested above that there is a latent identification between the queen of Navarre and the unfortunate lady as storytellers. This identification is strengthened by the fact that involuntary actions characterize both the naked narrator and the privileged listener, who "ne s'en peut tenir à ce dernier mot," who cannot keep from laughing. The involuntary laughter and witty rejoinder are a mediated form of the shame/desire that the naked narrator experiences.[27] Female laughter is then both an admission of the embarrassment of (self-) assertion and a defense against it, as the very act of laughter means that one is laughing about someone else. "Faire rire les autres à ses despens" (379; 486) means that one is either the object of laughter, or one laughs, and if one laughs, one laughs at the expense of another ("faire le compte d'une aultre").[28] Novellas allow this laughter, and indeed are entertaining to the extent that one does laugh.

But the naked narrator and the laughing princess are not the only ones to perform involuntary actions. The gentleman who hastily leaves the bedchamber accidentally uncovers the protagonist; if his spur had not caught on the sheet, no one would have noticed: "Et ne s'en fust personne aperceu, sinon l'esperon qui s'estoit attaché au linceul de dessus l'emporta tout entier" (378;486). The male attacker is therefore at the beginning of this series of involuntary revelations; he is also earlier described as being "folastre" and does not have the "sens" to close the door. The physical, material accident of his caught spur is transformed by the women into linguistic relief from boredom. This series of involuntary actions is an analogue to the move from physical, visible unruliness of desire in men to linguistic unruliness in women.

The displacement of self-revelation from the actual rape to its discovery is, in this line of interpretation, produced by the involuntary original action of the man, who in turn sets in motion a chain of involuntary actions: the narrator's self-incrimination and the queen's laughter. The very existence of involuntary movements of desire is a sign of original sin, and in this sense the novella is about the phenomenon of sin and its literal pervasiveness in secular society. Of course the original sinner here is the man.

In the theological interpretation offered by Longarine the focus shifts from the spectacle of disgrace and the reaffirmation of decorum to the pseudopsychological mechanism of desire and sin. The theological is, however, not incompatible with courtly ideology, as the theological account of desire is one that involves lack of voluntary control. As we have seen, voluntary control is also of utmost importance in the maintaining of a feminist position in the face of the insistently self-serving undermining of feminine resistance by the male *devisants*. Courtly civilization is in a profound sense a dream of control; it is an ideology that defines its own perfection by, in the *Heptameron*, excluding servants, bears, *bandouliers*, and monks in order to achieve the atmosphere of play in the circle protected from the rays of the noonday sun. Within this circle Marguerite de Navarre has been able to evoke and keep at bay the violent dynamics of truth, pleasure, and honor.

Notes

1. The authors wish to thank Laura Gates for her translation of certain portions of this chapter.

2. Castiglione, *Il libro del Cortegiano*, ed. Ettore Bonora (Milano: Mursia, 1972).

3. For example, Quintilian (*Institutio oratoria*, 8.3.61–63) makes the point that oratory, in order to be truly effective, must make you think you are seeing what is being recounted before your (mind's) eye.

4. Parlamente, in the prologue, speaks of the initial courtly project, which consisted of "n'escripre nulle nouvelle qui ne soit veritable histoire"; the dauphin wished the truth of the stories to be untarnished by the beauty of rhetoric (9;68). The execution of this project is how the noble company wishes to prevent death by boredom.

5. Cicero, *De officiis*, ed., trans. Walter Miller (Cambridge, Mass.: Harvard University Press, 1913), "Loeb Classical Library."

6. See also, on this point, the discussion of novella 62 in John D. Lyons, *Exemplum: The Rhetoric of Example in Early Modern France and Italy* (Princeton, N.J.: Princeton University Press, 1989), 105.

7. It should be clear from our discussion, nevertheless, that the self-revealing narration is motivated mostly by the intense courtly investment in observation and discovery, and the resulting "amusement." Self-revelation seems to stem only in a highly mediated way from a basic desire to narrate as a way of making sense of things. For an evocation of this desire, see Peter Brooks, *Reading for the Plot: Design and Intention in Narrative* (New York: Alfred A. Knopf, 1984), 54: "[The narrative as narrating] is in essence the desire to be heard, recognized, understood, which, never wholly satisfied or indeed satisfiable, continues to generate the desire to tell, the effort to enunciate a significant version of the life story in order to capture a possible listener." See, for a reading of the *Heptameron* that sees many of the stories as an attempt by Marguerite de Navarre to tell her own story, to *express* her own reaction to her attempted rape by Bonnivet, Patricia F. Cholakian, *Rape and Writing in the "Heptaméron" of Marguerite de Navarre* (Carbondale: Southern Illinois University Press, 1991).

8. There is an interesting contrast between novella 62 and 11, told by Nomerfide to make the company laugh. In it, Madame de Roncex (whose name is revealed) is surprised with her skirts up in the privy of the Franciscan monastery. The laughter in this scene, to which the "victim" herself finally gives in, is born of a cleared-up misunderstanding. In light of the monks' reputation, when screams are heard, everyone assumes there has been a rape. The scatological nature of the "ord et sale" story is therefore perfectly inoffensive. Even better, it momentarily eases the sexual anguish which is weighing on the universe of the novellas.

9. See Nicole Cazauran, *L'Heptaméron de Marguerite de Navarre* (Paris: SEDES-CDU, 1976), on the strategic opposition between masculine and feminine "honneurs."

10. Dagoucin's technique, despite appearances, is perhaps not all that different, only more subtle. See in particular the discussion which follows novella 24

(the story of Elisor). Oisille has to intervene in order to contain the overflow of misogyny provoked by the queen of Castille's case.

11. In Sigmund Freud, *Jokes and Their Relation to the Unconscious*, in *Complete Works*, ed. J. Strachey (New York: W.W. Norton, 1961, vol. 8). See below, note 28.

12. Montaigne, *Essais*, 2.3, "Coustume de l'Isle de Cea," ed. Pierre Villey and Verdun-L. Saulnier (Paris: Presses Universitaires de France, 1966), 356.

13. One might recall Geburon's ominous maxim (novella 18): "place qui *parlamente* est demy gaingnée!" (142;219, italics ours).

14. Titus Livy, one might say, is an anti-Saint Paul. His Lucretia fiercely denies all sin, rather than recognizing it, but she commits suicide instead of trusting herself to God.

15. Stephanie H. Jed, *Chaste Thinking, the Rape of Lucretia and the Birth of Humanism* (Bloomington: Indiana University Press, 1989).

16. Titus Livy is adapted by Jean de Meun, among others, in the *Roman de la rose*, 8578–8620, and copied by Boccaccio in his *De mulieribus claris*, 48. In Jean de Meun, the topos is that there are no more Lucretias, which is precisely what Estienne and Montaigne will say.

17. Livy, *Ab Urbe condita*, 1.58.9–11, ed. B. O. Foster (London: W. Heinemann, 1919).

18. *Shakespeare's Rape of Lucrece*, ed. I. Gollancz (London: Aldine House, 1896).

19. Christine de Pisan, *La Cité des dames*, 44, ed. Th. Moreau and E. Hicks (Paris: Stock, 1986).

20. Livy, 1.58.11.

21. This is to some extent the case of Françoise, the virtuous heroine of novella 42 (told by Parlamente), who successfully resists the repeated advances of a young prince (most probably the future François I). She states: "[J]'ay mon honneur si cher, que j'aymerois mieulx mourir, que de l'avoir diminué, pour quelque plaisir que ce soit en ce monde" (290;384). Oisille regrets that "les actes vertueux de ceste fille n'ont esté du temps des historiens, car ceulx qui ont tant loué leur Lucresse l'eussent laissé au bout de la plume, pour escripre bien au long les vertuz de ceste-cy" (294;389). Thus a woman might have achieved historic fame without trading her own life for an exemplum of eternal virtue. Yet, as an alternative to Lucretia's tale, the story sets aside the issue of masculine violence: the young prince fears his mother's wrath, and "ne voulloit poinct user d'autres moiens que ceulx que l'honnesteté commande" (292;387).

22. For a more general approach to the strategies of female narrative, see for example Nancy K. Miller, "Emphasis Added: Plots and Plausibilities in Women's Fiction," *PMLA* 96 (1981): 36–48.

23. The Vulgate does not mention God's grace: "Beati sunt quorum remissae sunt iniquitates, / Et quorum tecta sunt peccata." However, justification is connected to this image in the Pauline gloss on Ps. 32:1–2 in Rom. 4:4–8, which is the basis for Marot's paraphrase. The verses in Psalm Thirty-two are often taken to be a reference to the fruits of baptism, for example by Augustine in his *De nuptiis et concupiscentia* (1.33.38). The metaphor of the cover of God's grace is also found in the correspondence between Marguerite de Navarre and Guillaume Briçonnet. Mar-

guerite asks Briçonnet for a "robbe de nopces" to be able to appear at the table of the Lord (referring to Matt. 22:1–14). Briçonnet responds by commenting in length on the meaning of the nuptial robe, which when worn covers all sins: "[La robe] est sans cousture, comme doibt aussy estre Dieu ayme [sic] sans mixture. Qui la peult avoir ne doibt craindre la froidure: elle est sy grande qu'elle couvre innumerables pechéz. Le corps est le cheval que l'ame doibt maistriser par esperons de mortificacion et pauvretté d'esperit, pour . . . obtenir l'union de l'excellente et très-digne robbe nuptiale." This robe cannot be soiled: "L'on ne sçauroit maculer ceste digne robbe nuptiale, car c'est toute puretté non susceptible d'ordure" (in letter of November 11, 1521, *Correspondance* (1521–1524), ed. Christine Martineau and Michel Veissière, with the assistance of Henry Heller [Geneva: Droz, 1975, 1979] 1:52 and 53). The spur of the gentleman does in fact reveal the sin of the body. See also Briçonnet's commentary on Gen. 3:22 in his letter of August 31, 1524: "Helas, il est bien nud qui de péché se vest, lequel ne se peult celler! C'est ung hoste corrosif et irrequiet qui trop se monstre et mal paye son escot" (Vol. 2, p. 242). Jan Miernowski pointed out to us that Marguerite de Navarre uses the cover image in a similar way in her *Chansons spirituelles*, ed. Georges Dottin (Geneva: Droz, 1971), 10.31–36, p. 32.

24. Augustine, *City of God*, 14.17, trans. Philip Levine (London: W. Heinemann, 1966).

25. Blushing, one can argue, is that involuntary "movement" common to the sexes: Augustine speaks about the "necessity of blushing" (*haec erubescendi necessitas*, in *Contra duas epistulas Pelagianorum*, 1.16.33) in all human beings. However, blushing is, strictly speaking, only a sign of shame, not of desire itself; it is unruliness mediated.

26. See Robert J. Clements and Joseph Gibaldi, *Anatomy of the Novella: The European Tale Collection from Boccaccio and Chaucer to Cervantes* (New York: New York University Press, 1977), 4, on the connection between "novella" and "newness."

27. Whether laughter is involuntary or voluntary is an issue in medical literature of the sixteenth century; see for example Laurent Joubert, *Le Traité du ris* (Latin 1560; French trans., Paris: N. Chesneau, 1579), 3.11, where Joubert argues that although laughter forces itself out by necessity, that does not mean it is involuntary, as one can decide to stop laughing if reason persuades one to, etc.

28. See also Freud's discussion (in *Jokes and Their Relation to the Unconscious*) of the structure of obscene jokes that suppose a woman's body as the object at the expense of which the joke is made, between two men. The scheme does not fit here, at least on the surface, as it is not men projecting their possession of the female body, but women laughing at the expense of other women.

Mary B. McKinley

9. Telling Secrets: Sacramental Confession and Narrative Authority in the *Heptameron*

> Confession is to be made before the eyes of all in an open place, to prevent a rapacious wolf from sneaking into corners and causing unthinkably shameful things.
>
> —Jean Gerson, c. 1409

In *Heptameron* story 41 Saffredent tells of the countess of Aiguemont, who sends for a priest to administer the sacrament of penance to her household. On Christmas Eve, he hears the confessions of the countess, her maid of honor, and the lady's young daughter. Something in the young girl's confession—the narrator calls it "son secret"—emboldens the confessor to chastise her for the gravity of her sins and to impose upon her an unusual penance: she must wear the confessor's cord against her bare flesh ("de porter ma corde sur vostre chair toute nue") (284;377). The girl at first accepts the penance, but tearfully refuses when the priest insists on attaching the cord with his own hands. The priest suggests that she is a heretic, but the girl remains steadfast in her refusal. The priest then will not grant her absolution, and she leaves, frightened and confused.

The plight of the lady-in-waiting's daughter, like that of the other women represented confessing to a priest in the *Heptameron*, reflects the early-Reformation polemic on sacramental confession and indicates Marguerite de Navarre's position in that debate. At the same time, these stories also raise broader questions about narrative technique, authority, and gender in the work.

Recent feminist scholars have described the experience of women in early modern Europe as one of enclosure. They portray women as being contained by patriarchal power structures in their homes, in their bodies, and in their speech. A woman's sexual freedom, like her vocal participation in public life, was controlled by the culturally sanctioned dominion that first her father, then her husband had over her. Traditional authority had long linked an outspoken character with sexual licentiousness in a woman, but with eloquence, a highly prized Renaissance virtue, in a man.[1] The discourse of misogyny portrayed woman as naturally wanton, out of control, and tending toward chaos both in her sexuality and in her speech. Husbands were cautioned to contain their wives in these areas and warned of the woes that could follow if they did not.[2] Sacramental confession was one institution that required women to speak. In fact, it made women become storytellers, narrating the circumstances of their sins to the confessor. Marguerite skillfully uses the confession stories, not only to make an ideological statement about her evangelical criticism of the institution, but to figure the complex emerging narrative voice of women, especially that of one woman named Marguerite. Early feminist ideology, narrative textual practices, and authorial self-representation come together and interact in these stories. This chapter explores that dynamic.

*   *   *

The Fourth Lateran Council decreed in 1216 that all Christians had to confess their sins to a priest at least once a year.[3] Those who failed to do so incurred excommunication. Although the decree, *Omnis utriusque sexus*, did not initiate the practice of private auricular confession, by codifying it under the authority of the pope, it made the sacrament of penance the essential instrument of forgiveness and justification. It thereby invested the priest with crucial authority. The penitent's contrition alone was no longer sufficient to guarantee remission of guilt and reconciliation with God. Only the priest's pronouncing the words *absolvo te* over the contrite penitent could effect sacramental forgiveness. The decree thereby countered contritionists such as Abelard (d. 1142) who had argued that internal sorrow inspired by the love of God was the essential element in the forgiveness of sins. In that view, successful repentance was principally a matter between the sorrowful sinner and God.

Later medieval theologians continued to debate contrition versus absolution. Thomas Aquinas (d. 1274), while accepting the importance of contrition in the remission of guilt, nevertheless moved toward absolutionism by declaring that the words *absolvo te* were what scholasticism called the "form" or essential agent of the sacrament's grace. For Thomas, penance, like all sacraments, was effective not from the work of the person receiving it, *ex opere operantis*—even though a proper disposition of the penitent was necessary—but *ex opere operato*, from the action of the sacrament itself. Emphasis on absolution became much stronger in the writings of Duns Scotus. For him, perfect contrition was an ideal too lofty to be realized by any but the most saintly, and the normal way to forgiveness was through attrition, an imperfect but efficacious sorrow. The power of the sacrament made up for the insufficiencies in the penitent's sorrow. Contrition was no longer necessary, or even possible, in most cases. The Scotist doctrine gave penitents security against uncertainty about the quality of their contrition, but it also gave to the priest an ecclesiastically validated authority over the penitent's access to forgiveness and justification.[4]

Story 41 illustrates the domination of the absolutionist position in the late medieval church, as well as the corruption that was its consequence. In practice an unscrupulous priest could withhold absolution as a means of coercion, and literature recounts that such coercion was often sexual, although estimates of its frequency differ.[5] In story 41, the exchange between the young girl and the priest after she accepts his initial penance—to wear his cord against her flesh—is a striking portrayal of coercion and solicitation.

> "Baillez-la-moy, mon pere, et je ne fauldray de la porter." "Ma fille," dist le beau pere, "il ne seroit pas bon de vostre main; il fault que les myennes propres, dont vous debvez avoir l'absolution, la vous aient premierement seincte; puis après, vous serez absoulte de tous vos pechez." La fille, en pleurant, respond qu'elle n'en feroit rien. "Comment!" dist le confesseur, "estes-vous une herecticque, qui refusez les penitences selon que Dieu et nostre mere saincte Eglise l'ont ordonné?" (284;377)

The story's emphasis on the cord is richly significant.[6] The cord linguistically as well as literally represents the priest's attempt to secure the woman in sexual bondage (*corde* + *lier*). It also evokes metonymically the priest's sexual organs. Finally the cord reminds the reader that the offending confessor is a Franciscan, or Cordelier.

Yet, this is a story of foiled coercion. In spite of her inner conflict—the narrator tells us that the girl "ne luy vouloit desobeir" (284;377)—in her response, the girl distinguishes clearly between church doctrine on confession and her confessor's abuse of it. She reclaims the maternal authority of the church that the priest has misappropriated, and refusing to be coerced, responds with an eloquence that belies her youth: "'Je use de la confession,' dist la fille, 'comme l'Eglise le commande, et veulx bien recepvoir l'absolution et faire la penitence, mais je ne veulx poinct que vous y mectiez les mains; car, en ceste sorte, je refuse vostre penitence.'" Her refusal costs her that essential absolution: "'Par ainsy,' dist le confesseur, 'ne vous puis-je donner l'absolution.'" (284;378)

*   *   *

Confession and its practices were often indicted by the advocates of church reform. In general, Reformist notions of justification challenged absolution's role in the process of reconciliation between the faithful and God.[7] Disillusion about confession was a central factor in Martin Luther's alienation from the Catholic church. Luther's ninety-five theses, posted at Wittenberg in 1517, reacted to the abuses of indulgences and challenged the church's view of the sacrament of penance. The first two theses set the tone for all that would follow:

> 1. When our Lord and Master Jesus Christ said, "Repent" [Matt. 4:17], he willed the entire life of believers to be one of penance.
> 2. This word cannot be understood as referring to the sacrament of penance, that is, confession and satisfaction, as administered by the clergy.[8]

Although the positions of these early reformers differed in many respects, they all challenged absolutionism and taught the primary importance of contrition and faith in divine reconciliation. In a letter written to Marguerite on March 6, 1522, Guillaume Briçonnet, her spiritual director, shows his affinity with them:

> Mais tant est Dieu beneficque donnateur et liberal qu'il ne reste que à demander que n'ayons tout. Qui demande obtient ("Dixi: confitebor adversum me injusticiam meam et tu remisisti impietatem peccati mei") [Ps. 31.5]. Qui demande pardon de ses pechéz par vraie repandance et foy, ilz sont pardonnéz avant que les confesser. Ce n'est à dire pourtant qu'il ne faille les confesser; mais est necessaire qui a le temps et opportunité. (1.182, no. 36)[9]

Briçonnet is clearly a contritionist. Forgiveness is an issue resolved solely between an accepting God and a contrite, believing penitent who asks for it. Yet, Briçonnet maintains a moderate position by adding the last sentence. Confession, presented almost as an afterthought ("pourtant") and in a double negative phrase, is necessary, but that necessity is attenuated by circumstance.

The *Heptameron*'s critique of sacramental confession reflects the Reformers' position. By reworking the same basic plot in all of the confession stories, Marguerite criticizes the absolutionists and challenges the sacerdotal role in repentance and justification. In story 41, after the priest refuses her absolution, "[l]a damoiselle, se leva de devant luy, ayant la conscience bien troublée, car elle estoit si jeune, qu'elle avoit paour d'avoir failly, au refuz qu'elle avoit faict au pere" (284;378). At Christmas mass, when the countess and her retinue prepare to receive communion—the narrator calls it the *corpus Domini*—the young girl's mother asks her daughter if she is ready. Weeping, she responds "qu'elle n'estoit poinct confessée." In spite of her convictions and her defense of them to the priest, even though she did, in fact, "confess" her sins—she told the priest her "secret"—she feels that the process of her forgiveness is incomplete: "refusant la penitence qu'il m'a baillée, m'a refusé aussi l'absolution" (284;378). Her words imply her understanding that absolution depends on her acceptance of the penance that the priest imposes. Such a notion was vehemently contested by the Reformers, who viewed confessional penance as an erroneous assertion that good works could help a Christian merit salvation. The phrase *corpus Domini* links the girl's rejection of the confessor's body with her exclusion from receiving communion, the body of Christ. The priest is inappropriately confused with Christ, which is just what Reformers said happened in absolutionist confession.

If the young woman's youth gives her a troubled conscience about these issues, a worry shared by many Christians according to Reformers like Luther, her mother's understanding of the situation is more incisive: "La mere s'enquist saigement et congneut l'estrange façon de penitence que le beau pere vouloit donner à sa fille; et après l'avoir faict confesser à ung aultre, receurent toutes ensemble" (284;378). In this brief sentence the narrator shows the mother resolving her daughter's problem, a problem created by a "beau pere." The mother becomes the agent of her daughter's successful confession to another priest and thereby makes possible her reunion with Christ, the *corpus Domini*. Where the corrupt patriarchal institution excludes the young woman from communion and community, a maternal intervention reconciles her daughter with God, with the church, "la mere saincte Eglise," and with the community of women who "receurent toutes ensemble." The phrase "après l'avoir faict confesser à ung aultre," like Briçonnet's sentence, concedes the necessity of sacramental confession. In both cases, the short references to confession help to moderate the anti-absolutionist tone of the passages, but their brevity seems almost dismissive. We learn nothing of the second priest, "l'aultre," who expedites the penitential process. It is the mother and, at her request, the countess who orchestrate the final justice of the story:

> Et, retournée la contesse de l'eglise, la dame d'honneur lui feit la plaincte du prescheur, dont elle fut bien marrye et estonnée, veue la bonne oppinion qu'elle avoit de luy. Mais son courroux ne la peult garder, qu'elle ne rist bien fort, veu la nouvelleté de la penitence. Si est-ce que le rire n'empescha pas aussy, qu'elle ne le feit prendre et battre en sa cuisine, où à force de verges, il confessa la verité. (284;378)

The countess, a woman of authority, in a comic inversion of penitential practices, makes the priest go to confession in her kitchen. In return for the novel penance he had proposed, she has inflicted upon him a common medieval penance, flagellation. The *verges*, rods or switches—but *verge* is also a slang word for penis—recall the *corde* that the priest wanted to attach to the woman's body. The priest is beaten at his own game by a woman who, although angry, laughs. Her laughter stands in contrast to the young woman's earlier tears. We might say that her laughter wipes away those tears, because it is through the countess's intervention that the victim sees the villain brought to justice. The laughter punctuates a sentence that began with the tearful young woman's decisive words refusing to comply with the priest's coercion. As Bakhtin argues, laughter in the Renaissance always relates "to the freedom of the spirit, and to the freedom of speech."[10] The story ends with women on top.

*   *   *

The *Heptameron* troubles the categorical distinction between silent, confined, and sexually chastened women on the one hand, and outspoken, public, and sexually wanton women on the other. The stories and discussions examine many different cases of vocal and of silent women, show different outcomes, and make different judgments. In story 41, for example, the woman's speech in an ecclesiastically approved context, her confessing of her sins to a priest, gets her into trouble. The narrative emphasizes that the priest is aroused by hearing her story: "Et, après qu'elle eut tout dict ce qu'elle sçavoit, congneut le beau pere quelque chose de son secret; qui luy donna envie et hardiesse de luy bailler une penitence non accoustumée" (284;377). This is no Petrarchan *innamoramento*; the narrator records no visual details about the young woman. Only the priest is, ironically, *beau*.

Eros works through the ears, here and in all the confession stories, thereby foregrounding woman's voice.[11]

However, if the woman unwittingly ensnares herself through her speech, she also uses it to her advantage. She speaks out to defend her chastity and her autonomy.[12] The clarity and force of the woman's short speech is quite striking, especially since the narrative frames it by details that emphasize her emotional distress: her tears, her troubled conscience, her youth, her fears ("en pleurant . . . ayant la conscience bien troublée, car elle estoit si jeune, qu'elle avoit paour . . .") (284;378). Nothing in her speech betrays that emotional state. Her single sentence seems somehow implausible. It merits reexamination:

> —"Je use de la confession," dist la fille, "comme l'Eglise le commande, et veulx bien recepvoir l'absolution et faire la penitence, mais je ne veulx poinct que vous y mectiez les mains; car, en ceste sorte, je refuse vostre penitence."

The grammatical structure of the sentence indicates that the young woman is in dauntless control. She utters a complex series of six clauses and delivers them in flawless grammatical form. All of the independent clauses have active verbs in the first person singular; the word *je* occurs three times. Of the four first-person verbs, all in the unattenuated present tense, the first declares that the woman is the agent in the confessional process, supported by church authority. The next two express decisive positions of the woman's will. With the final clause, she refuses the priest's coercion. The clauses are clearly connected by conjunctions that express a logical sequence of thought leading up to the final refusal. Recalling that, at least since Augustine, the word *confession* has had two meanings—to declare one's beliefs and to acknowledge one's sins—we can see that the woman confesses in the sentence. This is not the discourse of an intimidated victim nor of a woman whom cultural conventions have succeeded in silencing. As is generally true in the *Heptameron*, the story gives us practically no detail that would help us discuss the woman's character development. Indeed, the very notion of character development, as modern readers understand that concept, can be applied to Renaissance texts only at great risk of anachronism.[13] But, for that very reason, the young woman's eloquent rebuff of the confessor calls for comment. It is as if someone else were helping her here—lending her a voice, so to speak—someone who anticipates the subsequent intervention of her mother and of the countess of Aiguemont. It is as if, we might argue, there has been "emphasis added."

In her essay by that title, Nancy Miller explores the ways in which women novelists tend to shape their plots differently than men do. Responding to Freud's 1908 essay, "The Relation of the Poet to Daydreaming," she asks, "Now, if the plots of male fiction chart the daydreams of an ego that would be invulnerable, what do the plots of female fiction reveal?" She concludes that female fiction does not reveal a consistent model, but she identifies a category of "women writers" in contrast to what George Eliot referred to pejoratively as "lady novelists." Women writers assert egoistic desires that arise from a repressed impulse to power. Their works articulate "a fantasy of power that would revise the social grammar in which women are never defined as subjects; a fantasy of power that disdains a sexual exchange in which women can participate only as objects of circulation." Their fictions express a sense of invulnerability in ways that may seem implausible, in "modalities of implausibility."[14]

The tearful young woman's decisive speech is just such an implausibility. From a position of vulnerability she asserts her right to subjectivity. Her ego prevails over that of her confessor. And if evangelical doctrine aids and abets her in establishing her integrity against the institution of absolutionism, she is equally strengthened in her egoistic stance by another woman, by the author of her story, Marguerite de Navarre. Margaret Miles has argued that, in representing the naked female body, male artists have generally deprived woman of subjectivity.[15] The *Heptameron* often depicts situations where a woman's subjectivity is denied or stifled by another character. However, the book frequently dramatizes a struggle in which a woman defends her subjectivity aided not only by other characters but by a subtle form of authorial intervention. In story 41, that intervention, the emphasis added, begins well before that of the young woman's mother and then of her mistress, the countess of Aiguemont—a woman who is herself in the service of another woman, named, perhaps not coincidentally, Marguerite.[16]

If the saving intervention of the two women does not occur until the end of the story, someone has prepared us for it right from the start, with the story's opening lines: "L'année que madame Marguerite d'Autriche vint à Cambray, de la part de l'Empereur son nepveu, pour traicter la paix entre luy et le Roy Très Chrestien, de la part duquel se trouva sa mere madame Loïse de Savoie; et estoit en la compaignye de la dicte dame Marguerite la comtesse d'Aiguemont" (283;377). By introducing the story in the context of the 1529 Peace of Cambrai, the "Paix des Dames," the narrator evokes for the reader women who replace men in traditional roles of power, who intervene to promote harmony in a world of discord.[17] These are women—

including Marguerite de Navarre's own mother, Louise de Savoie—who speak in public from a position of strength. The story not only ends but also begins with women on top. It is framed by female authority, and that frame surges into the voice of the young woman alone with her confessor "en une chapelle bien fermée" (283;377), a woman standing up to ecclesiastical authority and transgressing the rule of female silence.[18] Although Saffredent is the fictional narrator of story 41, we can read that tale and its women characters as a self-figuration of the author, Marguerite de Navarre.

That is not to say, in facile *roman à clef* fashion, that the *Heptameron*'s characters are masks that cryptically convey portions of Marguerite de Navarre's biography. Such an attitude, like the once commonly-held notion that Parlamente is in some way Marguerite, clouds more important issues. It is more fruitful to examine the work's textual processes: how the author took the raw material of her *véritables histoires* and shaped them into *nouvelles*; how she infused plot and characters with the signature of her own experience and convictions. Nancy Miller quotes Virginia Woolf on George Eliot in the *Common Reader*: "Her self-consciousness is always marked when her heroines say what she herself would have said" (Miller, 39). Although we can only make informed speculations about what Marguerite herself would have said, what we do know about her suggests that her authorial subjectivity speaks decisively through the young woman's words.

In several ways, that woman's plight figures Marguerite's own experience as a writer. One of her earliest poems, *Le Miroir de l'âme pecheresse*, was condemned by the ecclesiastical authorities of the Sorbonne. In spite of that attempted suppression, she continued to write mystical poetry, a genre that has been recognized as a voice of dissent.[19] In so doing she acknowledged her affinity with another Marguerite, Marguerite Porete, a woman who was burned at the stake in 1310 for refusing to abjure the radical mysticism expressed, or more precisely, confessed in her *Miroir des simples âmes*. Marguerite de Navarre extols the author of that *Miroir* in her longest mystical poem, *Les Prisons*.[20] The mystical voice both confesses belief and confesses sin directly and powerfully to God and reader, often outside of and in conflict with ecclesiastical authority. In his study of mystical discourse, Michel de Certeau argues that the church used sacramental confession to correct and control the subversive voice of mysticism.[21] And in her own mirror poem, *Speculum de l'autre femme*, Luce Irigaray describes the woman mystic's confessor as an antagonist in her relationship with God: "Therefore, she is condemned by confessors or inexperienced voyeurs who are horrified to see and hear her."[22]

Throughout her life Marguerite worked from her often tenuous position of power as the king's sister to protect other Reformers and enable them freely to confess their beliefs. According to a letter written in 1555 by her daughter, Jeanne d'Albret, the physical threat to her free expression followed Marguerite even into the intimacy of her immediate family:

> The said queen [was] warned by her late brother the King, François of good and glorious memory, my much honored uncle, not to get any new doctrines in her head [*mettre en cervelle dogmes nouveaux*] so that from then on she confined herself to amusing stories [*romans joviaux*]. Besides, I well remember how long ago, the late King, my most honored father . . . surprised the said Queen when she was praying with the ministers Roussel and Farel, and how with great annoyance he slapped her right cheek and forbade her sharply to meddle in matters of doctrine. He shook a stick at me which cost me many bitter tears and has kept me fearful and compliant until after they had both died.[23]

The letter is intriguingly suggestive about the cause of Marguerite's genre shift from mystical poetry to *nouvelles*. For our immediate purposes, the account of fraternal duress and of wife and child abuse in the royal family casts a new light on the portrayal of women's discourse in the *Heptameron*. If it appeared to Jeanne d'Albret that François I's attempt at intimidation had worked, we know that Marguerite's move to *romans joviaux* did not stifle her ideological voice, nor did it cause her to abandon mystical poetry. And if her biological daughter was made fearful and compliant by a physically abusive father, Marguerite gave voice to fictional daughters whose resolute discourse brought down the most domineering of fathers. Rolandine, in story 21, is the most eloquent of those daughters, and the young woman in story 41, who thwarts "le beau pere" her confessor, is one of Rolandine's sisters in spirit.[24]

*   *   *

The confession stories further dramatize women's enclosure by emphasizing the physical confinement and secret nature of the confessional space. The narrator of story 41 notes that the women's confessions were heard "en une chappelle bien fermée, afin que la confession fut plus secrette . . ." (283;377). The detail of the enclosed chapel would have signaled to an early Reformation audience that the priest was motivated more by concupiscence than by concern for the young woman's privacy. Allusions to closed secret spaces were common in the ecclesiastical admonitions against sexual solicitation during confession.

Jean Gerson's stern warning about rapacious wolves in corners,[25] that I quote as the epigraph to this chapter, is echoed by Bishop Robert of Aquino: "Nam ego nescio laudare illos qui audiunt confessiones mulierum in locis secretis, in cameris, in angulis latebrosis in quibus etiam quandoque et saepe qui boni et justi creduntur ad enormissima sacrilegia et vitupera-biles dissolutiones labuntur" (quoted in Lea, 1.394–95). Confessionals, structures in which a grill or screen separated the confessor from the penitent, were instituted by the church later in the sixteenth century not so much to protect the privacy of the penitent as to prevent such *enormissima sacrilegia et vituperabiles dissolutiones*.

The reference to the enclosed chapel "afin que la confession fut plus secrette," articulates the figurative relationship between the spatial enclo-sure and the material of the confession itself—*son secret*, what the woman told the priest. The story also makes it clear that *son secret* stands for the woman's sexuality as well, since the priest assigned his invasive penance only after he "cogneut . . . quelque chose de son secret" (284;377). Finally, *son secret* refers to the woman's relationship to narrative, to her right to tell her own story.

Absolutionist confession gave priests the power to manipulate a peni-tent's narrative. Although official church doctrine discouraged prurient questioning, some penitential manuals encouraged confessors to ask de-tailed, voyeuristic questions that forced the penitent to tell his or her story in specific ways.[26] Confession required a mastery of rhetoric, because peni-tents had to persuade the confessor to grant them absolution. The shaping of their narratives, the way they told their *secrets*, was a central aspect of that rhetoric.[27] Story 41 portrays the young woman as a storyteller whose narrative arouses the confessor's erotic desire. Her rhetoric has an unin-tended effect. Or we might say that the priest is a bad reader. He imposes a lascivious interpretation on the woman's narrative, much as Hircan often does in reacting to another's stories.[28] At the same time the story, by its narrative structure, eschews the probing, voyeuristic invasion of the peni-tential manuals. The young woman's *secret* remains secret: we never read the story that the confessor heard. It is as if the person who shaped story 41's narrative respected the seal of confession, the rule forbidding confessors to reveal what they had heard from penitents. Within story 41 is an ellipsis, the absent story which arouses the priest's erotic desire and generates the story we are reading. The *chapelle bien fermée* where the young woman's secret emerges reminds us that closed spaces are where narrative is born. The closed chapel is, like a Russian doll, found within another closed space: "dedans ce beau pré le long de la riviere du Gave, où les arbres sont si foeillez que le soleil ne sçauroit percer l'ombre ny eschauffer la frescheur; là, assiz à noz aises, dira chascun quelque histoire qu'il aura veue ou bien oy dire à quelque homme digne de foy" (Prologue, 10;69).

And the libidinous priest is not far removed from the storytellers, who agree on their pastime after hearing Hircan's suggestion that they spend the afternoons making love. As Peter Brooks reminds us in *Reading for the Plot*, "Desire is always there at the start of a narrative, often in a state of initial arousal, often having reached a state of intensity such that movement must be created, action undertaken, change begun."[29] The opening sentence of the prologue to the second day illustrates Brooks's assertion: "Le lendemain, se leverent en grand desir de retourner au lieu où le jour precedent avoyent eu tant de plaisir; car chascun avoit son compte si prest, qu'il leur tardoit qu'il ne fust mis en lumiere" (87;155).

The complex dynamic among eros, secret, and narrative is the mainspring of the *Heptameron*.[30] Here narration is figured by an absence, by a story told but not recorded. The young woman's *secret* and, indeed, all of story 41 call attention to a dark, sheltered place ("le soleil ne sçauroit percer l'ombre ny eschauffer la frescheur") that figures early modern woman's narrative; a cave-like space that while appearing hollow, is productive: "Car Nature leurs a dedans le corps posé en lieu secret et intestin un animal, un membre, lequel n'est es hommes, on quel quelques foys sont engendrées certaines humeurs salses, nitreuses, bauracineuses, acres, mordicantes, lancinantes, chatouillantes amerement" (Rabelais, *TL*, 32).[31]

The physician Rondibilis's garrulous and misogynist declamation on women in the *Tiers Livre* contains one of the more colorful Renaissance descriptions of the uterus as *animal avidum generandi*.[32] Appropriately, his speech is followed by a series of stories that interrupt the progression of Panurge's consultations. Occupying chapters thirty-three and thirty-four, the stories "dilate" Rabelais's narrative before it returns in chapter thirty-five to the counsel of Trouillogan.[33] All three of the stories betray fear of women out of control: the feast of Cuckoldry evokes unbridled female sexual desire, while the nuns of Coingnaufond (another enclosed space) and the mute wife reflect popular versions of female garrulity. The second of these tells of nuns who confess their sins to each other and whose respect for the seal of confession the pope tests by leaving in their care ("en quelque lieu sceur et secret" *TL*, 34) a sort of Pandora's box which they waste no time in opening. The farce of the mute wife features a husband who first desires to hear his wife's voice, but who, when she is cured and becomes garrulous, regrets the satisfaction of that desire. When the doctor who cured her muteness tells him that there is no cure "contre cestuy interminable parlement de femme," the husband chooses to become deaf.

This brief dilation out of the *Heptameron* and into the *Tiers Livre*, a work published in 1546 and dedicated by Rabelais to Marguerite de Navarre, invites comparison between two figurations of the womb relating to narrative. The form of the *Heptameron* suggests dilation, "cestuy interminable parlement de femme" (*TL*, 34). It is no doubt going too far to see in these words an allusion to Marguerite's book and her leading *devisante*.[34] But, as a corrective to Roland Barthes's model of narrative, and to the aspects of Peter Brooks's use of that model that similarly tend to gender narrative as masculine, the texts under consideration here recognize, albeit differently, a feminine narrative principle.[35] Looking ahead, it is interesting to recall that for the subject matter of the earliest novels, women authors in the seventeenth century turned to the secret inner desires of their female protagonists.[36] The *Heptameron* eschews sexism in its figurations of narrative; men as well as women are presented as internal narrators: Bernage in story 32; the duke of Burgundy in 70; the widow in 4, whom Brantôme identified as Marguerite; the naked narrator in 62.[37] But the confession stories as a group chronicle the larger emergence in the *Heptameron* of an *animal avidum narrandi*, of woman's narrative voice, and, as we shall see, of one woman's authorial voice within the generally inhospitable climate of early-Reformation France.

∗   ∗   ∗

Focusing on the details that I have emphasized in story 41, the shortest of the confession stories, helps us to delineate problems of narrative, authority, and gender that emerge in the longest one, story 22, the story of Marie Héroet. The same elements of enclosure, coercion, spoken resistance, reprisal, and ultimate vindication recur in that story, as if it were a rewriting and elaboration of the shorter one. Erotic reaction to the woman's voice is more explicitly detailed: "Marie Heroet, dont la parolle estoit si doulce et agreable, qu'elle promectoit le visaige et le cueur estre de mesme. Parquoy, seullement pour l'ouyr fut esmeu en une passion d'amour" (177; 256). The family drama is more complex, because along with the young outspoken daughter, the concupiscent, threatening "father" ("Je suis votre pere," 181;261), and the powerful, rescuing mother, there are two surrogate mothers, one good, one evil, represented by the two abbesses, a good father confessor who is destroyed by the bad one, and finally, one brother who mediates in the mother's rescue of the daughter. That rescue is effected through the intervention of "la Royne de Navarre," who, like the countess of Aiguemont, hears the offending priest's "confession" and reestablishes order in the end (184–85;264). Marie Héroet strikingly figures woman's appropriation of narrative, because she writes her story after she has been silenced and negotiates her own liberation by slipping her text to her brother, who, although nameless in the story, probably represents another writer, the poet Antoine Héroet, a courtier of Marguerite de Navarre.[38]

However, I would like to leave Marie Héroet for now and focus instead on the last story in the collection as we have it. Story 72 takes place in a hospital. One night when a poor man is dying there, a monk arrives to hear the man's confession and administer extreme unction. A young nun stays to help the monk assist the dying man and prepare his body for burial. The narrator says that the nun feared the monk "plus que le prieur ny aultre, pour la grande austerité dont il usoit tant en parolles que en vie" (425;540). As they enshroud the cadaver, austerity gives way to desire:

> commencea le religieux à parler de la misere de la vie et de la bienheureuseté de la mort; en ces propos passerent la minuyct. La pauvre fille ententivement escoutoit ces devotz propos, et le regardant les larmes aux oeilz: ou il print si grand plaisir, que, parlant de la vie advenir, commencea à l'ambrasser, comme s'il eut eu envye de la porter entre ses bras en paradis. La pauvre fille, escoutant ces propos, et l'estimant le plus devost de la compaignie, ne l'osa refuser. Quoy voiant, ce meschant moyne, en parlant tousjours de Dieu, paracheva avecq elle l'oeuvre que soubdain le diable leur mit au cueur. (425; 540–41)

Unlike Marie Héroet and the young woman at Marguerite of Aiguemont's court, the naive young nun is silent. She fails to distinguish between the monk's improper advances and the ecclesiastical authority he represents, but above all, her fear makes her fail to speak out and challenge him.

It is worth noting that, unlike stories 41 and 22, in which the young women come from families of wealth and status, in story 72, the young nun is a *pauvre fille* both affectively and economically. She is intimidated by the priest's reputation as *devost* and *austere* and overcome more than seduced by the discourse he misappropriates from his duties as a preacher ("parlant de la vie advenir . . . parlant tousjours de Dieu").[39] In contrast to his speaking, she only listens. "[E]scoutant ces propos," she is as passive as the dying man who, "peu à peu perdit la parolle." The narrator suggests that the priest perverts the pastoral duty he was called to perform for the dying man and lustfully misdirects it toward the nun ("comme si 'il eut eu envye de la porter entre ses bras en paradis"). The narrator records no reaction from the young nun except her listening, while the priest continues to speak, "l'asseurant que ung peché secret n'estoit poinct imputé devant Dieu, et que deux personnes non liez ne peuvent offencer en tel cas, quant il n'en vient poinct de scandalle; et que, pour l'eviter, elle se gardast bien de le confesser à aultre que à luy" (425;540).

Here again the word *secret* is highly resonant. The *peché secret* refers to their sexual intercourse, the sin of fornication. Such a sin, the priest main-tains, is not blameworthy before God; its "secrecy" somehow protects them from divine reproach.[40] However, this time, we as readers witness the secret. We know that the monk is the agent of the "secret," and although the sexual transgression does not occur in the context of confession, he lodges it there so that he may control its narrative.[41]

Leaving the monk, the nun goes into a chapel dedicated to Our Lady, and there she speaks for the first time in the story, addressing her words to another woman: "Vierge Marie!"[42] Those words remind her "qu'elle avoit perdu ce tiltre de virginité, sans force ny amour, mais par une sotte craincte" (425;541). That thought makes her weep bitterly.[43] The priest, overhearing her, "se doubta de sa conversion, par laquelle il povoit perdre son plaisir." To prevent that loss, he reproaches her harshly and tells her that "si elle en faisoit conscience, qu'elle se confessast à luy et qu'elle n'y retournast plus, si elle ne vouloit, car l'un et l'autre sans peché estoit en sa liberté." If the priest's argument seems muddled to the reader, it succeeds nevertheless in convincing the nun: "La sotte religieuse, cuydant satisfaire envers Dieu, s'alla confesser à luy, mais pour penitence, il luy jura qu'elle ne pechoit poinct de l'aymer, et que l'eaue benoiste povoit effacer ung tel peccadille. Elle, croyant plus en luy que en Dieu, retourna au bout de quelque temps à luy obeyr; en sorte qu'elle devint grosse" (426;541).

As in story 41, the confessor uses penance as a means of sexual coer-cion. The practice of imposing penance as part of the ritual of penitence grew from a belief that sinners must not only be forgiven but must also pay for their sins in the form of some kind of punishment. The nun confuses the penance with confession itself. Penance was a bone of contention in the early Reformation, not only because it implied the efficacy of good works, but because of the passionately contested practice of indulgences as a means of accelerating the expiatory process. To assign as a penance the repetition of the very sin that had brought the penitent to confession would have required a striking perversion of the confessor's role.

The nun's pregnancy moves her to regret her actions and to accuse the monk. Her dilating womb requires that she tell her story. The first woman she turns to for help fails her: "Elle suplia la prieure de faire chasser hors du monastere ce religieux, sçachant qu'il estoit si fin, qu'il ne fauldroit poinct à la seduire. L'abbesse et le prieur, qui s'accordoient fort bien ensemble, se moquerent d'elle, disans qu'elle estoit assez grande pour se defendre d'un homme, et que celluy dont elle parloit estoit trop homme de bien" (426; 541). The nun then seeks a solution that typifies the superstitious ideas that the Reformers decried: "A la fin, à force d'impétuosité, pressée du remords de la conscience, leur demanda congé d'aller à Romme, car elle pensoit, en confessant son peché aux piedz du pape, recouvrer sa virginité" (426;541).

Filled with remorse, the nun has what the contritionists considered the requisite disposition for divine forgiveness, but her request indicates that she trusts only absolution, and only papal absolution at that. The extent of her confidence in the pope's power shows that just as she had shown misplaced faith in the priest, "croyant plus en luy que en Dieu," she attributes to the pope god-like powers.[44] Seizing the opportunity to be rid of her, the prior and prioress send the nun on her way. But it is not the pope who saves her. "Mais Dieu voulut que, elle estant à Lyon, ung soir, après vespres, sur le pupiltre de l'eglise Sainct Jehan, où madame la duchesse d'Alençon, qui depuis fut royne de Navarre, alloit secretement faire quelque neufvaine avecq trois ou quatre de ses femmes, estant à genoulx devant le crucifix, ouyt monter en hault quelque personne" (426;542). Seeing that the person is a nun,

> afin d'entendre ses devotions, se retira la duchesse au coing de l'autel. Et la religieuse, qui pensoit estre seulle, se agenouilla; et, en frappant sa coulpe, se print à pleurer tant, que c'estoit pityé de l'oyr, ne criant sinon: "Helas! mon Dieu, ayez pitié de ceste pauvre pecheresse!" La duchesse, pour entendre que c'estoit, s'approcha d'elle, en luy disant: "M'amye, qu'avez vous, et d'où estes-vous? Qui vous amene en ce lieu cy?" (426–27;542)

Here the nun seeks forgiveness following Briçonnet's advice: admitting her guilt ["frappant sa coulpe"], she asks for pardon directly from God. And as if to illustrate Briçonnet's assurance, "il ne reste que à demander que n'ayons tout. Qui demande obtient . . . ," her prayer is immediately answered. To the *devisants*, who had listened to Oisille read that morning from the "Canonicque de sainct Jehan" (420;535) the scene might well have recalled the words that stand behind Briçonnet's: "Et quelque chose que nous demanderons nous le receverons de luy" (1 John 3:22).[45] It is surely not a coincidence that the scene takes place in the *eglise de Sainct Jehan*. The duchess appears, like a *dea ex machina*, to facilitate the nun's reconciliation with God.

As if to reinforce the remarkable—we might even say implausible—quality of the encounter, the nun unwittingly reveals that the duchess's arrival at that moment is the answer to a yet unuttered prayer. "La pauvre religieuse, qui ne la congnoissoit poinct, luy dist: 'Helas! m'amye, mon malheur est tel, que je n'ay recours que à Dieu, lequel je suplie me donner moien de parler à madame la duchesse d'Alençon, car, à elle seule, je conterai mon affaire, estant asseurée que, s'il y a ordre, elle le trouvera'" (426–27;542). The nun's statement, as indeed the entire exchange between the two women, is striking for both its theological and its narratological implications. Her recognition that her only recourse is God is correct evangelical doctrine. The narrator corroborates that position by introducing the scene in the church as an act of divine providential intervention: "Dieu voulut que. . . ."

In the course of the story the nun has moved from beliefs about repentance and reconciliation that the Reformers attacked: that holy water could efface her sin and that a pilgrimage to Rome could restore her virginity, to the belief that she is totally powerless and that only "Dieu beneficque, donnateur et liberal" will save her. And she respects Briçonnet's admonition that even the pardoned sinner should confess her sins. However, in a curious displacement of hierarchy, she asks God to give her the opportunity both to "confess" her sin and to tell her story ["je conterai mon affaire"] not to a priest but to the duchess of Alençon, and she expresses her assurance that, if there is order to be found in that "affaire," the duchess will find it.

In answering the nun, the duchess creates a fictional double to hide her true identity: "'M'amye,' ce luy dist la duchesse, 'vous povez parler à moy comme à elle, car je suis de ses grandes amyes'" (427;542). It is not entirely clear at this point why the duchess does that, but it makes the nun resist: "'Pardonnez-moy,' dist la religieuse, 'car jamais aultre qu'elle ne saura mon secret.'" The formula "Pardonnez-moy" evokes confession as the nun insists on the duchess's exclusive right to know her secret, to hear her story. "Alors la duchesse luy dist qu'elle povoit parler franchement et qu'elle avoit trouvé ce qu'elle demandoit." The second part of the duchess's statement to the nun makes the reader pause. What is the antecedent of *ce*? Taken generally, the word could simply refer to "her wish," as in the Chilton rendering "her wish was granted" (542). But what wish? If it is the wish to speak to the duchess, *celle* seems more appropriate: she had found the woman she was asking for. *Ce* allows for ambiguity. It could also mean the forgiveness for her sins, the answer to her plea: "mon Dieu, ayez pitié de ceste pauvre pecheresse." The duchess told her that she could speak freely and that she had (already) found what she was asking for. The duchess would then be reassuring her with Briçonnet's message: "Qui demande pardon de ses pechéz par vraie repandance et foy, ils sont pardonnéz avant que les confesser."

The ensuing scene reinforces the image of the duchess as evangelical confessor: "La pauvre femme se gecta à ses piedz, et, après avoir pleuré et cryé luy racompta ce que vous avez ouy de sa pauvreté. La duchesse la reconforta si bien, que, sans lui oster la repentance continuelle de son peché, luy mist hors de l'entendement le voiage de Romme" (427;542).[46] The duchess hears the story of the nun's sin, comforts the sinner and shows a reformer's attitude toward the practice of imposing a penance. She removes the traditional penance of pilgrimage but leaves in place "la repentance continuelle de son peché." The notion of continual repentance recalls Luther's first thesis: "When our Lord and Master Jesus Christ said, 'Repent,' he willed the entire life of believers to be one of penance."

The story ends, as do stories 22 and 41, with a woman of authority reestablishing order, helping the female victim to resume normal life in a community of women and having the wicked priest punished. The duchess sends the nun back to her convent, "avecq des lettres à l'evesque du lieu, pour donner ordre de faire chasser ce religieux scandaleux" (427;543). She exercises her authority by writing letters that give an order. The word *ordre* in the story's final sentence echoes the nun's statement that she would tell her story, "mon affaire," only to the duchess of Alençon, "estant asseurée que, s'il y a ordre, elle le trouvera" (426–27;542). The duchess has indeed put the nun's affairs back in order. But her task of finding and giving order assumes a larger dimension in the light of the duchess's double identity: "madame la duchesse d'Alençon, qui depuis fut royne de Navarre" (426; 542). The woman represented in the third person, whose authoritative intervention saves the nun, is of course the author herself, Marguerite de Navarre. The story figures her as consoling confessor and powerful rescuer but just as pointedly as storyteller, as narrator, and as author. A storyteller must learn the secrets of others in order to find the material for her narrative. When Dagoucin introduces "la duchesse d'Alençon, qui depuis fut royne de Navarre," the duchess is hiding her true identity, casting a veil of secrecy about herself as she entered the church: "[elle] alloit secretement faire quelque neufvaine" (426;542). She is entering the secret space of narrative. When she first hears, then sees the nun, she becomes an eaves-dropper: "afin d'entendre ses devotions, se retira la duchesse au coing de l'autel." She thereby enters the intimate space of the nun, "qui pensoit estre seulle." When she hears the pitiful prayer, she approaches the nun, "pour entendre que c'estoit" and asks her a series of questions that will draw out her story. The duchess shows the curiosity of a voyeur, and in that respect she figures all narrators. In this case the nun willingly recounts her *affaire*, but it becomes the story we read only after the duchess has found and given it order ("s'il y a ordre, elle le trouvera," 427;542).

In the discussion opening the day in which this story is told, the narrator says that the *devisants* spent their midday meal "parlans encore de la Journée passée, se defians d'en povoir faire une aussy belle" (421;535). In response to the challenge of creating stories worthy of those in the preced-ing day, "pour y donner ordre, se retirerent chascun en son logis." The *devisants* withdraw into a private space in order to begin the task of fabula-tion, the work of giving order to the secrets they have found in the hidden corners of human experience. When the last sentence of the story describes the duchess giving an order that will punish the priest, it is not just a coincidence that the words echo those of the day's prologue. Political authority and narration are linked in the expression *donner ordre*, just as the politically powerful female figure in the story and the author of the *Hep-tameron* are linked. Dagoucin, the fictional narrator of the story, acknowl-edges the duchess in the next line of text, the first line of the discussion following the story: "Je tiens ce compte de la duchesse mesme" (427;543).

The phrase "la duchesse d'Alençon, qui depuis fut royne de Navarre" heralds the subtle but crucial dynamic between character, narrator, and author in the *Heptameron*. Just as the duchess hides her identity from the nun, presenting herself to the woman through the mediation of a fiction ("vous povez parler à moy comme à elle, car je suis de ses grandes amyes"), Marguerite de Navarre the author conceals her authorial identity from the reader and represents herself through the mediation of a powerful female authority figure, the historical character, Marguerite de Navarre. Whoever is responsible, author or editor, for making this story the final one in the collection, it is fitting that the *Heptameron*'s *nouvelles* end with such a striking signature of authorial control.

The confession stories portray strong, maternal women rescuing vulnerable younger women from threatening paternal figures.[47] And these stories reflect the relationship between the authorial voice of Marguerite de Navarre and the political authority of the same name represented in the *Heptameron*. One of the best-kept secrets in that book is the identity of its authorial voice. Just as the tearful young girl needed the help, first of her mother, then of the laughing countess, just as the nun sought help from the duchess, so the authorial voice in the *Heptameron*, an unobtrusive voice, seeks and appropriates authority by portraying powerful women characters, especially one named Marguerite de Navarre. That character becomes a signature of authority and a strategy allowing the author to remain anonymous. She is an advocate, "une grande amye" of the authorial voice. But, like the invisible hand that operates a puppet, the authorial voice is the stronger of the two, because she controls and manipulates self-representation. Like the untold but telling *secret* in story 41, the near-silent authorial voice of the *Heptameron* is a powerful absence.

If François I thought he had successfully bullied his sister into silence (thereby doing just the opposite of what Marie Héroet's brother did by carrying his sister's text forth into the public world), he underestimated her rhetorical strategies.[48] Her *romans jovials* continue the tradition of her mystical poetry by forcefully advocating *dogmes nouveaux*. The author silences herself so that she can speak louder.

Notes

As co-editor of this book I have been privileged to read the chapters of the other contributors while I was revising my own. I have tried to acknowledge particular debts, but my thinking has profited in a more general way from all of them.

1. Several important studies have called attention to the linking of women's speech and sexual licentiousness throughout history: R. Howard Bloch, "Medieval Misogyny," *Representations* 20 (Fall 1987): 1–24; Ann Rosalind Jones, *The Currency of Eros: Women's Love Lyric in Europe, 1540–1620* (Bloomington: Indiana University Press, 1990); Patricia Parker, *Literary Fat Ladies: Rhetoric, Gender and Property* (London and New York: Methuen, 1987); Margaret Ferguson, "A Room Not Their Own: Renaissance Women as Readers and Writers," in *The Comparative Perspective on Literature: Approaches to Theory and Practice*, ed. C. Koelb and S. Noakes (Ithaca, N.Y.: Cornell University Press, 1988), 93–116; Peter Stallybrass, "Patriarchal Territories: The Body Enclosed," in *Rewriting the Renaissance: The Discourses of Sexual Difference in Early Modern Europe*, ed. Margaret W. Ferguson, Maureen Quilligan,

and Nancy J. Vickers (Chicago: University of Chicago Press, 1986), 123–42. Constance Jordan's thorough analysis of the Renaissance texts that codified women's enclosure as well as those which defended women is extremely valuable. See *Renaissance Feminism: Literary Texts and Political Models* (Ithaca, N.Y.: Cornell University Press, 1990).

2. See Natalie Zemon Davis's essay, "Women on Top" in *Society and Culture in Early Modern France* (Stanford, Calif.: Stanford University Press, 1965–75), 124–51.

3. The literature on the history of sacramental confession is vast. For an accessible overview from a position sympathetic to but not uncritical of the church, see John T. McNeill, *A History of the Cure of Souls* (New York: Harper & Brothers, 1951), esp. chaps. 4–8. Lea's *A History of Auricular Confession in the Latin Church* (see note 1) is factually detailed but markedly anticlerical in tone. The article "Pénitence," by E. Amann and A. Michel in the *Dictionnaire de théologie catholique* 1st ed. (Paris, 1909–1950), vol. 12.1, 722–1127, is very informative, as is Jaroslav Pelikan's *The Christian Tradition: A History of the Development of Doctrine*, vol. 4, *Reformation of Church and Dogma (1300–1700)* (Chicago: The University of Chicago Press, 1984). Jean Delumeau considers the 1216 Lateran decree a turning point in the history of Western mentality and examines confessional manuals and practices in *L'Aveu et le pardon: Les Difficultés de la confession XIIIᵉ–XVIIIᵉ siècle* (Paris: Fayard, 1990). The study which most helped me in this chapter is Thomas Tentler's *Sin and Confession on the Eve of the Reformation* (Princeton, N.J.: Princeton University Press, 1977).

4. See Tentler, *Sin and Confession*, 18–27; Delumeau, *L'Aveu et le pardon*, 51–56.

5. See McNeill, *A History of the Cure of Souls*, 147–48; Lea, *Auricular Confession* 1.382–93; Tentler, *Sin and Confession*, 104.

6. Paul Chilton uses *cordelier* as an example of the difficulties in translating the *Heptameron*. See the introduction to his translation, p. 29.

7. Early Reformers, like John Wycliffe and John Hus, denied the priest's role and the necessity of sacramental confession for complete repentence and reconciliation. In 1415 the Council of Constance condemned such positions. *Dictionnaire de théologie catholique*, vol. 12.1, col. 1051–52.

8. *Martin Luther's 95 Theses: With the Pertinent Documents from the History of the Reformation*, ed. Kurt Aland (Saint Louis, Mo.: Concordia Publishing House, 1967), 50.

9. Guillaume Briçonnet and Marguerite de Navarre, *Correspondance (1521–1524)*, eds. Christine Martineau, Michel Veissière, and Henry Heller, 2 vols. (Geneva: Droz, Travaux d'humanisme et Renaissance), I, 1975; II, 1979, vol. I, p. 182. For additional documents reflecting early-Reformation beliefs about confession, documents that Marguerite would have known, see Myra D. Orth, "Radical Beauty: Marguerite de Navarre's Illuminated Protestant Catechism and Confession," forthcoming in the *Sixteenth Century Journal*.

10. Mikhail Bakhtin, *Rabelais and His World*, trans. Helene Iswolsky (Cambridge, Mass.: M.I.T. Press, 1968), 70.

11. Margaret R. Miles has described a shift in emphasis from the visual to the auditory in Reformation theology and culture. See *Image as Insight: Visual Under-*

standing in Western Christianity and Secular Culture (Boston: Beacon Press, 1985), chap. 5, "Vision and Sixteenth-Century Protestant and Catholic Reforms," 95–125.

12. On chastity and virginity as strategies of independence in the early church, see Joyce E. Salisbury, *Church Fathers, Independent Virgins* (London/New York: Verso, 1991); V. Burruss *Chastity as Autonomy: Women in the Stories of Apocryphal Acts*, (Lewiston, N.Y.: E. Mellen Press, 1987). With allowances made for the different time period under consideration, the general conclusions of these studies seem applicable to women and the church in Marguerite's time.

13. On character and characterization in the early sixteenth century, see Daniel Russell, "Conception of Self, Conception of Space, and Generic Convention: An Example from the *Heptameron*," *Sociocriticism* 4–5 (1986–87): 159–83; and Russell's article in this book, "Some Ways of Structuring Character in the *Heptameron*."

14. Nancy K. Miller, *Subject to Change* (New York: Columbia University Press, 1988), 25–46.

15. In *Carnal Knowing: Female Nakedness and Religious Meaning in the Christian West* (Boston: Beacon Press, 1989; rpt. New York: Vintage Books, 1991), Margaret R. Miles examines the way that artists representing the naked female body generally deprived woman of subjectivity.

16. John Bernard notes that some of the stories allude to "a highly placed, titled female who can be viewed as a surrogate for Marguerite" (265). See "Sexual Oppression and Social Justice in Marguerite de Navarre's *Heptaméron*," *Journal of Medieval and Renaissance Studies* 19, no. 2 (1989): 251–81. In story 41 that surrogacy is signaled by the apparent coincidence of Marguerite d'Autriche's name.

17. Cotgrave gives among his definitions of *traicter*: "to deale in, or meddle with, to discourse, debate, or make mention of; also, to covenant, or contract with." Randle Cotgrave, *A Dictionarie of the French and English Tongues*, reproduced from the first edition, London, 1611, intro. William S. Woods (Columbia: University of South Carolina Press, 1950;1968). Peacemaking was one of the few public exercises of power allowed to women. See the catalog of a recent exhibition by H. Diane Russell with Bernadine Barnes, *Eva/Ave: Women in Renaissance and Baroque Prints* (Washington, D.C.: National Gallery of Art; and New York: The Feminist Press at The City University of New York, 1990), 30.

18. Colette Winn has analyzed the rule of silence and its transgressions in "La Loi du non-parler dans l'*Heptaméron* de Marguerite de Navarre," *Romance Quarterly* 33 (1986): 157–68.

19. See Stephen Ozment, *Mysticism and Dissent* (New Haven, Conn.: Yale University Press, 1973); Sarah Beckwith, "A Very Material Mysticism: The Medieval Mysticism of Margery Kempe," in *Medieval Literature: Criticism, Ideology and History*, ed. David Aers (Brighton, England: The Harvester Press, 1986), 34–57; and Michel de Certeau, *La Fable mystique, 1: XVIᵉ–XVIIᵉ siècle* (Paris: Gallimard, 1982).

20. See Marguerite de Navarre, *Les Prisons*, ed. Simone Glasson (Geneva: Droz, 1978), Introduction, 45–53; and 3.11.1313–1375; Robert D. Cottrell, *The Grammar of Silence: A Reading of Marguerite de Navarre's Poetry* (Washington, D.C.: The Catholic University Press, 1986), 299–302; Jean Dagens, "Le 'Miroir des simples âmes' et Marguerite de Navarre," in *La Mystique rhénane*, Colloque de Strasbourg, May 16–19, 1961 (Paris: Presses universitaires de France, 1963), 281–89.

21. "Les campagnes ecclésiastiques de la fin du Moyen Age développent les procédures qui font 'revenir' les expériences 'mystiques' dans le champ de l'institution visible. Le ressort commun de ces méthodes—leur modèle technique—semble être la confession." Michel de Certeau, *Fable*, 117.

22. And again: "Her confessor will not always lend an approving ear to this," Luce Irigaray, *Speculum of the Other Woman* (Ithaca, N.Y.: Cornell University Press, 1985; trans. of *Speculum de l'autre femme* [Paris: Editions de Minuit, 1974]), 198, 202.

23. Jeanne d'Albret to the Vicomte de Gourdon, August 22, 1555. B.N., F fr 17,044, fol. 446. Translated and quoted in part by Nancy Lyman Roelker in *Queen of Navarre: Jeanne d'Albret* (Cambridge, Mass.: Harvard University, The Belknap Press, 1968), 127.

24. John Lyons's analysis of Rolandine's discourse first drew attention to the women in the *Heptameron* who speak forcefully in response to others' attempts to limit and control them. See his *Exemplum: the Rhetoric of Example in Early Modern France and Italy* (Princeton, N.J.: Princeton University Press, 1989), chap. 2, "The *Heptameron* and Unlearning from Example," 72–117. Carla Freccero explores further the politics of voice in "Rewriting the Rhetoric of Desire in the *Heptameron*," in *Contending Kingdoms: Historical Psychological and Feminist Approaches to the Literature of Sixteenth-Century England and France*, ed. Mary-Rose Logan and Peter L. Rudnytsky (Detroit: Wayne State University Press, 1991), 298–312. For a careful reading of how such women might relate to questions of authorial and narrative voice, see Deborah N. Losse, "Authorial and Narrative Voice in the *Heptaméron*," *Renaissance and Reformation*, 23, no. 3 (1987): 223–42. Patricia F. Cholakian has proposed that the entire *Heptameron* is its author's voicing her protest after she was the victim of an attempted rape. See *Rape and Writing in the "Heptaméron" of Marguerite de Navarre* (Carbondale: Southern Illinois University Press, 1991).

25. "Fiat confessio coram oculis omnium, in patente loco, ne subintroeat lupus rapax in angulis suadens agere quae turpe est etiam cogitare." *Orat. in C. Remens.* ann. 1409 (Gousset, Actes etc., 2.657), quoted in Henry Charles Lea's *A History of Auricular Confession in the Latin Church*, 3 vols. (Philadelphia: Lea Brothers and Company, 1896), vol. 1, 394.

26. "Priests were guided on how to lead the penitent through a detailed, specific recollection of each occasion of sin—what prior actions had led up to it, what emotions surged while committing it, when remorse set in, whether the resolve truly was there to avoid a similar temptation in the future." Rudolph Bell, "Telling Her Sins: Male Confessors and Female Penitents in Catholic Reformation Italy," in *That Gentle Strength: Historical Perspectives on Women in Christianity*, ed. Lynda L. Coon, Katherine J. Haldane, and Elisabeth W. Sommer (Charlottesville: University of Virginia Press, 1990), 118. Bell's article contains colorful excerpts from the penitentials. For a more balanced view of the confessional manuals, see Anne Jacobson Schutte, "Consiglio Spirituale e controlo sociale: Manuali per la Confessione stampati in volgare prima della Controriforma," in *Città Italiane del '500 tra Riforma e Controriforma: Atti del Convegno Internazionale di Studi, Lucca, 13–15 ottobre, 1983* (Lucca: Maria Pacini Fazzi Editore, 1988), 45–59. Michel de Certeau argues further that "la confession auriculaire ou privée introduit dans le savoir clérical les dérives cachées du vécu quotidien, tous les escapismes dont les secrets

sont poursuivis, nommés, convoqués sous le nom de 'péchés.' La confession s'in-
sinue dans le dédale des existences, elle les interroge, elle les fait parler, ainsi elle les
exorcise" (*Fable*, 117). See also Tentler, *Sin and Confession*, 88–95.

27. Natalie Zemon Davis argues that similar rhetoric was needed by suppli-
cants petitioning the king for pardon. See *Fiction in the Archives* (Stanford, Calif.:
Stanford University Press, 1987). The situation of a woman using storytelling skills
before a man in order to assure her salvation recalls the narrative frame of *The
Arabian Nights*.

28. Augustine attributes faulty reading of the Bible to a refusal of charity and
"the reign of cupidity." See *On Christian Doctrine*, trans. D. W. Robertson (New
York: Bobbs, Merrill, 1958), 2.41.62 and 3.9.13–10.16.

29. Peter Brooks, *Reading for the Plot* (New York: Vintage Books, 1985), 38.

30. The association of sexuality, narrative, and confession is the focus of
Michel Foucault's *Histoire de la sexualité, 1: La Volonté de savoir* (Paris: Gallimard,
1976). As is often the case with Foucault's illuminating analyses, his time frame
seems inaccurate for the sixteenth century. Foucault places the twilight of frank
expression of sexuality only at the beginning of the seventeenth century. However,
although many sixteenth-century texts might illustrate Foucault's thesis, Montaigne, in his "Sur des vers de Virgile," records his struggles to articulate sexual
experience in a culture that he says has already made it impossible to talk about sex.
See *Les Essais de Montaigne*, ed. Pierre Villey and V. L. Saulnier, 2 vols. (Paris:
Presses Universitaires de France, 1978), vol. 2, pp. 840–97.

31. Rabelais, *Oeuvres complètes*, ed. Pierre Jourda, vol. 1 (Paris: Classiques
Garnier, 1962), 540. Quotations from Rabelais's *Tiers Livre* are cited in the text using
the abbreviation *TL* and chapter number.

32. For an explanation of that anatomical tradition, see Ian Maclean, *The
Renaissance Notion of Woman: A Study in the Fortunes of Scholasticism and Medical
Science in European Intellectual Life* (Cambridge: Cambridge University Press, 1980),
40–42.

33. I call here on Patricia Parker's notion of dilation as a rhetorical trope
associated with women. See *Literary Fat Ladies*, chap. 2, 8–35.

34. Although Tom Conley's and Hope Glidden's chapters in this book encourage me in that direction.

35. Glidden examines Barthes's notion of the probing motivation of narrative
in her chapter in this book. In *Reading for the Plot*, Peter Brooks distinguishes
between a male and female dynamic of plot motivation in nineteenth and twentieth-
century literature. See in particular, chap. 2, "Narrative Desire," 37–61. Susan
Winnet has taken issue with Brooks's gendering anatomy of narrative in "Coming
Unstrung: Women, Men, Narrative, and Principles of Pleasure," *PMLA* 105 (1990):
505–18.

36. John Lyon's paper, "The 'Cueur' in the *Heptaméron*," delivered at the
conference on Marguerite de Navarre held at Duke University in April 1992,
suggested that connection to me. Acts forthcoming, ed. Marcel Tetel.

37. For more on the internal narrators in those stories, see the chapters by
François Rigolot, François Cornilliat and Ullrich Langer, and Hope Glidden in this
book. Response to my paper on the duke of Burgundy as a voyeuristic narrator,

"The Poetics of Desire in *Heptameron 70*," delivered at the Kentucky Foreign Language Conference in 1991, helped me a great deal in this present chapter.

38. See the biographical notice in F. Gohin's critical edition of Antoine Héroet, *Oeuvres poétiques*, Société des Textes Français Modernes (Paris: Cornély, 1909), ix.

39. Cathleen M. Bauschatz argues that the *Heptameron* frequently portrays men as unfit to teach or preach to women. See her contribution to this book, "Voylà, mes dames . . .": Inscribed Women Listeners and Readers in the *Heptameron*."

40. For *Imputé*, Cotgrave gives "Imputed, attributed, ascribed unto; laid unto the charge of" and for "Imputation" he gives "An imputation; reproach, blame, or fault laid to the charge of" (*A Dictionarie of the French and English Tongues*).

41. Late medieval theological debate about the seal of confession argued whether a penitent was morally bound—or morally forbidden—to reveal the name of the partner with whom he or she had committed a sin. The distinctions the priest raises as mitigating circumstances—that their act was not adultery because neither is married and not a serious offense because there was no scandal—echo the refinements found in the penitentials.

42. See François Cornilliat's analysis of this story in "Pas de miracle: La Vierge et Marguerite dans l'*Heptaméron*," *Travaux de Littérature*, forthcoming.

43. Her reaction is understandable. Loss of virginity was considered the greatest catastrophe that could happen to a nun. Virginity, its maintenance and its loss, was a favorite topic in the patristic writings that continued to prescribe monastic life. Saint Jerome's "Letter to Eustochium" gives a chastening description of the end awaiting the woman who fails to protect her virginity. For a study of this tradition in the monastic rules of the Middle Ages, see Jane Tibbetts Schulenburg, "The Heroics of Virginity: Brides of Christ and Sacrificial Mutilation," in *Women in the Middle Ages and the Renaissance: Literary and Historical Perspectives*, ed. Mary Beth Rose (Syracuse, N.Y.: Syracuse University Press, 1986), 29–72.

44. In the patristic literature on virginity and the consequences of its loss, there was doubt that even God could save a fallen virgin. Saint Jerome warns, "although God can do all things, He cannot raise up a virgin after she has fallen." See *The Letters of St. Jerome: Ancient Christian Writers*, trans. Charles Christopher Mierow (Westminster, Md.: Newman Press, 1963) 1.138. Quoted in Schulenburg, "The Heroics of Virginity," 33.

45. 1 John 3:22, *Le Nouveau Testament*, trans. Jacques Lefèvre d'Etaples (Facsimile de la première édition Simon de Colines, 1523, Yorkshire: S.R. Publishers Ltd.; New York: Johnson Reprint Corporation; Paris: Editions Mouton & Co., 1970). John's epistle echoes in turn Matt. 21:22.

46. Briefer suggestions of women assuming the priest's role as confessors include story 67, where a man dies, "n'aiant service ne consolation que de sa femme, laquelle le servoit de medecin et de confesseur" (393–504). Again, in story 25, where the prince's curious sister, presumably a representation of Marguerite de Navarre, seeks information about her brother's secret life: "La seur, qui eut envie de sçavoir quelle congnoissance ce beau pere avoit de la bonté de son frere, l'interrogea si fort, que, en luy baillant ce secret, sous le voile de confession" (206;289).

47. These stories of maternal support provide another dimension of what Carla Freccero has called the *Heptameron*'s "mother-daughter dialogue." See her "Marguerite of Navarre" in *A New History of French Literature*, ed. Denis Hollier (Cambridge, Mass.: Harvard University Press, 1989), 145–48. If, as Freccero notes, the book often depicts maternal authority serving the patriarchal order, it also offers models of maternal figures protecting and empowering young women against that order.

48. Several recent studies have heightened my awareness of such strategies. Annabel Patterson has examined the way censorship pressured English Renaissance writers into developing rhetorical strategies that also led to thematic, formal, and stylistic innovations. Although she does not discuss the *Heptameron*, in her introduction she uses the example of Clément Marot. See *Censorship and Interpretation: The Conditions of Writing and Reading in Early Modern England* (Madison: University of Wisconsin Press, 1984). Alison Weber argues that Teresa of Avila used complex rhetorical strategies to negotiate her place in Inquisition Spain. See *Teresa of Avila and the Rhetoric of Femininity*, (Princeton, N.J.: Princeton University Press, 1990). In a different area, but one that has been very suggestive for my present work, Joan DeJean has shown how Lafayette maintained and manipulated a posture of anonymity surrounding the publication of *La Princesse de Clèves*. See "Lafayette's Ellipses: The Privileges of Anonymity," *PMLA* 99, no. 5 (1984): 884–902. Susan Sniader Lanser's *Fictions of Authority: Women Writers and Narrative Voice* (Ithaca, N.Y.: Cornell University Press, 1992), brings together feminist and narratological theory to analyze the emerging voices of women authors. Finally, Catherine Randall Coats has studied the effect of Calvinist theological conventions on the shaping of d'Aubigné's authorial voice. See *Subverting the System: D'Aubigné and Calvinism*, Sixteenth Century Essays and Studies, vol. 14, Kirksville, Mo.: Sixteenth-Century Journal Publishers, Inc., 1990). All of these studies suggest that examining extra-textual constraints may lead to a richer understanding of the authorial voice in the *Heptameron*.

Philippe de Lajarte

10. The Voice of the Narrators in Marguerite de Navarre's Tales

Of the many problems of narrative roles in the *Heptameron*, this chapter will concentrate on two: First, the various ways in which the voices of the narrators become present and manifest themselves and, second, the relationship between the voices of the storytellers (the fictive authors of the tales) and the voice of the author of the *Heptameron*. Before considering each of these problems, we will define some important terms.

Narrative Utterance and Reception in the Tales of Marguerite de Navarre

Since the storytellers in the *Heptameron* comprise one speech role in a complex structure which has many other such roles, it may be useful for the reader to see a general table of how these roles give Marguerite de Navarre's tales a highly original structure (Figure 1).

In order to make a clear distinction between them and to give an unambiguous idea of how they are interrelated, I will give a brief definition of these roles.

THE AUTHORS
The author's role is surely the hardest to define. Since Proust and Valéry it has been the center of numerous discussions, and its problematical nature cannot be ignored.

I do not think of the author as the biographical individual who is a person independent from her work. But neither do I consider the author, as do Booth, Schmid, and Lintvelt, as the "abstract author" who "represents the deep meaning, the global meaning of the literary work."[1] Such a view is not acceptable because a literary work does not have *one* meaning, but a

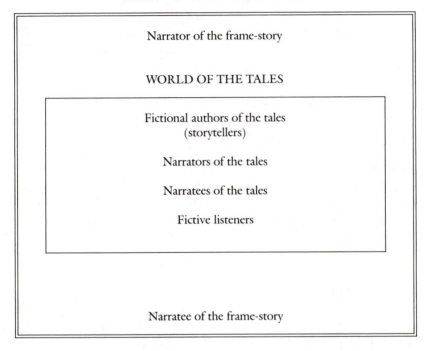

Figure 1. The narrative structure of Marguerite de Navarre's *Heptameron*.

virtual multitude of meanings which give rise to different readings and interpretations according to the period and the cultural groups to which readers belong.

The notion of the author is complex, but it will, in the theoretical basis of this study, consist of three elements. The first two correspond to two contrary but inseparable properties of the literary work universally recognized today. A literary work forms a unique *system* whose elements are closely interdependent. I will thus define the author first as the *role or entity which produces this unique system*. Every literary work also appears as a unit belonging to two categories which subsume it: the literary genre as part of the reader's "horizon of expectations" on which that work is silhouetted (even when it violates generic rules),[2] and the whole system of genres which constitutes literature itself at each moment of its history.[3] Literary genres are contractual in nature; a genre is the implicit or explicit contract offered by the author to the reader, a contract that determines "the way the text is read."[4] My second definition of the author is *the subject of the generic contract* which serves as the basis of both the work's process of production and its process of reception. Moreover, the author of a narrative work—a work of representation in which, by definition, the author does not make her voice directly heard—may be at the same time (as is the case with the author of the *Heptameron*) the author of non-narrative works in which she expresses herself in her own name and voice, a voice which may on occasion coincide directly with those of certain speech roles of her narrative work—an inter-textual phenomenon of obvious importance. My third definition of the author of a narrative work will thus be: *the subject of the voice or voices in which, outside the work, the author expresses herself in her own name.*

Since Marguerite de Navarre's tales have a frame-story, the authorial role appears in two semiotic layers: as the real author at the level of the work as a whole and as the fictive authors, the storytellers, at the level of the tales.

THE AUDIENCE

As the role that is symmetrical to the authorial role, the audience role is arranged, like the former, in two layers: the real readers at the level of the whole work, and the fictive audience of the individual tales.

THE NARRATORS

The narrator is the fictive speech role to which every author of a story *necessarily* delegates the responsibility of narrative discourse. Unlike the author's role, which, in one major respect, transcends the story, the narrator is a role entirely immanent to the story: a pure being of discourse, the narrator is the *discursive role* which the author takes up within her story and which, like the borrowed role may be highly variable in status and aspect.

Like the authorial role, the narrative role is arranged in two semiotic degrees: the frame-story has its own narrator (the hypernarrator) and the tales have theirs (the hyponarrators).

THE NARRATEES

A symmetrical and corollary role to the narrator but located at the opposite pole of the story—in the receiving position—the narratee is the *role* which the author attributes to the reader *within the story, the fictive image of the reader*, made up from scratch by the author who assigns the narratee as the narrator's interlocutor or addressee. Like the narrator and unlike the reader, the narratee is a purely discursive entity.

Like the narrator's role, the narratee's role is arranged in two levels: one in the frame-story and the other in the tales.

Having defined the nature and function of the speaking and receiving roles in the tales, we can now address the first topic of this study: the different ways the narrators are manifest within the tales of the *Heptameron*.

Manifestation of the Narrators in the *Heptameron* Tales

The mode of enunciation chosen by the storytellers in the *Heptameron* is the one universally known, since Benveniste's classic studies on this subject, as *history*.[5] Benveniste defined *history* as the mode characterized by the absence, within the story, of any linguistic marker of the narrator's presence: "As a matter of fact, there is then no longer even a narrator. The events are set forth chronologically, as they occurred. No one speaks here; the events seem to narrate themselves. The fundamental tense is the aorist, which is the tense of the event outside the person of a narrator" (p. 208). This conception of a story without a narrator had already been proposed by Käte Hamburger in her brilliant book, *The Logic of Literature*: "Epic fiction, the product of narration, is not an object with respect to the narrative act. Its fictivity, that is, its nonreality, signifies that it does not exist independently of the act of narration, but rather that it only *is* by virtue of its being narrated. . . . That is, the narrative poet is not a statement-subject. He does not narrate about persons and things, but rather he narrates these persons and things."[6] This thesis has recently been taken up again, with very solid arguments, by A. Banfield and S. Y. Kuroda.[7] Beyond their differences, these theories which argue for the existence of stories without narrators are all based on two series of arguments, the first of which is meant to support the second: (1) stories uttered in the *history* mode have an assortment of linguistic and semiotic features which are peculiar to them and set them apart from other types of stories; and (2) the presence of these features excludes a communicational conception of these stories and its correlate, the existence of a subject of narrative enunciation or narrator.

Although the first of these two series of arguments seems useful and is a very positive contribution to narratology, the reasoning which leads these authors to the second series of arguments does not seem valid. Just because stories narrated in the mode of *history* differ by a series of specific features from the classic type of communicational discourse, we cannot conclude that these stories are without a subject of enunciation: all discourse is projected against a "horizon of expectations" and bases its legitimacy on an explicit or implicit *contract*; any discourse constitutes in this way a discursive *practice*. And every discursive practice, to the very extent that it is a *practice*, requires by definition a *subject*.[8] The error of the theorists of stories without narrators is to confuse the notions of the subject of enunciation and the personal subject. As Barthes observed appositely, the narrator of a story may indeed choose to take on the semblance of impersonality without ceasing to be a narrator: "The story [*Histoire*] may seem to tell itself. . . . In fact, in such a case, the speaking subject suspends his emotive personality but substitutes another persona, the objective persona: the subject exists fully but as an objective subject."[9]

Although uttered in the *history* mode, the tales of the *Heptameron* thus do have narrators whose "impersonal" voices manifest certain characteristic features that I will attempt to define. But *history*, as we know, is never found in its absolutely pure form: it always includes elements of *discourse* in which the narrator appears as a personal subject. These intermittent manifestations of a personal narrator are all the more normal in the *Heptameron* tales in that the tales are narrated by strongly individualized storytellers to an audience that is also individualized. Moreover the narrator's appearances occur within a conversational exchange which gives them a specific rhetorical function.

The *Heptameron* narrators appear as personal subjects in many varied forms. The first consists of all the narrators' references to the moment of their act of storytelling. A second series of such appearances corresponds to certain essential functions that devolve on the narrative role: the witnessing function, the function of overseeing the general narrative operation (*régie narrative*), the adjudicating function, the comparative function, and the communicative function. The final way for the *Heptameron* narrators to appear as personal subjects is irony.

REFERENCES TO THE PRESENT IN THE NARRATIVE ACT
References to the present—the time the story is told—occur in three kinds of narrative acts.

The first such utterances are those which situate the tales chronologically with reference to the moment the story is told. The *Heptameron* narrators usually use objective indications to situate their stories in time;

sometimes, however, they use *deictics*[10]: "*Depuis dix ans en ça*, en la ville de Florence, y avoit un duc de la maison de Medicis . . ." (90;158).[11]

The second kind of narrative utterance are the fragments of *discourse* with an identifying function. In a small number of tales certain places or characters are identified by means of utterances in *discourse*: "*Il y a ung villaige* entre Nyort et Fors, nommé Grip, *lequel est au seigneur de Fors*" (250;341).

The third category of utterances are those which, in some tales, make the transition from *history* to *discourse* at the end of the story. Closural utterances in some of the tales are marked by their substitution of *discourse* for *history* as the speech mode. Such a substitution is transitional: it effects the change from narration to dialogue by returning attention to the speech act which *history* had covered up during the tale and by redirecting attention to the real moment in which the storytellers are physically alive and in which they communicate with one another: "Et, par son bon vouloir, fut fait le mariage, *où elle a vescu toute sa vie en bonne réputation. Et luy a fait le jeune prince beaucoup de grands biens*" (294;388).

NARRATOR'S INTERVENTION AS WITNESS

The second category of narrators' interventions—narrator as witness—consists of utterances in which the narrators attempt to give credibility to their stories by a direct affirmation that they personally knew one of the principal characters of their tale: "En la court du Roy François premier, y avoit ung gentil homme, *duquel je congnois si bien le nom que je ne le veulx point nommer*" (116;189).

UTTERANCES CONCERNING GENERAL NARRATIVE OPERATION

Utterances concerning general narrative operation, relatively infrequent interventions, fall into three categories.

The first is the topos which appeared long before the *Heptameron* and has continued: the narrator tells the narratee either that she will abridge the story of actions or events too numerous to be retold in detail, or that she cannot give an exact rendition of sentiments or passions of such intensity that words cannot describe them. "Je ne sçaurais entreprendre de vous compter par le menu les propos qu'ilz eurent pour rompre cette jalousie" (66;134). "Je n'entreprendz point vous dire la douleur que sentoit Amadour escoutant ces paroles, car elle n'est seullement impossible à escripre, mais à penser, sinon à ceulx qui ont experimenté la pareille" (75;143).

The second category of such general operation consists of those interventions concerning the organization of time in the story. Most of these are anticipations of coming events and use the formula *vous verrez* (you will see): ". . . La Bonté divine, qui print pitié des pauvres brebis esgarées, ne voulut plus endurer la gloire de ce malheureux regner, *ainsi que vous verrez*" (177;256).

The third category of narrative operation is more specific to the *Heptameron*. It consists of comments on the French translation which the narrators give or refuse to give of characters' letters or messages written in Italian or Spanish: "Quant il fut en sa chambre enfermé . . . , luy va escrire trois motz en espaignol, que j'ay trouvé de si bonne substance que je ne les ay voulu traduire pour en diminuer leur grace . . ." (386–87;495).

Adjudicating Interventions

The narrator exercises her adjudicating function by making judgments of truth or value, whether this judgment takes a morphemic or propositional form.

The narrators' adjudicating function appears most often in evaluative morphemes. Most concern characters in the stories and can be divided into two nonexclusive semantic categories: first, moral praise or blame, and second, pity. In the first category the two most frequently occurring morphemes are the adjectives *saige* and *meschant*: "La duchesse, ayant oy ceste *saige* response, l'ayma plus fort que paravant" (401;514). "Quoy voiant, ce *meschant* moyne, en parlant tousjours de Dieu, paracheva avecq elle l'oeuvre que soubdain le diable leur mit au cueur" (425;540).

The most current morpheme of the second category is the adjective *malheureux*; significantly, this qualifier is usually applied, not to the victims of evil characters, but to the evil characters themselves, whose behavior inspires in the narrators a sentiment of moral commiseration: "Après qu'elle eut perdu la parolle et la force du corps, ce *malheureux* print par force celle qui n'avoit plus de deffense en elle" (20;80).

Less common than evaluative morphemes, the narrators' judgments and commentaries in statement form are nonetheless frequent in the *Heptameron*. The *Heptameron* narrators often make judgments about the characters' conduct: "Ainsy vesquit ceste jeune dame, soubz l'ypocrisie et habit de femme de bien, en telle volupté que raison, conscience, ordre ne mesure n'avoient plus de lieu en elle" (212–213;297). Often these judgments concern features of the characters' moral or psychological makeup and appear as psychonarrative statements or statement fragments: "Parquoy, ayant mis dehors toute la craincte qu'elle debvoit avoir de monstrer sa folye devant ung si saige homme, son vice et sa meschanceté à un si vertueux homme de bien, se meist à luy escripre l'amour qu'elle luy portoit . . ." (256;347). There are five kinds of such judgments.

1. *General maxims.* One of the more original features of the *Heptameron* is the inclusion of numerous maxims within the main narrative line: "Sçachant que *le despit faict faire à une femme plus que l'amour, principalement à celles qui ont le cueur grand et honorable*, print la hardiesse, ung jour, en parlant à la Royne, de luy dire qu'il avoit grand pitié dont elle n'estoit autrement aymée du Roy son mary" (23;84).

One very special category of maxim stands out in the *Heptameron*: statements about the fundamental tenets of the evangelic faith. Most of them occur within psychonarrative utterances intended to elucidate the deep-seated reasons for certain characters' sinful behavior, for instance, the unfortunate wife's suicide in tale 23, when she is the victim of the lecherous Franciscan who slipped into her bed pretending to be her husband: "Et alors, elle . . . qui du tout ignoroit *la grace donnée par nostre bon Dieu par le mérite de son Filz, la remission des pechez par son sang, la reconsiliation du pere avecq nous par sa mort, la vie donnée aux pecheurs par sa seulle bonté et misericorde*, se trouva si troublée, en l'assault de ce desespoir fondé en l'enormité et gravité du peché . . . qu'elle estima la mort trop plus heureuse que sa vie" (190–91;271).

2. *Narrators' suppositions concerning characters' motivation.* The *Heptameron* narrators are usually omniscient and thus know the inner thoughts and feelings of their characters. Sometimes, however, they momentarily adopt the stance of spectators, seeing the characters only from the outside. This stance leads them to utter various suppositions about the characters' motivation: "La Royne, ou pour se monstrer autre qu'elle n'estoit, ou pour expérimenter à la longue l'amour qu'il luy portoit, ou pour en aymer quelque autre qu'elle ne voulloit laisser pour luy, ou bien le reservant, quand celluy qu'elle aymoit feroit quelque faulte, pour luy bailler sa place, dist, d'un visage ne content ne courroucé . . ." (196;277).

3. *Narrator's interventions concerning the operations of divine Providence or of Fortune.* Since divine Providence was universally held to be a real, albeit transcendent entity in the sixteenth century, the narrative utterances that mention it—and they are numerous in the tales of the *Heptameron*—should be considered as belonging to the *history* mode of utterance. However, several of them include, as inserted subordinate clauses, maxim-like utter-

ances that are formulated as *discourse*: "La Bonté divine, *qui est parfaicte charité et vraye amour*, eut pitié de sa douleur et regarda sa patience" (173;252).

The same is true for utterances about the operation of Fortune: though some fall in the category of *history*, most of them include maxim-like observations formulated as *discourse*: "... mais, au bout de quelque temps, la felicité de ce monde, *qui avecq soy porte une mutabilité*, ne peut durer en la maison, qui estoit trop heureuse" (312;410).

4. *Narrator's hypotheses concerning the end of the story.* In some *nouvelles*, the denouement is not narrated, but takes the form of a hypothesis formulated by the narrator as *discourse*: "*Il est à presumer* que, s'il y eut des gens de bien pour juges, ilz ne laissèrent pas la chose impugnye" (351;454).

5. *Narrator's formulation of the lesson to be learned from the story.* It is almost always the storyteller's role to formulate the moral and pragmatic lesson of the stories; indeed, that is one of the two specific discursive marks of the storytellers. However, in a small number of tales that lesson is included within the body of the story and therefore becomes part of the narrator's role: "et fut le dit monastère spolyé de ses larcins et des belles filles qui estoient dedans, et les moynes y enfermez dedans bruslèrent avecq le dit monastère, pour perpétuelle mémoire de ce crime, *par lequel se peult cognoistre qu'il n'y a rien plus dangereux qu'amour, quant il est fondé sur vice, comme il n'est rien plus humain ne louable, que quant il habite en ung cueur vertueulx*" (240;329).

SIMILES

Similes within the tales, like judgments made by the narrator but occurring less frequently, are indications of narrative authority in its personal form. Such similes almost always have a psychonarrative function, and their comparative terms, like certain narratorial judgments, are generally composed of maxim-like utterances formulated as *discourse*: "*Tout ainsy que ung bon gendarme, quand il veoit son sang, est plus échauffé à se venger de ses ennemis et acquerir honneur*, ainsy son chaste cueur se renforce doublement à courir et fuyr des mains de ce malheureux" (19;80).

INTERVENTION FOR THE PURPOSE OF COMMUNICATION

Within the tales, communication is the particular aim of the narrative interventions formulated as *discourse*. But here I am referring to one particular type of narrative intervention: those interventions that refer explicitly to the group listening to the tales. They can be divided into three categories:

interventions of narrative control; narrator's judgments; and strictly narrative utterances.

The majority of the narrative interventions concerning narrative control include an address to the listeners designated by the pronoun *vous*, as in the following utterance: "Je ne puis entreprendre de *vous* racompter l'ennuy de la duchesse, car il estoit tel que doibt avoir une dame d'honneur et de cueur, qui sur sa foy voyoit mourir celle qu'elle désiroit de saulver" (331; 430–31).

Narratorial judgments accompanied by an address to the listener are all judgments of a general nature, as in the following example: "*Vous, qui sçavez le prompt chemyn que faict ce feu quant il se prent à ung des boutz du cueur et de la fantaisie, vous jugerez bien* que entre deux si parfaictz subjectz ne s'arresta guères Amour, qu'il ne les eust à son commandement" (138;214).

The majority of narrative utterances that include an address to the listeners are utterances in the form of a proposition of the type "*je*" + "*vous*" + *verb of thinking* + *complement*. These are utterances whose function could be called superlative insofar as they lead the listeners to give great weight to their semantic content: "Je ne sçaurais *vous* dire lequel estoit *plus* aise des deux, ou luy de tromper sa femme, ou elle de tromper son mary" (44;109).

Narrative Irony

The last form of the narrators' personal intervention within their stories is irony, more precisely irony in the form of a trope (we will not deal here with instances of narrative irony that concern only the content of the story). Such narrative intervention is distinguished from the preceding forms by the fact that it does not include any syntactical mark (the use of *discourse*), but instead is lexical and semantic.

As a trope, narrative irony is obvious in most cases through one or several lexical syntagmas, as in the following sentence from tale 61 which, like many others in the same story, plays on the substitution of a sacred lexical register (justified by the clerical status of one of the main characters) for the profane lexical register that the situation would normally require (an adulterous liaison between a married woman and a canon): "Ainsy que l'on vouloit fermer la porte d'Autun, y arriva *ceste pelerine,* et ne faillit d'aller tout droict où demeuroit *son corps sainct*, qui fut tant esmerveillè de sa venue, que à peyne povoit-il croyre que ce fut elle" (374;481).

Less frequently narratorial irony goes beyond the level of lexical syntagma to that of several main or subordinate clauses, as in this sentence from tale 56 where the irony operates at the expense of a lady whose excessive confidence in Franciscans makes her a victim of their swindling. In order to pocket the dowry, one of them persuades her to marry her daughter to one of his young companions from the monastery: "Il advint que ung matin il print grant devotion à ceste dame et a sa fille d'aller oyr la messe à Sainct-François, et *visiter leur bon pere confesseur, par le moyen duquel elles pensoient estre si bien pourvues l'une de beau filz et l'autre de mary*" (350;453).

Relationships Among the Voices of the Narrators, Storytellers, and Author

The evidence of the narrator's voice as *personal* authority—whose principal forms we have just categorized—represents only one of the original traits of this voice in Marguerite's *nouvelles*. There is another which helps even more to confer on the narrator's voice its singular profile within the tales: that is the interactions of that voice with those of the fictional authors, on the one hand, and with the voice of the author of the whole work (the hyperauthor) on the other. The last part of this chapter concerns the nature of those interactions.

Let us be clear at the outset: Even though the voices of the narrators and of the characters are included in every kind of tale, the voice of the author, on the contrary, is not necessarily present. Crafter of the tale and contractual subject of the narrative pact, the author can in effect choose to disengage herself from her work on the level of utterance and not to let her own voice be heard in it at any moment. That means that, in the *Heptameron*, the voices of the fictional authors of the tales, the storytellers, and the voice of the real author (the hyperauthor) are not necessarily present in the tales. It is only after doing an *intervocal* analysis that we will be able to know if they are there or not, and, if they are, what their relationships are with the voices of the narrators.

Voices of the Narrators and Storytellers

In the *Heptameron*, the storyteller's voice can be heard clearly in the introductory and concluding utterances of the tales. These utterances stand out by clear linguistic marks from the narrative discourse of the tales. We can look for a correspondence between the narrator's voice and the storyteller's voice to determine whether the storyteller's voice is present within its own utterances. The storyteller's introductory and concluding utterances announce and sum up the moral and pragmatic lesson of the tale: they are essentially *ideological*. When we hear the storyteller's voice in a tale, we confront an ideological utterance. In other words, when the storyteller's voice and the narrator's voice coincide, this merging reveals an ideological statement.

In their argumentative goals and their exemplarity, the *Heptameron*'s tales diverge. Yet, as long as we remain within the universe of the tales, they are less important than the ideological convergence that characterizes the discourse of the tales. A close examination of that discourse reveals its inherent double ideological agreement: agreement, on the one hand, between the storyteller's voice and the narrator's voice; and, on the other hand, among the voices of the different storytellers/narrators.

This agreement, which, significantly, does not come from any purely narratological necessity is the rule throughout all of the tales. To prove this would be tedious, but it can easily be verified. Here is an illustration in which Longarine has given Saffredent the floor to tell tale 26, and he begins his story as follows:

> J'ay en main l'histoire d'*une folle* et d'*une saige*: vous prendrez l'exemple qu'il vous plaira le mieulx. Et congnoistrez que, tout ainsy que amour faict faire aux *meschans* des *meschancetez*, en ung cueur *honneste* faict faire choses dignes de *louange*: car . . . amour ne change poinct le cueur, mais le monstre tel qu'il est, *fol* aux *folles*, et *saige* aux *saiges*. (207–208;291)

This opening remark stands out because of two antinomic lexical classes whose opposition corresponds to the opposition between Good and Evil that the Christian ethos of the time established in the area of human conduct. The reader who thinks that this is only normal is seriously mistaken, as much about the work's protocol of reading as about the facts themselves: the proof will be demonstrated by the text that follows. But first it is helpful to note that the same axiological opposition on which the argumentative goals of the storyteller's introductory remark are founded recurs within the narratorial discourse in the scattered but insistent form of terminology dominated by abundant reminders of the opposition of *saige and fol(le)*: "Combien qu'il eust plus voluntiers aymé *la saige dame* que nulle, si est-ce que la paour qu'il avoit de perdre son amityé . . . le feit taire et se amuser ailleurs" (210;294); "Audatieusement se coucha auprès d'elle où il feut reçu ainsy que le plus beau filz qui fust de son temps debvoit estre de la plus belle et *folle dame* du pays" (212;296); "Combien qu'il eust faict *les follyes* que vous avez oyes, contre la volunté et conseil de *la saige dame*, si ne diminua-elle jamais l'amour vertueuse qu'elle luy portoit" (214;298). In addition to this agreement between the storyteller's and the narrator's voice on a deep ideological level, there is also agreement among the voices of the different narrators, or rather among the voices of the different storytellers/ narrators of the tales.

Countless examples relating to different thematic domains could be cited here. We will limit ourselves to just one, one that concerns a specific thematic field of extreme importance in Marguerite's tales: the evangelical doctrine of salvation by faith and grace. This is the doctrine supporting the psychonarrative by which the storyteller/narrator of tale 23, Oisille in this case, meticulously explains the suicide of a young woman, the unwitting victim of a *cordelier*'s Machiavellian lubricity:

> Et, alors elle, qui n'avoit jamais aprins des cordeliers, sinon la confiance des bonnes oeuvres, la satisfaction des pechez par austérité de vie, jeusnes et disciplines, qui du tout ignoroit la grace donnée par nostre bon Dieu par le merite de son Filz, la remission des pechez par son sang, la reconsiliation du pere avecq nouz par sa mort, la vie donnée aux pecheurs par sa seulle bonté et miséricorde, se trouva si troublée . . . qu'elle estima la mort trop plus heureuse que la vie. (190–91;271)

It is by a psychonarrative supporting the same fundamental principles of the evangelical faith that, in tale 30—the story of the tragic destiny of an incestuous mother—Hircan laboriously explains the infernal mechanism by which each of the unfortunate mother's efforts to escape the grasp of sin only made her more inextricably its prisoner. This is notwithstanding the fact that Hircan's personal "ideology" is the polar opposite of Oisille's and that in this case he gives to his tale an argumentative goal that is totally different from the one that supported Oisille's tale of the suicide quoted above.

> Mais, en lieu de se humilier et recongnoistre l'impossibilité de nostre chair, qui sans l'ayde de Dieu ne peult faire que peché, voulant par elle-mesmes et par ses larmes satisfaire au passé et par sa prudence eviter le mal de l'advenir, donnant tousjours l'excuse de son peché à l'occasion et non à la malice, à laquelle n'y a remede que la grace de Dieu, pensa de faire choses parquoy à l'advenir ne sçauroit plus tomber en tel inconvenient. . . . Mais la racine de l'orgueil que le peché exterieur doibt guerir, croissait toujours, en sorte que, en evitant ung mal, elle en feit plusieurs aultres. (231;318–19)

We could cite many other examples of similar agreements; they would each bear witness to this paradoxical phenomenon: in spite of divergences, even radical oppositions, in the argumentative goals that grow from their respective ideological orientations, there is, on a more fundamental ideological level, a single, consistent voice (that of the storytellers/narrators) that speaks from within the *Heptameron*'s tales. It is this paradox which we now must try to explain. That task leads us to consider the role of the narrative utterance at the very top of the hierarchy: that of the author.

AUTHOR'S VOICE

The agreement of the storytellers' voices in the tales of the *Heptameron*, that is, the voices of their fictional authors and those of their narrators, is only one expression of a phenomenon of writing that is, almost without exception, particular to the sixteenth century. Generally, the author's voice is heard through the voice of the narrator. The modern notion of representing the narratorial role as a specific and independent role of utterance to which the author of a story delegates automatically (because of an inherent necessity within the narrative discourse) the responsibility of telling the story is a notion foreign to the minds of sixteenth-century narrative authors. More generally, they would find strange the idea that the writing of narrative implies the choice of a *discursive role*, the idea that writing narrative is essentially a *game* offering the writer the possibility of appropriating a *ludic voice* distinct from the non-ludic voice which the same writer would adopt in genres in which, conventionally, the author speaks in his or her own name. To conclude from this that narrators do not exist in the semiotic reality of sixteenth-century narrative texts would be as absurd as to deny the presence of the unconscious in the works of Racine because the concept of the unconscious did not exist in the seventeenth century, or to argue that the distinction between *langue* and *parole* cannot be applied to old French texts because Saussure's *Cours* dates only from the twentieth century. Since narrators are nothing more than subjects of narrative discourse, their existence is as old as narrative. However, all the possibilities of writing offered by the narratorial role were not used by sixteenth-century writers the way they are by writers today.

But the obliteration of the narrators' role in the *Heptameron*'s tales gives no additional consistency to the storytellers' roles. *Fictional* authors of the tales, the storytellers, like the narrators, are *discursive roles* that the author of the work assumes in a ludic mode. And the logic of writing which diverts that author from exploiting the possibilities of semiotic autonomy offered by the narratorial role leads her simultaneously to neglect the similar possibilities of autonomy inherent in the storytellers' role. Instead she makes *her own* voice heard through the storytellers' voices. This explains the double agreement that we observed on a profound ideological level in the enunciatory structure of the *Heptameron*'s tales: agreement between the voices of the narrators and the storytellers, and agreement among the voices of the different storytellers/narrators. Behind the commotion of multiple narratorial voices whose discordance takes center stage and whose confrontation dominates the surface of the tales' discourse, a single voice speaks at the heart of this discourse: the author's voice.

The *univocality* that profoundly characterizes the narrative discourse of Marguerite's tales contrasts sharply with the fundamentally antagonistic structure of interlocutory discourse within which this narrative discourse is inscribed and from which it receives its sense and its function. An interlocutory discourse whose plurivocity, as radical as it is irreducible, pulverizes the ideological unity that the underlying voice of the author conferred on the profound layers of narrative discourse. Pulverization is evident by its sometimes spectacular effects. For example, in tale 26, Saffredent's palinode reverses purely and simply in the dialogue following the story he has just told the very meaning of the lesson which *as storyteller* he felt just moments before he must—the verb (*devoir*) takes on its full meaning here—assign to the story.

The singularity, as much structural as it is generic and historical, of Marguerite's tales comes from the fact that they are constituted by the intricate interweaving and interaction of two discursive universes: a narrative discursive universe and an interlocutory discursive universe, that explicitly but rigorously control enunciatory protocols that are not only different but in many ways contradictory. A "realist" logic—of a realism that is ours but not that of sixteenth-century writers—would imply that the deep ideological antagonisms that set the speakers of the dialogues in opposition to each other are also found in the tales that those speakers tell each other, not only for the simple pleasure of telling, but because they assign to them an essential function in the framework of their individual argumentative strategies. If the *Heptameron* violates that logic which seems so evident to us, it is because the enunciatory protocol that controls its narrative universe is not, as ours has become, a ludic protocol.

Notes

1. W. C. Booth, *The Rhetoric of Fiction* (Chicago: University of Chicago Press, 1961 and 1983); W. Schmid, *Der Textaufbau in der Erzählungen Dostoievskys* (Munich: Fink, 1973); J. Lintvelt, *Essai de typologie narrative: Le "point de vue"* (Paris: Corti, 1981). I quote from the last of these works, p. 18.

2. H. R. Jauss, *Toward an Aesthetic of Reception*, trans. Timothy Bahti (Minneapolis: University of Minnesota Press, 1982), p. 25ff.

3. "L'oeuvre littéraire constitue un système et . . . la littérature en constitue également un" (J. Tynianov, "De l'évolution littéraire," in *Théorie de la littérature* [Paris: Le Seuil, 1965], 122–23).

4. Philippe Lejeune, *Le Pacte autobiographique* (Paris: Le Seuil, 1975), 44.

5. Emile Benveniste, "Relationships of Person in the Verb" and "The Correlations of Tense in the French Verb," in *Problems in General Linguistics*, trans. Mary Elizabeth Meek (Coral Gables, Fla.: University of Miami Press, 1971), 195–215.

6. Käte Hamburger, *The Logic of Literature*, 2d rev. ed., trans. Marilynn J. Rose (Bloomington: Indiana University Press, 1973), 136.

7. A. Banfield, "Le Style narratif et la grammaire des discours direct et indirect" in *La Critique générative*, Collectif Change (Paris: Seghers-Laffont, 1973), 186–226, and "Où l'épistémologie, le style et la grammaire rencontrent l'histoire littéraire: Le Développement de la parole et de la pensée représentées," *Langue française* 44 (1979): 9–26. S. Y. Kuroda, "Réflexions sur les fondements de la théorie de la narration," in *Langue, Discours, Société* (Paris: La Seuil, 1975), 260–93.

8. "A statement . . . differs from any series of linguistic elements by virtue of the fact that it possesses a particular relation with a subject" (Michel Foucault, *The Archaeology of Knowledge*, trans. A. M. Sheridan Smith [New York: Harper and Row, 1972]), 92.

9. Roland Barthes, "Le Discours de l'histoire," *Informations sur les sciences sociales*, 6, no. 4 (1967): 68–69.

10. *Deictics* are pronouns or demonstrative adverbs with referents that are only identifiable (like the first-person and second-person pronouns, with which the deictics are related in linguistics) within the context of the speech act.

11. Emphasis here, and in the following quotations, is added.

André Tournon

11. Rules of the Game

Ten characters in search of a pastime rather than an author turn themselves into authors to pass the time. Does their success manage to dispel the nostalgia one feels for the novel in which they would otherwise have appeared? Things seemed to be off to such a good start in the prologue: flash floods, perilous routes, ambushes, rescues, reunions—the swings in action are as lively as one could wish. But everything comes to a standstill in Sarrance, the space shrinks, a meadow, a monastery, days go by to the rhythm of Lady Oisille's homilies, the rhythm of tales in tens giving rise to debates at regular intervals, the ringing of the bells, and the evening service. The contrast is striking enough to prompt the reader to reduce these characters, destitute of adventure, to voices recounting and commenting upon others' adventures. One willingly grants them personality, ideas, and even, as ballast, the historical reality that lay behind their probable models; but it would seem that they lack the consistency which a fictional fate— even of a rudimentary nature—can bestow upon imaginary beings, plausible or not. Stuck in between the actual narrator and the stories' heroes, the storytellers assume the role of pseudo-witnesses and judges without jurisdiction; they are not *dramatis personae*. Such, at least, is the impression left when the heroic and courtly adventures outlined in the opening of the prologue abruptly miscarry.

Under these conditions, each character's individual features will serve principally to qualify the remarks he or she makes: one comes to expect in Hircan and Saffredent's declarations a somewhat cynical hedonism, while Dagoucin tends to close himself off in ethereal speculation; among the ladies, the stern Oisille and the wise Parlamente, along with Longarine, will serve as contrast to the flighty Ennasuite and the merry Nomerfide . . . Nothing in these features is particularly subtle or out of the ordinary. But let us push this character-typing to its logical conclusion: the relationships hinted at, which would have animated the group had the novel promised in the prologue been accomplished, need to be considered first and foremost in how they affect the discussion and the stories—how they function as markers in a scheme of enunciation which underlies the work as a whole and which is insistent enough to alter the work's overall scope and meaning. If it should turn out that this scheme has left its stamp upon the choice and handling of the tales' themes, we will find ourselves dealing with a complex narrative and discursive system where what is said can mean something entirely different from the words' manifest sense. This second signification would occur not out of any inherent semantic ambiguity, but according to an ulterior motive, by which one character addresses another, intentionally disguising secrets which the others are curious to learn. A study of the first day can help pinpoint clues which suggest the major outlines of the rules of the game,[1] and afterward, allow one to measure the impact of such rules upon any overall interpretation in order to draw certain conclusions as to the kind of fictional language devised by Marguerite de Navarre.

*   *   *

The very first story makes explicit the fact that the tales are selected out of personal motives: Simontaut addresses Parlamente, who alone fathoms his intentions, in order to air a private resentment.[2] It is also clear that his message can only be deciphered by detecting a false analogy: Madame de Saint-Aignan's crimes have nothing whatsoever to do with Parlamente's "cruauté" toward her unrequited suitor. In other words, between the tale presented as an example to the others (a story of ambushes and murder) as well as the interpretation which it is explicitly given (all women since Eve are depraved) and what that tale intimates to its recipient (why are you so mean to me?), there exists a distance great enough to appreciably compromise the tale's didactic effectiveness as an example. At the stories' threshold, this rather simple play on meaning warns us from the outset that the system of expression at work in the *Heptameron* can conceal pitfalls, and this is what makes things interesting.

Such a preliminary assessment is emphasized through contrast, and at the same time rectified, by the second tale, a hagiographical and entirely unequivocal story recounted by Oisille, who is obviously beyond the others' amorous intrigues. The reader thus cannot even be sure whether subsequent speeches will be skewed: they might not be, and one will have to determine each, case by case. It is also evident that not every clue to the enigma, should there be an enigma, will be made available to the reader.

Saffredent, to whom falls the responsibility for the third tale, wanted to speak of "quelque chose qui bien eut esté agreable à la compaignye, et sur toutes à une . . ." (22;82); he recounts the story of an adultery avenged in kind, wishing, says he, to share the hero's marital misfortune provided he obtain similar liberties which make up for his trouble. Ennasuite pokes fun at him, imagining that the compliment was directed toward her; but another, who remains unnamed, "se print bien fort à rire," confident that she is the favorite—and "quant Saffredent apperceut que celle qui ryoit l'entendoit, il s'en tint trop content . . ." (27;89). This is a tale with a hidden agenda if ever there was one, but to whom is it addressed? At this point in the work, there is no way of knowing,[3] and that is what counts: the narrator's aims, and along with those aims at least one of the tale's meanings, depend upon a piece of information that has been partially left out; to presume upon the tale's meaning would be to flaunt a naïveté comparable to that of Ennasuite, but in order to laugh knowingly, one needs to be let in on the secret like the other lady. An analogous situation is hinted at shortly afterward, but this time within one of the stories: answering Nomerfide who accuses him of wanting "par ung bruit en veult couvrir ung autre" (40;103), Hircan amuses his listeners by recounting how a merchant made a pretense of courting a youthful woman next door "pour couvrir ung amour plus haulte et honnorable," even managing to camouflage this relationship in turn by rushing to meet the mother, who has caught them unawares, and pretending to passionately embrace her. Snare follows upon snare, both within the stories and between their tellers. Longarine takes hold of Hircan's tale as a pretext to invent a quarrel between Hircan and his wife over imagined infidelities; after which, she maliciously follows up with a story of her own about a man called Bornet ["Dullfellow"] who, thinking to deceive his wife, unknowingly delivers her into the arms of a comrade—or, if one prefers, the story of this wise wife who, intending to catch her husband in the act, gives herself without realizing it to another man. Finally, in a parting shot, Longarine redirects her aim at Saffredent, who reacts violently (47;112). Playing or fighting, everything points obliquely toward a web of possible complicities and conflicts capable of twisting the meaning of that which is said openly.

But could not all this be only fun and jest of little consequence, brought out by stories told in a frivolous tone? When the group launches into serious topics, the implicit rules of the game should change. And they do change, but not in the way one would expect. The turning point is indicated right after the eighth tale's discussion winds up in mirth: the group "se prindrent tant à rire qu'*ilz misent fin en leurs propos.*" Here interrupts Dagoucin, "*qui encores n'avoit sonné mot,*" (47;112, emphasis added) and from the opening words, his speech takes on a moralistic tone: "L'homme est bien desraisonnable quand. . . ." He severely reproaches infidelity, and in response to an objection raised by Simontaut (based upon a misappropriation of the platonic theory of the androgyne), he exposes his doctrine of altruistic love, unalterable and incommunicable unto death. His masculine partners make fun of these ideas, but in vain for the tone is no longer humorous: the ninth tale, presented in the style of a sermon ("A fin que les signes et miracles, suyvant ma veritable parole, vous puissent induire à y adjouster foy," 49;114), is the tragic story of a martyr for "parfait amour." Nor can one describe as trifling the following tale of Floride and Amadour's love which, thwarted, drives each to the point of despair. Everything has been set up as if Marguerite de Navarre wished to highlight the contrast of these two last tales—and the commentaries they elicit—with the preceding stories, sorts of fabliaux embedded in dialogues taken straight out of comedy.[4] Now will begin the serious debates.

Despite having abandoned a frivolous tone, the play on encoded messages proves here no less disconcerting. From the start, the discourses which introduce the tale are invalidated. Dagoucin prefaces his tale by professing an absolute circumspection, grounded not upon rules of caution nor upon social disapproval, but upon the demands of love itself, demands which he makes out to be restrictions: "j'ay si grand paour que la démonstration fasse tort à la perfection de mon amour, que je crainctz que celle de qui je debvrois desirer l'amitye semblable, l'entende; et mesme je n'ose penser ma pensée . . . car, tant plus je tiens ce feu celé et couvert, et plus en moy crois le plaisir de sçavoir que j'ayme parfaictement" (48;113). But in fact, Dagoucin's protestations are perfectly "entendues" by Parlamente, "qui soupsonnoit ceste fantaisye" (48;114), to the point that his overly eloquent silence functions as a "démonstration" of love which wins a form of consent from Parlamente through her benevolent warning: "Donnez-vous garde, Dagoucin; car j'en ay veu d'aultres que vous; qui ont mieulx aymé mourir que parler" (48;114).

Her tacit approval is further suggested by the distribution of roles during the introduction to the ninth tale: Parlamente is the one who, by means of the phrase just mentioned, reorients the theme of silence toward one of sacrifice, thus presenting the tale by exactly that which makes it unique, placing it beyond the pale of the debate's point and counterpoint, and turning it into an astonishing liturgy upon love and death. This will need to be examined in greater detail; for the moment, let us simply take note of a certain number of contrasts between the statements' literal signification and the meaning which is assigned to those statements through their role as messages and the relationship they actually establish among their transmitting and receiving parties. Dagoucin's eloquent praise of silence, undertaken in his role as an adept at self-sacrifice, ends up conveying the very love that he has supposedly renounced as well as leading the object of his affection into acknowledging his conception of love. Further, he possibly intends by this to trap his lady into implying her assent, which could be interpreted as a sign of her favor toward him.

What comes next in this maneuvering proves no less subtle. Parlamente refrains from accepting Dagoucin's advances, leaving to Oisille the task of responding to the tale, and she only intervenes to refute those who disparage acts of self-renouncement in love, when they raise the seemingly casual question of whether a less timid suitor might not have attained success. Ostensibly addressed to Hircan and Saffredent, Parlamente's rejoinder might secretly acquiesce in Dagoucin's disguised message: by assuring that added daring would not have achieved success, she lets on that abnegation and discretion were the best possible attitudes to have adopted and the most apt to spark her feelings in response. Thus Dagoucin eagerly accepts that Parlamente recount a tale symmetrical to his own, which would establish between them a sort of complicity of sensitive spirits:

> Ma dame, puis que j'ay prouvé par exemple l'amour vertueuse d'un gentil homme jusques à la mort, je vous supplye, si vous en sçavez quelcune autant à l'honneur de quelque dame, que vous la nous veuillez dire pour la fin de ceste Journée (54;12).

Parlamente relates the story of Floride and Amadour. The tale opens with an idyllic sketch figuring characters whose names evoke etymological echoes with Guillaume de Lorris's *Roman de la rose*; but here, Amadour's virtuous discretion offers a way to communicate his feelings to Floride and encourage her to return them. Floride detects the stratagem and accepts to play along (63–65;131–33); Amadour's marriage with Aventurade, and then his affair with Poline, serve as means by which to cover his genuine purpose (60,62;128–30). Finally, when his plans turn out to be star-crossed, he suddenly decides to "se payer en une heure du bien qu'il pensoit avoir mérité" (72;140), attempts to rape Floride, is driven off, comes back several years later, and repeats the offense. The intentions concealed beneath the "vertueux propos," the timidity, and the respectfulness of the courtly suitor are thus laid bare (74;142). Parlamente gives a lesson in wariness to the other ladies and to herself, leaving her admirer dissatisfied with a closing formula in which one perceives a hint of malice: "Je sçay bien [. . .] que ceste longue nouvelle pourra estre à aucuns fascheuse" (83;152).

But in order to thus give the impression of allusively replying to Dagoucin's advances, the tale had to be contorted to the point of altering its role as example.[5] According to Parlamente's introduction, the story should have demonstrated that a virtuous woman can resist the most insistent and clever of solicitations; instead, it ends up showing that the followers of platonic love are no less to be feared than those who openly seek sensual pleasure and that, depending on the circumstances, men can cut short their ethereal speeches and pass from words to deeds, regardless of the beloved's will. This shift of emphasis, without going so far as to overturn the message's meaning, maintains the margin of ambiguity found to be peculiar to the storytellers' coded exchanges: if one reads between the lines of the explicit formula addressed to Hircan—"Vous semble-il pas que ceste femme ayt esté pressée jusques au bout, et qu'elle ayt vertueusement resisté?" (83;153)—one discovers a reply to Dagoucin: " 'I am not fooled by your protests of self-sacrifice.' " This is confirmed later, in broad terms, by doubts which are raised concerning claims of honest intent (tale 12, 94–96;162–65, and 35, 260;351–52). The discrepancy between these two replies is sharp enough to compel the reader to be wary of unequivocal interpretations, whatever be their aim. Restricting the meaning of the tales to the hidden significations which they acquire within the network of relationships between the storytellers would be to lay oneself open to errors of an opposite—yet parallel—nature to those committed by the kind of reading which confines itself to finding a moral in each tale, disregarding the ulterior purposes which the context assigns to the narrator and the listeners.

Moreover, Marguerite de Navarre has taken care to warn against this type of naïveté by indicating, through a detail in form, an additional complication of the rules of the game, this time to be applied not by the storytellers, but by the reader. Parlamente does not place herself in the position of eyewitness to the story of Floride and Amadour; instead, she repeats secondhand what she has been told by an earlier narrator. Is this in order to protect the story's plausibility, given that Parlamente is young, whereas the events recounted stretch out over many years? Perhaps (if one prefers to assume that the fiction's chronology was not entirely up to the author to arrange as she wished), but our narrator not only cites her earlier informant, she also relays his opinion upon the circumstances while, in the same breath, she underscores her esteem for him: this story, says Parlamente, was told to her "par ung de [s]es plus grands et entiers amys, à la louange de l'homme du monde qu'il avoit le plus aymé" (54;120). Thus the spotlight is turned upon the demeanor of Amadour (which accredits the hypothesis above concerning a discrepant, confidential message directed at Dagoucin), but now Amadour is proclaimed as being worthy of praise. Hircan and Saffredent also adopt this viewpoint at the story's end, of course, but their assessment can be discounted since it comes from characters whose bias is both known and criticized (in this passage, by Oisille when she bruskly rebuffs Hircan, 83;153). The anonymous second narrator, on the other hand, is not a member of the group, and nothing is known about him except that he is a friend of Parlamente. His verdict escapes any qualification which would relativize or limit its force; his assessment is pronounced peremptorily, and is invulnerable to challenge. Thus, a system of values is introduced which vies with Parlamente's, can contest her judgment, and even influence her opinion (for at the end of the story, Parlamente faults Floride's conduct as "cruel," in spite of her "vertu," 83;153). In short, the gratuitous reference to someone outside the group who vouches for the story is used in order to muddle or to oppose the different criteria by which the story will be judged. Why this extra complication?

The answer is to be found within the tales themselves. For however much the work's overall shape is affected by the fact that the tales are embedded within the concerns and the world of the storytellers, one might consider this as merely a contrivance to link together otherwise unconnected stories—a framework as extraneous as ornamental borders which enclose engravings—and refuse to admit that such a context can condition the tales' meaning.[6] As a matter of fact, it is far from certain that throughout the entire work the connection between the discussions and the tales is as carefully orchestrated as during the first day. In any event, it so happens here that the internal composition of the two tales corresponds exactly to the protocols of reading which we have determined in referring to indications outside of the tales proper.

Other critics have already drawn attention to the fact that the tenth tale, due to its length and the span of time over which its events occur, sheds its appearance as an anecdote and begins to resemble more a full-fledged novella. The characters take on complex and protean traits, their acts and their motives no longer offer the transparency expected of supposedly exemplary deeds, but instead acquire the disconcerting irregularity of real actions. The narrative text here can fittingly be considered as "dialogic" in the Bakhtinian sense of the term: its different voices intersect and join, sometimes discordantly. The pages which recount Amadour's plans and calculations, his talent at eloquent conversation, his capacity for dissimulation, in short the skill and willpower with which he carries out his aims, are the same pages which also paint him as speechless and love-struck in Floride's presence (57,61;124,129), and prepared to make any sacrifice upon learning she is unhappy (70;138). On this same tack, the story presents his first attempt at rape first as the side effect of a fit of madness provoked by despair (71;140 and 73;141: "Amadour, qui avoit perdu toute raison . . ."), then as a premeditated act, a conscious gamble inspired by what he stands to gain: "il se délibéra de jouer à quicte ou à double pour du tout la perdre ou du tout la gaigner, et se payer en une heure du bien qu'il pensoit avoir merité" (72;140).

At the cost of coherence, the scene's actual description combines gestures conveying love and sorrow with that of fainting, the very act which Amadour feigns in order to bring Floride within the reach of his embrace (72;140). Later, Floride's reprobation and declaration of their separation, despite every justification, is qualified as a "cruelle conclusion" (75;143), whereas Amadour's rather shifty positioning close to the countess of Arande in order to re-obtain Floride's favor is passed off as the effect of the vitality of "son cueur, qui estoit si grand qu'il n'avoit au monde son pareil" (76;144). Still other details (77, 80–81;143,149–50) confirm Amadour's "honesty" and "virtue," in contrast to his errors; finally, his heroic death as a soldier for Christendom and the funeral homage paid to him ("Ainsy morut le pauvre Amadour, autant regretté que ses vertuz le meritoient," 82;152) round out the glorious portrait that was announced by the anonymous witness who transmitted the story, and that is now corroborated by Geburon, who believes he has recognized Amadour's identity and affirms that he "estoit ung aussy honneste et vertueulx chevalier qu'il en soit poinct" (84;154).

The indecision thus achieved is not limited to Amadour's role, but affects what is at question in the overall work, in the tales as well as the debates, in the attitudes and the ulterior purposes of the speakers: the courtly conduct and mannered discourse which they appear to uphold. At every level, the work is beset by a fundamental ambiguity: first and foremost, of the "honnestes propos" by which not only the tales' lovers, but also the storytellers, and even the *Heptameron*'s readers, allow themselves to be charmed. Does such speech serve as a means of seduction, or rather as the mark of true intellectual and moral distinction? And can one really distinguish between the two? Neither Parlamente nor Marguerite de Navarre gives a conclusive answer, and for a reason. The codes of courtly love aggravate desire through frustration, both enjoining and condemning audacity at the same time, prescribing at once gracious reception and extreme reserve—those "Nenni" which signify "yes," "no," or "perhaps," according to the apparent tenderness of the smile. The subtlety of courtly dialogue favors equally discretion and dishonesty, half-spoken collusion and deception; in short, one must resign oneself to live with the contradiction and to employ a language of double-entendres. Elements of the verbal play between Parlamente and Dagoucin, which is reproduced *en abîme* within the first dialogue between Floride and Amadour (". . . lequel vault mieulx, parler ou mourir?," 62–65;129–33), inform and regulate the task facing the reader: the collection's overall arrangement and the narrative techniques used demand an investigation which proceeds hesitantly and which must continually search for a meaning that is deeper—by virtue of its very obscurity—than what seems at first able to be formulated into a lesson from "example." This wariness cannot, however, be reduced to a principle of generalized doubt, for systematic suspicion proves here hardly less rash than blind trust, and applying an interpretive grid suited, for example, to *Les Liaisons dangereuses* would be as brutally simplistic as naively reading the episodes to be gallant chivalric adventures. The labyrinths of language and desire can lead blindly to pure love and self-sacrifice as easily as they can lead to pitfalls and ambushes.

This is what underlies the enigmatic ninth tale, which has only been examined as yet for its repercussions upon the storytellers' debate. Here once again the way in which the tale is presented betrays disagreements, in order to array alternating perspectives around a sort of vanishing point. The story's theme is first outlined in Parlamente's reply to Dagoucin's praise of silence: "J'en ay veu [. . .] qui ont mieulx aymé mourir que parler" (48;114). In the commentary following the story, Dagoucin reorients the theme: he esteems that through the tale, he has shown "que parfaicte amour mene les gens à la mort, par trop estre celée et mescongneue" (53;119), which suggests that mutism and mutism's lethal consequences are intrinsic to the perfection of love. But meanwhile, the preamble has made the hero out to be an example of those "qui ne sont mortz d'autre maladye que d'aymer parfaictement" (49;114); and this formula is alone confirmed by the story, which only mentions the suitor's discretion in the preliminary lines ("il n'osoit descouvrir son affection," 49;115) and drops this theme after the fifth sentence (in which one learns that the young woman knew of "l'honnête amitié qu'il lui portoit," and took a liking to him to the point of giving rise to suspicion and gossip). The lover's death is thus not the result of his silence.

Is his death provoked by the chagrin of being shown to the door by the beloved's parents? This conjecture, seemingly plausible as far as the narrative skeleton goes, is invalidated by the astonishing scene in which the tale culminates, for the emphasis given to the gestures and the words of the perishing lover suggests something entirely different: a sacrifice "joyeusement" consented to (50,52;116,118), in which the *consolamentum* of the first and only kiss intermingles with the hero's dying sigh and with the act of mercy which he implores of God.[7] Signs of death's approach pile up one upon the other: in order to receive the privilege of a kiss which was only granted to him because "il n'y avoit plus en luy sentiment ne force d'homme vif" (52;118), the "pauvre languissant" stretches out "ses bras tout dénués de chair et de sang," embraces his beloved "avecq toute la force de ses os," kisses her "de sa froide et pasle bouche." Following upon these macabre images, a final touch equates erotic ecstasy with the spasm of death: "Et, en ce disant, la reprint entre ses bras par une telle vehemence, que, le cueur affoibly ne pouvant porter cest esfort, fut habandonné de toutes ses vertuz et esperitz; car la joye les feit tellement dilater que le siege de l'ame luy faillyt" (52;118). And the young woman reacts with an equally convulsive vigor, to the point that onlookers barely manage to pull her away from the embrace in order to "[ôter] la vive, pire que morte, d'entre les bras du mort." Few texts exist which express with such force this strange interplay between Eros and Thanatos, especially when one takes into account the customarily discreet style in which the tales have been written. Far more than any psychological or moral motivation rationally identifiable as such, what shows through here is the death-wish complex in its most undiluted state. Hircan does not err in speaking of madness and in being shocked by the final gesture, "embrass[er] le corps mort (chose répugnante à nature)" (53;119); his outburst of unreflected hedonism and of common sense bears witness to the fact that Dagoucin's possibly contrived doctrine has brought the group to the brink of hidden zones where nothing can be directly expressed except in a poetic form; all of which, in the conclusion, does indeed turn his story into a celebration of silence and of a love that is "celé et méconnu," but in an entirely different sense from what could have been expected by the initial debate which provided the excuse to tell the story.

However clear be the characters' statements, either in the discussions or within the tales, the *Heptameron*'s language thus partakes in pretense and secrecy by virtue of the montage invented by Marguerite de Navarre in order to indicate, emphasize, and sometimes complicate the work's dialogic structures. At the precise center of the work as planned (in ten days), the rationale for this system of expression is revealed in theological terms when Oisille wonders about what resources the storytellers can still call upon, in other words, about the text's mode of production. Geburon reassures her: "Tant que malice et bonté regneront sur la terre, ilz la rempliront tousjours de nouveaulx actes, combien qu'il est escript qu'il n'y a rien de nouveau soubz le soleil. Mais, à nous, [= "as for us"] qui n'avons esté appellez au conseil privé de Dieu, ignorant les premieres causes, trouvons toutes choses nouvelles tant plus admirables, que moins nous les vouldrions ou pourrions faire" (327;427). Like Scève, and later Montaigne, it is through postulating that language is never perfectly transparent—that human motivations and behavior can never be entirely deciphered—that Marguerite de Navarre creates a literary form whose wellspring never runs dry, a literary form arranged around a blind spot which she defines as the "conseil privé" of the God of novelists.

Notes

1. This decision to focus upon the fiction's explicit indications distinguishes our study from the structural analysis of Philippe de Lajarte, "Modes du discours et formes d'activité dans les 'Nouvelles' de Marguerite de Navarre," *Littérature* 55 (1984): 64–73. Such differing approaches nevertheless lead to complementary conclusions.

2. The scene appears fleetingly at the moment of transition between the opening discussion and the tale. Following up a comment made by Hircan, Simontaut has just expressed the wish that he could "commander à toute ceste compaignye"; Parlamente "l'entendit très bien, que se print à tousser; parquoy Hircan ne s'apperceut de la couleur qui luy venoit aux joues, mais dist à Simontault qu'il commencast, ce qu'il feit [. . .] Mes dames, j'ay esté si mal recompensé de mes longs services que, pour me venger d'amour et de celle qui m'est si cruelle . . ." (10–11;70).
See the more detailed analysis given by John D. Lyons in his *Exemplum: The Rhetoric of Example in Early Modern France and Italy* (Princeton, N.J.: Princeton University Press, 1989) 91–93, of how this first tale alerts the reader to a distortion of the concepts of "testimony" and "example." Our work also follows from Lyons's study of tales 21 and 40 upon the following pages ("Rolandine and her Aunt," 93–103).

3. One has learned from the prologue (3;61–62) that Dagoucin and Saffredent are the suitors of Longarine and Parlamente; in tale 8 (48;113, see discussion below), one will find out that Dagoucin pines for Parlamente, and thus it then becomes

possible to infer that Saffredent is courting Longarine. But at the conclusion of the third tale, this second bit of information is not yet available. Besides, everything is still not cleared up: it is difficult to see how the third tale's story of mutual adultery can especially apply to Longarine, just bereft of her husband! Its circumstances would better fit the case of Parlamente, wife of the inconstant Hircan (who seems to have set his designs upon Nomerfide, 34, 40, 391, 420; 97, 103, 501, 534). But the story's theme could have been selected so as to lead the others onto a false track.

4. Tale 8 happens to be taken from the fabliau of the *Meunier d'Arleu*, already borrowed by Italian writers (Poggio, Sacchetti, Sermini); tales 5,6, and 7 are in the same vein. Only the second tale, beyond the pale of gallant banter and as if set apart, approaches the "tragique" style of the ninth, with respect to which it has been placed symmetrically.

5. At the outset, Amadour is silent concerning his feelings: Floride herself suspects nothing for several years. He introduces his declaration of love by the very question which had sparked Dagoucin and Parlamente's exchange (48;113): "M'amye, je vous supplie me conseiller lequel vault mieulx, parler ou mourir" (62;129). Last but not least, when Amadour trys to take advantage of Floride, he pretends to faint ("comme ung homme à qui la force default," 72;140) in order that she take him into her arms; a restaging disquietingly similar to the central scene of tale 9 (see following).

6. All the more in that in an earlier version, the *Heptameron* may have been envisaged without discussions among the storytellers. One must nonetheless note that the fragment upon which this conjecture is based, published in the appendix of the François edition (445), appears to introduce a final (and tenth) tale appreciably longer than the others, stating that it comes from a story told to the narrator by an "amy" who related what had "advenu au plus grand amy qu'il eust en ce monde." It is as if, even before having invented the roles of the storytellers, Marguerite de Navarre already wished, in this first draft, to explicitly split into two the act of narration.

7. This is indicated in an expression so unexpected that Adrien de Thou's manuscript corrects its reading. One finds in the Bibliothèque Nationale manuscript Fr 1512 (according to the reference edition's transcription): "Je rendray joyeusement mon esperit à Dieu . . . le suppliant, ayant mon desir entre mes bras, recepvoir entre les siens mon esperit." "Mon désir" here amounts to the object of that desire, through synecdoche. De Thou gives a more trivial reading, ". . . laissant le corps entre vos bras, recevoir entre les siens mon esperit."

Part III

Character and Community

Daniel Russell

12. Some Ways of Structuring Character in the *Heptameron*

In *Hamlet and Oedipus*, Ernest Jones appears to take Hamlet's custom (in Danish and Icelandic proto-Hamlet stories) of sleeping in his mother's chamber to be a sign of some Oedipal abnormality.[1] Such communal sleeping arrangements were of course quite normal from before the time Tristan left tracks in the flour on his way to Iseult's bed well into the sixteenth century, and occur from time to time in the world of Marguerite de Navarre's stories without provoking concern or comment of any apparent kind.[2] A psycho-historian today would probably not fall into this trap of anachronism, but the anecdote does serve to remind us that the dynamics of self and society were very different in the late Middle Ages and Renaissance, and this difference had a profound effect on characterization and the structure of narrative in the Renaissance *nouvelle*.[3]

At the surface of the narration, characterization unfolds in two ways in the *Heptameron*. The storytellers take shape almost exclusively through their discussion of the stories; in her book on the *devisants*, Betty Davis attempted to put the pieces of each puzzle together to produce a series of portraits.[4] But in the *nouvelles* themselves pictures of the characters, such as they are, take shape only through the way the storytellers recount their tales; these characters emerge more through the way the story is structured than through any concerted effort at portrayal of the kind one might expect to find, for example, in a nineteenth-century novel.

In this chapter, I will examine the presentation of various characters in several *nouvelles* of the *Heptameron* in an attempt to explain what may appear, from the perspective of a modernist reading, to be disconcerting anomalies or technical flaws in the narrative construction. The premise underlying this study assumes that each period of history develops a prevailing conception of the self, and that those conceptions exercise considerable influence on the projection and presentation of characters in any anecdote or other narrative exposition. Stable periods produce stable conceptions of the self, and these conceptions may appear to be universally valid models for self-structuring in the period that produced them, and sometimes, at least for a society's more conservative members, even long after that society has changed quite radically. But the sixteenth century was a period of transition in many respects and did not, therefore, develop so firmly fixed a conception of the self as either the Middle Ages that preceded it or the classical period that followed. This situation, I believe, permitted the kind of social mobility one can see in the Renaissance, but it also had the effect of producing characters in narrative fiction that emerge in surprisingly various and different ways.[5]

This is not the place to discuss the psychology of the self in the Renaissance, but I wish rather to use the presentation of character in the *Heptameron* as evidence of the various ways character may have been perceived at the time and show how the perception of character was in transition in ways that reflect the tensions of different conceptions competing in the same social space. Long before the relativity of the subject became a fashionable theme among Marxists, Krister Stendahl claimed "that one of the most important insights of biblical studies in the twentieth century" "questions the often tacit presupposition that man remains basically the same through the ages." Following an Augustinian tradition, Luther perceived Saint Paul as an introspective individual, but this view of Paul is quite different from the one presented by the earliest texts, or the surprisingly homosexual Saint Paul imagined recently by Bishop Spong, who was promptly and severely taken to task by psychiatrists with a different diagnosis for Paul. We cannot, of course, know Paul, but looking at different interpretations of his life and works can tell us much about the conceptions of the self at different periods in history. Likewise the presentation of characters by the *devisants* in the *Heptameron* can shed light on the process that was powering an evolution from one stable conception of the self to another.[6]

*   *   *

Physical and psychological descriptions are, by and large, absent from the *Heptameron*, and they are replaced by other kinds of characterizing techniques. Even though physiognomy was considered in the Renaissance to be a precious key to the understanding of character, few physical details emerge in descriptions of characters in the *nouvelles*. But if physiognomy, as

Ronsard advised Charles IX, will help kings "juger de leurs sujets seulement à les voir,"[7] it is logical to assume, conversely, that physiognomy, the general contours of the physical self, could be imagined from some knowledge of one's behavior, thus paradoxically making a physical description of characters redundant within the economy of the storyteller's art.

There may, however, be other reasons why a physical description of characters would be superfluous to this art. Characters were still types to a certain extent; not pure types as we think of them appearing alongside personifications in medieval allegories, but hybrid, social types like the wicked and lecherous priest, the handsome, dashing, and brave young hero, or the clever, deceiving wife, types that need to be described by a combination of epithets rather than by a single one as was often the case for earlier types. As such, many characters followed certain relatively fixed models one might encounter in the theater or in woodcuts. So once again the audience could be expected to have a sufficiently clear theatrical or iconographical model in mind to conjure an image distinct enough that it could serve to unite the character and his actions into a more or less coherent entity. And what differentiation we should imagine in characters comes more from their place of origin (country, province, and so on), their rank, or their profession, than from the individuation of Romantic or post-Romantic subjectivities. Finer distinctions in such elements of differentiation could be expressed in clothing among the great, or in festival garb. And proverbial typecasting associated certain nationalities with certain characteristics, such as cleverness, a propensity to drink, or deceitfulness; the motivation of *nouvelle* 16 in the *Heptameron*, for example, turns partially on the assumption that Italians are more cowardly than the French.

The ever greater variety of proverbial typecasting at the time of Marguerite was beginning to diversify and fragment earlier, more general types in ways that were beginning to produce a kind of individuation of character.[8] The process was, however, usually still far from complete, and generally reflected the drama of some effort to escape from, or accommodate oneself to, an intolerable situation imposed by the old order, or caused by some breakdown of that old order, a situation that reflected the strains of an aging and now basically inadequate system. Real individuation in the post-Renaissance sense seems to have emerged, if we can take the *Heptameron* as typical, through a process of resistance to the kind of typecasting that relegated individuals to rigidly defined roles and places in a hierarchically structured social system. For this resistance to be effective in tailoring a truly sui generis, autonomous self, it needed to be persistent, and ongoing.

Through such persistence, the rebellious individual might win the grudging, or not so grudging, admiration and, eventually, acceptance of society, acceptance of the kind accorded to the religious martyr, through some kind of heroic denial of that society. The stories of the early Christian martyrs in works ranging from the lives of the saints through Boccaccio's *De claris mulieribus* and Christine de Pisan's *Cité des dames* to Antoine Du Four's compendium of *Vies des femmes celebres*, prepared for Anne de Bretagne in the very early years of the sixteenth century,[9] may well have provided models for this kind of exceptional self-generation.

This stubborn, persistent resistance sometimes must have come to be perceived as an admirable consistency of character, often characterized, as for example by Montaigne in "De la vertu" (*Essais*, 2.29), as constancy. When such constancy was the subject of a *nouvelle*, its demonstration required an extension of the story line that permitted certain characters to emerge as much more fully developed, or at least in higher relief, than those we would typically find, for example, in the *Cent nouvelles nouvelles*. And often these characters are marked by personal names, whereas the typecast characters usually are "named" only as types or through a designation that situates them within a family or societal structure. At the beginning of *nouvelle* 35, for example, we sense that we will be dealing with a type when Hircan characterizes the heroine of his story as "estant en l'aage de trente ans, que les femmes ont accoustumé de quicter le nom de belles pour estre nommées saiges" (255;346). Epithets provide the names for types, and these are the only "names" Hircan's heroine will have in this story.

The case of Rolandine will serve as my model of the individuated character in the *Heptameron*. One of the longest stories in Marguerite's collection, *nouvelle* 21 recounts the drama of a plain, but virtuous young woman who is neither appreciated by her mistress nor properly dowered by her miserly father. Although her virtuous ways attracted numerous marriage proposals in her youth, the queen always vetoed them. Our heroine faced life as an old maid with equanimity until, as she was approaching thirty, she met a poor and unattractive bastard son of a good family. They were attracted to each other "comme souvent ung malheureux cerche l'autre" (159;236) and forged an idyllic and chaste relationship that provided them with much happiness until the queen discovered their relationship and did her best to separate the couple. The story then becomes first one of their resistance to all efforts to separate them, then increasingly, the story of Rolandine's persistent defense of her ideal love and the unauthorized marriage she had secretly contracted with the bastard.

She confronts the queen and upbraids her, recalling explicitly the obligations of the great to assure the well-being of the members of their retinue and, implicitly, the queen's earlier opposition to possible marriages within the conventions of society; Rolandine concludes that it is "une faulte qui doibt estre imputée plus à vous que à moy" (170;248). The queen characterizes "son visage si constant et sa parole tant veritable" as signs of "l'obstination et la dureté de vostre cueur" (169;247–48). Although imprisoned by her father, Rolandine stands firm in her love, and that love seems all the more admirable in contrast to her husband's conduct in exile where he betrays the hypocrisy of his earlier professions of love by marrying a wealthy German lady. But in the end Rolandine's constancy triumphs, for after divine Providence (*la Bonté divine*) has miraculously conspired to kill off her husband, she returns to the good graces of her father and marries a worthy gentleman who admired her "congnoissant que sa fin n'avoit esté que pour la vertu" (173;252). Still, her troubles are not over; her husband is not wealthy and, at the death of her father, her brother opposes her claims to any inheritance because of her disobedience. Providence intercedes once more, and upon her brother's death she inherits both shares of her father's fortune to insure a comfortable life thereafter for herself and her husband.

Rolandine figures as the complete outsider in this story. Neither the eldest daughter, nor the preferred younger sister; neither beautiful nor ugly; neither rich nor poor, she is spurned by her mistress and could not then epitomize any type in the system. Her only choice then was either to fade into the anomalous state of a nonentity or to assert a unique personality. Meeting the bastard, another outsider, provided the opportunity and impetus to pursue an independent course of conduct. But it is the way she followed that course of action that made her unique.

Throughout the *nouvelle* words like *constant* and *constance* underline a tenacity that will earn Rolandine a reputation different from that of typical women whom men, we discover in the discussion, consider to be "tant inconstantes." This ideal of consistency of character, that contrasts with the psychological unpredictability of the characters in earlier *nouvelles*, is powered by concerns of honor within a rigid social hierarchy. For as the conditions of honor changed, consistency of character became increasingly a dominant concern and an essential structuring requirement of the self as it began to liberate itself from the hierarchies of medieval society.

The story of Rolandine's aunt (*nouvelle* 40), superficially so similar to that of Rolandine, actually highlights the exceptional quality of Rolandine's struggle as Parlamente portrays it. The aunt is presented as the very type of foolish young lover who hears only what she wants to hear and then suffers the consequences for not following the rules of her society. True, she does suffer her fate with "patience," an eminently admirable quality for Marguerite, but despite her travails so like those of Rolandine, and even though, after her death, people "y couroit comme à une saincte" (277;370), she comes across quite differently from Rolandine: she passively submits to her fate and remains unnamed. The reason is that Parlamente, who tells both tales, is setting out to show something different here; this story is meant to convey a warning not to marry for pleasure without proper family consent. That is why, I believe, she remains unnamed, and that too is why the discussion following the tale centers not on the heroine, as in the case of Rolandine, but rather on the institution of marriage, that is, on an element of the medieval social hierarchy that conditioned and shaped the types that inhabited it. Hence, the aunt is presented as a type who has been transformed by circumstances into another type. This story makes it clear that the way characters are perceived and presented is conditioned by the lesson the *nouvelle* as exemplum is supposed to convey. That two characters so similar can be presented quite differently by the same storyteller highlights the transitional character of this society where there was no dominant, stable conception of the self, but where the model of medieval types was still feuding with the new ideal of the Renaissance individual.

Perhaps none of Marguerite's stories shows the link between the pursuit of honor and the structure of individuality more clearly than the one found in the longest *nouvelle* in the *Heptameron*, the story of Floride and Amadour, again two named characters. The handsome Amadour, a precocious champion on the battlefield and darling of the court, falls in love at first sight with the child Floride, whom he could never aspire to possess through marriage given the difference of social rank that separated them. He therefore begins to cultivate a chaste love in which all physical desire is sublimated to the ideal of *honeste amour*, and to this end he becomes a friend and confidant of the family, a young man whom Floride's mother trusts as her own son. To bring himself into closer and more intimate contact with his beloved, and at the same time deflect attention from his increasingly insistent passion, dissimulate the object of that passion, and protect her honor, Amadour even marries Floride's rather homely best friend, and then pretends to be in love with another lady of the court.

Perhaps the very process of deception by which he nurtured his love and defended the honor of his lady ended by corrupting him. The arts of dissimulation he had gradually cultivated could eventually serve to mask the growing libidinal conflict arising within him, perhaps even from himself. In any event, honor for Amadour was ultimately not the same as for Floride. She attains the ideal he has shown her, but she does not become a cold, rigid type; on the contrary, she slowly comes to love Amadour in her flesh, admits that love, to herself and to him, and then sees that love and trust, first betrayed, and then transformed, as if by grace, or at least without explanation, into a love of the good, and of God. Floride is lifted in a kind of mystical apotheosis by the Platonic ideal Amadour has shown her. In comparison with her figurative death to the world, that comes with her retreat into a monastery, Amadour's ineffectual and suicidal pursuit of another kind of honor brings only a literal death whose dry report has completely emptied it of all heroic mysticism, almost as completely as if it had been painted by Manet.

The tragic irony embedded in this story is that what Amadour pursues is, paradoxically, taken from him by the ideal he had inculcated in Floride in order to be close to her. But there is a larger tragedy on the horizon of this tale: Amadour fails because of the drives of the flesh, which Floride explicitly mortifies. Her sublimation is successful because her honor lies in chastity; it is a viable ideal that can be all-consuming for Floride. A man's honor still had, at least for Amadour, a different foundation; in the discussion following *nouvelle* 43, Parlamente distinguishes between the two kinds of honor this way: ". . . celles qui sont vaincues en plaisir ne se doibvent plus nommer femmes, mais hommes, desquelz la fureur et la concupiscence augmente leur honneur; car ung homme qui se venge de son ennemy et le tue pour ung desmentir en est estimé plus gentil compagnon; aussy est-il quant il en ayme une douzaine avecq sa femme. Mais l'honneur des femmes a autre fondement: c'est doulceur, patience et chasteté" (301;396–97). Amadour's honor is military and lies on the battlefield; it lies in conquest, whereas that of Floride lies in self-conquest, self-denial, and thus, paradoxically, self-affirmation. But the rather stereotyped account of Amadour's death makes his sacrifice seem somehow hollow, and indeed the *raison d'être* for his honor was slowly disappearing as the conduct of war changed into a more administrative pursuit in the sixteenth century.[10]

With the increasing anonymity of the individual combatant in the new kind of warfare, honor could no longer be easily won, lost, or upheld in any meaningful way in a single episodic adventure. No longer could the epic duel between two heroes yield a reputation that could characterize them forever. The poets could no longer transform such feats of combat into a heroic apotheosis. No longer could such a victory and its heralding bring the kind of glory that would dispense the hero from the need to affirm his reputation in the actual conduct of life outside the theatrical engagements of chivalric war, along the lines of Bayard's much admired model. Slowly, the ideal of masculine honor, like that of feminine honor, would turn into a more diffuse thing that would require consistency of conduct over time; and so too, the *noblesse d'épée* slowly gave way to the *noblesse de robe*.

The passive consistency of the medieval typecast character was no longer operative, for individual memory required a different conformity, and one that was more personal, active, and more broadly encompassing over time than the medieval type would allow. It would appear that this memory began to develop in the thirteenth century following the Fourth Lateran Council which decreed, in the canon *Omnis utriusque sexus*, obligatory individual confession for all faithful, both men and women, at least once a year.[11] This memory instituted the diachronic time of the *récit* as the basis for inner personal consistency and integrity, and linked moments and events in a way that points toward the classical self that was to become fully developed only in the seventeenth and eighteenth centuries.

We should probably not talk of a feminization of the ideal of the self, but it is certainly true that women appear to have been major contributors to a revision in that ideal as their glory could come only through *constancy* (or *patience* in another of Parlamente's characterizations), which carves out a new kind of path for self-realization to follow. The tension is between the new sense of a whole and unique self and the types within which people were more or less imprisoned in the late medieval social structure to the extent that realism provided its philosophical base or justification. That is, the tension arises between ideals imposed from without and those that are generated from within as an integral sense of a uniquely personal identity began to differentiate the individual from his or her role in society.

Generally, typecast characters in the *Heptameron* appear driven by dark forces beyond their control and incarnate human frailties with little apparent resistance or understanding. Typing, as I understand it here, is based on several traditional models such as the ages of man or the virtues and vices, which provide a system of epithets that go beyond description to become substantives. Such typing does not produce immutable, personification-like characters; it is not impervious to changes in the role that the character plays in the structure of society. Changes can occur, for example, with a change of age, and it is no coincidence, I think, that Marguerite is particularly interested in women who are *entre deux âges*, for these are the women who are most often faced with change and confront it in different ways.

When age or the vicissitudes of fortune effect such changes, the transition is sometimes highlighted or explained in proverbial or emblematic terms. Hence, Rolandine's attraction to the *bastard* is explained, as we have seen, in proverbial terms: "comme souvent ung malheureux cerche l'autre." The incestuous encounter in *nouvelle* 30 can take place only with some breakdown in the typecast role the mother is playing; the events leading up to it could have produced another outcome and the collision between pride and human frailty is a rather unexpected explanation for the outcome that actually does occur, since pride, in some regards, does not seem to be a major component of her character. No, she is shown as simply, and perhaps imperiously, confident of her strength as it was attributed to her by the type she had worked so hard to incarnate. The seeds of the breakdown as I visualize it are neatly contained in the only name Hircan gives her as he recounts her sad story: "la jeune dame vefve" (229;317). A palpable tension between nature and culture is invoked by the epithets "jeune" and "vefve," positioned on either side of the noun like two persuasive companions tugging in opposite directions; "jeune" pulls her in the direction of nature while "vefve" asserts the claims of culture.

At first she denies nature, and puts all her energies into the culture-based role of the mother as an educator. As her son grows, Nature, Hircan tells us, teaches him other lessons, and one of his mother's maids tells her that he is trying to seduce her. The mother unwisely decides to teach her son a lesson in a very dramatic way; following her directions, the maid sets a meeting where the mother will take her place, disguised by darkness, until she wishes to reveal her identity and chastise the surprised and errant boy. But Nature takes the upper hand, and leads her too far along the treacherous path upon which she has embarked. Her precipitous fall into incest is succinctly explained in an emblematic image:[12] ". . . tout ainsy que l'eaue par force retenue court avecq plus d'impetuosité quant on la laisse aller, que celle qui court ordinairement, ainsy ceste pauvre dame tourna sa gloire à la contraincte qu'elle donnoit à son corps" (230;318). This emblematic variation on a fairly common image provides the transitional explanation for her fall in which she forgets "le nom de mere," that is, in which she abandons the "mother" type that she had put all her energies into living to perfection. The pivotal image replaces causal explanation in structuring the transition, or at least its presentation.

Several other *nouvelles* in the *Heptameron* contain emblematic images, and they often play crucial roles in the structuring of the story. *Nouvelle* 16, for example, and the ensuing discussion, provide a superb example of the way late medieval allegory evolved into, on the one hand, a dust of fragments that could be used emblematically to ornament a variety of texts with quite different meanings, and, on the other, a loose, general rhetorical frame for the presentation of a message or, as here, of a dialogue/debate. *Nouvelle* 16 tells the story of a Milanese widow who swore never to remarry or to love again. However, a Frenchman pursued her with such tenacity over a period of three years that she gave in to his entreaties, and they swore "amityé perpetuelle" to each other. In the telling of the tale, the metaphor of the hunt surfaces from time to time with verbs and similes like "pourchassa" and "elle le fuyoit comme le loup fait le levrier" (131;206). As the lady finally describes how she ended up by giving in to her lover's entreaties, she remarks that "comme la bische navrée à mort cuyde, en changeant de lieu, changer le mal qu'elle porte avecq soy, ainsi m'en allois-je d'eglise en eglise, cuydant fuyr celluy que je portois en mon cueur, duquel a esté la preuve de la parfaicte amityé qui a faict accorder l'honneur avecq l'amour" (132;207).

The image of the deer who aggravates his wound by fleeing the hunter had been common in the rhetoric of love since Petrarch, and following its use in a mourning device by René d'Anjou in the fifteenth century, was turned into emblems by Gilles Corrozet and Maurice Scève.[13] Is this emblematic image simply rhetorical ornamentation? Its appearance is carefully prepared earlier in the story, as we have seen, by other evocations of the hunt, and indeed, it would appear that the listeners understood it to be the governing metaphor of the tale, as they pick up the metaphor of the stag, and use the verb "chasser" on two occasions in their discussions. The metaphor sets the story squarely within a traditional context of male-female relations and orients it toward a conclusion that would be suitable to male and female *devisants* alike, conforming as it does to medieval social norms. But as a result, this "widow" is even less individualized than the one in *nouvelle* 30.

Sometimes, the structuring of the tales goes beyond this kind of simple emblematic articulation, and the characters are so rigidly typecast, at least in appearance, that the story turns into an allegorical tableau devoid of purely narrative action. Such is the case in *nouvelle* 26 where a young nobleman finds himself torn between a wise lady and a foolish one. A total lack of what one might today call psychological realism in the "adoption" of the handsome young nobleman by a wealthy old commoner and his beautiful young wife removes the story from the space of everyday reality and into that of the fairy tale, which is an allegorical space, the space of parable.[14] The young man was attracted to his beautiful adopted mother, but "la paour qu'il avoit de perdre son amityé" (210;294) moved the young man to look elsewhere for love, only to find someone as full of vices as his stepmother was full of virtues.

In the context of other stories about widows in the *Heptameron*, the warning signs of some psychological fault lines in this model housewife come early on as she is described as being dressed "si honnestement qu'elle sembloit plus vefve que mariée" (208;292), and the reader is alerted to the allegorical dimensions of the tableau that emerges by the way the two ladies are contrasted through the implicit parallel between a good and a bad housekeeper. The heroine reminds one of the *Venus domestique*, presented by Guillaume de La Perrière in one of his emblems as a good manager, who talks little and does not venture far from the house.[15] The heroine is so reserved that her foolish old husband asks the young *seigneur* to dance with her; we notice that there is little or no dialogue when she appears early in the story—in clear contrast to the foolish lady who is revealed to us in good measure through dialogue.

Then, the young man is compared, quite in passing, to Hercules. That comparison sets the story, for the knowledgeable reader, against the mythological background of Hercules at the crossroads, trying to choose between vice and virtue.[16] The static story is comparable to a Renaissance painting of Hercules, in contemporary dress, trying to make his choice between good and evil. And indeed, the memory of some painting may have prompted the organization and choice of metaphors used to structure the telling of this tale. While Veronese's *Allegory of Virtue and Vice* (*The Choice of Hercules*, The Frick Collection, New York) was painted around 1580, and is hence too late to be suggested as a model, it does provide a good idea of how some painting of this popular subject might have worked to provide a visual model *against* which the story might be elaborated.

For there is a very real difference between the mythological model and its use in this story. The virtuous heroine, the Venus of domesticity, is still a Venus, and her love for the young man slowly becomes contaminated by Eros despite all her efforts to embody her husband's ideal of the perfect wife and *ménagère*. That is why she rebukes Monsieur d'Avannes in his enthusiastic attempt to characterize her as a personification of virtue (215;299). Indeed, not only is she no personification, she cannot even defend her typecast role as the ideal wife from the incursions of erotic love, given the implicitly unnatural conditions in which she tries to live that role. And it is the tension between her developing passion and the artificial situation in which she finds herself that leads to her death. Types are not personifications, and they are fragile at best when they are lived out in circumstances where culture is at odds with nature.

*   *   *

Against this background, how might we profitably compare the three female characters, Rolandine, Floride, and "la jeune dame vefve," as they are presented in their stories? First, I take Rolandine and Floride, two named characters, to be primarily emergent individuals whereas the young widow is, I would submit, like the Milanese widow or the good and bad housekeepers, primarily a type. The evolution or crystallization of character in the first two, as it becomes more conscious, appears seamless, the progression, logical within the context of their beliefs. The widow changes abruptly from one type to another, from the proud, self-sufficient mother to the penitent sinner who relies more on her own tears and self-imposed penitence to atone than on any petition to the grace of God. These changes are the result of powerful forces beyond her control that produce shattering consequences for the identity she is trying so hard to incarnate. In one respect, the contrast is clearest between Rolandine and the widow. Whereas Rolandine is lifted by the intercession of divine grace, so clearly signaled by two utterly improbable deaths, but two deaths that were absolutely essential for Rolandine's self-fulfillment, the widow believed, foolishly, in the power of works, and

> en lieu de se humilier et recongnoistre l'impossibilité de nostre chair, qui sans l'ayde de Dieu ne peult faire que peché, voulant par elle-mesmes et par ses larmes satisfaire au passé et par sa prudence eviter le mal de l'advenir, donnant tousjours l'excuse de son peché à l'occasion et non à la malice, à laquelle n'y a remede que la grace de Dieu, pensa de faire chose parquoy à l'advenir ne sçauroit plus tumber en tel inconvenient. (231;318–19)

Tears and works fit into a framework of medieval realism, whereas an emphasis on grace emerges with William of Ockham and nominalism in the fourteenth century, as it must in a world where objects do not incarnate a higher reality, where only that which is experienced may be the object of intellectual study, where everything that is of the other world may be only the subject of faith, and where the individual's relation to that world can only be a matter of grace.[17]

Not having petitioned divine grace, the widow is overwhelmed by the complexity of human nature and the forces that work upon it; hence, she is doomed to cling to the model of a type, only to be violently catapulted into a situation that attaches her to another type. There can be no consistent, constant coming-to-terms with her self, and in the end her life appears as a mosaic of typecast roles she has played in this Oedipal casting of the struggle between nature and culture.

As medieval culture and society slowly ceased to be as monolithic as they were once perceived to be, the difficulties of living a typecast role loomed increasingly larger. Nominalism took account of the problematics of a system in which Foulques de Toulouse, when rebuked for giving alms to an Albigensian heretic, replied that he was giving alms to the "poor woman" not to the "heretic."[18] He could just as well have refused to give to the heretic, and the conundrum this anecdote evokes is but one sign of the increasingly complex situation of the self toward the end of the Middle Ages. The triumphant characters in the *Heptameron*, most often women like Rolandine or Marie Heroet (*nouvelle* 22), manage to take account, with some help from divine grace, of that complexity and fashion highly individuated selves. Tragic destinies, like that of the young widow, founder in the shoals and eddies of a typology of the self that was increasingly becoming a backwater to currents producing new social frameworks and new models for the self in early modern Europe.

Notes

1. Ernest Jones, *Hamlet and Oedipus* (1949; New York: Norton, 1976), p. 98, note.

2. See for example, *nouvelle* 30, where the widow's son is pursuing one of his mother's *demoiselles*. The young lady slept in her mistress's chamber, and the assignation is made to take place, without comment and without provoking surprise or shock on the part of the audience, in that very chamber!

3. See Jonathan Culler, *Structuralist Poetics* (Ithaca, N.Y.: Cornell University Press, 1975), 29: "The discourse of a culture sets limits to the self; the idea of personal identity appears in social contexts . . . ," and Jacques Lacan, "Le Stade du miroir comme formateur de la fonction du je," in *Ecrits* (Paris: Seuil, 1966), 93–100, esp. p. 97, where he speaks of a "temporal dialectic" which "projette en histoire la formation de l'individu . . . et qui pour le sujet, pris au leurre de l'identification spatiale, machine les fantasmes qui se succèdent d'une image morcelée du corps à

une forme que nous appellerons orthopédique de sa totalité." "Ce corps morcelé . . .
apparaît alors sous la forme de membres disjoints et de ces organes figurés en
exoscopie, qui s'ailent et s'arment pour les persécutions intestines, qu'à jamais a
fixées par la peinture le visionnaire Jérôme Bosch, dans leur montée au siècle
quinzième au zénith imaginaire de l'homme moderne." Might we not imagine that
the Renaissance played out at a macrocosmic level what Lacan imagines that we all
play out in the microcosm of ourselves as we go about the formation of those
"selves"?

4. Betty J. Davis, *The Storytellers in Marguerite de Navarre's* Heptaméron,
French Forum Monographs, 9 (Lexington, Ky.: French Forum Publishers, 1978).
For some pertinent differences between the characters of the storytellers as narrators
and as *devisants*, see Philippe de Lajarte, "Des *Nouvelles* de Marguerite de Navarre à
La Princesse de Clèves: Notes sur quelques transformations de l'écriture narrative de
la Renaissance à l'Age classique," *Nouvelle revue du XVIe siècle* 6 (1988): 45–56.

5. Here and throughout, see also my study of "Conception of Self, Conception of Space, and Generic Convention: An Example from the *Heptaméron*," *Sociocriticism* 4–5 (1986–87): 159–83. There I attempt to explain what might appear to be
inconsistencies in François I's conduct in the famous *nouvelle* 25 by proposing a
transitional conception of the self that effects not only Parlamente's perception and
presentation of her hero, but also effects the structuring of her account of the
anecdote. This chapter is intended as a sequel to my earlier study.

6. See Krister Stendahl, "The Apostle Paul and the Introspective Conscience
of the West," *Harvard Theological Review* 56 (1963): 199–215. For Bishop Spong's
reading of Paul as a repressed homosexual and Wallace K. Tomlinson's reply that "a
body of medical literature" inclines to the assumption that Paul had temporal lobe
epilepsy, see *The New York Times*, Feb. 2, 1991, and Feb. 12, 1991. As these conflicting
views of Paul suggest, we may be living through another unstable period of
evolution that may have begun as long ago as the early years of this century.

7. Pierre de Ronsard, *Institution pour l'adolescence du roy tres-chrestien Charles
IX de ce nom*, ll.37–40:

Ils [les Princes mieux naiz] deviennent appris en la Mathematique,
En l'art de bien parler, en Histoire et Musique,
En Physiognomie afin de mieux sçavoir
Juger de leurs sujets seulement à les voir.

8. On the importance of the proverb as matrix for thought and wisdom in the
early Renaissance, see V.-L. Saulnier, "Proverbe et paradoxe du XVe au XVIe
siècle," in *La Pensée humaniste et la tradition chrétienne aux XVe et XVIe siècles*, ed.
H. Bedarida (Paris: Centre national de recherche scientifique, 1948), 87–104.

9. Antoine Du Four, *Vies des femmes Celebres*, ed. G. Jeanneau, Textes Littéraires Français (Geneva and Paris: Droz and Minard, 1970).

10. See Michael West, "Spenser's Art of War: Chivalric Allegory, Military
Technology, and the Elizabethan Mock-Heroic Sensibility," *RenQ*, 41 (1988): 654–
704.

11. See Jacques Le Goff, *L'Imaginaire médiévale* (Paris: Gallimard, 1985), 99–102.

12. On the notion of an emblematic image, see D. Russell, "Emblematic Structures in Sixteenth-Century French Poetry," *Jahrbuch für Internationale Germanistik* 14 (1982): 54–100; "Montaigne's Emblems," *French Forum* 9 (1984): 261–75, and Jerome Schwartz, "Emblematic Structures in Yver's *Printemps*," *Journal of Medieval and Renaissance Studies*, 17 (1987): 235–55.

13. Vergil, *Aeneid*, 4.69; and Petrarch, *Rime sparse*, in *Canzoniere*, ed. Gianfranco Contini (Turin: Einaudi, 1964), 209. For emblematic parallels, see Gilles Corrozet, *Hecatomgraphie* (Paris: Denys Janot, 1540), sig. e7v; Maurice Scève, *Délie*, diz. 159, and preceding *emblesme*, "Fuyant ma mort, j'haste ma fin" or dizain 46, "Plus fuit le Cerf, & plus on le poursuyt," etc. For a poetic variation, see Du Bellay's *L'Olive*, son. 70, and my discussion of it in "L'Emblématique et la description dans la poésie française de Du Bellay," in *Du Bellay: Actes du Colloque International d'Angers du 26 au 29 Mai 1989* (Angers: Presses de l'Université d'Angers, 1990), 237–247. For René d'Anjou's device see my "Emblematic Structures in Sixteenth-Century French Poetry."

14. On the notion of allegorical space, see Walter J. Ong, S.J., "From Allegory to Diagram in the Renaissance," *Journal of Aesthetics and Art Criticism* 17 (1955): 423–40.

15. Guillaume de La Perrière, *Le Theatre des bons engins* (Paris: Denys Janot, 1539), emblem 18.

16. It thus reminds us of the allegory of the young man at court in d'Aubigné's *Tragiques*, Princes, ll. 1107ff. See too Henkel and Schöne's *Emblemata: Handbuch zur Sinnbildkunst des 16. und 17. Jahrhunderts* (Stuttgart: J. B. Metzler, 1967), cols. 1642–43, esp. the examples from Corrozet, Coustau, and Junius.

17. See for example, Jacques Paul, *Histoire intellectuelle de l'occident médiéval* (Paris: Armand Colin, 1973), 441–44.

18. Recounted by J. Huizinga, *The Waning of the Middle Ages*, trans. F. Hopman (New York: Doubleday Anchor Books, 1954), 216.

François Rigolot

13. The *Heptameron* and the "Magdalen Controversy": Dialogue and Humanist Hermeneutics

> Dictes-moy si la Magdelaine n'a pas plus d'honneur entre les hommes maintenant, que sa soeur qui estoit vierge?
>
> —*Heptameron* (246;335)

> Dicat age, nonne sublimior est status innocentiae atque impeccantiae: quam post contracta peccati contagia, poenitentiae salutaris atque resipiscentiae?
>
> —Josse Clichtove, *Disceptationis de Magdelena Defensio*

In novella 32 of the *Heptameron* the envoy from King Charles VIII (1470–98), a gentleman by the name of Bernage, receives lodging one night in a German castle. Unexpectedly, at suppertime Bernage becomes the unwilling witness to a strange scene as his host's beautiful wife emerges, dressed in black and with her head shaved, from behind a tapestry: "Et ainsy que la viande fut apportée sur la table, [Bernage] veid sortir de derriere la tapisserye une femme, la plus belle qu'il estoit possible de regarder, mais elle avoit la teste tondue, le demeurant du corps habillé de noir à l'alemande" (242;331).

As the servant brings a drinking cup to the lady, Bernage is taken aback when he realizes that the cup is actually made of "la teste d'un mort, dont les oeilz estoient bouchez d'argent" (242;331). He soon learns the reason for such a sinister ritual: as a daily punishment for her past infidelity, the lady is forced by her vengeful husband to drink out of her dead lover's skull. Bernage is immediately moved by the lady's suffering and resignation. Allowed by his host to enter into conversation with her, he hears her pitiful confession: " 'Monsieur, je confesse ma faulte estre si grande, que tous les maux, que le seigneur de ceans [lequel je ne suis digne de nommer mon mary] me sçauroit faire, ne me sont riens au prix du regret que j'ay de l'avoir offensé.' En disant cela, se print fort à pleurer" (244;333).

The next morning, before leaving the castle to resume his royal mission, Bernage urges the German gentleman to recognize his wife's true remorse for her sin and to consider granting her his forgiveness. At the end of the narrative we learn that the husband eventually realizes that Bernage is right and, combining his compassion for his wife with his desire to have children, he takes her back and the story has a happy ending: "Il la reprint avecq soy, et en eut depuis beaucoup de beaulx enfans" (245;334). When Bernage returns to the French court, he reports the strange events to the king who, after hearing of the German lady's unusual beauty, dispatches his favorite painter, Jean Perréal, alias Jean de Paris, to bring back her "living likeness" to him ("pour luy rapporter ceste dame au vif," 245;334). Ultimately the truth of the story will be recorded on canvas for the king by the greatest French painter of his time.

Every detail in the story seems to function referentially. The narrative is made authentic by virtue of historical names (Charles VIII, Bernage, Jean de Paris), social functions (king, messenger, painter), and geographical locations (Germany, Sivray, Amboise). Such a relentless preoccupation with authentic details is very much in keeping with the theoretical premises of the book's prologue. As the ten assembled *devisants* look for a proper pastime until the bridge is repaired, Parlamente proposes to complete the forgotten court project to produce a new *Decameron*, but with one major difference: that all the stories be truthful. ("[Les Dames de la Court] se delibererent d'en faire autant, sinon en une chose differente de Boccace: c'est de n'escripre nulle nouvelle qui ne soit veritable histoire," 9;68). Because of this insistence on authenticity, embellishments through rhetorical devices will be banned from the stories lest they might "falsify the truth of the account" ("de paour que la beaulté de la rethoricque feit tort en quelque partye à la verité de l'histoire," 9;68).

Yet, as scholars have not failed to point out, analogues to novella 32 can be found both in the French and the Italian literary traditions. The most plausible source of Marguerite's story is probably the medieval *Violier des histoires romaines*, a French version of the fourteenth-century *Gesta Romanorum*, which features a skull turned into a drinking cup.[1] Furthermore, as a long exegetic tradition has shown, the search for truth rarely remains on the referential plane. In fact, in the discussion following novella 32, we move from a purely literal narrative of the events to a figurative interpretation on some crucial aspects of these events. To use Genette's terminology, the shift from a "récit d'événements" to a "récit de paroles" is accompanied with a much more consequential change in terms of the hermeneutic status of the *nouvelle*.[2] The question is no longer: "Do all the recorded events conform to the ideal of truthfulness established in the prologue?" It has become: "How exemplary can this story be for the *devisants* who are listening?"

A particularly clear allegorical stance is represented in novella 32 by Ennasuite who, in her usual provocative manner, glosses the German lady's sinfulness in terms of the gospel story of Mary Magdalen. Since this is a key starting point for our discussion, the dialogue between Parlamente, Longarine, and Ennasuite will be reproduced here in its entirety:

> —"Je trouve," dist Parlamente, "ceste punition autant raisonnable qu'il est possible; car, tout ainsy que l'offense est pire que la mort, aussy est la pugnition pire que la mort."
> Dist Ennasuitte: "Je ne suis pas de vostre opinion, car j'aymerois mieulx toute ma vie veoir les oz de tous mes serviteurs en mon cabinet, que de mourir pour eulx, veu qu'il n'y a mesfaict qui ne se puisse amender; mais après la mort, n'y a poinct d'amendement."
> —"Comment sçauriez-vous amender la honte?" dist Longarine, "car vous sçavez que, quelque chose que puisse faire une femme après ung tel mesfaict, ne sçauroit reparer son honneur?"
> —"Je vous prye," dist Ennasuitte, "dictes-moy si la *Magdelaine* n'a pas plus d'honneur entre les hommes maintenant, que sa soeur qui estoit vierge?"
> —"Je vous confesse," dist Longarine, "qu'elle est louée entre nous de la grande amour qu'elle a portée à Jesus Christ, et de sa grande penitence; mais si luy demeure le nom de *Pecheresse*."
> —"Je ne me soulcie," dist Ennasuitte, "quel nom les hommes me donnent, mais que Dieu me pardonne et mon mary aussy. Il n'y a rien pourquoy je voulsisse morir." (245–46;334–35)

To Parlamente who finds the punishment reasonable and to Longarine who holds that nothing can ever make up for the loss of a woman's honor, Ennasuite is quick to respond by proposing the image of the greatest of penitent sinners, Mary Magdalen. What might be perceived by modern readers as a passing reference to a popular saint may, in fact, have had quite an important meaning in the context of the hermeneutic debates in the early 1500s. As a result, the reader is faced with a double question. First, if Ennasuitte is right, must novella 32 be read as an allegorization of the Magdalen story? And, second, if that is so, is the greatest sanctity and honor for those who have never sinned (Longarine's position) or for those who have sinned and have been forgiven (Ennasuite's position)? Before answering these questions it is important to consider the problem of the "Magdalen Controversy" as it was formulated by several major humanists and theologians of the time, especially Jacques Lefèvre d'Etaples, Josse Clichtove, and John Fisher.

The cult of Saint Mary Magdalen was a very popular one in the Middle Ages.[3] As the prostitute converted by Christ's love, she was the object of numerous sermons, especially in churches devoted to her, around July 22, her feast day. Pilgrimages to Vézelay and La Sainte-Baume, near Marseilles, were often led by kings and queens. Louise de Savoie, the queen mother, had a particular devotion to Mary Magdalen. She had commissioned François du Moulin de Rochefort, a close friend of the royal family, for a biography of the saint.[4] In January 1516, as an act of thanksgiving after her son's victory at Marignan, Louise de Savoie went on a pilgrimage to La Sainte-Baume and was joined there by her son, François I, his wife, Claude de France, and Marguerite herself. At nearby Saint-Maximin they all prayed in front of the famous reliquary of Saint Mary Magdalen.[5] An inscription commemorating the royal visit was placed in the crypt. In the years following the event, François I and his mother contributed considerable sums of money toward the completion of the churches of Saint-Maximin and La Sainte-Baume. The world's famous people congregated at Saint Mary Magdalen's holy places in the first decades of the sixteenth century, including Charles V who voiced his claims over the saint's relics.[6]

One is not therefore surprised that novella 32 should be told by Oisille, the old devout widow who is commonly identified by scholars with the queen mother. Marguerite, whose voice is often thought to be echoed by Parlamente's, was brought up in a spirit of veneration for the saint; but this does not explain why, in novella 32, Parlamente sides with Oisille on the crucial issue of the sinner's punishment. One must turn to other sources, namely contemporary philological and theological debates, to better understand the lively debate between female *devisants* which follows Oisille's narrative.

Among Christian humanists the controversy around Saint Magdalen started around 1515, and focused on a new philological reading of the gospels. The debate revolved around the question of the saint's identity as it could be reconstructed from the text of the New Testament. According to the commonly accepted patristic tradition, three women in the gospel narrative had come to be regarded as various incarnations of Mary Magdalen. First, there was the unnamed woman who anointed Jesus's feet, wiped them with her hair, and was absolved from sin through her faith in Christ (Luke 7.36–50). Then there was Mary of Bethany, Martha's and Lazarus's sister (John 11.1–45), who also poured ointment on Jesus's head (Matt. 26.6–12; Mark 14.3–9) and feet (John 12.1–8) on the occasion of a supper in their home. Contrary to her sister, Martha, who devoted herself to domestic affairs, Mary was inclined to a more contemplative life. Finally, there was the woman named Mary Magdalen or Mary of Magdala "from whom seven demons had been expelled" (Luke 8.2; Mark 16.9). She had followed Jesus throughout Judea and assisted him until his death (Matt. 27.55–56; Mark 15.40–41; Luke 23.49; John 19.25). On Easter morning, as she and still another Mary, mother of Saint James the Less, went to Christ's tomb with spices and ointment, they discovered that the body of Christ had vanished (Matt. 28.1–10; Mark 16.1–8; Luke 24.1–10; John 20.1–10). She was the first to bring the news of the Resurrection to the disciples.

In the early 1500s the question was raised among Christian humanists whether Mary Magdalen was really one person or a composite of several women, mentioned at different places in the New Testament.[7] This was, of course, a rather subversive question as it implicitly denied the very existence of the saint as she was known to most Christians. Jacques Lefèvre d'Etaples, the great humanist and Bible translator, played a crucial part in the controversy.[8] For him as for his fellow humanists in general, "no interpretation of any kind could be valid unless it was founded on a solid understanding of the meaning of the words of the text, of the verbal context in which the words appeared, and of the historical and cultural milieu that produced the text."[9] In two tersely written theological tracts, *De Maria Magdalena* (1518) and *De Tribus et Unica Magdalena* (1519), he critiqued the established tradition of a unified persona and argued for the distinction between the unnamed converted sinner (in Luke 7), the sister of Martha (in Luke 10) and "Mary called Magdalen" (in Luke 8).[10] Through an exemplary close reading of the four gospel stories, and particularly of the Luke narrative, Lefèvre showed that there was indeed no philological ground to sustain a popular belief abusively sanctioned by the church.

Without entering further into this very complicated debate between many scholars (by the early 1520s there were some twenty tracts on the controversy which, by then, had reached Italy and Spain[11]), it should be pointed out that Lefèvre's two important *disceptationes* were dedicated to close friends of Marguerite: the first, to François du Moulin de Rochefort, her brother's former tutor and soon to become grand almoner at the court; and the second, to Denis Briçonnet, a brother of Guillaume, the famous bishop of Meaux who had an extensive correspondence with Marguerite.[12] After the downfall of the Meaux group, Lefèvre continued to enjoy the protection of Marguerite and ultimately retired to her court at Nérac in 1531.[13] It is therefore quite conceivable that some aspects of the controversy may have been reflected to some degree in the text of the *Heptameron*. After all, Lefèvre's thesis had been solemnly condemned by the Sorbonne in 1521, and Marguerite's negative feelings about the powerful Paris institution are well known.[14]

Returning to the text of the *Heptameron*, one observes that the Magdalen model is twice proposed by Ennasuite as an example for sinners to follow.[15] Already in novella 19, two lovers whose marriage plans were opposed by their families decide to enter religious orders. This is how Ennasuitte's account of the story ends:

> Et depuis vesquirent Poline et son serviteur si sainctement et devotement en leurs Observances, que l'on ne doibt doubter que Celluy duquel la fin de la loy est charité, ne leur dist, à la fin de leur vie, *comme à la Magdelaine*, que *leurs pechez leur estoient pardonnez, veu qu'ilz avoient beaucoup aymé*, et qu'il ne les retirast en paix ou lieu où la recompense passe tous les merites des hommes. (150–51;228, emphasis added)

This is not only an allusion to the popular Magdalen figure but a clear paraphrase of the gospel narrative: "So I tell you, her sins, many as they are, are forgiven, for she has greatly loved" (Luke 7.47). Curiously enough, Ennasuite is not aware of the new distinction Lefèvre had drawn between Luke's popular contrite sinner and "Mary called Magdalen," the saintly woman who accompanied Jesus throughout Judea, stood weeping at the foot of the cross, and was the first to announce the news of Christ's Resurrection. Ennasuite simply "follows" (as suggested, perhaps, by the onomastic pun in her name) the traditional teaching of the church, ignoring Lefèvre's important *distinguo*. Indeed this may cast some doubt on the representativeness of her discourse as a defender of exemplarity in Marguerite's fiction.

As a matter of fact, one of the consequences of Lefèvre's philological approach to the Magdalen textual puzzle was the questioning of the hierarchical order of moral exemplarity. Lefèvre and his supporters were especially keen on distinguishing Mary of Bethany, Martha's sister, from Luke's unnamed converted sinner because they wanted to promote Mary of Bethany as a model figure for contemplative life. To them she represented the greatest Christian ideal. In his defense of Lefèvre against conservative theologians committed to traditional liturgy, Josse Clichtove, Lefèvre's disciple and close collaborator, formulated the problem as follows:

> Which is the higher condition: that of innocence and sinlessness or that of repentance and sorrow for the acquired stains of sins? Here is one [Mary of Bethany] who is said never to have sunk into the stains of vice. Is she not given

greater praise for virtue than the one [Luke's sinner] who, after a fall, is said to have been raised up by the merciful grace of God and washed from her filth? Surely one's life becomes finer and more praiseworthy to the extent that it is assimilated to divine perfection. Truth itself, speaking in the gospel, declares that each one will be perfect if he is like his master. A life lived without falling into serious sin appears to be more similar to divine perfection and purity, which is totally foreign to sin, than one which, after the downfall of sin, is cleansed and washed by the help of divine mercy.[16]

Ennasuite's position appears to be the exact opposite of Lefèvre's and Clichtove's. In her own narrative (novella 19), when Poline, after renouncing her human love, decides to enter the order of Saint Clare ("la religion de saincte Claire," 150;228), she acts like "Mary Magdalen" whose sins were forgiven through Christ's mercy. This is a traditional view of "la Magdelaine" which was opposed by the new evangelical scholars. Choosing contemplative over active life meant to pattern oneself on Mary of Bethany, not on Luke's penitent sinner; and, to the critics of the Magdalen tradition, it was important to recognize the superior order of a life totally foreign to sin. To be sure, Ennasuite's voice is a clear departure from what we know of Marguerite's own ideas, given Lefèvre's prominent influence over the Meaux evangelical circle.

Returning now to novella 32, one can see a similar problem in the discussion following the story. As she finishes her narrative, Oisille admonishes her fellow women not to follow the example of the fallen wife but, instead, to recognize their weaknesses and place their trust in God:

> Mes dames, si toutes celles à qui pareil cas est advenu beuvoient en telz vaisseaulx, j'aurois grand paour que beaucoup de coupes dorées seroient converties en testes de mortz. Dieu nous en veulle garder, car, si sa bonté ne nous retient, il n'y a aucun d'entre nous qui ne puisse faire pis; mais, ayant confiance en luy, il gardera celles qui confessent ne se pouvoir par elles-mesmes garder; et celles qui se confient en leurs forces sont en grand dangier d'estre tentées jusques à confesser leur infirmité. Et en est veu plusieurs qui ont tresbuché en tel cas, dont l'honneur saulvoit celles que l'on estimoit les moins vertueuses; et dist le viel proverbe: *Ce que Dieu garde est bien gardé.* (245;334, emphasis added)

From this speech it is clear that Oisille follows the ideal of the "groupe de Meaux" as expressed so eloquently by Lefèvre. In her first lines she makes a grim joke about the number of golden goblets that should be replaced by human skulls if all unfaithful wives were to be administered the same punishment. Obviously she approves of the vengeful husband's attitude.

Then, switching to a more straightforward preaching stance, she offers the sole possible alternative, namely that only by turning to God one can surely avoid one's own downfall: "He will guard those women who confess that they cannot guard themselves" (245;334). She even quotes an old proverb to seal her advice into the stone of immemorial wisdom: "*Ce que Dieu garde est bien gardé*" (245;334). Therefore, in the *doyenne*'s discourse, it is clear that the exemplary condition can only be gained through God, by preserving a state of innocence and sinlessness.

This strictly idealistic position on Christian ethics is echoed by Parlamente whose speech immediately follows Oisille's: "'Je trouve,' dist Parlamente, 'ceste punition autant raisonnable qu'il est possible; car, tout ainsy que l'offence est pire que la mort, aussy est la pugnition pire que la mort'" (245;334). Parlamente's unequivocal statement reduplicates both the husband's words to Bernage ("Je luy ordonnay une peyne [. . .] *plus desagreable que la mort,*" 243;332, emphasis added) and the 1559 editorial summary ("*Punition, plus rigoureuse que la mort,* d'un mary envers sa femme adultere").[17] The weight of the authorial voice can hardly be mistaken here. Let us recall that, from the very beginning of the *Heptameron*, Parlamente had been second-in-command, only after Oisille. In the prologue, when Oisille prescribed the reading of the holy Scripture to deliver the company from boredom and sorrow, Parlamente objected to Hircan's alternative ("pastimes that require only two participants") and proposed to complete a forgotten courtly project, a new *Decameron*, in which "each of us will tell a story which he has either witnessed himself, or which he has heard from somebody worthy of belief" (10;69).

Thus, in discussing novella 32, Parlamente follows Oisille once again, and reiterates her uncompromising position: there is no way around the fact that betraying one's husband is a crime "worse than death." This staunch ethical statement takes on patriarchal overtones as it reduplicates both the fictional husband's dictum and the editor's liminary comment. The Father's Law is thus maintained at the three main levels of the narrative structure. In Gérard Genette's parlance, the "extra-diegetic instance" (Gruget's editorial and thus quasi-authorial voice) reiterates the message given "intra-diegetically" (by Oisille and Parlamente as *devisants*) and "meta-diegetically" (by the vengeful husband of the story).[18]

Such an absolute position is not shared, however, by all the company, as witnessed by Ennasuite who does not hesitate to voice her strong disagreement: "'Je ne suis pas de vostre opinion, car j'aymerois mieulx toute ma vie veoir les oz de tous mes serviteurs en mon cabinet, que de mourir pour eulx, veu qu'*il n'y a mesfaict qui ne se puisse amender*; mais après la mort, n'y a poinct d'amendement'" (245;334, emphasis added). Interestingly, the focus of the discussion shifts from the rigid ideal of sinlessness to a more flexible understanding of human imperfection. For Ennasuite there is no sin for which one cannot make amends while one is alive. Repentance is always possible through the merciful grace of God. And Mary Magdalen's example is quoted here as a case in point. As Ennasuite is prompt to remark to Longarine: "Tell me, I beg you, whether the Magdalene does or does not have more honour amongst men than her sister, who was a virgin?" (246;335). Here Ennasuite falls into the trap of the "united persona" by confusing the unnamed converted sinner (in Luke 7) and Martha's contemplative sister (in Luke 10). Worse, she calls "la Magdelaine" the two wrong persons and ignores the real Magdalen of the gospel narrative (in Luke 8). In the context of philological humanism Ennasuite becomes an obvious caricature of the unlearned reader who fails to recognize the elementary *distinguo* of textual interpretation.

Yet, from a different perspective, Ennasuite's position can also be understood as a direct application of the second Christian commandment: "Love thy neighbor." Moved by the sinner's sincere repentence, she is ready to argue in favor of forgiveness and dismiss the husband's inhumane treatment of his wife. The king's envoy, Bernage, is her model inasmuch as he advocates charitable over harsh repressive methods. Before leaving the castle to carry out his mission, one recalls, Bernage had made the following suggestion to his host:

> —Monsieur, l'amour que je vous porte et l'honneur et privaulté que vous m'avez faicte en vostre maison, me contraingnent à vous dire qu'il me semble, *veu la grande repentance de vostre pauvre femme, que vous luy debvez user de misericorde*; et aussy, vous estes jeune, et n'avez nulz enfans; et seroit grand dommage de perdre une si belle maison que la vostre, et que ceulx qui ne vous ayment peut-estre poinct, en feussent heritiers. (333–34;244–45, emphasis added)

The vengeful husband is thus invited to open his heart and follow Christ's forgiving attitude vis-à-vis the penitent sinner of the gospel narrative (in Luke 7). By showing compassion to his wife and returning to a normal marital life, the gentleman will regain his honorable status; he will have children and his property will remain a source of pride within his family. Her *caritas* joins *ubertas* to restore the lost plenitude of Christian matrimony.[19]

Strangely enough, Bernage's and Ennasuite's moving pleas for forgiveness recall "conservative" views expressed by some of the humanists' adversaries during the Magdalen controversy. This is particularly true of Lefèvre's most eminent and vocal opponent, John Fisher, bishop of Rochester and one of the most famous chancellors of Cambridge University.[20] In his various polemical tracts, Fisher questioned the theological basis of the reformers' thesis with an impressive array of patristic exegesis.[21] To him, humanist exegesis might be intellectually appealing but its practical consequences were disastrous as they harked back to Pharisaic justice. Weren't Christ's Apostles weak and sinful men, redeemed and sanctified by God's mercy? The same could be said of Mary Magdalen. The validity of biblical and textual arguments had to be weighed against the possible destruction of centuries of popular piety and tradition. For purely philological reasons it might be productive to separate the three aspects of Magdalen's conflated personality, and rank the contemplative mystic over the contrite sinner. But in practical Christian ethics it was more important to fuse the three women's characters into one pragmatic typology. In the traditional interpretation of the gospel narrative, Mary Magdalen had moved from a state of sinfulness to purgative, active, and finally contemplative life. The example of her conversion could help all sinners recognize the limitless font of God's mercy and thus provide them with the kind of encouragement they needed to repent and amend their ways.[22]

In his *De unica Magdalena* Fisher wrote:

> I immediately thought of how many difficulties would confront the whole Church if Lefèvre's opinion were ever to be accepted. How many authors would have to be rejected, how many books would have to be changed, how many sermons formerly preached to the people would now have to be revoked! And then, how much uneasiness would arise among the faithful, how many occasions for the loss of faith! They will soon doubt other books and narratives, and finally the mother of us all, the Church, who for so many centuries has sung and taught the same thing.[23]

Indeed all of Fisher's discourse stemmed from a pastor's concern for the edification of his faithful; it was in diametrical opposition to the "Groupe de Meaux" humanists' belief in the philological restitution of truth, even at the expense of liturgical customs and the devotion of the faithful. There were, of course, other thinkers who, in those same years, had a more moderate attitude and who, while expressing some doubts about certain aspects of the liturgy, refrained from openly criticizing the church's tradition. This was the case of François du Moulin de Rochefort who, in his biography of Saint Magdalen commissioned by Louise de Savoie, adopted a middle-of-the-road position. In his *Vie de sainte Madeleine* François du Moulin de Rochefort writes: "Maiz si ceste femme pecheresse estoit seur de Marthe j'en ferois doubte et non sans cause, si ce n'estoit la determinacion de l'Eglise. [. . .] Passer oultre ne m'est permis car je ne veuil rien innover. [. . .] Tout ce qui s'ensuit est selon la tradicion de l'Eglise."[24]

Yet, between Lefèvre's and Fisher's positions we can witness the expression of the typical rift, which was to become crucial during the Reformation, that is between the general consensus of the whole universal church and the critical awareness of a few enlightened individuals who independently defended their claims to truth.[25] To a large extent, thus, the fundamental disagreement which can be observed between the *devisants* at the end of novella 32 seems to reflect the polarized positions of Fisher and Lefèvre in the Magdalen controversy. This does not mean, however, that Marguerite's own position can be identified as easily. True, Oisille and Parlamente speak in favor of the humanist *distinguo* whereas Ennasuite sides with the defenders of the traditional consensus. Yet at no point in the *Heptameron*, not even in the prologue, can we find clear authorial markings of intentionality: there is no ultimate voice to deliver a didactic, univocal message of truth.[26]

It might be argued that by the mid-1540s the controversy had lost much of its impetus. Lefèvre had died in 1537, and Marguerite had probably distanced herself from the vain aspects of the polemics. At any rate, an allegorical reading of novella 32 in terms of the "Magdalen Controversy" can only highlight the tension which existed in Marguerite's world between the elevated ethical ideals of the humanists and the less refined, practical morality of late medieval Christianity. In the *Heptameron* no attempt is ever made to resolve this tension: the two sorts of sensibility exist side by side and interact with one another in an imperfect, open-ended, often heart-rending dialogue. Such a textual situation may partly reflect Marguerite's own feelings as she was herself torn between her respect for a profound devotion to a popular saint and her intellectual support for a critique of this worship by her humanist friends.

Notes

1. On the identification of this source see Pierre Jourda, *Marguerite d'Angoulême, Duchesse d'Alençon, Reine de Navarre (1492–1549): Etude biographique et littéraire* (Paris: Champion, 1930; Geneva: Slatkine, 1978), 2: 726–27; Nicole Cazauran, *L'Heptaméron de Marguerite de Navarre* (Paris: SEDES, 1976), 142–43. More remote

analogues can be found in day four of the *Decameron*, which is devoted to lovers whose passion leads to tragic adventures. For instance, in 4.1 Tancredo kills his daughter's lover and sends her the victim's heart in a golden goblet (see also 4.9 about William of Roussillon). *Tutte le opere di Giovanni Boccaccio*, ed. Vittore Branca (Milan: Mondadori, 1976), vol. 4. For another interpretation of the image of the skull, see the companion article, François Rigolot, "Magdalen's Skull: Allegory and Iconography in *Heptameron* 32," *Renaissance Quarterly*, in press.

2. Gérard Genette, "Discours du récit," in *Figures III* (Paris: Editions du Seuil, 1972), 186ff.

3. There is a large bibliography on the worship of Saint Mary Magdalen in the Middle Ages and the early modern period. See in particular: Etienne Michel Faillon, *Monuments inédits sur l'Apostolat de Sainte Marie Madeleine en Provence . . .* (Paris: J.-P. Migne, 1865); "Mary Magdalen" in the index to Karl Young, *The Drama of the Medieval Church* (Oxford, Clarendon Press, 1933), 2 vols.; Madeleine Delpierre, *L'Iconographie de Sainte-Marie Madeleine dans l'art français, de l'époque romane à la fin du XVIe siècle* (Paris [Thèse de l'Ecole du Louvre], 1948); Victor Saxer, *Le Culte de Marie Madeleine en Occident: Des origines à la fin du Moyen Age* (Auxerre: Publications de la Société des fouilles archéologiques et de monuments historiques de l'Yonne, 1959), 2 vols.

4. François du Moulin de Rochefort, *Vie de sainte Madelaine* (1517). B.N. fr. 24955. See also Marie Holban, "François du Moulin et la querelle de la Madeleine," *Humanisme et Renaissance* 2 (1935): 26–43 and 147–71.

5. Interestingly enough, François du Moulin de Rochefort, the author of the *Vie de sainte Madeleine*, was made abbot of Saint-Maximin by the queen mother as a recompense for his hagiographic work. See Holban, "François du Moulin," 155.

6. See Faillon, *Monuments inédits*, 1033ff.

7. Margaret Mann touches upon the history of the episode in her book, *Erasme et les débuts de la Réforme française (1517–1536)* (Paris: Champion, 1934), 55ff. But the most thorough account of the controversy is given by Anselm Hufstader in his article, "Lefèvre d'Etaples and the Magdalen," *Studies in the Renaissance* 16 (1969): 31–60.

8. About Jacques Lefèvre d'Etaples, see Augustin Renaudet, *Préréforme et humanisme à Paris pendant les premières guerres d'Italie (1494–1517)* (Paris: Librairie d'Argences, 1953), and Guy Bedouelle, *Lefèvre d'Etaples et l'intelligence des Ecritures* (Geneva: Droz, 1976), as well as Eugene F. Rice's edition of *Prefatory Epistles of Jacques Lefèvre d'Etaples and Related Texts* (New York and London: Columbia University Press, 1972). In his *Marot, Rabelais, Montaigne: L'Écriture comme présence* (Paris-Geneva: Champion-Slatkine, 1987), Gérard Defaux gives a new, invigorating view of sixteenth-century evangelical writing.

9. Edwin M. Duval, "Interpretation and the 'Doctrine absconce' of Rabelais's Prologue to *Gargantua*," *Etudes Rabelaisiennes* 18 (1986): 2.

10. Jacques Lefèvre d'Etaples, *De Maria Magdalena, & triduo Christi disceptatio, ad Clarissimum virum D. Franciscum Molineum . . .* (Paris: Henri Estienne, 1517 old style, 1518 new style); *De Tribus et Unica Magdalena Disceptatio secunda: ad Reverendum in Christo Patrem Dionysium Briconnetum episcopum Maclouiensem . . .* (Paris: Henry Estienne, 1519).

11. See Hufstader, "Lefèvre d'Etaples and the Magdalen," 40.

12. Guillaume Briçonnet and Marguerite d'Angoulême, *Correspondance (1521–1524)*, ed. Christine Martineau and Michel Veissière, with the assistance of Henry Heller (Geneva: Droz, 1975, 1979), 2 vols.

13. See Anthony Levi, "Humanist Reform in Sixteenth-Century France," *The Heythrop Journal* 6 (1965): 456ff.

14. Marguerite's own *Miroir de l'âme pécheresse* had been condemned by the Sorbonne in 1533. "C'est elle [Marguerite] peut-être autant que la régente qui soulève la question des Madeleines, laquelle devait amener un des premiers conflits entre la Sorbonne et les novateurs: déjà elle est en relation avec Lefèvre d'Etaples sans qu'on puisse préciser la date où elle le connut." Jourda, *Marguerite d'Angoulême*, 1:53.

15. In Suzanne Hanon's concordance to the *Heptameron* one finds only two references to Mary Magdalen: J2N9 (i.e., novella 19) and J4N2 (i.e., novella 32). *Le Vocabulaire de l'"Heptaméron" de Marguerite de Navarre: Index et Concordance* (Paris-Geneva: Champion-Slatkine, 1990, microfiche), p. 1748. The same can be found in the *Index* compiled by the "Groupe de Lexicologie" of the University of Clermont under Guy Demerson's leadership. I wish to thank Nicole Cazauran for these useful references.

16. Josse Clichtove, *Disceptationis de Magdalena, Defensio: Apologiae Marci Grandivallis illam improbare nitentis, ex adverso respondens* (Paris: Henri Estienne, April 1519), fol. 7v.

> Dicat age, sublimior est status innocentiae atque impeccantiae: quam post contracta peccati contagia, poenitentiae salutaris atque resipiscentiae? Nonne maiori honoratur eulogio atque virtutis praeconio, quae praedicatur nullatenus in lutum cecidisse: quam ea quae post prolapsionem dicitur miseratrice dei gratia fuisse erecta, et a sorde luti purgata? Nimirum quanto aliqua vitae humanae conditio, divinae perfectioni magis assimilatur: tanto ea et praestibilior est et commendatior, cumm summa veritas in Evangelio proloquatur: *Perfectus autem erit omnis: si sit sicut magister eius.* Atqui vita humana sine gravis peccati labe transacta, evadit similior divinae perfectioni atque puritati quae omnimodam habet impeccantiam: quam ea quae post ruinam in peccatum, detergitur et abluitur divinae miserationis ope.

Quoted by Hufstader, "Lefèvre d'Etaples and the Magdalen," p.57, n.89. Clichtove was responding to Marc de Grandval, a canon of Saint Victor, who had attacked Lefèvre in his *Apologia* published by Josse Bade in September 1518.

17. See *Heptameron*, ed. M. François, p.476, n.538.

18. See Genette, "Discours du récit," 238–39.

19. This attitude is fully in accordance with the contemporary formulation of Christian matrimony. On the question of marriage and evangelical morality, see M. A. Screech, *The Rabelaisian Marriage* (London: E. Arnold, 1958), 84–103.

20. A symposium on Bishop Fisher was held at Cambridge in 1985, on the 450th anniversary of his death. What emerged from the volume of proceedings is a troubling multifaceted personality: both conservative and controversialist, mystically pacifist and insurrectionist, persecutor and martyr. *Humanism, Reform and the*

Reformation: The Career of Bishop Fisher, edited by Brendan Bradshaw and Eamon Duffy (New York: Cambridge University Press, 1989).

21. Fisher's three main publications on the Magdalen question are the following: *De unica Magdalena, Libri tres* (Paris: Josse Bade, March 1519); *Confutatio Secundae Disceptationis par Jacobum Fabrum Stapulensem* (Paris: Josse Bade, September 1519); and *Eversio Munitionis quam Iodocus Clichtoveus erigere moliebatur adversus unicam Magdalenam* (Louvain: T. Martens, 1519). See Edward Surtz, *The Works and Days of John Fisher* (Cambridge, Mass.: Harvard University Press, 1967), esp. 274–89.

22. *Confutatio*, fols. 12v, 34r-v. See Hufstader, "Lefèvre d'Etaples and the Magdalen," 57–58.

23. *De unica Magdalena, Libri tres*, fol. A3v:

Cogitavi subinde quot ex hac opinione Fabri, si reciperetur, incommoda toti ecclesiae provenirent, quot autores essent damnandi, quot emendandi codices, quot ad populum olim factae conciones iam revocandae sint. Quantos praeterea scrupos inde multi conciperent, quot ansas arriperent malae fidei, parum deinceps aut libris aut historiis credituri: sed et de communi matre ecclesia, quae iam per tot saecula id ipsum et cecinit et docuit, sinistre admodum suspicaturi.

The English translation is borrowed from Hufstader, "Lefèvre d'Etaples and the Magdalen," 44.

24. *Vie de Sainte Madelaine*, f° 03 v°, f° 80, f° 04. See Holban, "François du Moulin," 36, n.6.

25. In his important scholarly work Jean-Pierre Massaut looks at the attitude of Lefèvre and Clichtove to several theological issues, including the Magdalen controversy, and concludes that they adopt a middle position between the Sorbonne and the Reform, scholarship and piety. *Critique et tradition à la veille de la Réforme en France* (Paris: Vrin, 1974), chap.5, 67–70, and apps. 1 and 2, 115–19. I wish to thank Gary Ferguson for this reference.

26. Let us recall that it is Parlamente, not Marguerite who sets the rules of the game in the prologue of the *Heptameron*. About Marguerite's ambivalence, as reflected in the composition and design of her book, see Marcel Tetel, *Marguerite de Navarre's* Heptameron: *Themes, Language, and Structure* (Durham, N.C.: Duke University Press, 1973). On the problematic status of exemplarity in the Renaissance, see Karlheinz Stierle, "L'Histoire comme exemple, l'exemple comme histoire," *Poétique* 10 (1972): 176–98 and, more specifically on Marguerite de Navarre, John D. Lyons, *Exemplum. The Rhetoric of Example in Early Modern France and Italy* (Princeton, N.J.: Princeton University Press, 1989), chap. 2. In her "La Nouvelle exemplaire ou le roman tenu en échec," Nicole Cazauran notices an interesting tension between "le souci d'un sens exemplaire" and "l'exégèse jamais achevée des devisants." *Cahiers Textuels* 10 (1992): 21–23. Novella 32 is given a prominent place in Giselle Mathieu-Castellani's analysis of what she calls "la poétique de l'histoire tragique." *La Conversation conteuse. Les Nouvelles de Marguerite de Navarre* (Paris: Presses Universitaires de France, 1992), 105–23.

Paula Sommers

14. Writing the Body: Androgynous Strategies in the *Heptameron*

Hélène Cixous and Luce Irigaray communicate the unicity of women's bodies by focusing on topics that have been excluded from traditional androcentric literature—female sexuality from the woman's point of view, menses, childbirth.[1] In a manner more acceptable to her contemporaries, Marguerite de Navarre draws upon conventional narrative tradition and portrays women's bodies as the object of male desire and aggression.[2] This aggression may be verbal, as in Geburon's use of the hunt topos to describe the relationship between the lover and his prey. More often it is physical— Floride's struggle with Amadour (novella 10), the shaved head and imprisonment of the German countess (novella 32), Sister Marie Heroet's suffering at the hands of a lustful prior (novella 22), the murder of the *muletière* (novella 2). Geburon's comments and the tales cited, however, are set in a dialogical context that includes the male body, the masculine point of view, and a pluralistic discussion of motivation. Gendered discourse in the *Heptameron* can, therefore, be frustrating and inconclusive. It is also only one thread in a complex work that includes an androgynous as well as a gendered point of view.

Given the queen of Navarre's interest in Neoplatonism, the term "androgynous" immediately evokes Ficino and his reading of the *Symposium*. Like Marguerite, Ficino situates androgyny in the realm of the spiritual and the psychological. While Aristophanes uses his male, female, and bisexual androgynes to express the flexibility of Greek sexual mores, the Italian Neoplatonist associates each of these androgynes with a specific virtue—masculinity with courage, femininity with temperance, and bisexuality with justice, suggesting that androgyny can be broadly interpreted as a balance of traits within the individual (*De Amore* 4.2). This approach was adopted by some of Marguerite's contemporaries and anticipates in some ways the theories of Carolyn Heilbrun.[3] There is, however, no similar sexual typology for virtue in the *Heptameron* and references to the Neo-platonic androgyne are rare.[4] Following the eighth tale Simontaut refers to the continuing search for love as a quest for the missing half that will establish perfect sexual and psychological unity, but Dagoucin refutes him:

> Pour ce que l'homme ne peult sçavoir où est cette moictyé dont l'unyon est si esgalle que l'un ne differe de l'autre, il faut qu'il, s'arreste où l'amour le contrainct; et que, pour quelque occasion qu'il puisse advenir, ne change le cueur ne la volunté; car, si celle que vous aymez est tellement semblable à vous et d'une mesme volunté, ce sera vous que vous aymerez, et non pas elle. (48;113)

Both these speakers restrict the concept to its use in contemporary love discourse. For one it justifies an endless search for gratification. For the other it is a quest that has no validity since a perfectly androgynous union, could it be found, would represent self-love rather than *caritas*. Simontaut and Dagoucin would, therefore, question contemporary iconographical representations of the androgyne as a symbol of married love.[5] Married couples in the *Heptameron* struggle in most instances to accommodate the character of an other who is far from being a harmonious "moicityé." If marital union does not evoke the androgyne, moreover, neither does the relationship between idealistic lovers who are few and fare poorly in the novellas.

Androgynous elements in the *Heptameron* owe little to Ficino's commentary on the *Symposium*, but they do suggest some affinity with his concept of God as a being who is himself androgynous and with biblical tradition that also admits, although without consistent emphasis, a creator who reconciles the characteristics of male and female within himself and within his church: "So God created man in his own image, in the image of God created he him; male and female created he them" (Gen. 1:27); "There is neither Jew nor Greek, there is neither bond nor free, there is neither male nor female; for ye are all one in Christ Jesus" (Gal. 3:28). Androgynous elements of the *Heptameron* appear first in the prologue as Marguerite shapes the reader's perception of the text and, through the familiar topos of the *peregrinatio*, introduces religious symbolism that is consistent with her evangelical perspective.[6] Prior to gendered discourse, sanctioned by scriptural and theological tradition, her androgynous strategies create an authoritative code that will subsequently oppose the subjective, divisive discourse of Hircan, Saffredent, Simontaut, and others. They are manifest in the description of the travelers as they make their way from Cauterets to

Notre Dame de Sarrance, in the inauguration of the storytelling game and in the representation of the *devisants*. Beyond the prologue they structure the frame-story and appear in the sequencing of the tales and the composition of the novellas themselves. With regard to the travelers, Marguerite's prologue is characterized by the progressive repetition of narrative elements that involve a threat to the physical body and, as a response, the formation of a collective, androgynous body in which men and women unite for a common purpose. Since these androgynous groups are able to control aggression and, most strikingly, the sexual conflict that is a constant focus of attention, they reflect to some degree the divine harmony and the balance that should prevail in the Christian community. They function, albeit imperfectly, as signs of *caritas*.

As the prologue begins, travelers from throughout Europe gather at Cauterets in the hope that the health-giving waters of the spa will cure their illnesses. The initial paragraph introduces a basic pattern—physical danger/collective response—that will be repeated throughout the prologue with significant variations. Initially, the physical danger, aside from the general concept of illness, is not specified. The travelers are characterized only by colorless pronouns—*ceux, quelcuns, plusiers, les ungs, les autres*—and there is only one reminder that the masculine generic includes a feminine presence—"les seigneurs et dames françoys" (1;60). Lack of individuation and failure to specify any relationships among most of those gathered at Cauterets draw attention to the basic themes and the symbolic value of the narrative, in this instance the quest for physical well-being and the reliance on natural sources. While the travelers gain some success, it is only temporary. The first collective body in the *Heptameron*, one whose androgynous composition is possible but not emphasized, is dispersed and decimated by the overflowing mountain streams. Confidence in the healing powers of nature is shattered, and a once familiar environment with well-known roads and paths is transformed into a hostile setting.

In the course of the perilous journey from Cauterets to Notre Dame de Sarrance, Marguerite describes new physical dangers and the formation of a second, more enduring and specifically androgynous body that is situated on both a physical and metaphysical plane. In naming the individual *devisants* who complete this journey, she introduces gendered discourse into the *Heptameron*, shifting the thematic focus of her prologue, at least apparently, from a broad consideration of human nature—*homo*—to an examination of *vir* and *femina*. Indeed, sexual tension in the prologue and the vigorous war between the sexes that sustains much of the storytelling in the body of the *Heptameron* suggest concentration on sexual dichotomy—the very opposite of androgynous balance.

Balance, nevertheless, persists. Marguerite reproduces the sexual typologies of the *querelle des femmes* only to subvert them. Already in the prologue sexual identity is shown to accommodate a broad range of character traits, since the travelers of both sexes differ in age, experience, and authority. If Ennasuite and Nomerfide flee in terror from marauding bears, behavior that might suggest stereotypical feminine cowardice or weakness, the slaughter of those who stay behind to resist confirms their wisdom in leaving the scene. Flight can also be a masculine response to danger. Geburon, pursued by robbers, dashes into the church where the *devisants* are gathered "tout en chemise, criant a l'ayde" (4;63). Dagoucin and Saffredent appropriately rescue Parlamente and Longarine, ladies in distress, but not before the latter's husband is killed and Hircan nearly defeated. Simontaut, a proud equestrian figure and symbol of masculine initiative, emerges from the flood humbled and unhorsed—"se trainant a quatre pieds . . . tant las et foible qu'il ne se pouvait soustenir" (5;64). The misadventures of the *devisants* in the prologue clearly demonstrate that neither sex has a privileged claim to specific virtues. Both men and women can display courage, cowardice, or tenacity. Whether male or female, moreover, the human body is characterized by vulnerability. Indeed, it is this common vulnerability that encourages the formation of the cooperative, androgynous community at Notre Dame de Sarrance.

The formation of this community is, given the symbolic structure of the prologue, the result of providential intervention. Marguerite de Navarre reminds her readers of the spiritual order that exists behind the natural order with its unpredictable storms and life-giving waters by including in her threatening landscape monasteries and kindly figures who intervene to save the beleaguered travelers. Simontaut, who is particularly fortunate in this regard, encounters both a shepherd and a humble religious who guides him to the place where his fellow countrymen have found refuge: "Et ce soir la Dieu y amena ce bon religieux qui luy enseigna le chemyn de Notre Dame de Sarrance" (5;64). Gathered by Providence, united by a common desire to give thanks and praise to God for their deliverance, the *devisants* represent the church as an androgynous community of believers. Caught up in the unity of the mystical body represented by mass and communion (6;65) and by scriptural reading (7–8;66–67), they nevertheless retain their sexual identities, and the female reader, who may identify with Oisille in her role as Christian widow, can decode the hidden meanings of biblical revelation as authoritatively as the male. The *devisants* as church, as God's chosen, thus model in their religious practice a sublime image of cooperation and interdependence that evokes the relationship of humanity to a God who includes in his own perfection and in his created order both male and female.

Celebration of mass is the culmination of a movement that brings the *devisants* from the spa to the eucharistic table and from a purely earthly unity to mystical participation in the nature of the Deity. Once this unity is achieved, the transcendent point of view that focused attention on the body in the distinct yet related realms of Providence and Nature gives way to more subjective views of the body in society.[7] While it functioned earlier in the prologue as a sign of mortality and vulnerability or a "container" for the eucharistic presence, the body now increasingly represents individuation, distinction, discrimination, and desire. The social importance of age and marital status appears immediately after mass. Parlamente requests the permission of her husband before speaking. She addresses Oisille before the others because she recognizes her as a source of motherly wisdom. Oisille, in turn, defers to Hircan, accepting his critique of her proposed pastime for the group. The brief scenario recalls the metatextual order with its careful respect for the authority of patriarchy and for rank and status. It anticipates the hierarchical social structures that occur in the tales to follow, but this is not to say that once the prologue "descends" to the social or human level androgyny disappears.

In effect, discussion of an appropriate activity for the group once the travelers have found refuge at the abbey repeats for the third time the narrative combination of physical threat/group response. The *devisants* are threatened by an illness as deadly as any that first inspired the trip to Cauterets: "'. . . si nous n'avons quelque occupation plaisante . . . nous sommes en danger de demeurer malades.' La jeune vefve Longarine adjousta à ce propos, 'Mais qui pis est, nous deviendrons fascheuses, qui est une maladie incurable; car il n'y a nul de nulle de nous, si regarde à sa perte, qu'il n'ayt occasion d'extreme tristesse'" (7;66). The common danger is now melancholy, and contemporary readers would have understood this as a very real danger even though they might have been able to discuss the precise way in which sadness deprived the heart and other organs of the body of their vital spirits, causing desiccation and death. The remedies proposed by the *devisants* appear, in fact, in treatises on melancholy and can be seen as a reflection of commonly accepted treatments for this particular illness.[8] Oisille's remedy correctly addresses the ordering of the soul. Hircan is wise to emphasize the importance of physical exercise: ". . . si nous sommes en noz maisons, il nous fault la chasse et la vollerye, qui nous faict oblier mil folles pensees, et les dames ont leur mesnaige, leur ouvraige et quelquesfois les dances" (8;67).

Parlamente effectively incorporates both Oisille's prayerful approach and Hircan's concerns into a balanced psychosomatic program. The banks of the river and the sheltering vegetation provide little opportunity for exercise, but the setting is attractive and comfortable. The storytelling offers intellectual stimulation while discouraging melancholy reverie. Like the communion service, it is a ritualized activity that occurs in a privileged space and time and transcends the hierarchical distribution of roles in society. The quest for divine truth symbolized by mass and the pursuit of secular truth in the tales both occur in androgynous communities where health is achieved and sexual differences are contained and balanced.

Upon review, the prologue shows that the French travelers participate in a series of androgynous "bodies" that relate to different, yet overlapping categories. Directed by Providence to the monastic setting, they represent the community of evangelical believers united by the mystical body of Christ in the Eucharist and governed by his word in Scripture. As participants in the storytelling exchange, they form a narrative and interpretative community that models both textual production and hermeneutics as collective, androgynous activities. What becomes of the androgynous emphasis once the storytelling begins, however, and the *devisants* turn to discussion of the secular/sexual body, the social conventions that constrain it and the carnal responses that it provokes? Even though the impersonal narrator now yields to the diverse and often discordant voices of the *devisants*, the cornice recalls the symbolism of the prologue.[9] Female narrators regularly succeed male narrators. Sequencing of the tales reveals a collective desire to balance male and female, misogyny and "feminism." The evangelical perspective initiated in the prologue is maintained by the practice of scriptural reading and the presence of Geburon and Oisille, an appropriately androgynous combination. Their discourse typically opposes the sexual dichotomies displayed in the tales by focusing on a universal moral predicament: "Car les maulx que nous disons des hommes et des femmes ne sont poinct pour la honte particulliere de ceulx dont est faict le compte, mais pour oster l'estime et la confiance des creatures, en monstrant les miseres où ilz sont subgectz, afin que nostre espoir s'arreste et s'appuye à Celluy seul qui est parfaict et sans lequel tout homme n'est que imperfection . . . " (317;416).

While diversity prevails in the novellas, it does so within textual structures that maintain the androgynous communities of the prologue. In a very profound sense these communities correct or criticize practices of sexual dominance that exist in the tales as well as in the metatextual environment. Androgynous patterns in the *Heptameron*, like those that Robert Kimbrough discovers in Shakespeare and other writers of the English Renaissance are, therefore, linked with a subtly feminist point of view.[10] Contrast between the cornice where women storytellers enjoy the same rights as men and the narratives where women speakers often have the greatest difficulty being heard provides an impressive illustration of the gap between the androgynous community at Notre Dame de Sarrance and an often harsh reality.[11] The painful struggles of the neglected wife in tale 15, the imprisonment of the Count de Jossebelin's sister (novella 40), and the hanging of the young woman who offended the duke of Urbino (novella 50) are but a few examples of injustices that can occur in an unbalanced secular order where the female voice has little or no authority. Numerous tales involving lascivious and treacherous monks show that equally dangerous consequences can occur in the androcentric and, therefore, equally unbalanced, ecclesiastical domain.

Androgynous strategies persist throughout the *Heptameron* and function both on an evangelical level that confirms Marguerite's perception of moral equality between the sexes and on a secular level where men and women, divided by sexual roles and acutely aware of gender differences, nevertheless remain partners in the demanding search for truth. The equal dignity of women in both situations gives legitimacy to the female voice, but without altering the subordination of women in the patriarchal order. Heilbrun's comments on *Wuthering Heights*, which she considers an androgynous novel, have, in this regard some relevance to the *Heptameron*: ". . . the sense of waste, of lost spiritual and sexual power, of equality of worth between the two sexes, is presented with no specific cry for revolution, but with a sense of a world deformed."[12]

Marguerite's sense of a world deformed derives from her Christian spirituality and her observation of the human reality depicted in her tales and the world around her. The sense of equal worth and of waste is omnipresent, whether we consider the prologue with its struggling community of travelers in an unpredictable environment or the multiple settings of the tales and their depiction of frustration and waste—the long years that Rolandine devotes to love for an unworthy husband (novella 21), the suffering and the corruption of the "mal mariée" (novella 15), the wretchedness of the German countess (novella 32), the failure of so many monks and priors to achieve their spiritual ideal, and the portrayal of so many couples who, for social or personal reasons, experience neither understanding nor fulfillment. The androgynous patterns that Marguerite weaves into the *Heptameron* through the model community of *devisants* and the contrast between tale and dialogue offer no "revolutionary" possibilities for reform, but they do provide some means of understanding the deformity of the world and, perhaps, of resisting it.

Notes

1. A short reading list for attitudes of this kind would include selected works by Hélène Cixous, "The Laugh of the Medusa," trans. Keith Cohen and Paula Cohen, *Signs* 1 (Summer 1976); 875–93; *La Venue à l'écriture*, (Paris: Union Générale d'Editions, 1977); and, coauthored with Catherine Clément, *La Jeune Née* (Paris: Union Générale d'Editions, 1975). See also Luce Irigaray, *Ce sexe qui n'en est pas un* (Paris: Editions de Minuit, 1977), and *Speculum de l'autre femme* (Paris: Editions de Minuit, 1974). For more theoretical background consult Jane Gallop, *Thinking Through the Body* (New York: Columbia University Press, 1988); *New French Feminisms*, ed. Elaine Marks and Isabelle de Coutivron (Amherst: University of Massachusetts Press, 1980); Ann Rosalind Jones, "Writing the Body: Toward an Understanding of L'Ecriture féminine," *Feminist Studies* 7 (1981): 247–63; and Susan Rubin Suleiman, ed., *The Female Body in Western Culture: Contemporary Perspectives* (Cambridge, Mass.: Harvard University Press, 1985).

2. Background for Marguerite's portrayal of the body can be drawn from a number of sources who discuss the Renaissance and late medieval mentality. See esp. Caroline Walker Bynum, *Fragmentation and Redemption: Essays on Gender and the Human Body in Medieval Religion* (New York: Zone Books, 1991); Constance Jordan, *Renaissance Feminism: Literary Texts and Political Models* (Ithaca, N.Y.: Cornell University Press, 1990); Ruth Kelso, *Doctrine for the Lady of the Renaissance* (Urbana: University of Illinois Press, 1956); Margaret R. Miles, *Carnal Knowing: Female Nakedness and Religious Meaning in the Christian West* (Boston: Beacon Press, 1990); Peter Stallybrass, "Patriarchal Territories: The Body Enclosed," in *Rewriting the Renaissance: The Discourses of Sexual Difference in Early Modern Europe*, ed. Margaret W. Ferguson, Maureen Quilligan, and Nancy J. Vickers (Chicago: University of Chicago Press, 1986); and Ian Maclean, *The Renaissance Notion of Woman: A Study in the Fortunes of Scholasticism and Medical Science in European Intellectual Life* (New York: Columbia University Press, 1980). Among the most comprehensive discussions of the body as subject of desire in the *Heptameron* is the recent study of Patricia F. Cholakian, *Rape and Writing in the "Heptaméron" of Marguerite de Navarre* (Carbondale: Southern Illinois University Press, 1991).

3. For background on androgyny in general see Achim Aurnhammer, *Androgynie: Studien auf einem Motiv in der europaischen Literatur* (Vienna: Bohlau, 1986), and Elémire Zolla, *The Androgyne, Fusion of the Sexes* (London: Thames and Hudson, 1981). For androgyny and feminism, see Carolyn Heilbrun, *Toward a Recognition of Androgyny* (New York: Harper and Row, 1974), and *Reinventing*

Womanhood (New York: Norton and Company, 1979), and June Singer, *Androgyny: Toward a New Theory of Sexuality* (Garden City, N.Y.: Doubleday, 1976).

4. Marguerite evokes the Neoplatonic androgyne in her religious poetry, on occasion, with reference to "honnête amour." François I, in *La Navire*, ed. Robert Marichal (Paris: Champion, 1956) is, thus, Marguerite's "moitié" (v.373–75).

5. Barthelemy Aneau in his *Picta Poesis* illustrates married love with the figure of an androgyne, a man and a woman whose bodies have fused so that one side of the body is feminine, the other masculine, according to Elémire Zolla in *The Androgyne*, 72. Zolla also notes parallels with this type of imagery and scenes in Spenser's *The Faerie Queene*.

6. The prologue has inspired and continues to inspire thoughtful analysis. The *peregrinatio* theme is best developed by Glyn P. Norton in "The Emilio Ferretti Letter: A Critical Preface for Marguerite de Navarre," *Journal of Medieval and Renaissance Studies* 4 (1974):297–300. Also by Norton is "Narrative Function in the *Heptaméron* Frame Story" in *La Nouvelle française à la Renaissance*, ed. Lionello Sozzi (Geneva: Slatkine, 1981), 437–47. See also Yves Delègue, "Autour de deux prologues: *L'Heptaméron* est-il un anti-Boccace?" in *Travaux de Linguistique et de littérature de l'Université de Strasbourg* 4.2 (1966): 23–37; Claude-Gilbert Dubois, "Fonds mythique et jeu des sens dans le 'prologue' de l'*Heptaméron*," in *Etudes seiziémistes offertes à M. le professeur V.-L. Saulnier par plusieurs de ses anciens doctorants* (Geneva: Droz, 1980), 151–68; Doranne Fenoaltea, "Brigands and Bears in the Prologue to the *Heptaméron*," *French Studies* 39 (1985):395–40; Dora Polachek, "Narrating the 'Truth': The Problematics of Verisimilitude in the *Heptaméron* Prologue," *Romance Languages Annual* 1 (1989): 301–5; and Paula Sommers, "Marguerite de Navarre's *Heptaméron*: The Case for the Cornice" *French Review* 57 (1985): 786–93.

7. To some extent Marguerite's prologue recalls the hierarchical pattern of medieval theology and law with their tertiary division into divine, natural, and human. For Marguerite, as for Augustine or Aquinas, the lowest division of the hierarchy, that of human behavior and human perception, is characterized by the greatest degree of ambivalence, imperfection, and error.

8. For discussion of typical cures consult Robert Burton, *The Anatomy of Melancholy* (London: George Bell, 1896; rpt. 1903). See also (for remedies and bibliography) Lawrence Babb, *The Elizabethan Malady: A Study of Melancholia in English Literature from 1580 to 1642* (East Lansing: Michigan State College Press, 1951), and Raymond Klibansky, *Saturn and Melancholy* (New York: Nelson, 1964).

9. Deborah N. Losse studies problems relating to narrative voice in her article "Authorial and Narrative Voice in the *Heptaméron*," *Renaissance and Reformation* 23, no. 3 (1987):223–42.

10. Robert Kimbrough, *Shakespeare and the Art of Humankindness* (Atlantic Highlands, N.J.: Humanities Press International, 1990).

11. For a more thorough exploration of gaps between novellas and cornice discourse see Gisèle Mathieu-Castellani, *La Conversation conteuse: Les Nouvelles de Marguerite de Navarre* (Paris: Presses Universitaires de France, 1992).

12. Heilbrun, *Toward a Recognition of Androgyny*, 59.

15. "Et puis, quelles nouvelles?": The Project of Marguerite's Unfinished Decameron

> *Nihil sub sole novum*, nec valet quisquam dicere: Ecce hoc recens est;
> Iam enim praecessit in saeculis quae fuerunt ante nos.
> —Ecclesiastes 1:10

> *Mandatum novum* do vobis: Ut diligatis invicem, sicut dilexi vos, ut et
> vos diligatis invicem. In hoc cognoscent omnes quia discipuli mei estis,
> si dilectionem habueritis ad invicem.
> —John 13:34–35

If Marguerite de Navarre had completed the book we improperly refer to as the "Heptameron," she would certainly have called it *Les Cent nouvelles*. Not only is this the title by which she designates the Italian work on which she explicitly modeled her own—"les *cent Nouvelles* de Bocace" (Prologue, 9;68)—but Brantôme consistently refers to Marguerite's collection, unfinished though it is, as "les *Cent Nouvelles* de la reine de Navarre."[1]

But what does this projected title tell us about the book? What, precisely, are "nouvelles"? Marguerite's modern readers, who are for the most part professors and students of literature, naturally assume that these are something essentially literary, "nouvelle" being a piece of short narrative fiction that can be defined historically or formally in relation to similar genres like the *fabliau*, the *conte*, the *novella*, and the novel. But the nonprofessional readers for whom Marguerite wrote her book, and by whom she meant it to be understood, would never have construed her title in this way, for "nouvelle" in the sixteenth century was not a literary term borrowed from the Italian "novella," but an old, familiar word commonly used in everyday conversation to mean "news," a piece of "news," or the report of anything "new."[2]

Works by contemporaries and associates of Marguerite contain countless indications that the word remained in active use with its native, non-literary meaning even among those most interested in literature and most familiar with the Italian novella. Marguerite's valet de chambre Clément Marot, for example, addresses his beleaguered evangelical patroness in the following terms:

> J'ay entendu, tres illustre compaigne,
> Que contre toy se sont mys en campaigne
> Les haulx quantons du lac pharisien.
> Par quoy soudain du camp Elisien
> J'ay faict sortir troys de mes damoyselles
> Pour te monstrer le plus grand de mes zelles,
> Qui est d'*oyr nouvelles* briefvement
> De la deffaicte et prompt definement
> De ceste race inutille et contraire
> A ce bon Christ . . .

> ("Epistre presentée à la Royne de Navarre
> par Madame Ysabeau," lines 1–10, in *Epîtres*, p. 186)

"Nouvelles" in this typical passage are clearly not novellas, but *news* in the ordinary sense of a live report of recent events. Elsewhere Marot uses the word frequently with the same meaning, sometimes in the plural (usually to request or relate personal or public news to a friend), and sometimes in the singular (usually to mean the report or "word" of a single fact or crucial event).[3]

That Marguerite understood "nouvelles" in precisely this mundane sense is made abundantly clear by the *Cent nouvelles* themselves, for within the narratives of Marguerite's book the word occurs dozens of times to mean any news one character hears about another or, more frequently, the report by which a character learns of specific events that have taken place elsewhere. A typical example of the first meaning occurs in the story of Elisor and the queen of Castille: "Luy seul avecq ung varlet s'en alla en ung lieu si solitaire, que nul de ses parens et amys durant les sept ans n'en peurent avoir *nouvelles*. De la vie qu'il mena durant ce temps et de l'ennuy qu'il porta pour ceste absence, ne s'en peut rien sçavoir" (198;279). Examples of the more common meaning occur in the first two stories of the collection: "Après que l'homicide fut faict, et que les deux serviteurs du trespassé s'en furent fouys pour en dire les *nouvelles* au pauvre pere . . ." (15;74); "Arriva son pauvre mary, qui veid premier le corps de sa femme mort devant sa maison, qu'il n'en avoit sceu les *nouvelles*" (21;81). "Nouvelles" in both these senses occurs frequently throughout the collection, and no fewer than eleven times in the story of Floride and Amadour alone (*nouvelle* 10).[4]

For Marguerite, as for Marot, such "nouvelles" can be either plural or singular. The former tends to mean news in general or multiple reports of the same fact, the latter a report of a single, specific event, as the following examples from the famous story of Rolandine (*nouvelle* 21) show: "[Le] bastard . . . craignant que son affaire fust revelé, s'eslongna du dangier, et fut long temps sans revenir à la court, mais non sans escripre à Rolandine par si subtilz moyens, que, quelque guet que la Royne y meist, il n'estoit sepmaine qu'elle n'eust deux fois de ses *nouvelles*" (165;243). "Le pere, sçachant ceste piteuse *nouvelle*, ne la voulut poinct veoir, mais l'envoya à ung chasteau dedans une forest" (172;250). "Ceste *nouvelle* apporta une si extreme douleur au cueur de ceste pauvre Rolandine, que, ne la pouvant porter, tumba bien griefvement mallade" (173;251). In these and all other occurrences throughout the *Cent nouvelles*, "nouvelles" are nothing more than news, a "nouvelle" nothing more than the true report of a recent event.[5] Furthermore, as these examples suggest, the most specific "nouvelles" typically involve events that have already been narrated in detail. In all such cases the reader knows for a fact that the nouvelle is a true and accurate account of what has actually happened.

Not only are "nouvelles" merely news or reports, but, as all the major authors associated with Marguerite bear witness, the expression "Quelles nouvelles?" was the most common form of greeting in sixteenth-century France, exactly equivalent to our "Quoi de neuf?" or "What's new?" Marot, for example, begins his rondeau "Aux Damoyselles paresseuses d'escrire à leurs Amys" with:

Bon jour, *et puis, quelles nouvelles?*
N'en sçauroit on de vous avoir?
S'en brief ne m'en faictes sçavoir,
J'en feray de toute nouvelles.
        (Rondeau, "Bon jour," lines 1–4, in *Oeuvres diverses*, p. 107)

In Bonaventure Des Périers's *Cymbalum mundi* (1537) Curtalius greets Mercury in the first dialogue with the words: "*Et puis*, monsieur, *quelles nouvelles?*" as does Cupido in the third dialogue: "Qui est-ce là? Hé! bon jour, Mercure; est-ce toy? *Et puis, quelles nouvelles?* Que se dict de bon là-hault en vostre court celeste?" And in Rabelais's *Pantagrueline prognostica-tion* (1532) Alcofrybas observes that in France, "le premier propos qu'on tient à gens fraischement arrivez sont: '*Quelles nouvelles?* Sçavez-vous rien de nouveau?'"[6]

The expected response to the greeting "quelles nouvelles?"—and the unavoidable answer to our question, "what *are* nouvelles?"—is obviously nothing remotely resembling a novella. In the world in which the *Cent nouvelles* were written and read, nouvelles were something quite ordinary that people asked for and got every day of their lives—not pieces of literary writing but pieces of orally reported news: information ranging from the kind of *faits divers* that eventually become *petite histoire*, to personal tidbits and gossip. Properly construed, the title of Marguerite's book announces nothing more than a hundred "reports" or pieces of "news"—"stories" only in the modern journalist's sense of the word.

Such indeed are the "stories" of the *Cent nouvelles*. The nouvelles told by the interlocutors are no different from those told by characters within their narratives. They are offered, and received, as orally transmitted news— functional, factual, eyewitness reports (or at least authenticated reports whose source is guaranteed by the interlocutor-reporter to be reliable) of real events that have occurred recently in the lives of real people. Because these nouvelles are news, they typically begin by situating their subjects in relation to political events and noble personages known to the listeners (and presumably to Marguerite's intended readers as well). And because the news is authentic, the listeners (and presumably Marguerite's readers) can frequently identify the individuals involved even when names are concealed or changed to protect the honor of a well-known family.

It is in the context of this a priori factual, reportorial value ascribed to all nouvelles in general, and to the nouvelles reported by Marguerite's interlocutors in particular, that we must understand the famous principle of veracity established in the prologue of the *Cent nouvelles*. When Parlamente decrees that the hundred nouvelles related at Notre Dame de Sarrance are to differ from the "cent Nouvelles de Bocace" in that there is to be "nulle nouvelle qui ne soit *veritable histoire*" (9;68),[7] she is not adding a criterion of truth to the definition of a literary genre, as modern professional readers are naturally inclined to believe. Rather, she is reaffirming the true nature of French *nouvelles* in the face of what in Italy had degenerated into fiction. It is crucial to understand that for Marguerite and her readers, nouvelles are not Boccaccian *novelle* that just happen to be true. On the contrary, Boccac-cio's *novelle* are *false* nouvelles. They are fake news, simulated reports of things that never actually happened, Italian fabrications. In a word, they are nothing but literature. The crucial point is that unlike Boccaccio's narrators, Marguerite's interlocutors do not tell tales. They relate incidents. They report news.

All of these observations would of course apply to earlier collections of French nouvelles as well, and indeed similar points have been made, most incisively and pertinently about the two works whose title, like Marguerite's, signals a direct response to Boccaccio: *Les Cent Nouvelles nouvelles*.[8] But the point is especially important in the case of Marguerite's *Cent nouvelles* because the fact that her nouvelles are new is crucial to the unique project of the work as a whole. If we are to understand the meaning and importance of Marguerite's unfinished decameron we must begin by taking completely seriously its thoroughly French pretensions to faithful, accurate, nonliterary reportage.

This does not mean, of course, that we must necessarily accept all the news reported by Marguerite's interlocutors as historical or biographical fact. (Much of it *is* factual and can be corroborated by nonliterary records, but much is also borrowed from the fictions of "artists" like Boccaccio and simply disguised to look like real news.) Even less does it mean we must refrain from reading Marguerite's narratives as literary texts. (Even if the rewards of doing so were not sufficiently obvious to everyone, the fact would remain that all these "news" are contained within a larger narrative whose story is, in the first half of the prologue especially, self-consciously and even ostentatiously fictional and literary.) It does mean, however, that we must accept the fundamental premise of the work—its controlling fiction, if we prefer—which is that the interlocutors' nouvelles are not fiction. And it means that we must not allow our professional preoccupation with literature, or our modern suspicions of language, to stand in the way of a clear view of what is fundamentally at stake in the all-important discussions that follow each nouvelle.

Contrary to what we might like to think, the interlocutors are sublimely indifferent to the telling of the stories they hear, and they never once engage in anything that would pass today for "interpretation." Indeed they cannot, for according to the controlling fiction of the work there is nothing for them to interpret in any hermeneutic sense of the word: no text, no narrative, no words, only facts and events that have been faithfully set before them. The aristocratic, honor-bound *devisants* never show the slightest sign of suspicion that one of their number might betray his or her constantly reaffirmed oath to tell the truth, the whole truth, and nothing but the truth;

nor that a reporter might slant a story to fit his or her own sense of its significance or in any way put a spin on the news; nor even that any slippage might ever occur between events and the language that narrates them. Confident in the perfect candor and competence of their fellow reporters, in the perfect adequacy and transparency of language, and in the perfect congruence between narration and narrated events, they never once doubt that with each nouvelle—with each new piece of news—they are getting the whole story and they are getting it straight.[9]

In such utopian circumstances as these, which the fiction of the *Cent nouvelles* requires that we accept whether we believe they are possible in the real world or not, there can be no room for hermeneutics. On the other hand there is ample room for direct judgments and evaluations of people and events, unhindered by any opacity of medium or any doubt concerning the facts—that is, for a utopian form of what we would perhaps call "news commentary." And indeed what the interlocutors interpret in each and every nouvelle, often with frightening intensity and conviction, is not the intentions of the reporter or the implications of his or her words but the intentions of other people and the implications of their actions. Their arguments are concerned exclusively with questions of good and bad character, motives, and behavior; of right and wrong opinions, actions, and ways of living; of guilt and innocence in the performance of specific deeds by specific people in specific circumstances. In discussing their nouvelles they do not discuss narratives, they discuss the news.[10]

*   *   *

This pleasant pastime may not strike us as particularly surprising, given the well-known preoccupation of the early sixteenth century with questions of practical moral philosophy. But the interlocutors' enterprise is in fact a problematic and even a potentially harmful one, for in addition to being factual reports, "nouvelles" can be something highly undesirable for Marguerite and her contemporaries. Two of the greatest writers associated with Marguerite can help us to see this clearly.

In Rabelais's *Pantagrueline prognostication*, Alcofrybas prefaces his satirical attack on astrological prognostication by condemning all curiosity, not only about the unknowable future but about all "new things" in general. The condemnation is predicated on the virtual identity of "news" and "novelty" within the single term "nouvelles." People are so "curieulx de sçavoir choses nouvelles," he says, that they are easily taken in by liars and charlatans. The French are especially susceptible because they are notoriously curious, always greeting everyone they meet with "Quelles nouvelles? Sçavez-vous rien de nouveau?" and becoming angry when travelers do not bring them "pleines bougettes de nouvelles." And they are as credulous as they are "promptz à demander des nouvelles." Pantagruel's solution to this typically French problem was to establish a special agency to "examiner les nouvelles" and admit into Utopie and Dipsodie only nouvelles proven (like those of the *Cent nouvelles*) to be "veritables."[11]

Des Périers's *Cymbalum mundi* is even more explicit in its condemnation of curiosity about "nouvelles" and in its association of "news" with "new things." Mercury, having been dispatched to earth by Jupiter to discover "aulcune nouvelle" of his stolen book of fates (3.24)—and by Juno to fetch a copy of the "les *Cent Nouvelles nouvelles*" (3.25)!—and having twice been met with the characteristically French greeting "Et puis, quelles nouvelles?" (1.6 and 3.27), exclaims: "N'est-ce pas pitié? Soit que je vienne en terre ou que le retourne aux cieulx, tousjours le monde et les dieux me demandent si j'ay, ou si je sçay, rien de nouveau. Il fauldroit une mer de nouvelles, pour les en pescher tous les jours de fresches" (3.30). In exasperation he makes a horse talk to its master, thus giving humans what they seem to want most—namely, "quelque chose de nouveau" (3.30,33) that will be talked about, written about, published, sold in bookstores . . . and that will generate "quelques aultres nouvelles" (3.33).

Similarly, the talking dog Hylactor hopes to become famous by exploiting the folly of humans, who are so "curieux de nouveauté" (4.34) that they despise "choses presentes, accoustumees, familieres et certaines, et ayment tousjours mieulx les absentes, nouvelles, estrangeres et impossibles" (4.41). Yet Hylactor and his interlocutor, Pamphagus, are guilty of the same curiosity. When they discover a message from the lower Antipodes they exclaim excitedly: "Je croy qu'il y aura quelque chose de nouveau. . . . Voyla bien des nouvelles! . . . J'espere qu'il y aura quelques bonnes nouvelles" (4.42). The work ends with a final jab at the same weakness in all humans: "tant sont les hommes curieux et devisans voluntiers des choses nouvelles et estrangeres!" (4.43).

While such curiosity about "new things" is not a particularly important theme within the narratives of the *Cent nouvelles*, it is a motivating force for the interlocutors themselves, whose desire for "nouvelles" is insatiable and who see quite plainly the connection between news and novelty. As one of the interlocutors points out, there can be no "nouvelles" without "nouveaulx actes" to report (327;427). A nouvelle is only a "nouvelle" if it is an account that can be "tenu pour nouveau" (400;512). In this respect the interlocutors are typically French.

To modern readers this French thirst for nouvelles may appear harm-less enough and perhaps even endearing. To the author and readers of the *Cent nouvelles*, on the contrary, it was implicitly understood to be extremely dangerous. Here again, Rabelais and Des Périers will help us to see the problem as we are meant to see it. In condemning French curiosity about "choses nouvelles" Rabelais borrows directly and conspicuously from a well-known passage in *De bello gallico* in which Caesar notes a regrettable national defect ("infirmitas") in the Gauls.[12] From this explicit borrowing we are to infer that when a Frenchman says: "Quelles nouvelles? Sçavez-vous rien de nouveau? Qui dict? Qui bruit par le monde?" he is behaving in precisely the way that made his feckless ancestors unfit for civic duty.

Des Périers, in condemning the same curiosity, alludes to a different ancient authority in such a way as to suggest an even more negative aspect to this hereditary Gallic flaw. He situates the dialogues of the *Cymbalum mundi* in "Athenes" (1.5,6), in "Grece" (4.34), in order to portray his curious compatriots as "Atheniens" (1.5). Now his portrait of these "Athe-nians" is borrowed directly from a well-known episode in the Acts of the Apostles in which the apostle Paul visits Athens and preaches on the Areopagus. Luke observes here that the Athenians "spent their time in nothing except telling or hearing something new"—"ad nihil aliud vaca-bant nisi aut dicere aut audire aliquid novi" (Acts 17:21).[13] Just so, Des Périers's Mercury complains that the Athenians "tousjours me demandent si j'ay, ou si je sçay, rien de nouveau" (3.30) and the crucial phrase "quelque chose de nouveau" ("aliquid novi") is repeated three more times in the work (3.30, 3.33, 4.42). In their weakness for nouvelles the modern-day Gauls are thus exactly like the citizens of first-century Athens.

In this resemblance lies a terrible truth, for the Athenians of Luke's description, as any reader of Marguerite certainly knew, were those worldly and wordy philosophers, the Epicureans and Stoics, who were interested in the apostle Paul only as long as they thought he was preaching some *new* divinities ("novorum daemoniorum"), had some *new* philosophy for sale ("nova doctrina"), and could fill their ears with strange *new things* ("nova quaedam"). When they learned that these new things were only Jesus and the Resurrection, most of them mocked and lost all interest (Acts 17:18–20,32). Readers of Rabelais, Des Périers, and Marguerite would surely have understood the implications of the resemblance that Marguerite's own protégé Des Périers had made it impossible to ignore: namely, that the *nouvelle*-hungry French, like the curious Athenians, are interested only in the vain and variegated wisdom of men, not in the immutable wisdom of God.

This is a point about which the evangelical author of the *Cent nouvelles* was bound to be extremely sensitive. Marguerite never ceased condemning worldly wisdom as something vain and prideful. In *Les Prisons*, for example, "Athenian" curiosity about learning and philosophy is presented as one of the prisons from which the narrator must be freed by the Word of God. More fundamentally, Marguerite consistently denounced attachments to all worldly things. In virtually everything she wrote she returned tirelessly to the same passage in the First Epistle of John that warns against the three temptations of the world: "Do not love the world or the things in the world. If any one loves the world, love for the Father is not in him. For all that is in the world, the lust of the flesh [*concupiscentia carnis*] and the lust of the eyes [*concupiscentia oculorum*] and the pride of life [*superbia vitae*], is not of the Father but is of the world. And the world passes away, and the lust of it; but he who does the will of God abides forever" (1 John 2:15–17). In the *Cent nouvelles* alone Marguerite quotes and alludes to this key passage at least five times (see especially *nouvelles* 19, 147–48; 224–25 and 40, 280; 374).

Thus, in the intellectual, spiritual, and artistic sphere of which Marguerite de Navarre was the center, "nouvelles" were doubly dangerous. At worst they were indistinguishable from "new things" like the forbidden knowledge of an unknowable future promised by charlatan prognosticators and the vain knowledge of the past and present pursued by pagan philosophers and lovers of human wisdom. At best they were frivolous "news" about the oddities and vanities of this world. What is common to all *nouvelles*, moreover, is the one thing that Marguerite condemns most vigorously in this and all her works, for a nouvelle by any definition is that which distracts curious people from the love of God and binds them ever more closely to the world and its vanities.

In this respect the *Cent nouvelles* appears to be an anomaly in Marguerite's work. By indulging their French passion for nouvelles and whiling away their time with chitchat about other people's news, the interlocutors would appear to be guilty of two things Marguerite consistently and vigorously condemned—idle curiosity and a vain attachment to the world. Worse yet, they would appear, like those unredeemed Gentiles encountered by Paul on the Areopagus, to neglect the one thing that truly matters in favor of anything new.

*   *   *

In these decidedly negative, anti-evangelical associations of *nouvelles* lies the crux of the project of Marguerite's *Cent nouvelles*. For the one thing that truly matters and from which one must never be distracted, according to Marguerite and the writers around her, is also a *nouvelle*. It is the "Good News," or εὐαγγέλιον (euangelion), that is reported in the New Testament and consists in the strange new words and deeds of Christ, the Word of God made flesh. Marguerite identifies the Gospel explicitly as a "nouvelle" from the very beginning of her book, when Oisille begins to describe her daily Bible readings in the following terms: "Incontinant que je suys levée, je prends la Saincte Escripture et la lys, et, en voiant et contemplant la bonté de Dieu, qui pour nous a envoié son filz en terre anoncer ceste saincte parolle et *bonne nouvelle*, par laquelle il permect remission de tous pechez, satisfaction de toutes debtes par le don qu'il nous faict de son amour, passion et merites . . ." (7;66, emphasis added). According to this orthodox formulation, the Good News of which Christ is both the teller and the subject, is a report, or a story of redemption through love. This is the "nouvelle" that Oisille proposes as a suitable pastime for the entertainment of her fellow travelers stranded at Notre Dame de Sarrance.[14]

Oisille's proposal is accepted enthusiastically by all and faithfully put into effect. Each of the following days begins with a reading from the New Testament, followed by Oisille's commentary and a general discussion of the passage. The travelers thus amuse themselves exactly according to plan, by hearing and discussing the one completely true and authentic nouvelle—a nouvelle that is literally (to quote a common sixteenth-century expression) "aussi vraye que Evangile"—namely, the "bonne nouvelle" whose plot, in Hircan's synopsis, is "la vie que tenoit nostre Seigneur Jesus-Christ, et les grandes et admirables euvres qu'il a faictes pour nous" (8;67).

It is only as an afterthought, and as an explicit concession to the imperfection of mortals not yet dead and dissolved in Christ, noted by Hircan ("Mais si fault il que vous regardez que nous [ne] sommes encore si mortiffiez qu'il nous fault quelque passetemps et exercice corporel", 8; 67),[15] that a second pastime is added to the first. And it is only after Hircan's own suggestion is dismissed as excessively corporeal that Parlamente offers, as a compromise between pure spirituality and pure physicality, the well-known proposal that is accepted and carried out in the following pages of the book. The telling of news is thus presented by Marguerite, and understood by all her characters, as something less important and less worthy than the principal activity of reading the Bible. The "nouvelles" of the *Cent nouvelles* are a sop for weak mortals, a secondary object appended and clearly subordinated to the primary object that is the "bonne nouvelle."

But this secondary, subordinate pastime is at the same time strictly parallel to the primary one. Just as the sojourners will spend their mornings recounting and discussing "*the* News," so they will spend their afternoons recounting and discussing "news." The projected "cent Nouvelles" (9;68) are thus the exact, postprandial counterpart of the unique, matutinal "bonne nouvelle" (7;66).[16] Furthermore, the two activities prove in practice to be interconnected and complementary. Oisille herself makes an explicit connection between them at the precise midpoint of the entire project. In the prologue to the sixth day she says: "Il me desplaist que je ne vous puis dire, à ceste après disnée, chose aussy proffitable que j'ay faict à ce matin; mais, à tout le moins, l'intention de mon histoire ne sortira poinct hors de la doctrine de la saincte Escriture, où il est dict . . ." (328–29;428).

And in fact, news reported by the interlocutors frequently involves the importance and proper use of the Good News. Thus, for example, the good wife of nouvelle 67, "qui avoit toute consolation en Dieu," is admired because she "porta pour sa saulve garde, norriture et consolation, le Nouveau Testament, lequel elle lisoit incessamment" (393;503), whereas a monk or priest might be condemned for failing to "prescher la parolle de Dieu" (285;378), "prescher l'Evangille" and "presch[er] purement et simplement l'Escripture" (303;399), or because he maintains that "l'Evangille n'estoit non plus croyable que les *Commentaires* de Cesar ou autres histoires escriptes par docteurs autenticques [var.: etniques]" (303–4;400).

Conversely, a truth revealed in the Good News is occasionally illustrated by a particular piece of news: "Voylà, mes dames, une histoire qui est bien pour monstrer ce que dict l'Evangile: Que Dieu par les choses foybles confond les fortes [1 Cor. 1:27]" (185;265). Or more frequently, the Good News is invoked by the interlocutors in their discussion and interpretation of the news. The discussions of the *Cent nouvelles* are in fact crammed full of quotes and paraphrases of the New Testament, some of them identified as such, but most of them offered casually and without attribution for the benefit of an audience perfectly capable of recognizing them without a gloss, and for whom the Bible is the common point of reference. It is as though the afternoon discussions of news were a kind of *travaux pratiques* during which the interlocutors considered problems of practical application of the theoretical evangelical lessons heard and discussed in the morning.

In this carefully drawn and deliberately executed relationship between "la bonne nouvelle" and a hundred "nouvelles" lies not only the antidote to the pestilence of curiosity about "news" and "new things," but the basis of the entire project of Marguerite's *Cent nouvelles*. The whole point, it would seem, is to probe the articulation between the Good News of redemption and daily news in a fallen world—that is, between the one truly new thing that has befallen humanity since its original fall from grace and the innumerable, apparently new things that befall it every day even now, fifteen centuries after redemption.

Virtually every nouvelle and every discussion finds its place within this larger project. Day after day, nouvelle after nouvelle, the underlying questions remain the same: How are we to understand the Gospel, immersed as we are in the contingencies of this world and adrift in a sea of nouvelles? And conversely, how are we to understand the new things that happen around us in light of the Good News of the Gospel? What points of contact, what mediation, can there be between the distant extremes that are Christ and man, "la saincte parolle" and human "parolles," the perfect and the unfinished, the immutable and the unpredictable, the eternal and the transitory, the unique and the multifarious—in short, between the single, definitive "bonne nouvelle" and a hundred, variegated "nouvelles." These questions lie at the very heart of Marguerite's project. They lend to the work as a whole its meaning, to each nouvelle its interest, and to each discussion its purpose.

If the afternoon news is dominated by stories about lovers (fortunate or otherwise) it is because the morning News is founded on a single commandment that is paradoxically both "new" (John 13:34 and 1 John 2:8) and not "new" (1 John 2:7 and 2 John 5), the commandment of love: "A new commandment I give to you, that you love one another; even as I have loved you, that you also love one another" (John 13:34). Similarly, if monasticism and marriage are such important subjects, it is because these are the two institutions by which Christians live together in the world according to the Word. And if crime and punishment, guilt and innocence are such common themes, it is because the Gospel contains, along with the good news of redemption, a report on justification and judgment.

The clearest statements about all of these subjects are in fact contained in the specific parts of the Good News that are read and discussed each morning at Notre Dame de Sarrance."[17] On the subject of love, the Epistle to the Romans states as a fundamental principle and an absolute truth that "love is the fulfilling of the law" (Rom. 13.10), and the first Epistle of John, "qui n'est plaine que d'amour" (328;428), states repeatedly that "God is love" (1 John 4:8, 16) so that "he who loves is born of God and knows God" but "he who does not love does not know God" (1 John 4.7–8; compare 1 John 4.16). On the subject of Christian communities in the world, the Acts of the Apostles gives the best contemporary description we have of the

paleo-Christian church, one that describes the "unyon" in which "les apostres faisoient leur oraison" and a "vie apostolicque" so perfect it makes the
interlocutors desire to "veoir ung tel temps et pleurer la difformité de
cestuy-cy envers cestuy-là" (370;476). And as for questions of guilt and
innocence, these are addressed directly by the Epistle to the Romans, which
contains the fullest elaboration of the doctrine of justification by faith alone
as a gift of grace (Rom. 3:21–28).

But if love is the divine and perfect thing the New Testament says it is,
then what are we to make of the havoc wrought by love in the particular
cases of real men and women witnessed and reported by the interlocutors?
And if marriage is a "great mystery" signifying the relation between Christ
and his church, as the Good News says (Eph. 5:32; compare nouvelle 19,
150;228 and the discussion of nouvelle 54, 343–44;446–47), then how are
we to understand the realities of infidelity, of infernal cruelty and suffering,
and even of murder that take place within the real marriages reported in the
daily news? And if the saved are justified by faith alone and not by the merit
of their works, then how can we know whether certain behavior or opinions are good or bad, or judge the appropriateness of punishments and
rewards in this world?

Such are precisely the questions that are raised and debated during the
afternoon discussions of recent events in the lives of friends and acquain-
tances. All of the themes so familiar to readers of Marguerite's book derive
directly from the single issue of the relation between the Gospel and the
world. Can the "amour parfaicte" that is God exist among God's imperfect
creatures? If so, what is it? Mystical love? Neoplatonic love? Courtly love?
Marital love? Brotherly love? Natural love? Bestial love? Incest? Are all of
these partial emanations of the unique, divine love that is God? Do any of
them really participate in the perfection that is God?

Or put another way, is love between a man and a woman equivalent to
the love of God? Or analogous to the love of God? Or merely a rung on the
ladder to the love of God? Or rather an obstacle to the love of God that
must be overcome? Or a source of suffering good only for credit in Purga-
tory? Does God love and justify those who love, even if they love imperfectly or love an unworthy object? Then what distinguishes agape from eros
and holy union from fornication? What is the relation between a man's lust
for a woman and his love for a fellow creature who happens to be of a
different sex? Or between a godly woman's modesty and honor and a
worldly woman's hypocrisy and pride? When is a monk not a brother in
Christ, or a husband not an image of Christ? At what point does love cease

to be God to become *concupiscentia carnis*, when does honor cease to be a Christian woman's virtue to become *superbia vitae*? How can love possibly exist *in* the world without becoming love *of* the world (1 John 2:15–16)? And behind all these questons, the most fundamental one: How can we live in the world of news, yet still live according to the Word of the Good News?

*   *   *

If Marguerite had completed her *Cent nouvelles* she would almost certainly not have allowed her interlocutors to resolve their disputes about these questions, for what characterizes the human world in this book is precisely that it can never attain the fullness, stability, and perfection of the Word of God. This is why the interlocutors must struggle to discover some way of mediating between news and the Good News in the first place, and why all their efforts to do so here in the world of news are doomed to go on indefinitely.

Marguerite states this crucial aspect of the project explicitly and strategically at the precise midpoint of her unfinished book. At the end of the fifth day, when the project is exactly half finished, Oisille expresses the fear that completion will be prevented for want of sufficient news. Even if we were to invent stories, she says, we could not hope to match the true accounts we have heard so far. To which Geburon answers that, on the contrary, news is so abundant that the project could go on forever, well beyond the projected ten days. "Car," he explains:

> La malice des hommes mauvais est toujours telle qu'elle a esté, comme la bonté des bons. Tant que malice et bonté regneront sur la terre, ilz la rempliront tousjours de *nouveaulx actes*, combien qu'il est escript qu'il n'y a *rien nouveau* soubz la soleil [Eccles. 1:10]. Mais, à nous, qui n'avons esté appellez au conseil privé de Dieu, ignorans les premieres causes, trouvons toutes *choses nouvelles* tant plus admirables, que moins nous les vouldrions ou pourrions faire: parquoy n'ayez poinct de paour que les Journées qui viendront ne suyvent bien celles qui sont passées, et pensez à faire vostre part de bien faire vostre debvoir. (326–27;427, emphasis added)

From the divine perspective of "la bonne nouvelle," nothing is new and there can never be any news. But from the human perspective of the reporters and subjects (and readers) of "nouvelles," everything seems new and there can be no end to news. Like Montaigne's *essais*, which could go on as long as there is ink and paper in the world, Marguerite's nouvelles, and the project of her *Cent nouvelles*, could go on as long as people live and love in the world. The only possible conclusion to the work is an arbitrary end imposed by the completion of a bridge and a round number. The only possible conclusion to the project it illustrates is the arbitrary end imposed by death—that final piece of news in which each reporter will inevitably leave the world of multiplicity and change, generation and corruption, to be dissolved in Christ and enter the "conseil privé de Dieu."[18]

But although the project consists in an endless dialectic of irresolvable points of view, it is founded on a profound consensus—not a conclusive consensus to be arrived at and revealed at the end of the *Cent nouvelles* but a provisional one that is operative from the beginning. For not one of the interlocutors ever doubts for a moment that the "bonne nouvelle" is the absolutely authentic and authoritative Word of God and that "nouvelles" are, on the contrary, contingent and open to different interpretations. And all implicitly acknowledge that it is imperative to live according to the Gospel, and therefore essential to understand how the Gospel may be applied to the news. Their disagreements focus on the nature—not on the fact or the importance—of the articulation between the two. The assembled friends thus form an evangelical community founded on a spiritual consensus greater than any of their particular disagreements and on mutual bonds stronger than any personal tensions and rivalries.

In her prologue Marguerite shows us clearly what we are to make of this evangelical community. Many details conspire to identify it as a kind of church. First, the community is designated throughout the prologue as an "assemblée," which is the exact French equivalent of the Greek "ἐκκλησία" (ekklesia). Second, it is identified literally as a community of the saved. Its members have all survived, like Noah and his family, a flood in which all other French visitors to Cauterets seem to have perished, including most members of their own parties.[19] What has saved them and "miraculously" brought them together, moreover, is the "grace" and "bonté" of God (Prologue, 6;65). Third, it is a kind of secularized monastic, or metamonastic, community that lives within the monastery at Sarrance and follows the monastic routine, structuring its days around ten o'clock mass and four o'clock vespers, but at the same time is separate from, and clearly superior to, the community of regular monks—those monks who listen to the interlocutors' news as avidly as the interlocutors listen to the monks' vespers (epilogues to day one, 85;154; day two, 156;234; day three, 234;323; and day four, 369;534) and whose abbot, in contrast to Oisille, is a hypocritical and avaricious lecher (6;65 and 282;376).

And finally, this is a community that constantly reaffirms itself *as* a community of the saved through eucharistic thanksgiving and communion in God. These are in fact their first acts as a group after all the saved have been reassembled at Notre Dame de Sarrance:

> La joye fut si grande en ceste compaignye miraculeusement assemblée, que la nuict leur sembla courte à louer Dieu dedans l'eglise de la grace qu'il leur avoit faicte. Et, après que, sur le matin, eurent prins ung peu de repos, allerent oyr la messe et tous recepvoir le sainct sacrement de unyon, auquel tous chrestiens sont uniz en ung, suppliant Celluy qui les avoit assemblez par sa bonté parfaire le voiage à sa gloire. (6;65)[20]

These acts are repeated every day when the members hear mass and then dine together, thus participating in both kinds of communion—the one holy, the other fraternal—at the precise midpoint of their daily schedule, at the pivot between the antemeridian "bonne nouvelle" and the postmeridian "cent nouvelles."

All of this is to suggest that the little group of refugees stranded at Sarrance constitutes a genuine church—not a monastic travesty of Christian brotherhood but the real thing: a lay community of individuals elected and miraculously assembled by the grace of God, held together by the Good News of redemption and the love that is God, and constituted in the image of those paleo-Christian communities about which they read in the Acts of the Apostles.

And in this identity lies the profoundest aspect of the project of the *Cent nouvelles*. For as they debate the application of the Gospel to human life, the interlocutors are simultaneously living the "vie apostolicque" (370; 476) as it is described in the Gospel.[21] The true church is not an institution defined doctrinally once all disputes have been resolved. It is a community of saved individuals actively engaged in irresolvable disputes. In the very process of debating the articulation between the Good News and the news, the interlocutors may be said to participate in the Good News as fully as it is possible to do in the world of news.

And when at the end of ten privileged days the members of this evangelized *brigata liete* cross a frail wooden bridge over angry waters to reenter the fallen world of passions and acts, they will presumably continue to do this by putting into actual practice the conclusions each has drawn from events in the lives of others. They will go their separate ways, exactly as they came by separate ways—"parquoy, tant pour sercher *chemin nouveau* que pour estre de *diverses opinions*, se separerent. Les ungs traverserent, . . . les autres s'en allerent, . . . les ungs allerent à . . . et les autres à . . ."

(Prologue, 2;60–61, emphasis added)—and exactly as they have maintained their separate opinions during the ten days spent discussing the news. What new things await them in the real world of news? What will be *their* news? Of all this, *nulle nouvelle*. Nor does the curious reader need to know, for only one piece of news really matters: in their diaspora the members of the dispersed church will confront the multitude of apparently new things in their own lives with one eye always fixed on the single new thing that remains always truly new—the Good News and its new commandment, which all have possessed from the beginning.

Notes

1. Pierre de Bourdeille, seigneur de Brantôme, *Oeuvres complètes*, ed. Ludovic Lalanne, 11 vols. (Paris: Jules Renouard, 1864–82). See for example vol. 9, pp. 38, 84, 211, 236, 309, 388, 544, 678, 703, 716–17. The earliest manuscripts and editions of Marguerite's work respect this title in a way that modern editors do not. Bibliothèque Nationale manuscript Fr. 1512, for example (on which Michel François based his edition), is titled "Eptameron *ou nouvelles* de la Reine de Navarre," and Claude Gruget's first printed edition is titled even more accurately "L'Heptameron *des Nouvelles* de très illustre et très excellente Princess Marguerite de Valois" (emphasis added).

2. Godefroy (vol. 10, pp. 212–13) defines "novele" as the "premier avis qu'on reçoit d'une chose, renseignement sur quelque chose de lointain, de caché, d'ignoré," or a "renseignement sur l'état, la situation de quelqu'un qu'on n'a pas vu depuis un certain temps." Frédéric Godefroy, *Dictionnaire de l'ancienne langue française et de tous ses dialectes du IXe au XVe siècle*, 10 vols. (1891–1902; rpt. Geneva and Paris: Slatkine, 1982).

Huguet (vol. 5, p. 458) gives a few examples of "nouvelle" in these meanings and many more illustrating the sixteenth-century expressions "nulle nouvelle" and "nulles nouvelles," which mean "il n'en est pas question, on n'en parle pas" and "il n'en est rien, il n'en fut rien," respectively. Huguet records *no* examples of "nouvelle" in the sense of "novella." Edmond Huguet, *Dictionnaire de la langue française du seizième siècle*, 7 vols. (Paris: Champion and Didier, 1927–67).

3. Typical examples of the former are found in the *Coq-à-l'âne*: "*Des nouvelles* de pardeça: / Le Roy va souvent à la chasse" (1.116–17, in *L'Enfer*, p. 30);

> *Des nouvelles* de par deça:
> L'autre jour, quant il trepassa,
> L'empereur, il ne l'estoit pas
> Et n'avoit pas passé le pas
> Pour dire qu'il fust trespassé.
>
> (3.117–81, in *L'Enfer*, p. 54, emphasis added)

A typical example of the latter is found in *L'Enfer*:

Les infernaulx feront saults et hullées;
Chaines de fer et crochets sonneront,
Et de grand' joye ensemble tourneront,
En faisant feu de flamme sulphurée,
Pour *la nouvelle ouyr* tant malheurée.

(II.476–80, in *L'Enfer*, p. 21)

Clément Marot, *L'Enfer. Les Coq-à-l'âne. Les Élégies*, ed. C. A. Mayer (Paris: Champion, 1977, emphasis added).

4. In the François edition, see pp. 66 (twice), 68 (twice), 69, 70, 71, 76 (twice), 81, 82. Emphasis throughout this discussion is added. For other uses of "nouvelles" within the nouvelles of Marguerite's book see nouvelles 12 (93 and 94), 13 (105), 14 (114), 21 (165), 22 (183), 24 (198, two times), 33 (247), 43 (300), 61 (375), 64 (384), and 70 (403).

5. All emphasis is mine. For other occurrences of "nouvelle" in the singular, see *nouvelles* 12 (92), 13 (107), 23 (189), 24 (197, 200), and 64 (385).

The only technical use of "nouvelles" in the *Cent nouvelles* is a revealing one. It has to do not with literature but with epistemology: "L'ame, qui n'est creée que pour retourner à son souverain bien, ne faict, tant qu'elle est dedans ce corps, que desirer d'y parvenir. Mais, à cause que les sens, par lesquelz elle en peut avoir *nouvelles*, sont obscurs et charnelz par le peché du premier pere, ne luy peuvent monstrer que les choses visibles plus approchantes de la parfection, après quoy l'ame court" (151, emphasis added). Strictly speaking, "nouvelles" are the means by which we have access to facts in the world around us.

6. Clement Marot, *Oeuvres diverses*, ed. C. A. Mayer (London: Athlone, 1966), p. 107. Bonaventure Des Périers, *Cymbalum mundi*, ed. Peter Hampshire Nurse, 3d ed. (Geneva: Droz, 1983), 6 and 27. François Rabelais, *Pantagrueline prognostication pour l'an 1533*, ed. M. A. Screech (Geneva: Droz, 1974), 5. All emphasis is added.

Cf. lines 10–12 of Marot's second *Coq-à-l'âne*:

Et puis, que dict on de nouveau?
Quand part le Roy? aurons nous guerre?
O la belle piece de terre!

(in *L'Enfer*, p. 33)

7. "Histoire" is another word we are likely to misconstrue. But here again the use of the word within the nouvelles indicates that unless "histoire" happens to mean "history" of the kind Caesar and other classical authors wrote (303–4;400), it is always an exact synonym of "nouvelle" in the narrowest sense of a single report of an event known by the reader to be true. Typical examples are: "La religieuse [Marie Heroët] . . . bailla par la grille à son frere tout le discours de sa piteuse histoire" (184;264); "Tout soubdain, s'en alla la duchesse à la Royne et à madame la Regente, leur compter ceste histoire; qui, sans autre forme de procès, envoierent querir ceste pauvre malheureuse" (375;482).

As this last example suggests, the verb "compter," like "racompter," consistently means to give a true report, or account of what has happened. And the ubiquitous word "compte," whether appearing within a nouvelle or a discussion, always means the true and accurate "account" of an event, never a literary "conte." Thus the evangelical Oisille can refer in perfect conscience to the Acts of the Apostles as "comptes" (370;476, see note 17 below).

8. On the Burgundian *Cent nouvelles nouvelles* (1462), see Roger Dubuis, *Les Cent Nouvelles nouvelles et la tradition de la nouvelle en France au Moyen Age* (Grenoble: Presses Universitaires de Grenoble, 1973), 11–33. On the *Cent nouvelles nouvelles* of Philippe de Vigneulles (1515), see Armine A. Kotin, *The Narrative Imagination: Comic Tales by Philippe de Vigneulles* (Lexington: University of Kentucky Press, 1977), esp. 13, 22–24, and 79–96; and Gabriel-A. Pérouse, *Nouvelles françaises du XVIe siècle: Images de la vie du temps* (Geneva: Droz, 1977), esp. 31–37.

Pérouse's discussion of this and other earlier collections of nouvelles is particularly illuminating, and his observations are as valid for Marguerite's collection as they are for earlier ones. Pérouse occasionally hints at this (e.g., pp. 105–6), but studies of Marguerite's *Cent nouvelles* do not seem to have taken the point sufficiently into account.

9. This unmodern faith is not so naive as to be universal. It is strictly limited to the circle of aristocratic speakers whose nobility is a sufficient guarantee of their oath to speak the truth. Nouvelles heard outside this circle are subject to caution, as the story of Alexander of Medici's murder by Lorenzaccio shows (92 and 93;161–62), and as one of the interlocutors explicitly states: "Je croy, mes dames, que vous n'estes pas si sottes que de croyre en toutes les *Nouvelles* que l'on vous vient compter, quelque apparence qu'elles puissent avoir de saincteté, si la preuve n'y est si grande qu'elle ne puisse estre remise en doubte. Aussy, sous telles especes de miracles, y a souvent des abbuz" (246;335, emphasis added).

To my knowledge these are the only cases of false nouvelles in the entire *Cent nouvelles*. It is significant that the first case involves a deliberate lie concocted by an Italian (N.B.) as part of an assassination plot, the second a false miracle faked by a vicious, cynical priest and believed by superstitious innocents.

10. The closest modern equivalent to their discussions might be conversation at a dinner party during which the guests would discuss, each from his or her own personal and political point of view, a late-breaking news report that all had heard an hour earlier from the lips of Peter Jennings (let us say, the story of Marion Barry's arrest on drug charges). Even the most hermeneutically inclined of the guests would probably have more to say about the manner of the arrest and the possible motives behind it, the status of black men and of black politicians in America, and the character, guilt, and innocence of Marion Barry than about the plot structure of Peter Jennings's story or the quality and significance of his prose style and narrative technique. The difference is that even the least hermeneutically inclined of the guests would be infinitely more sensitive to the relevance of these questions than are Marguerite's interlocutors, for whom the report would be indistinguishable from the events themselves.

11. The *Prognostication* was reedited in 1533, 1535, 1537, 1538, and 1542, the later editions being appended to the *Pantagruel* in all collective editions of Rabelais's epics.

On the theme of curiosity in the early sixteenth century see Gérard Defaux, *Le Curieux, le glorieux et la sagesse du monde dans la première moitié du XVIᵉ siècle: L'exemple de Panurge* (Lexington, Ky.: French Forum, 1982). Defaux's general observations on the subject are actually more germane to Marguerite de Navarre than they are to Rabelais.

12. Julius Caesar, *Commentarii de bello Gallico* 4.5:

His de rebus Caesar certior factus, et infirmitatem Gallorum veritus, quod sunt in consiliis capiendis mobiles, et novis plerumque rebus student, nihil his committendum existimavit. Est autem hoc Gallicae consuetudinis ut, et viatores etiam invitos consistere cogant, et, quod quisque eorum de quaque re audierit aut cognoverit, quaerant; et mercatores in oppidis vulgus circumsistat, quibus ex regionibus veniant, quasque ibi res cognoverint, pronunciare cogant.

Compare:

le povre monde qui est curieulx de sçavoir choses nouvelles. Comme de tout temps ont esté singulierement les Françoys, ainsy que escript Cesar en ses *Commentaires*. . . . Ce que nous voyons encores de jour en jour par France, où le premier propos qu'on tient à gens fraischement arrivez sont: 'Quelle nouvelles? Sçavez-vous rien de nouveau? Quy dit? Qui bruit par le monde?' Et tant y sont attentifz que souvent se courroussent contre ceulx qui viennent de pays estranges sans aporter pleines bougettes de nouvelles, les appellant veaux et idiotz. Si doncques, comme ilz sont promptz à demander des nouvelles, autant sont ilz faciles à croyre ce que leur est annoncé. . . . (Rabelais, *Pantagrueline prognostication*, 4–5)

13. The versions of the Bible quoted here and in the following pages are those of the Revised Standard Version and the Vulgate, as they appear in the following editions: *The New Oxford Annotated Bible with the Apocrypha, Containing the Second Edition of the New Testament and an Expanded Edition of the Apocrypha*, eds. Herbert G. May and Bruce M. Metzger (New York: Oxford University Press, 1977).

14. It should be recalled here that the connection between Christ and news is much more evident in French than in English, since the feast we call the Mass of Christ ("Christmas") is called "news," or "a new thing" by the French: "Noël" < novel. The connection was even more evident to French readers of the sixteenth century, because "noëls" were a much-practiced poetic subgenre in which the etymological force of "noël" was habitually stressed. See, for example, Clément Marot's ballade "Du jour de Noel": "L'Ange me dist d'ung joyeulx estomach: / 'Chante Noel en Françoys ou en Grec, / Et de chagrin ne donne plus ung zec'" (ballade 11, lines 25–27, in *Oeuvres diverses*, 158). "Noël en grec" is of course "εὐαγγέλιον," or "gospel" (cf. Luke 2:10).

It should be noted in passing here that if "nouvelles" had any literary associations for Marguerite and her readers these were less likely to be Italian short stories than French Christmas carols.

15. The "ne" in brackets is omitted in the Michel François edition but clearly required by the sense. I have supplied it on the authority of the Le Roux de Lincy and Montaiglon edition of the same manuscript (*L'Heptaméron des nouvelles* [Paris: Auguste Eudes, 1880], 1:245). The reading given by the de Thou manuscript (Fr. 1524) as edited by Yves Le Hir (*Nouvelles* [Paris: Presses Universitaires de France, 1967], 17) is clearly superior: "mais si faut il que vous regardez que *ne* sommes encores si mortifiez, qu'il *ne* nous *faille* quelque passetems et exercice corporel" (emphasis added).

16. This deliberate parallel between the "bonne nouvelle" and "nouvelles" is reaffirmed in the prologue to the seventh day where, after the interlocutors have referred countless times to their own reports as "comptes," Oisille is quoted indirectly as referring to the book of Acts, similarly, as "ces comptes-là" (p. 370;476). On this day, news of things done by contemporaries is to follow and parallel the news of things done ("acta") by the apostles.

17. The Epistle to the Romans is read every day for the first five days (253–54); the First Epistle of John is read on days six and eight (328,421;428;535); the beginning of Acts is read on day seven (370;476). Quotes from all these texts echo frequently throughout the *Cent nouvelles*.

The first scholar to take these indicated readings seriously was Christine Martineau. See her brief but very useful remarks in "La Voix de l'Evangélisme dans l'*Heptaméron* de Marguerite de Navarre," in *Mélanges Jean Larmat: Regards sur le Moyen Age et la Renaissance (histoire, langue et littérature)*, Annales de la Faculté des Lettres et Sciences Humaines de Nice, 39 (Nice: Les Belles-Lettres, 1983), 385–91.

18. It is only an accident, of course, that Marguerite met her own arbitrary end—which she was said to have embraced "comme quelque bonne et joyeuse *nouvelle*" (see Charles de Sainte-Marthe, "Oraison funèbre de Marguerite de Navarre," in *L'Heptaméron des nouvelles*, ed. Le Roux de Lincy and Anatole de Montaiglon, 1:113)—before imposing an end on her creation. In other works of roughly the same period Marguerite showed her mastery at completing a work without resolving the problems it is designed to raise. *La Coche*, for example, purports to be the faithful record of a debate in which each of three ladies claims to suffer most and love best. Marguerite presents herself in the poem as a mere witness and scribe, unable and unwilling to decide among the conflicting claims, barely worthy even to transcribe the debate and transmit it in a book to a suitable judge. We never learn what that judge's supposedly unerring decision might be.

See also the farce called *Comédie des quatre femmes* in Saulnier's edition of Marguerite's *Théâtre profane* 2d ed., Textes Littéraires Français, 3 (Geneva: Droz and Paris: Minard, 1963), pp. 96–125. Like the *Cent nouvelles* it brings together five women and five men in an unresolved debate ("only time will tell") about love and sorrow before, during, and after marriage.

19. This biblical analogy is made explicit on the first page of the book: "Mais sur le temps de ce retour vindrent les pluyes si merveilleuses et si grandes, qu'il sembloit que Dieu eut oblyé la promesse qu'il avoit faicte à Noé de ne destruire plus le monde par eaue" (Prologue, 1;60).

20. The twin formulas "louer Dieu de la grace qu'il leur avoit faicte" and "recepvoir le sainct sacrement de union, auquel tous chrestiens sont uniz en ung"

correspond exactly to the two principal meanings of the Greek word "εὐχαρισ-τία"—etymological (thankfulness, gratitude, thanksgiving, *actio gratiarum*) and liturgical (Holy Communion).

21. It can hardly be a coincidence that Acts is the one book of the New Testament that makes the interlocutors momentarily forget their "entreprinse" so that they have to be reminded to "[se] preparer à racompter [leurs] nouvelles" (370;476). Acts is the book that not only describes the "unyon que les apostres faisoient leur oraison" but goes on to condemn Athenian curiosity about "new things" as irredeemably anti-evangelical (see above).

Critical Tales: An Epilogue

The preceding studies can be read as individual articles, part of the large and growing body of scholarship on the *Heptameron*. Yet they also constitute a network in which each study allows us to read the others, and Marguerite's work, with new insight. As editors we would like to show some of the ways in which these chapters interconnect. Although there are many threads that can be followed through from contribution to contribution, we feel that the contributors' reflections on the *Heptameron* as narrative offer a particularly central theme.

In a book containing seventy-two tales and ten storytellers, the act of telling attracts considerable attention. The *Heptameron* prevents readers from falling into the world of the story and forgetting that they are confronted, not with a window on reality, but with verbal reports about the world. This consciousness is all the more noteworthy in that the prologue explicitly stresses fidelity to the real world as the goal of the stories. Yet the anonymous narrator and each of the storytellers contribute to our awareness of narration as an act and of narrative as a product or construct. Many of the studies collected here concern the nature of narrative in the *Heptameron* either as the principal focus or as an important secondary component of the study. For the purposes of showing how the studies relate to one another we will follow three major and interlocking emphases: the *Heptameron*'s place in the history of narrative genres, theoretical issues of narrative raised by Marguerite's work, and the representation of the person or human individual, including the issue of gender, in the *Heptameron* narrative system.

The *Heptameron* in the History of Narrative Genres

The *Heptameron* is now recognized as a major step in the evolution of narrative from such medieval forms as the romance, the fabliau, and the Boccaccian novella to the novelistic narratives which dominate prose fiction from the seventeenth century on. Some critics point to the connection between the *Heptameron* and the seventeenth-century French novel which has assumed symbolic, canonical status as the prototype of the modern novel, Marie de Lafayette's *La Princesse de Clèves*. Yet one scholar (Duval) takes exception here to this generic history and points out that this evolutionary account is an artifact of professional literary history. In his view, the term *nouvelle* had a very different meaning for Marguerite and her contemporaries. Duval's caution on this score can be generalized to remind us that in any historical approach our views of the past will differ—spontaneously and at least on a first approximation—from the author's and first audience's view. This is true not only because of all that contemporaries brought to the text which we do not (assumptions about social structure, religious knowledge and beliefs, familiarity with idioms, and so on) but because of what we bring to the text ourselves. Among the assumptions that we bring is the idea of progress, the tendency to define a text like the *Heptameron* backward from the literary forms that appear later. In fact, as Duval reminds us (along with de Lajarte), the very assumption that Marguerite's stories should be read as literature gives a cast to our reading that her initial readers did not impose.

In following our modern practice of historical and comparative readings, scholars of the *Heptameron* have addressed the potential for anachronistic readings by stressing the historic specificity of Marguerite de Navarre's situation and by gauging the *Heptameron*'s place in history in part from the text's own intertextual references. The earliest and clearest of these references is the narrator's mention of the courtly pastime conceived by King François I, his sister Marguerite, and their circle to make a collection of stories like Boccaccio's *Decameron*, "sinon en une chose differente de Bocace: c'est de n'escripre nulle nouvelle qui ne soit veritable histoire" (9;68). Duval points out that this design indicates that Marguerite's text would therefore have comprised one hundred tales if it had been carried through to completion. Because the title *Heptameron* was given to the collection of Marguerite's stories by Pierre Gruget, editor of the 1559 edition, and does not figure in the text itself, Duval declines to use this common modern title and refers to the collection as the *Cent nouvelles*. Although this title is used by a contemporary of Marguerite, Brantôme, the internal evidence of its attachment to this collection of tales comes only from the expression, which Duval quotes, the "cent Nouvelles de Bocace." This question of the title illustrates how strongly Marguerite's text is influenced by generic expectations, for even the scholar most critical of our relaxed equation of the term *nouvelle* with the Italian (and now also English) literary term *novella* locates the design of Marguerite's tales in the reference to Boccaccio. Hence both titles, *Cent nouvelles* and *Heptameron*, derive from the Boccaccian tradition.

Nouvelle, as Duval shows with solid documentation, "was not a literary term borrowed from the Italian 'novella,' but an old, familiar word commonly used in everyday conversation to mean 'news,' a piece of 'news,' or the report of anything 'new.'" Two aspects of the *Heptameron* thus appear in tense confrontation. On one hand there is the *formal* expectation of ten days of ten stories each, told by different narrators of both genders, according to an Italian model. On the other hand, there are expectations of *content* based on contemporary French use of the term *nouvelles*. Duval explores in detail how the temporal, fallen meaning of *nouvelles*, as the latest new event, is contrasted with the positively valued *bonne nouvelle* of the Gospel. Marguerite's prominence in the history of narrative is based in part on a change of the content within an existing, inherited structure. This shift marks the *Heptameron* as part of a national, or even nationalistic, tradition: "reaffirming the true nature of French *nouvelles* in the face of what in Italy had degenerated into fiction." In other words, the similarity of Marguerite's form to that of Boccaccio is precisely what permits the difference in her content to declare itself so clearly. An important, long-range implication of Duval's study is its forceful delineation of the specifically French claim to have redeemed narrative from the hands of the Italian falsifiers or fiction-makers. He notes that this claim characterizes earlier French collections of *nouvelles*, and we can also extend his remarks to later French texts. The attempt to produce narratives that are not fictitious is a strong link to several important texts of French classicism, notably *La Princesse de Clèves*, whose recognized author, Marie de Lafayette, denied it the status of fiction and referred to it as memoirs.[1]

Agreement that the *Heptameron* is generically related to the *Decameron* is matched by agreement on what the *Heptameron* is not, a *roman*. While it is fairly easy to see why the *Heptameron* is not a *roman*, it is somewhat harder to express the distinction in English, which has two terms where French has one. We speak of "romance" for works such as *Orlando furioso* or *The Faerie Queene* and of "novel" for works like *Les Liaisons dangereuses* or *La Princesse de Clèves*. In this conclusion we will simplify matters by using the term "novel" for all cases in which the French speak of *roman*, unless there is a special reason to remember the romance connotation. Several studies in this volume discuss the difference between the *Heptameron* and the novel structure, but some contributors nevertheless detect traces of the novel structure within certain *Heptameron* tales. Tournon writes of the frame-narrative as a novel in which the storytellers would have been the primary characters. In this view the *Heptameron* opens onto a "virtual novel" (*le roman resté virtuel*) consisting of the relationships among the frame-characters, whose intentions in telling their respective tales are mostly omitted or rather suppressed: "the narrator's aims, and along with those aims at least one of the tale's meanings, depend upon a piece of information that has been partially left out [*oblitérée*]." The narratives themselves are hence coded messages or connotative systems in Barthes's sense, that is, the relationship between the plot of the tale and the frame-character's narrating act becomes the mark or signifier of another sense.[2]

Tournon's formulation of a coding system goes beyond this simplified connotational version, because in his account of the *Heptameron* it is the relationship between narrator and receiver that gives meaning to the expression/content relationship. We can never fully understand the meaning of the tales as narrative gestures because most of the novel in the *Heptameron* has been reduced to a tantalizing absence. Tournon's view that the *Heptameron* will always frustrate—and is apparently intended to frustrate—readers' attempts at interpretation is widely shared (see, for example, Duval, Jeanneret), but his description of the nature of the obstacles to understanding is unique and has a particular pertinence to an account of the *Heptameron*'s place in the history of narrative genres. Where Duval posits a ten-day, one-hundred-tale format for Marguerite's book on the basis of the *Decameron* tradition, Tournon locates the *Heptameron* within the novel conventions. Only such an assumption can underpin the argument that Marguerite has "obliterated" the novel that might have been presented about the ten storytellers, for we conclude that the meaning of the narrative acts (and therefore of the tales themselves) escapes us in part (compare Conley's description of the *Heptameron*'s "infinite process of deferment"). The Boccaccian conventions of one hundred tales and indirect amorous communication are both alluded to in the *Heptameron*.

The "nostalgia for the novel" appears not only in the frame-narrative but in some of the tales themselves. Tournon points specifically to the tenth tale, of Floride and Amadour, which by its textual length and the duration of its incidents is more like a novel than are most of the tales. Amadour's indirect approach to Floride—which will also be a crucial element in Russell's study of the narrative structure of characters (representations of human individuals)—echoes the ambiguous and complex courtly dialogue of the frame.

The specter of the novel appears in Jeanneret's study, which asks why Marguerite and her contemporaries did not write novels. The four characteristics of the *Heptameron* which Jeanneret notes at the outset (brevity of narrative units, collection format, periodic commentaries, disagreement of interpretations) are manifestations of a much larger transformation of the presentation of texts and the management of information in the sixteenth century. The disappearance, or at least the eclipse, of the novel in the sixteenth century, is not simply a modulation in the generic patterns of narrative fiction, but a change that affects all textuality—that is, all that is produced or reproduced in written form. Due in part to the invention of the printing press, in part to the rise of new classes eager for practical information, in part to the humanists' drive to accumulate knowledge, the new presentation of texts was segmented and modular: collections of adages, handbooks, lists, and so on, which the reader could dip into in any order and read discontinuously, or as Montaigne said, "à pieces descousues" (*Essais*, 3.3). Jeanneret sees the novella collection as a format particularly appropriate for such a discursive environment. The tales, for the most part without internal connection (that is, without characters, plots, or time continuities which extend from one tale into another), are related by juxtaposition in a collection which, as Jeanneret points out, is ordered differently in early editions.[3] Humanist books, in Jeanneret's account, are provisional gatherings of information which can be selected, recombined, and moved for various purposes. The *Heptameron* fits this modular structure not only by virtue of the discontinuous nature of the tales but also by reason of the subordination of the tales to the discussion. Like humanist knowledge in general, claims Jeanneret, the tales are available for the argumentative purposes of the discussants, who segment a story to make examples. As we have already seen, the *Heptameron* stories are set forth as pieces of reality. To that initial segmentation is brought the refinement that examples accentuate certain aspects of each tale and that different discussants (as Bauschatz points out also, 7) will make quite different use of the same tale. The presence of these commentaries, as much as the brevity of each tale, contributes to the *Heptameron*'s modularity, for Jeanneret's view of Renaissance intellectual life with its quickened pace of change supposes not only the availability of but also a variety of uses for these units of knowledge.

The *Heptameron* is, finally, associated with a genre that only appeared in the late sixteenth century, the *histoire tragique*, a genre practiced by the *Heptameron*'s first editor, Pierre Boaistuau, whose 1558 edition bore the title, *Histoires des amans fortunez*. Conley notes that the *Heptameron* has certain things in common with the collection that Boaistuau would later publish as the *Histoires tragiques* (1559)—its claim to historical veracity and exemplarity, and a certain use of visual—or visualizable—representation. Although the *Heptameron* shares many features with this new genre of the sixteenth century, Conley concludes that Marguerite's fragmentary and mosaic-like structure contrasts with the centralizing character of the *histoire tragique*. The latter provides a moral and ideological hierarchy among the elements of its tales through "pitiful spectacle" which brings the plot to resolution (see Conley, Chapter 5).

Narrative Theory

In addition to the historical context of the *Heptameron*, critics who deal with the narrative structure of Marguerite's work draw attention to features that take on particular prominence in the context of late twentieth-century narrative theory. Since this aspect of their remarks is sometimes implicit, we will try to bring out the theoretical import of their observations. The two principal narrative issues to which the contributors return frequently are narrative omission, or ellipsis, and narrative distance.

The *Heptameron* frame is organized into days. Each of these days is explicitly divided into three major segments, morning, afternoon, and evening. Almost the entirety of Marguerite's text concerns the storytelling and discussion of each afternoon. Most of the duration of the frame-narrative is obliterated (to use Tournon's apt phrase). The two other parts of the day are mentioned so briefly that they can be considered elliptical.[4] If this narrative schema is projected onto the ideological evaluation of activities, one might argue—though this scale is challenged by the content of the tales—that the theoretically most valuable (religious study) and least valuable (bodily restoration) have been elided in favor of the representation of the middle ground. However, Marguerite takes pains to remind us of what has been left out—most of the ellipses are explicit: "Après qu'ilz eurent ouy la leçon de madame Oisille, et la messe, où chascun recommanda à Dieu son esperit, afin qu'il leur donnast parolle et grace de continuer l'assemblée, s'en allerent disner, ramentevans les ungs aux autres plusieurs histoires passées" (87;155).

The elliptical character of the *Heptameron* as narrative is mentioned by several of the contributors. As Cottrell says, "Oisille's biblical 'lessons' are not recorded in the text itself." Duval refers to the part of the *Heptameron* story to which we have access as a kind of discussion section, or *travaux pratiques*, "during which the interlocutors considered problems of practical application of the theoretical evangelical lessons heard and discussed in the morning."[5] Ellipsis is also a feature of one of the three *Heptameron* tales about sacramental confession, for the woman's narrative of her actions or thoughts to the priest, her *secret*, remains unknown to the reader. This part of the story disappears into an implicit ellipsis: "It is as if the person who shaped story 41's narrative respected the seal of confession, the rule forbidding confessors to reveal what they had heard from penitents" (McKinley).

Although recent narrative theory treats ellipsis as a category of narrative time, we can also consider it as a phenomenon of narrative distance, tied closely to modal issues of point of view. After all, the narrator of the *Heptameron* limits our access to certain types of information, specifically the combination of the canonical ten daily stories and the more ample discussions which Marguerite contributes to narrative tradition (Bauschatz). What we learn about depends on whose view we share. In the *Heptameron* there seems to be an abstract Boccaccian-like generic witness who is only present for the afternoon sessions. We call this witness "generic" on the grounds that she (or he) limits most of the report to the storytelling scene itself (including the words of the tales), conforming to the tradition of the novella collections. This focalizing component of the narrative can be distinguished from the general narrator by virtue of its presence during the days of storytelling. Although abstract and unnamed this witness is functionally as real as the nameless general narrator who transmits to us both the prologue and the storytellers' narratives.

Narrative distance—both in terms of point of view (mode) and narrator's position (voice)—is also studied in this volume with reference to the tales themselves.[6] One of the interesting qualities of Marguerite's writing is that she is aware of the possibility of distinguishing point of view and narrative position but that she takes great liberties with these theoretical boundaries. The structure of the novella collection makes readers aware from the start that there is a distance between the reader and the narrators. The prologue is narrated by one anonymous narrator (the general narrator or hypernarrator), who introduces the next layer of narrators (the *devisants* or storytellers), whose narratives often contain an additional narrator, such as the lady in tale 62 (see Cornilliat and Langer), the narrators of included verses (Tetel), or Bernage who transmits the strange case of the penitent adulteress in tale 32 (Rigolot). While this enumeration of layers probably represents general usage, de Lajarte even more rigorously distinguishes between the storytellers and the narrators of the *Heptameron* tales (see Chapter 10). For de Lajarte there are two sets of authors, one real (Marguerite de Navarre) and the other fictitious (the storytellers), and two sets of narrators, the hypernarrator and the narrators of the tales (hyponarrators).[7] In other words, for this contributor the storytellers as fictive but named and characterized individuals are theoretically distinct from the voice which enunciates the tale, just as Marguerite is theoretically distinct from the general narrator. This set of distinctions underscores the distance which, in principle at least, separates the author from so much of what is said in the *Heptameron*. Such carefully contrived distance actually gives greater impact to the return of Marguerite as a character in several tales in which she functions as an inscribed authority figure (and perhaps in other ways as well), for example, in story 62 as the "dame du sang roial . . . qui sçavoit bien dire ung compte et de bonne grace" (377;485).

Attention to narrative distance is not, for Marguerite, an abstract play on the possibilities of narrative structure. Instead, the consciousness of distance between the reader and the events retold is almost certainly based on the concern for factual truthfulness which Duval emphasizes. Parlamente had proposed, in the opening prologue: "dira chascun quelque histoire qu'il aura veue ou bien ouy dire à quelque homme digne de foy" (10;69). From the beginning, the *Heptameron* stories are intended to include some validating account of the relay between the event (*quelque histoire*) and its disclosure at the storytellers' circle in the Pyrenees. The number of times the information has been conveyed from one person to the next and the credibility of the conveyer of this information are given special attention in the first tale in such a way as to sensitize the reader to these distinctions.[8]

In their study of tale 62, Cornilliat and Langer consider an especially complex case of the relationship between the teller and the tale. This "obvious *mise en abyme* of narration" (Cornilliat and Langer) contains a frame in which the outward storytellers of the Pyrenees are mirrored—though with a limitation of gender—within the tale itself. One of the major features of story 62 is the collapse of the distinction between narrator and character when the lady reveals that she is the raped woman of her own story. The forcefulness of this implosion of narration into the event itself is accentuated not only by the reactions of the lady's listeners or by the delayed revelation which arrives only at the end of the story-with-a-story, but by the elaborate distinction of narrative levels in so many preceding tales.

Cornilliat and Langer bring forth a major corollary to the *Heptameron*'s concern with truthfulness: the desire to escape boredom. The characters assembled by chance in the monastery in the Pyrenees fear boredom ("la compaignie . . . commença fort à s'ennuyer," 6;65), according to the prologue. On these grounds and by reference to the established model of courtly discourse in Castiglione's *Cortegiano*, they argue that the exposure of truth, not truth itself, is the greatest antidote to boredom. We can extend this statement toward an understanding of the entire narrative machinery of the *Heptameron* as productive of pleasure to the extent that pleasure is created by distance and its sudden collapse, a libidinous and illicit "fallen" activity which recurs frequently in Marguerite's book of tales, this "sop for weak mortals" (Duval, Chapter 15). It seems to us, in other words, that a narrative collection which establishes such a multiplicity of relays for distancing the event from the teller of the event is creating the conditions necessary for the release of a tremendous force when these checks and boundaries are swept away. Such a use of boundaries to build up and then suddenly release an artificially increased energy is echoed thematically in certain of the tales themselves.[9] McKinley argues that "the complex dynamic among eros, secret, and narrative is the mainspring of the *Heptameron*" (Chapter 9). This account gives us a good foundation for understanding the surprisingly scatological and erotological aspects of so much of the *Heptameron*, for Marguerite has displaced the interest in story 62 from the rape to its revelation—in other words from the event to the mechanisms of its transmission (see Chapter 8), or what Cornilliat and Langer also call the "seesaw movement in the locating of guilt between the act and its recounting."

Cornilliat and Langer show that truth, shame (derived from the exposure of certain truths), and relief from boredom are bound together in a tight interdependence. The flight from fiction announced in the prologue may thus be based on an aesthetic derivative of Marguerite's religious beliefs. The theoretical consequences for the *Heptameron* narrative are, first, that categories of mode and voice will be delineated with care only to be violated and, second, that the most extreme combinations of point of view and narrative position will provide the greatest relief from boredom.

While Genette's narratology separates the question of the focalizing character (a matter of mode) from the study of narrative position (a question of voice), it is essential to join the two in order to appreciate what is at stake in story 62. Indeed the "punch line"—if such a comedic term can be used in this case—turns on the simple switch from third-person to first-person narration. This change in voice also constitutes a change in focalization, since the story is presented generally from the man's point of view (for example, "Ung jour, se pensa le gentil homme, que, s'il la povoit trouver à son advantaige, que par adventure elle ne luy seroit si rigoureuse," 378;485). Cornilliat and Langer describe tale 62 as a narrative trap for the woman narrator, since she asks that it not be repeated. Its nonrepeatable quality brings the narrative closer to the event itself—if it were truly nonrepeatable it would have to be told by a person present at the scene. Such a quality, suggest the critics, may make the tale non-boring and truthful. After the apparently unintentional revelation it became retrospectively evident that the narrator had to be one of the two principals in the event.

This double presence, presence as principal in the event and presence as narrator in the tale, makes the lady's story a form of confession—we do not use the term here to imply guilt (and in the context of tale 62 it is the lady's words rather than any of her acts that incur blame)—in the sense of a narrative that is necessarily in the first person. Here story 62 has qualities in common with the tales that concern the institutional church confessions which form the topic of the three tales studied by McKinley. Each of these tales also concerns a woman's confession, but initially to a male priest. In these tales, as in story 62, the woman's first-person narrative seems to be fraught with peril, if not blameworthy. As McKinley points out, Marguerite's attitude toward oral confession seems to be at least partially aligned with that of religious reformers who considered confession entirely secondary in penance (see Chapter 9). A comparison of McKinley's study of confession and Cornilliat and Langer's reflections on story 62 indicates the great importance the *Heptameron* assigns to the distinction between third- and first-person narration. Women are warned against the risks of speaking in the first person. Such risks may explain why the third-person narrative is the basic format of the *Heptameron*, which mediates women's individual experiences through a discursive community dominated by women, as represented by Marguerite's own authorial control over the *Heptameron* (Chapter 9). An understanding of this narratorial and political logic can permit the decoding of personal experience as recounted in the third person, for example in tale 4 (see Cornilliat and Langer, Chapter 8).

Narrative is also at issue in Tetel's study of the long verse texts embedded in four of the tales, which are, at least in part, a further *mise en abyme* of the narrative, or, as Tetel writes, such a poem is "reductively representative of the whole span of the novella" (Chapter 3). If we consider the implications of some of the other studies for the structure described by Tetel, we encounter an intriguing and apparently insoluble problem. How do the storytellers reproduce verbatim—or improvise to perfection—texts of more than 150 decasyllabic verses (tale 13) or a complex polymetric translation from the Italian (tale 19) while telling the story orally under circumstances that do not lend themselves to extensive preparation?[10] The pressure on the storytellers to avoid literary artifice seems to be countered by these microcosmic or synecdochic narratives within the tales. In effect the oral narrative of the storytellers, which is in fact a written representation of an oral narrative (printed in the book we call the *Heptameron*), contains within itself a written narrative which is represented orally! Alerted by Cornilliat and Langer to the revelations that are encoded in the very structure of narrative—that is, the logical possibility of certain combinations of mode and voice—and by Duval to the "controlling fiction" of the *Heptameron* that all is true, we can return with greater understanding of Tetel's comment that the whole span of the novella is represented in a single poem. The span of the novellas is comprised not only of the events told but also of the narrative structure. The included poetic texts are essentially written, they represent a fall from the oral tradition revealed in the fictive attempt to make a written collection which eschews the ornaments of the *gens de lettres* (9;69). The poems may constitute a marker by which Marguerite acknowledges that the storytellers are themselves merely relays in a complex, multilayered narrative structure.

The Narrative and the Self

The human person is represented in the *Heptameron* both directly, as character or persona in the narrative, and indirectly, as part of the mechanism of narrative transmission. By this second category we mean the implicit indications about persons that are visible when we consider *how* certain storytellers tell or interpret stories. To distinguish between comments on character as a specific fictive person (for example, Parlamente or Amadour) and character as a conception of the human being in general terms, contributors often use the current terms "subject" or "self" for this broader concept.

The study which addresses the representation of the self in the broadest terms is Russell's (Chapter 12), which begins with the extremely useful warning that each period develops a distinctive conception of the self. He argues that the Renaissance idea of the self was not as stable as that of the Middle Ages or of post-seventeenth-century culture. It was an era of transition between anonymous typing and the more modern, highly individuated character. At the same time he indicates that the modern reader's occasional impression that a *Heptameron* character has not been described comes from the different items of information we seek in a description. For instance, place of origin, rank, and profession may suffice to outline a character. Within these identity tags characters bear epithets that classify them as types, generally in the absence of a proper name. Russell sees the named characters as more individuated, as developing forms of consistency distinct from the types derived from medieval hierarchies. The development of the modern individual is not, in Russell's view, a movement independent of institutions. Like McKinley, he takes the Roman Catholic requirement of annual individual confession (beginning in the thirteenth century) as an important factor in the development of a consistent character: "This memory instituted the diachronic time of the *récit* as the basis for inner personal consistency and integrity, and linked moments and events in a way that points toward the classical self that was to become fully developed only in the seventeenth and eighteenth centuries." Russell sees the rebellious individual—like Rolandine in story 21, who opposes her father, the queen, and clerics—as the new self of the Renaissance. It is at least an interesting coincidence that rebellion and confession should be united in two of the studies in this volume. For McKinley the women characters develop through rebellion against confession as an ecclesiastical institution. Russell likewise cites Rolandine's discourse as a factor in her individuation ("She confronts the queen and upbraids her"), and this confrontation is an instance of woman's first-person discourse, which is often risky for the woman speaking (as it is for Rolandine) and for the social structures.

The *Heptameron* presentation of self includes the older typed character as well as the new rebellious and consistent individual. Russell sees many instances of characters who are closer to types, even to medieval allegory. Here Russell's view of the Renaissance self intersects with Jeanneret's account of the modular narrative, since Russell describes medieval allegory as having evolved into "a dust of fragments," an expression which evokes the rearrangement of segmented information ascribed to the humanists by Jeanneret and recalls Conley's perception of allegory in the very letters which compose characters' names (Chapters 6 and 5). Some tales thus present a partial reuse of allegorical materials for nonallegorical ends while others remain basically allegorical. Rigolot's study of the Mary Magdalen figure, principally in tale 32, brings an unusual insight into Marguerite's use of allegory. The traditional figure called "Mary Magadalen" was discredited by the textual studies of Jacques Lefèvre d'Etaples and other reform-minded humanists—close to Marguerite herself—who maintained that there were three distinct biblical persons who had been merged by tradition into the Magdalen. Mary Magdalen functions therefore as a popular allegorical figure for the penitent sinner. When the frame-character Ennasuite articulates a parallel between the punished wife of tale 32 and the penitent Magadalen, she adopts a traditional allegorical practice (and invites us to an allegorical reading of the tale) in opposition to Lefèvre's learned humanist position. Does Marguerite take an anti-allegorical stand, making Ennasuite a parodic character, a traditional Catholic who had not returned to the study of the sacred text but lived in a secondhand devotional world? Or does Marguerite use Ennasuite and the wife Magdalen figure of tale 32 to maintain an allegorical position in contrast to the potentially divisive and purely textual erudition of Lefèvre and his partisans?

De Lajarte's contribution (Chapter 10) concerns the human subject in narrative as it grows out of the activity of language itself. Although the author of the *Heptameron* is historically real, she becomes an author (rather than a historical personage) by virtue of writing and speaking. This author creates the other subjects which appear in the *Heptameron*: the general narrator, the storytellers, and the narrators of the individual tales. Despite this multiplicity of speech roles, each one of which supposes the existence of a subject, however fictitious, de Lajarte argues that Marguerite de Navarre (and, more broadly, the sixteenth century) did not make use of the ludic potential of these subjects. According to de Lajarte, the author does not distance herself from the narrative voices of each of the tales: "Generally, the author's voice is heard through the voice of the narrator. The modern notion of representing the narratorial role as a specific and independent role of utterance . . . is a notion foreign to the minds of sixteenth-century narrative authors." This is a challenging notion, and one that demands to be carefully nuanced. It appears to us that de Lajarte sees Marguerite as exploiting a ludic, varied subject through the contrasts between the conversational subjects (the storytellers) but maintaining a single ideological framework that comes through the narrators of the tales: "The *univocality* that profoundly characterizes the narrative discourse of Marguerite's tales contrasts sharply with the fundamentally antagonistic structure of inter-

locutory discourse within which this narrative discourse is inscribed."
Stone also detects the author, Marguerite, distancing herself from the
character Parlamente, in a description that reinforces de Lajarte's argument
that the major locus of contradiction is at the level of the storytellers
(Chapter 4). Like Russell, de Lajarte reminds us not to impose our modern
"realistic" expectations of consistency on the human subjects of the *Heptameron*. The major boundary at which this consistency is absent in the
Heptameron as a narrative system, for de Lajarte, is the contradiction between what each storyteller says when he or she is conversing and arguing
and what comes out of the narrative each tells (in other words, an opposition between the storyteller and the "hyponarrator" of the tale). The
questions that de Lajarte leaves for us are, first, how do our "realistic" and
our "ludic" expectations differ (are they not contradictory—one urging
consistency and the other playful inconsistency?), and, second, how do
these expectations bias our reading of the *Heptameron*?

The multiplicity of levels at which the author manifests herself and the
dispersion of the subject somewhere between the ludic and the realistic are
the points on which Conley's study goes farthest of all in the location of the
subject at the interstices of linguistic units, "an atomistic play of letters and
spaces" (see Chapter 5). Under Conley's readings the shifts in identity occur
not just with changes of speaker but from word to word, or even from
syllable to syllable. In the *Heptameron*, Conley says, the "play of form
begins with the dissolution of the characters into the physical form of the
discourse telling of their adventures."

One of the most widely discussed manners of describing or classifying
the self in the *Heptameron* is gender. An interest in gender is not only a
feature of late twentieth-century criticism, nor only a matter of particular
personal interest to Marguerite de Navarre. In a sense, gender is one of the
three external parameters of the literary genre within which (or against
which) the *Heptameron* inscribes itself, the Boccaccian novella collection
(ten days, ten stories per day, ten storytellers equally divided between
women and men). As we have seen, gender issues are very important in the
studies of Cornilliat and Langer and McKinley. Russell also turns to gender
to argue that women were culturally associated with virtues that facilitated
the transition to the modern individuated self. Since their virtue was to be
based on constancy or patience, whereas male virtue had sometimes been
based on the recurrent narration of a single great feat, the consistent self of
modern society was closer to a feminine ideal than to earlier masculine ones
(see Chapter 12).

Three studies deal primarily with the topic of gender as the fundamental category of the self and arrive at quite different conclusions about the *Heptameron*'s position on the importance of gender. Bauschatz studies Marguerite's representation of male storytellers and female audience in the frame-narrative, showing an expansion of the female audience's role (Chapter 7). In order to appreciate properly Bauschatz's analysis of the male and female frame-characters as they relate to and through narrative, it is important to stress that she does not deal with men and women but with male and female *characters*. Although some parts of her study, taken out of context, might seem to assert permanent traits of men and women in the world, she is really probing how Marguerite depicted men and women in the frame-narrative of the *Heptameron*. Behind this approach is the view of Marguerite, as female author, making a competing or corrective representation of male and female storytellers to overcome the depiction made by Boccaccio, a male author. Not surprisingly, Bauschatz says, the male storytellers of the *Heptameron* "do not really take into account women's perspectives as receivers of the stories." The male characters address stories to women to provoke an affective reaction, whereas, argues Bauschatz, the women storytellers are interested in hearing stories which will give serious models applicable to their own lives. On this account the male storytellers of the *Heptameron* seem to be Boccaccian characters who find themselves in a book that is at great variance with their own preferences. What Boccaccio and the *Heptameron* males have in common is a lack of interest in "the mechanism of didacticism," says Bauschatz, that is, "even if the stories told by male *devisants* present positive models of female behavior, they will not go far enough to indicate how and whether these models may be applied."

While Bauschatz stresses the dualism of gender opposition in the frame-narrative, Sommers describes the "formation of a collective, androgynous body in which men and women unite for a common purpose" (see Chapter 14). In a description that seems to agree with Duval's description of the frame-characters as forming an *ekklesia*, she finds that this androgynous group controls the sexual tension of the *Heptameron* and reflects "the divine harmony and the balance that should prevail in the Christian community." Marguerite seems to have broken down the typing of male and female among the frame-characters even before they begin to tell their stories.

Glidden's view of "gender as a classificatory system" in the *Heptameron* departs from both Bauschatz and Sommers. Unlike Bauschatz she does not find a dualistic classificatory system in which the major differences are between male and female characters, and, yet, unlike Sommers she does not stress spiritual harmony. For Glidden the complexity of gender roles occasionally pits the female storytellers against the female characters in the tales (see Chapter 2). Sexual desire and the freedom to speak one's desire openly and without shame is denied to women characters by female frame-characters rather than by male frame-characters. In this context, stories like tale 43 seem to unsettle the system: "Jambicque . . . exhibits lust as part of her 'nature,' and thereby challenges the notion that women place honor above all," says Glidden. In Glidden's view, Jambicque's arrangements to hide her identity from her lover are not merely an attempt to conform to customs of female modesty but rather a way of playing a sexually dominant role traditionally assigned to the male. Using the terms of the female storytellers, Glidden notes, "Jambicque should be called a man, because she desires."

This crossing of the boundary of "appropriate" conduct for her gender recalls McKinley's description of the way the character Marguerite d'Alençon occupies the role of *voyeur* in story 72. Jambicque's mask and her secrecy are meant to increase her pleasure and not merely to protect her from reprisals. Thus while Sommers seems to limit the *Heptameron*'s presentation of female sexuality to a portrayal of "women's bodies as the object of male desire and aggression," Glidden sees Jambicque's mask as "a redundancy within the story . . . [that] points beyond itself toward role playing, performance, and the carnivalesque." Under the mask she can fully enjoy being the desiring subject. Glidden notes that the mask can be read two ways: "masking is affirmative of feminine desire but is interpreted otherwise as a sign of shame—the patriarchal culture's way of foreclosing the idea of women's pleasure." Although she views the *Heptameron* as presenting patriarchal values through the women characters of the frame-story (it is interesting to note that Stone also mentions a reversal of gender roles in the exposition of values, Chapter 4), Glidden restores a female affirmation to the book by refusing to grant priority to one narrative level (the frame) over the other (the tale). It is interesting to speculate on the consequences that could be drawn from a combination of Glidden's and de Lajarte's descriptions. Where does the author place herself ideologically in the series of relays between general narrator, storyteller, and tale narrator? Has Marguerite subverted her storytellers through this and other tales?

The case of Jambicque is an appropriate one on which to close, for it unites many of the themes of this volume. This masked woman entertains secret desire and remains herself a secret. The omission and distance that characterize so much of the *Heptameron* narrative is represented in the plot Jambicque designed for herself. For her lover, the desire to know more, to have *nouvelles*, of her identity is the vice which costs him his happiness. Much of the interest of story 43 is the displacement of the plot from the simple sexual encounter to the mediated contact between man and woman through signs, including the simple chalk mark on Jambicque's shoulder. The sudden revelation—albeit here a private one—of Jambicque's identity resembles the sudden implosion of the lady's tale in story 62. Perhaps most of all, Jambicque's story returns us to the paradoxical nature of the *Heptameron*, with its combination of scriptural lessons and its tales of human sin and pleasure. The studies included in *Critical Tales* take us much farther toward understanding the *Heptameron* in its inexhaustible complexity.

Notes

1. Marie de Lafayette, letter to Lescheraine, April 16, 1678, quoted in Maurice Laugaa, *Lectures de Madame de Lafayette* (Paris: Armand Colin, 1971), 16.

2. Roland Barthes, *Eléments de sémiologie* (Paris: Gonthier, "Médiations" series, 1964 [1953]), 163ff.

3. We certainly do not deny that the *Heptameron* has other elements of continuity from tale to tale—notably the presence of the authorizing figure of Marguerite de Navarre herself in several tales, or the recurrence of ideological and institutional structures. In fact, it has occurred to us that one reading of the tales might produce a kind of novel about Marguerite herself. Finally, the celebrated pair of tales 21 and 40 may prefigure the dislocated sequential narrative that comes so much into vogue with the epistolary novel in the late seventeenth century.

4. Gérard Genette, *Figures III* (Paris: Le Seuil, 1972), 139. Genette's spectrum of completeness in narrative accounts of what happens during a given time ranges from the implicit ellipsis (at the minimum of inclusion) to the pause (at the maximum of inclusion). Marguerite's treatment of the morning and evening ranges from ellipsis to extremely brief summary.

5. Despite his very different emphasis, Jeanneret uses the same metaphor for the afternoons of the *Heptameron*: "The short narrative . . . provokes immediate and open reflection on significance, and functions as a laboratory where different reading styles can be tried out" (see Chapter 6).

6. Genette carefully distinguishes mode (Who sees the action?) from voice (Who tells the story?). Tradition had combined these two issues. For the purposes of our study we will relate the two while remaining aware of the theoretical reasons for separating them. Genette, *Figures III*, 203ff.

7. De Lajarte does not open here any question about the historical *mode* of Marguerite de Navarre's authorship, that is, whether she composed her text as sole creator and writer, or with secretarial assistance, or with collaborators who brought

their own invention to bear on the narrative. It should be noted that some recent scholarship has reopened the question of how the *Heptameron* was composed. See Paul Chilton, "The 'Epaves' of the *Heptaméron*: Some Quantitative and Qualitative Clues to Their Attribution," *Studi Francesi* 29 (1985): 449–67.

8. John D. Lyons, *Exemplum: The Rhetoric of Example in Early Modern France and Italy* (Princeton, N.J.: Princeton University Press, 1989), 82–93.

9. The case of the incestuous widow who becomes pregnant by her son in story 30 includes an illustration of the artificial accumulation of energy and its release: "Et, tout ainsy que l'eaue par force retenue court avecq plus d'impetuosité quant on la laisse aller, que celle qui court ordinairement . . ." (230;318).

10. The storytellers' reproduction of extensive written texts is a more obvious marker of the artifices of the collection, but we can ask the same questions about the supposedly faithful replication of the long speeches of tales 4 and 70.

Selected Bibliography

EDITIONS OF THE *HEPTAMERON*

L'Heptaméron des nouvelles. Edited by Le Roux de Lincy and Anatole de Montaiglon. 4 vols. Paris: Auguste Eudes, 1880.
L'Heptaméron. Edited by Claude Mettra. Classiques Garnier. Paris: Garnier, 1964.
L'Heptaméron. Edited by Michel François. Paris: Garnier, 1967.
Nouvelles. Edited by Yves Le Hir. Paris: Presses Universitaires de France, 1967.
Heptaméron. Edited by Simone de Reyff. Garnier-Flammarion. Paris: Flammarion, 1982.
Heptaméron. Edited by Renja Salminen. Helsinki: Suomalainen Tiedeakatemia, 1991.

ENGLISH TRANSLATION OF THE *HEPTAMERON*

The Heptameron. Translated by Paul A. Chilton. Harmondsworth: Penguin, 1984.

STUDIES OF THE *HEPTAMERON* OR CLOSELY RELATED ISSUES

Ames, Sanford S. "'A Severe and Militant Charity.'" *L'Esprit créateur* 28, no. 2 (1988): 89–95.
Baker, Mary J. "Aspects of the Psychology of Love in the *Heptaméron*." *Sixteenth-Century Journal* 19 (Spring 1988): 81–87.
———. "The Role of the Reader in the *Heptaméron*." *French Studies* 43, no. 3 (1989): 271–78.
Benson, Edward. "Marriage Ancestral and Conjugal in the *Heptameron*." *Journal of Medieval and Renaissance Studies* 9 (1979): 261–75.
Bernard, John D. "Realism and Closure in the *Heptaméron*: Marguerite de Navarre and Boccaccio." *The Modern Language Review* 84 (April 1989): 305–18.
———. "Sexual Oppression and Social Justice in Marguerite de Navarre's *Heptameron*." *Journal of Medieval and Renaissance Studies* 19 (1989): 251–81.
Berriot-Salvadore, Evelyne. *Les Femmes dans la société française de la Renaissance*. Geneva: Droz, 1990.
Bideaux, Michel. *Heptaméron, de l'enquête au débat: Marguerite de Navarre*. Paris: Editions Interuniversitaires, 1992.
Blum, Claude. *La Représentation de la mort dans la littérature française de la Renaissance*. 2 vols. Paris: Champion, 1989.

Briçonnet, Guillaume, and Marguerite de Navarre. *Correspondance (1521–1524)*. Edited by Christine Martineau and Michel Veissière, with the assistance of Henry Heller. Geneva: Droz, 1975–79.

Cazauran, Nicole. "Les Citations bibliques dans *L'Heptaméron*." In *Prose et prosateurs de la Renaissance: Mélanges offerts à Robert Aulotte*. Paris: SEDES, 1988.

———. *L'Heptaméron* de Marguerite de Navarre. Paris: SEDES-CDU, 1976; 1991.

———. "*L'Heptaméron* et les origines du roman moderne." *L'Information littéraire* 1 (1983):6–17.

Charpentier, Françoise. "A l'épreuve du miroir: Narcisse, mélancolie et honnête amour dans la 24e nouvelle de *L'Heptaméron*." *L'Esprit créateur* 30, no. 4 (1990):23–27.

Chilton, Paul. "The 'Epaves' of the *Heptaméron*: Some Quantitative and Qualitative Clues to Their Attribution." *Studi Francesi* 29 (1985):449–67.

Cholakian, Patricia F. *Rape and Writing in the "Heptaméron" of Marguerite de Navarre*. Carbondale: Southern Illinois University Press, 1991.

Clive, H. P. *Marguerite de Navarre: An Annotated Bibliography*. London: Grant & Cutler, 1983.

Cornilliat, François. "Pas de miracle: La Vierge et Marguerite dans l'*Heptaméron*." *Travaux de littérature* (Forthcoming).

Cottrell, Robert D. *The Grammar of Silence: A Reading of Marguerite de Navarre's Poetry*. Washington, D.C.: The Catholic University of America Press, 1986.

Dagens, Jean. "Le 'Miroir des simples âmes' et Marguerite de Navarre." In *La Mystique rhénane*, 281–89. Paris: Presses Universitaires de France, 1963.

Davis, Betty J. *The Storytellers in Marguerite de Navarre's* Heptaméron. French Forum Monographs 9. Lexington, Ky.: French Forum Publishers, 1978.

Davis, Natalie Zemon. *Fiction in the Archives*. Stanford, Calif.: Stanford University Press, 1987.

de La Garandière, Marie-Madeleine. *Le Dialogue des romanciers*. Paris: Minard, 1976.

de Lajarte, Philippe. "*L'Heptaméron* et la naissance du récit moderne: Essai de lecture épistémologique d'un discours narratif." *Littérature* 17 (1975): 31–42.

———. "*L'Heptaméron* et le ficinisme: Rapports d'un texte et d'une idéologie." *Revue des Sciences Humaines* 147 (July–September 1972): 339–71.

———. "Modes du discours et formes d'altérité dans les 'Nouvelles' de Marguerite de Navarre." *Littérature* 55 (1984): 64–73.

———. "Des *Nouvelles* de Marguerite de Navarre à *La Princesse de Clèves*: Notes sur quelques transformations de l'écriture narrative de la Renaissance à l'Age classique." *Nouvelle revue du XVIe siècle* 6 (1988): 45–56.

———. "Le Prologue de l'*Heptaméron* et le processus de production de l'oeuvre." In *La Nouvelle française à la Renaissance*, edited by Lionello Sozzi, 397–423. Geneva: Slatkine, 1981.

Delègue, Yves. "Autour de deux prologues: *L'Heptaméron* est-il un anti-Boccace?" *Travaux de linguistique et de littérature de l'Université de Strasbourg* 4, no. 2 (1966): 23–37.

———. "La Présence et ses doubles dans l'*Heptaméron*." *Bibliothèque d'humanisme et renaissance* 52 (1990): 269–91.

Dubois, Claude-Gilbert. "Fonds mythique et jeu des sens dans le 'prologue' de l'*Heptaméron.*" In *Etudes seiziémistes offertes à M. le professeur V.-L. Saulnier par plusieurs de ses anciens doctorants*, 151–68. Travaux d'Humanisme et Renaissance 177. Geneva: Droz, 1980.

Dubuis, Roger. *Les Cents Nouvelles nouvelles et la tradition de la nouvelle en France au Moyen Age.* Grenoble: Presses Universitaires de Grenoble, 1973.

Febvre, Lucien. *Amour sacré, amour profane: Autour de l'Heptaméron.* Paris: Gallimard, 1944.

Fenoaltea, Doranne. "Brigands and Bears in the Prologue to the *Heptaméron.*" *French Studies* 39 (1985): 395–402.

Ferguson, Gary. *Mirroring Belief: Marguerite de Navarre's Devotional Poetry.* Edinburgh: Edinburgh University Press for the University of Durham, 1992.

Ferguson, Margaret, Maureen Quilligan, and Nancy Vickers, eds. *Rewriting the Renaissance: The Discourses of Sexual Difference in Early Modern Europe.* Chicago: University of Chicago Press, 1986.

Fontaine, Marie-Madeleine. "L'Espace fictif dans l'*Heptaméron.*" In *Motifs et figures*, 233–48. Publications de l'Université de Rouen. Paris: Presses Universitaires de France, 1974.

Fontanella, Lucia. "Un codice sconosciuto delle *Nouvelles* di Margherita di Navarra: contributo allo studio della genesi della raccolta." In *La Nouvelle française à la Renaissance*, edited by Lionello Sozzi, 361–78. Geneva: Slatkine, 1981.

Frappier, Jean. "La Chatelaine de Vergi: Marguerite de Navarre et Bandello." In *Du Moyen Age à la Renaissance*, 393–473. Paris: Champion, 1976.

Freccero, Carla. "Rape's Disfiguring Figures: Marguerite de Navarre's *Heptaméron*, Day 1:10." In *Rape and Representation*, edited by Lynn A. Higgins and Brenda R. Silver. New York: Columbia University Press, 1991.

———. "Rewriting the Rhetoric of Desire in the *Heptameron.*" In *Contending Kingdoms: Historical, Psychological, and Feminist Approaches to the Literature of Sixteenth-Century England and France*, ed. Mary-Rose Logan and Peter L. Rudnytsky, 298–312. Detroit: Wayne State University Press, 1991.

Gelernt, Jules. *World of Many Loves: The Heptaméron of Marguerite de Navarre.* Chapel Hill: The University of North Carolina Press, 1966.

Hanon, Suzanne. *Le Vocabulaire de l'"Heptaméron" de Marguerite de Navarre: Index et Concordance.* Paris-Geneva: Champion-Slatkine, 1990. Microfiche.

Heller, Henry. "Marguerite de Navarre and the Reformers of Meaux." *Bibliothèque d'humanisme et renaissance* 33 (1971): 271–301.

Jeanneret, Michel. "La Lecture en question: Sur quelques prologues comiques du seizième siècle." *French Forum* 14, no. 3 (September 1989): 279–89.

Jordan, Constance. *Renaissance Feminism: Literary Texts and Political Models.* Ithaca, N.Y.: Cornell University Press, 1990.

Jourda, Pierre. *Marguerite d'Angoulême, Duchesse d'Alençon, Reine de Navarre.* 2 vols. Paris: Honoré Champion, 1930.

———. *Marguerite d'Angoulême: Etude biographique et littéraire.* 2 vols. Paris: Honoré Champion, 1930.

Kasprzyk, K. "L'Amour dans l'*Heptaméron*: De l'idéal à la réalité." In *Mélanges d'histoire littéraire (XVIe–XVIIe) offertes à Raymond Lebègue*, 51–57. Paris: Nizet, 1989.

———. "Marguerite de Navarre, lecteur du *Décaméron*, le Prologue et le Proemio." *Studi Francesi* 34, no. 1 (1990): 1–11.

———. "La Matière traditionnelle et sa fonction dans l'*Heptaméron*." In *Mélanges de littérature comparée et de philologie offerts à Mieczslaw Brahmer*, 257–64. Warsaw: Editions Scientifiques de Pologne, 1967.

Kelso, Ruth. *Doctrine for the Lady of the Renaissance*. Urbana: University of Illinois Press, 1956.

Kinney, Arthur. "The Poetics of Metaphysics and the Fiction of L'Inquiétisme." In *Continental Humanistic Poetics: Studies in Erasmus, Castiglione, Marguerite de Navarre, Rabelais, and Cervantes*. Amherst: University of Massachusetts Press, 1989.

Kritzman, Lawrence D. *The Rhetoric of Sexuality and the Literature of the French Renaissance*. Cambridge: Cambridge University Press, 1991.

Kupisz, Kazimierz. "A propos de l'honnesté." In *Kwartalnik Neofilologiczny*, vol. 31, 125–48. 1984.

Langer, Ullrich. "Interpretation and the False Virgin: A Reading of *Heptaméron* 33." In *Women in French Literature*, edited by Michel Guggenheim. Stanford French and Italian Studies 58. Saratoga, Calif.: Anma Libri, 1989.

Lefèvre, Sylvie. "*L'Heptaméron*: Codices et indices." In *Autour du roman*, 71–90. Paris: Presses de l'École Normale Supérieure, 1990.

Losse, Deborah N. "Authorial and Narrative Voice in the *Heptaméron*." *Renaissance and Reformation* 23, no. 3 (1987): 223–42.

———. "Distortion as a Means of Reassessment: Marguerite de Navarre's *Heptaméron* and the 'Querelle des Femmes'" *Journal of the Rocky Mountain Medieval and Renaissance Association* 3 (1982): 75–84.

Lyons, John D. "The *Heptameron* and the Foundation of Critical Narrative." *Yale French Studies*, no. 70 (1986). In *Images of Power: Medieval History/Discourse/Literature*. New Haven: Yale University Press, 1986.

Maclean, Ian. *The Renaissance Notion of Women: A Study in the Fortunes of Scholasticism and Medical Science in European Intellectual Life*. Cambridge: Cambridge University Press, 1980.

Martineau, Christine. "Le Platonisme de Marguerite de Navarre?" *Réforme, Humanisme, Renaissance* 2, no. 4 (1976): 13–14.

———. "La Voix de l'Evangélisme dans l'*Heptaméron* de Marguerite de Navarre." In *Mélanges Jean Larmat: Regards sur le Moyen Age et la Renaissance (histoire, langue et littérature)*, 385–91. Annales de la Faculté des Lettres et Sciences Humaines de Nice, 39. Nice: Les Belles Lettres, 1983.

Mathieu-Castellani, Gisèle. *La Conversation conteuse: Les Nouvelles de Marguerite de Navarre*. Paris: Presses Universitaires de France, 1992.

Miles, Margaret R. *Carnal Knowing: Female Nakedness and Religious Meaning in the Christian West*. Boston: Beacon Press, 1990.

Norton, Glyn P. "The Emilio Ferretti Letter: A Critical Preface for Marguerite de Navarre." *Journal of Medieval and Renaissance Studies* 4 (1974): 297–300.

———. "Narrative Function in the 'Heptaméron' Frame-Story." In *La Nouvelle française à la Renaissance*, edited by Lionello Sozzi, 435–47. Geneva: Slatkine, 1981.

Pérouse, Gabriel-A. *Nouvelles françaises du XVIe siècle: Images de la vie du temps.* Travaux d'Humanisme et Renaissance 154. Geneva: Droz, 1977.

Perrier, Simone, ed. *L'Heptaméron de Marguerite de Navarre: Actes de la journée d'étude Marguerite de Navarre, 19 octobre 1991.* Paris: Textuel, 1992.

Reynolds, Régine. *Les Devisants de l'Heptaméron: Dix personnages en quête d'audience.* Washington, D.C.: University Press of America, 1977.

Rossi, Daniela. *"Honneur* et *conscience* nella lingua e nella cultura di Margherita di Navarra." *Journal of Medieval and Renaissance Studies* 5 (1975): 63–87.

Russell, Daniel. "Conception of Self, Conception of Space and Generic Convention: An Example from the *Heptaméron.*" *Sociocriticism* 4–5 (1986–87): 159–83.

Sage, Pierre. "Le Platonisme de Marguerite de Navarre." *Travaux de linguistique et de littérature* 7 (1969): 65–82.

Sommers, Paul. *Celestial Ladders: Readings in Marguerite de Navarre's Poetry of Spiritual Ascent.* Geneva: Droz, 1989.

———. "Feminine Authority in the *Heptameron*: A Reading of Oysille." *Modern Language Studies* 13, no. 2 (1983): 52–59.

———. "Marguerite de Navarre's *Heptaméron*: The Case for the Cornice." *The French Review* 57, no. 6 (1985): 786–93.

———. "The Mirror and Its Reflections: Marguerite de Navarre's Biblical Feminism." *Tulsa Studies in Women's Literature,* 5, no. 1 (1986): 29–39.

Stogkovic-Mazzariol, Emma. "Le *piteuses histoires* di Margherita di Navarra." *Studi di letteratura francese* 18 (1990): 203–21.

Stone, Donald. *From Tales to Truth: Essays on French Fiction in the Sixteenth Century.* Frankfurt am Main: Klostermann, 1972.

———. "Narrative Technique in 'L'Heptaméron,'" *Studi Francesi* 33 (1967): 473–76.

Telle, Emile. *L'Oeuvre de Marguerite d'Angoulême, reine de Navarre et la querelle des femmes.* Geneva: Slatkine Reprints, 1969.

Tetel, Marcel. "Au seuil de l'*Heptaméron* et du *Décaméron.*" In *Prose et prosateurs de la Renaissance, Mélanges offerts à M. le Professeur Robert Aulotte,* 135–42. Paris: SEDES, 1988.

———. "*L'Heptaméron*: Première nouvelle et fonction des devisants." In *La Nouvelle française à la Renaissance,* edited by Lionello Sozzi, 449–58. Geneva: Slatkine, 1981.

———. *Marguerite de Navarre's* Heptaméron: *Themes, Language and Structure.* Durham, N.C.: Duke University Press, 1973.

———. "Marguerite de Navarre: The *Heptameron,* a Simulacrum of Love." In *Women Writers of the Renaissance and Reformation,* edited by Katharina M. Thilson. Athens: The University of Georgia Press, 1987.

Tournon, André. "'Amor de lonh': Thème et variations dans un groupe de quatre nouvelles de l'*Heptaméron.*" *Réforme, Humanisme, Renaissance* 5 (May 1977): 2–4.

Wiley, Karen F. "Communication Short-Circuited: Ambiguity and Motivation in the *Heptaméron.*" In *Ambiguous Realities: Women in the Middle Ages and Renaissance,* edited by Carole Levin and Jeannie Watson, 133–44. Detroit: Wayne State University Press, 1987.

Winn, Colette H. "La Dynamique appellative des femmes dans l'*Heptaméron* de Marguerite de Navarre." *Romanic Review* 77, no. 3 (1986): 209–18.

———. "Gastronomy and Sexuality: 'Table Language' in the *Heptaméron*." *Journal of the Rocky Mountain Medieval and Renaissance Association* 7 (1986): 17–25.

———. "An Instance of Narrative Seduction: The *Heptaméron* of Marguerite de Navarre." *Symposium* 39, no. 3 (1985): 217–26.

———. "La Loi du non-parler dans l'*Heptaméron* de Marguerite de Navarre." *Romance Quarterly* 33 (1986): 157–68.

Wright, Elizabeth C. "Marguerite Reads Giovanni: Gender and Narration in the *Heptaméron* and the *Decameron*." *Renaissance and Reformation* 15, no. 1 (Winter 1991): 21–36.

Contributors

CATHLEEN M. BAUSCHATZ is Associate Professor of French at the University of Maine. She has published numerous essays on readers and reading in French Renaissance literature and is currently completing a study of inscribed women readers in sixteenth-century France.

TOM CONLEY is Professor of French at the University of Minnesota. He is the author of *Film Hieroglyphics* (1991) and *The Graphic Unconscious in Early Modern French Writing* (1992), and he is completing a study of writing, space, and mapping in Renaissance literature.

FRANÇOIS CORNILLIAT is Associate Professor of French at Rutgers University. He is co-editor of *Rhétoriques fin de siècle* (1992) with Mary Shaw and of *What Is Literature? France 1100–1600* (forthcoming); and the author of *"Or ne mens"—Couleurs de l'éloge et du blâme chez les "Grands Rhétoriqueurs"* (forthcoming).

ROBERT D. COTTRELL is Professor of French at Ohio State University. His books include *Sexuality/Textuality: A Study of the Fabric of Montaigne's Essais* (1981) and *The Grammar of Silence: A Reading of Marguerite de Navarre's Poetry* (1986). He is the author of many articles on French Renaissance literature, including several on women writers of the period.

PHILIPPE DE LAJARTE teaches French literature at the Université de Caen, France. He is the author of several articles on the *Heptameron*, focusing in particular on the book's narrative structures and techniques.

EDWIN M. DUVAL is Professor of French and Renaissance Studies at Yale University. He is the author of *Poesis and Poetic Tradition in the Early Works of Saint-Amant: Four Essays in Contextual Reading* (1981); *The Design of Rabelais's Pantagruel* (1991); and many articles on writers such as Rabelais, Scève, and Montaigne.

HOPE GLIDDEN teaches French at Tulane University. Her publications include *The Storyteller as Humanist: The Serées of Guillaume Bouchet* (1981) and articles on Rabelais, Montaigne, French historiography, Marot, and other Renaissance topics. She is completing a manuscript on Rabelais, *Bodies of Knowledge*.

MICHEL JEANNERET teaches French literature at the University of Geneva. His work includes *Poésie et tradition biblique au XVIᵉ siècle* (1969) and, with Terence Cave, *Metamorphoses spirituelles: Anthologie de la poésie religieuse française, 1570–1630* (1972), as well as numerous articles on Renaissance literature and culture. His latest book is *A Feast of Words: Banquets and Table Talk in the Renaissance* (1991).

ULLRICH LANGER is Professor of French at the University of Wisconsin-Madison. He is co-editor of *What Is Literature? France 1100–1600* (1992) and the author of books on Agrippa d'Aubigné and Pierre de Ronsard. His most recent book is *Divine and Poetic Freedom in the Renaissance* (1990), and he has completed a book on friendship in early modern French and Italian literature.

JOHN D. LYONS is Commonwealth Professor of French at the University of Virginia. He is the author of *The Listening Voice: An Essay on the Rhetoric of Saint Amant* (1982) and *Exemplum: The Rhetoric of Example in Early Modern France and Italy* (1989) as well as articles on Corneille, Descartes, Lafayette, and Marguerite de Navarre. He is now completing a study of history and tragedy in the work of Corneille.

MARY B. MCKINLEY is Associate Professor of French at the University of Virginia. She is the author of *Les terrains vagues des «Essais»* (forthcoming), and she is completing a book, *Scriptural Speculum: Evangelical Authority and Authorial Identity in the Works of Marguerite de Navarre*.

FRANÇOIS RIGOLOT is Meredith Howland Pyne Professor of French Literature at Princeton University. His major books include *Les Langages de Rabelais* (1972); *Poétique et onomastique* (1977); *Le Texte de la Renaissance* (1982); and *Les Métamorphoses de Montaigne* (1988).

DANIEL RUSSELL, Professor of French at the University of Pittsburgh, and co-editor of *Emblematica*, has published widely on French Renaissance culture, including a book on *The Emblem and Device in France* (1985), and articles on Rabelais, Du Bellay, and Montaigne.

PAULA SOMMERS is Professor of French at the University of Missouri-Columbia. She is the author of *Celestial Ladders: Readings in Marguerite de Navarre's Poetry of Spiritual Ascent* (1989) and numerous articles on Marguerite de Navarre and the *Heptameron*.

꙳ DONALD STONE is Professor of Romance Languages emeritus at Harvard. He is the author of *French Humanist Tragedy: A Reassessment* (1974) and *Mellin de Saint-Gelais and Literary History* (1983). He is currently editing the French poetry of Mellin de Saint-Gelais for the Société des Textes Français Modernes.

MARCEL TETEL's *Marguerite de Navarre's Heptameron: Themes, Language and Structure* (1973) has been translated into French (1991). Recently he has focused on Franco-Italian Renaissance intertextuality in *Présences italiennes dans les Essais de Montaigne* (1992), and he is currently working on the French Renaissance novella in a similar context.

ANDRÉ TOURNON teaches French at the Université de Provence, Aix-Marseille. He is the author of *Montaigne: La Glose et l'essai* (1983) and of numerous articles on French Renaissance literature.

Index

This book has been set in Linotron Galliard. Galliard was designed for Mergenthaler in 1978 by Matthew Carter. Galliard retains many of the features of a sixteenth-century typeface cut by Robert Granjon but has some modifications that give it a more contemporary look.

Printed on acid-free paper.